A War of
Language a

[illegible]’s book considers national identity in relation to language, the way in which language can be manipulated to signal political, cultural or even historical difference. As a language with a long-recorded heritage and one spoken by the majority of those living in the Middle East in a variety of dialects, Arabic is a particularly appropriate vehicle for such an investigation. It is also, as Suleiman’s analysis reveals, an alternative and penetrating device for exploring the conflicts of the Middle East, and the diversity of its peoples and their viewpoints.

Suleiman’s book offers a wealth of empirical material, and intriguing, often poignant illustrations of antagonisms articulated through pun or double entendre. During the recent intifada, for example, Gazans would frequently respond ‘bomba’ (‘Couldn’t be better!’) to questions about their health. By making the phonetic connection between the Arabic ‘bomba’ and the English word ‘bomb’, they declared their defiance, their optimism in the face of Israeli bombings.

This is an important book which crosses disciplinary boundaries to offer rare and much-needed insights into Arabic linguistics, as well as contributing to broader debates on the politics of identity and nationalism.

YASIR SULEIMAN is Professor of Arabic and Middle Eastern Studies, and Director of the Edinburgh Institute for the Advanced Study of the Arab World and Islam at the University of Edinburgh. His publications include *The Arabic Language and National Identity: A Study in Ideology* (2003) and *The Arabic Grammatical Tradition: A Study in* Ta’līl (1999).

Sheffield Hallam University
Learning and Information Services
WITHDRAWN FROM STOCK

Cambridge Middle East Studies 19

Cambridge Middle East Studies has been established to publish books on the nineteenth- and twentieth-century Middle East and North Africa. The aim of the series is to provide new and original interpretations of aspects of Middle Eastern societies and their histories. To achieve disciplinary diversity, books will be solicited from authors writing in a wide range of fields including history, sociology, anthropology, political science and political economy. The emphasis will be on producing books offering an original approach along theoretical and empirical lines. The series is intended for students and academics, but the more accessible and wide-ranging studies will also appeal to the interested general reader.

A list of books in the series can be found after the index

A War of Words

Language and Conflict in the Middle East

Yasir Suleiman
University of Edinburgh

CAMBRIDGE
UNIVERSITY PRESS

CAMBRIDGE UNIVERSITY PRESS
Cambridge, New York, Melbourne, Madrid, Cape Town,
Singapore, São Paulo, Delhi, Mexico City

Cambridge University Press
The Edinburgh Building, Cambridge CB2 8RU, UK

Published in the United States of America by Cambridge University Press, New York

www.cambridge.org
Information on this title: www.cambridge.org/9780521546560

First published 2004

A catalogue record for this publication is available from the British Library

ISBN 978-0-521-83743-9 Hardback
ISBN 978-0-521-54656-0 Paperback

For Jerusalem, City of Peace and *Zahrat al-Madā'in*, and for all the freedom-loving people of the world

Contents

Illustrations

Figure

Plates

Tables

Acknowledgements

Many friends and colleagues have helped in various ways in writing this book, not all of whom I can acknowledge here. I would like to thank Norman Macleod of the Department of English Language at Edinburgh University for his painstaking reading of the manuscript and for commenting on many aspects of this research. His comments were illuminating on points of substance, formulation and style. Although I have not always followed his advice, his suggestions have enhanced the readability of the text and its style of presentation.

Several colleagues commented on earlier versions of this manuscript. I would like to thank them, especially Dr Dionisius Agius, whose comments helped sharpen my thinking on some aspects of this research. Professor Adrian Gully and Dr Ibrahim Muhawi read parts of this work and made valuable suggestions. My thanks go to them and to Mary Starkey, my copy-editor, for her interest and meticulous reading of the text. Needless to say, the responsibility for any errors is entirely mine.

As usual, Imad Saleh Awad was generous with his help. He pursued references for me when my UK sources dried up. I wish to thank him for his unstinting support. My thanks are also due to Marigold Acland at Cambridge University Press for her interest and encouragement. I am grateful to Oxford University Press for their permission to reprint plates 6a and 6b. Staff at the inter-library loan section of the Edinburgh University Library responded to my queries and requests for material with speed and care. To them many thanks.

Shahla, Tamir and Sinan were the best company I could have had throughout this research. In Jerusalem, they tolerated my obsession with street maps and street names. They walked with me for miles looking for signs wherever they could find them, becoming expert sign-spotters in the process. Comments they made often acted as a trigger to pursue a point beyond the limits I had put on it. At home, they put up with my absent-minded absorption in this research and allowed me to do as I pleased. I cannot thank them enough for this.

This book would not have been possible without the generous support of the Leverhulme Trust, which awarded me a three-year Major Research Fellowship to carry out the research upon which it is based. I am hugely indebted to the Trust for this support.

1 Introduction

Books have strange histories. This one is no exception. There is no doubt, however, that it is motivated by a combination of personal and professional interests. On the personal level, political conflict has touched my life on many occasions and in very tangible ways.

As a Palestinian Arab now living in the diaspora, I have grappled with the reality of conflict from afar, almost on a daily basis. But I have also been trying to make sense of my own identity. For the exile, parenthood accentuates these concerns in a myriad of ways. When, at an early age, my elder son asked me whether he should play for Palestine or Scotland in any World Cup final, I knew he was grappling with his own identity. The fact that there is no hope, I should perhaps say danger, of that happening in my lifetime or even his – although they say miracles do happen – does not negate the validity of his question. The question about football was in fact a question about 'Who am I?', a proxy for concerns of an existential kind. And when my children used to ask how a country (Palestine) could exist if it is not on the map, I knew that models of reality could be more meaningful than acts of memory and the mental images the imagination can conjure. I owe my interest in maps as cartographic-linguistic texts to these family encounters. Seeing my children sticking 'Palestine' on their school atlases, and doing so with so much care and deft scissor action, made me painfully aware of the effects of conflict on semiotic representation and the conceptualization of the self, whether in the cartographic or the linguistic field. My discussion of maps in chapter 5 derives its early impetus from those experiences of almost a decade ago.

To plug the gap between imagination and reality, we have taken several trips to our homeland, making Jerusalem our base for daily excursions to family, friends, olive fields, plum orchards, graveyards, old haunts, and places of historical and cultural interest. These excursions heightened my interest in language and political conflict, as the reader will see from chapters 2 and 5. But this interest goes back to an earlier period, to the tragic and cataclysmic events in Jordan in 1970–1 where I was a student at the time. Whereas in Palestine I could observe conflict between two languages, in Jordan the conflict was between dialects of the same language, as I explain in chapter 3. Sitting at home and watching Arab satellite TV in Edinburgh – Scotland's capital – or listening to the news about Iraq, Palestine or Israel, I picture the airwaves reverberating with conflict talk. When the Iraqi news-broadcaster referred to the American and British warplanes that attacked Iraqi targets in the 'illegally' imposed no-fly zones as *ghirbān al-sharr* (ravens of evil), I knew that the Iraqis wanted to denote, connote and satirize at the same time. The 'raven' is a hated bird in Arab culture; it is associated with bad omens, greed and treachery. It conjures images of destruction and desolation that go back to the story of Noah and the Ark. And, when collocated with the word *bayn* (in between), which it invariably recalls, it signals separation and death. Furthermore, when the Iraqi TV-broadcaster told the viewers that the 'ravens of evil' took off from military bases in Saudi Arabia, Turkey and the land/territory (*arḍ*) of Kuwait, we knew that the context for the last usage was one of conflict. It reminded us of the Gulf War in 1991. And it also signalled that, in the eyes of the Saddam regime, Kuwait did not enjoy the same claim to statehood as Saudi Arabia or Turkey. And even if it did, its involvement in the attacks on Iraq was conceived as more tangible and, therefore, as a greater act of treachery: its *land/territory*, and not some unnamed military bases in it, served as host to *ghirbān al-sharr* and was used to mount these attacks.

One of the most interesting features of the language of political conflict in the Arabic-speaking world is satire. We have seen one example of this above. The Libyan media are the undisputed masters of this mode of articulating conflict. When sanctions were imposed on Libya after the Lockerbie affair in the late 1980s, the country tried to end them by all available means. It sought the cooperation of the UN in the person of its Egyptian Secretary General, Butrus Butrus Ghali. But when the Secretary General was unable to help, the Libyan media turned against him. Instead of calling him Butrus Butrus *Ghālī* (his surname in Arabic means 'expensive' or 'precious'), they started to refer to him in their news bulletins as Butrus Butrus *al-Rakhīṣ*, which in Arabic means 'cheap', even 'trash'. Before, when President Sadat of Egypt was negotiating with the Israeli Prime Minister at Camp David in 1979, the Libyan media told its viewers what the leadership thought of these negotiations by referring to Camp David as *iṣṭabl Dāwūd* (David's Stables), the implication being that President Sadat was an animal, more specifically a horse, ready to be mounted by Menachem Begin, the new King David.

The Palestinians too have had their brand of humour and satire through the language of political conflict. A headline in the London-based daily *al-Quds al-Arabi* (18 July 2001) reads: 'Gaza Shopkeepers

Employ/Invest (*yastathmirūn*) the Language of War and Daily Clashes to Attract their Penniless Customers.' The article refers to the special vocabulary which the first Palestinian intifada (1987) against the Israeli occupation spawned. The second intifada (2000), which is still raging at the time of writing, has generated its own lexicon too. To attract cautious and uncertain customers to purchase their goods, some shopkeepers in Gaza announced early 'sales' in the hot summer of 2001. Earlier in the year, the Israelis used American-made F16s and Apache gunships to attack 'Palestinian targets', often killing many innocent civilians. Gaza shopkeepers satirized this action, describing their sales as 'an aerial bombardment on the prices' (*qaṣf min al-takhfīḍāt*). In one shop window, these words were accompanied by a picture of a rocket shooting through the word for 'prices' (*as'ār*). In another shop window, the words 'aerial bombardment on the prices' were written under the caption 'Breaking News' in Arabic (*khabar 'ājil*), which entered Arabic from English in the satellite-TV age. Some Gazans referred to this mode of speaking as 'real bombardment, but nice bombardment' (*innahu qaṣf ḥaqīqī, lākinnahu qaṣf laṭīf*). And when the Americans came to broker a ceasefire between Israel and the Palestinians, the Palestinians satirized this feeble conflict-resolution effort by urging the participants in a heated argument on the streets of Gaza to 'declare a ceasefire' (*waqf li-iṭlāq al-nār*).

The Gazans declared their defiance against the Israelis by using the slang word *bomba* (brilliant, in good health) when they were asked how they were. The phonetic similarity between this word and the word 'bomb' in English was of course the main point behind this usage. It is as though the Gazans were saying that the more bombs the Israelis drop on us, the better our health will be. Finally, to make light of their own situation, and to signal how extensive and deep Palestinian resistance to the Israeli occupation is, Gazans started to say of a person with dishevelled hair 'His head is on demonstration' (*rāsuh ṭāli' fī muẓāhara*). This is a clever way of saying that the Israeli siege and bombardment of Gaza is no excuse for unkempt appearance, but that since it is inevitable that people living under conditions of daily siege may not be able to pay enough attention to their appearance, then they should be given some credit for their departure from the norm. By laughing at themselves, the Palestinians make light of their own situation and declare that they can take the Israeli action against them in their stride. Laughter here is the cultural equivalent of that well-known British trait, the 'stiff upper lip'.

The examples from Iraq, Libya and Palestine show that the interaction between language and conflict is a complex one. This is why I have been drawn to this topic on a professional level. But it is not the only reason. The study of language and political conflict, which forms the major part of this book, allows us as scholars of language to interact with a variety of disciplines. Since the topic invites multi-disciplinarity, language and political conflict can create channels of scholarly interaction that may help repair the state of fragmentation that often obtains in the study of a single phenomenon, inevitable though this fragmentation is. Over the past few years, Arabic linguists have produced seminal studies of the structure of the language. Arabic sociolinguists have considerably enhanced our understanding of language in society. It is to the latter area that this study belongs; but it does so from a somewhat different angle, as the reader will see in the following pages. What is offered here stands as the second volume of a three-part study on language and society in the Arab world. The first of these volumes is *The Arabic Language and National Identity: A Study in Ideology* (Suleiman 2003).

Chapter 2 sets out the main parameters of this study and explains some of its basic concepts. It explains the interaction of power, conflict and language. And it does so by using a variety of examples from the Arabic-speaking world. Examples from outside this area are introduced for comparative purposes. The examples are examined in some detail to extract and contextualize some of the general principles that guide my approach to the study of language and socio-political conflict. One of the advantages of this way of treating the subject is to make the text accessible to a variety of readers – scholars and students, linguists and non-linguists, Arabists and non-Arabists. The chapter ends by outlining the major organizing principle of this study: the concept of linguistic collision between (1) a language and its dialects; (2) the dialects of a language; and (3) two (or more) languages in contact.

Chapter 3 focuses on the social dimension of language in conflict situations. It examines the debate between the modernizers and the language-defenders with respect to Standard Arabic and its colloquial forms. This debate is over 120 years old. It has a habit of igniting from time to time in Mount Etna style. The main arguments for and against the modernizers and the language-defenders are more or less the same at every eruption. If this means anything, it means that the debate has not exhausted itself yet. It is still simmering away under the surface of Arab linguistic and cultural life, ready to shoot its lava into the air whenever structural pressures build up in society. I believe that this is the case because the debate touches on issues of continuity versus change, tradition versus modernity, authenticity versus progress, the past versus the future – all of which help to enact the drama of identity and to inform the struggle over the place of the Arabs in history.

Chapter 4 takes the discussion towards language and political conflict in an intra-state setting (Jordan). We must not, however, enforce an artificial division between the political and the social in linguistic conflicts. The two always coexist, but their mix may differ from one situation to another. The linguistic conflict in Jordan is interesting because its beginnings can be dated with some confidence, and its correlation with a particular political conflict, building on the demographic dislocations of earlier and more cataclysmic conflicts, does not seem to be in doubt. This conflict is also interesting because it can provide a clear link between dialect, on the one hand, and national identity and state building, on the other. The fact that it provides a clear illustration of what is meant by language as a symbol, which tends to be accentuated at times of political tension, makes this conflict an excellent testing ground for some of the ideas that can be applied to other parts of the Arab world. The situation in Lebanon during the civil war (1975–92) would be a primary candidate for such a study. The Lebanese laugh now at how one's pronunciation of the Levantine word for 'tomatoes', a modern-day shibboleth, served as a clue to one's ethnic/national identity in a war situation. As a boundary-setter, a person's rendering of this shibboleth sometimes signalled the difference between life and death.

Chapter 5 continues the earlier discussion of linguistic conflict, but as a corollary of political conflict between people of different national and ethnic identities. The conflict between Arabic and Hebrew in Israel/Palestine combines the social and the political, although the latter is more dominant. Issues of national identity, state building, ethnic marking, map making and semiotic representation are involved in this conflict. The clash of irreconcilable ideologies in this conflict pervades the curriculum, the media and even the discourse of scientific investigation. The latter is a fascinating area. Studying the politics of sociolinguistics can help us understand that scholarly endeavour may not be as neutral or innocent as some members of the academy may sometimes think. In fact, an example of this is discussed in passing in chapter 4. My awareness of what may be dubbed 'the ideology behind the ideology' is a factor in my choice of opening paragraph in this chapter. It is meant to signal that only by being aware of our ideological commitments, national identities and personal trajectories can we minimize the bias created by political and other ideologies in our work. Often more unintentional than intentional, this bias leads to a distortion of our view of the data, of the way we study them and of the structures we choose to frame our findings.

Throughout this book, I have paid special attention to the rhetoric of linguistic conflict and to the role of language as a symbol in society. The analysis of the rhetoric of linguistic conflict enables us to tap into the values that inform and sustain conflict: the competition over resources, issues of moral probity and depravation, of purity and impurity, and of progress and decay. These values have an emotional pull in society. This is why the participants in linguistic conflicts make constant appeal to them for task-orientation purposes. People are often moved by these values, and this makes them act.

Two further points are in order here. The first concerns the scope of this work. I have decided to leave the linguistic conflict in North Africa out of consideration, preferring to restrict myself to the Middle East. I believe that there are sufficient differences between these two regions of the Arab world to justify this limitation of scholarly labour. North Africa deserves a study on its own, as do the southern regions of the Arab world. Sudan, Somalia and Mauritania hold enormous interest for the student of language and political conflict. Let us hope that they will be subjected to a study of this kind in the near future.

Finally, I have decided to use full transliteration of names in the reference list only. Arabic names in the text and the footnotes are given in the form that is nearest to their full transliteration. For example, Ṭarābīshī and Frayḥa will be rendered as Tarabishi and Frayha respectively. I have chosen to do this to reduce the impression of exoticization that full transliteration would give to the non-Arabist. I have, however, rendered other Arabic material (for example, book titles as in *Lughatunā al-ʿarabiyya fī maʿrakat al-ḥaḍāra*) in transliteration to enhance the recoverability of meaning for those readers who know Arabic and to give force to some of the interpretations I give.

2 Language, power and conflict in the Middle East

Language and power

In this work, language is viewed first and foremost as a form of cultural practice and as an inevitable site of ideological contestation involving asymmetrical power relations between groups and individuals. This is one of the major premises upon which this study is based, wherein power signifies the capacity to act in a way that involves the consent, acquiescence or resistance of others (see Barnes 1988; Hindess 1996). I am therefore not interested here in language as a structural system. Structural information – phonological, grammatical or lexical – will be given when it is necessary to contextualize a point of linguistic structure, and only in so far as this relates to the issue of language and society, which is the main focus of this research.

From an instrumentalist point of view, language is a means of communication. In this role, language links the members of a speech community to each other in the present. But it also serves to link these speakers to their history, endowing them with a sense of identity whose roots are located in the past. And it is this past, mythical or real, that animates the cultural practices and ideological concerns that drive the members of the community towards an imagined future. Language always stands at the crossroads of (social) time, linking the past with the present, and linking these two with the future. This is particularly poignant, both politically and culturally, for those languages with a long recorded heritage, of which Arabic is an example. It is also poignant for speakers in diasporic situations where questions of language maintenance and language loss operate at the individual, family and group levels.

Although communication is served through language, language itself often serves as the subject of communication in ways that exploit its capacity to signal ideological positions of various kinds. Most importantly, language serves as a marker of group identity and as a boundary-setter between the in-group (ourselves) and the out-group (others). I have dealt with this issue at length in *The Arabic Language and National Identity: A*

Study in Ideology (Suleiman 2003). In this current work, I am mainly interested in the interaction between language and national/ethnic identity in situations of intra- and intergroup conflict. Although the communicative function of language is always involved in this interaction, prominence will be given to its symbolic role as an emblem of identity. This symbolic function is brought to the fore in situations of language contact (see Weinreich 1966: 83–110). In these situations, language choice and language loyalty carry additional meanings which speakers can exploit to achieve specific objectives.

Let me exemplify the above premise concerning language and power by analysing the following two examples of my own linguistic behaviour, both as a form of cultural practice and as a site of ideological contestation. I am a Palestinian for whom Jerusalem is an ideological-cum-national home and the locus of many childhood memories. I left my native town in 1967, in the wake of the Israeli occupation of the West Bank and Gaza, to finish my schooling and undergraduate education in Jordan. In the mid-1970s I came to Scotland, where I have since been living and working. Although I had always dreamt of going back to visit my family in the Israeli-occupied territories, I was emotionally unable to do so until 1995. Since then, I have been back to visit several times, and I took the opportunity to travel with my family not just in the Occupied Territories, but also inside those areas of historical Palestine on which Israel was established in 1948. Negotiating many Israeli checkpoints, I found myself emotionally unable to use my native language, Arabic, with Israeli soldiers or policemen when they used it with me. This was true of my exchanges with the Druze serving in the Israeli army, although Arabic is as much their native language as it is mine. I was not actually aware of this aspect of my linguistic behaviour until my wife drew my attention to it. And since I could not speak Hebrew, I resorted to the only language I could use: English. To contextualize this aspect of my linguistic behaviour, I can report that, on my visits, I rarely used English with fellow Palestinians, even when some of them attempted to address me in that language because of my British passport or because my children, in their presence, spoke to me or to their mother in English. This was true of my interactions with members of the Palestinian police and ordinary people alike. I always used Arabic in dealing with them.

My use of Arabic with fellow Palestinians is not difficult to explain, even when English was available as an alternative medium of communication between us. It seems reasonable to suggest that this behaviour on my part was intended to create and express bonds of national solidarity with my interlocutors. It was meant to say to them, 'I am one of you', in spite of the fact that I carry a foreign emblem of identity, my British passport, and that I live in the diaspora. There is no doubt that my credibility and status would have been raised substantially if I had used English with them, particularly as my English is likely to have been a lot better than theirs. However, English would have acted as a barrier between us, not by virtue of its being a foreign language per se, but owing to the fact that it would have promoted the bonds of social status over those of national identity, in situations when the latter seemed to be situationally the most relevant. My avoidance of English and my preference for Arabic seemed therefore to be designed to promote the *national* over the *social* in the equation of language as a form of cultural practice and as a site of ideological contestation. In this situation, the symbolic function of language has transcended its instrumental utility as a means of communication. Arabic in this context served to bond me internally with other Palestinians, while at the same time bounding us externally vis-à-vis an occupying Other with whom I found myself refusing to use the language.

By refusing to use Arabic with Israeli soldiers and policemen, I was refusing to allow any bonds of solidarity, or even interpersonal understanding through the language, to obtain between us. I looked at the soldiers as members of a foreign force that illegally occupies my country. I must have reasoned therefore that my native language should never be 'sullied' in use with them, especially in the Hebraicized form used by Israeli Jewish soldiers. As far as the Druze soldiers are concerned, I felt that these soldiers were 'renegades' and oppressors of their 'kith and kin', although I am sure that they would not see themselves in this way. I therefore always adamantly refused to speak to them in Arabic, even when they were unable to speak English. The fact that they sometimes adopted a Hebraicized form of Arabic to address me added to my determination to refuse to respond in Arabic. On one occasion in Hebron, a West Bank town, I put myself in real danger because of this attitude. Listening to a torrent of abuse from two Druze soldiers in Arabic, I chose not to respond to their taunts. They knew that I understood every word, and clearly took pleasure in that, but I stuck to my linguistic guns while they continued to place their fingers close to the triggers of their rifles.

My refusal to use Arabic with Israeli soldiers, Jewish or Druze, is impregnated with symbolic meanings. It signalled an attitude of defiance on my part. It also represented an act of cultural resistance to the occupier; a token one perhaps, but one which nevertheless held a lot of political meaning for me. This refusal was also intended to redefine the power relationship between the Israeli soldiers and me as a Palestinian. Israeli Jewish soldiers hardly ever use the language in everyday intercommunity interaction inside Israel. Arabic for them is a language of occupation. It is a language that puts the soldiers in a privileged power position over the Palestinians, although their competence in it is often extremely limited. This differential allocation of power relations is reflected in the fact that (1) it is the Israeli soldier at the checkpoint who usually initiates the linguistic interaction with the Palestinians in (sometimes) a Hebraicized form of Arabic; (2) this interaction takes the form of demands to inspect identity papers, to ask questions and to issue commands; (3) the interaction is a truncated and a restricted one in which the Palestinian usually responds and normally does not initiate; (4) the dynamics of the interaction in terms of turn-taking is usually controlled by the Israeli soldier; (5) the extralinguistic behaviour of the Israeli soldier (in terms of gestures, body posture and eye contact) indicates a position of superiority; and (6) the Palestinian enters this interaction knowing that failure to comply or to play the game according to its tacitly set rules can result in various forms of punishment. For all of these reasons, I usually refuse to use Arabic with the Israeli soldiers, although they can tell by my name, my looks and my place of birth that I can speak the language. By so doing, I must be aiming to undermine the authority these soldiers can exercise over me, and to shift the balance of interactional power a little in my favour. It is this, I think, that the Druze soldiers particularly resent when dealing with people like me.

My use of English with the Israeli soldiers must be calculated to give me extra advantage over them.[1] The political, economic and cultural

[1] The following anecdote, related by Robert Cooper (in Spolsky and Cooper 1991: 121), provides an interesting example of the politics of language use in the Old City of Jerusalem:

> I once asked my students in a university seminar [Hebrew University] whether they thought parents would be willing to send their children to an English-medium school. They all agreed that such a school would find a ready market, in both the Arab and Jewish sectors, given parents' desire for their children to learn English well. I then asked whether Arab parents might be willing to send their children to Hebrew-medium Arab schools, and whether Jewish parents might be willing to send their children to Arabic-medium Jewish schools, in order to promote their children's acquisition of the other group's language. Both the Arab and the Jewish students in my seminar were deeply shocked. 'Oh, Professor Cooper,' one of my students replied slowly, in the tone of voice one might employ towards a dim-witted person, 'English is a neutral language in Israel, but not Arabic or Hebrew.'

Similar views about English as a politically neutral medium of internation communication in Israel and Palestine are reported in Spolsky et al. (n.d.). Bowman (1988: 33) deals with the deployment of Arabic, Hebrew and English in his treatment of the formation of Palestinian national consciousness; he writes:

> In Israel and the Occupied Territories the Arabic language is used to distinguish between Hebrew-speaking occupiers and the Arabic-speakers who suffer their occupation. Palestinians who [know] Hebrew . . . will rarely use the language when speaking with Israelis. They will instead use English, which, in a land which was previously occupied by the British, now serves as a *lingua franca*. Similarly, 'Oriental Jews' – Israelis whose original provenance was within the Arabic-speaking Middle East – will refuse in public to use the Arabic they speak with their families at home for fear that they might be thought to be 'Arabs'.

See Weber (1979) for the position of English in Jerusalem.

credentials of English as the primary lingua franca in the world today make it the language of power internationally. By using it with the Israeli soldiers, who are not always proficient in it, I often find myself able to redress the balance of power in my favour. The Israeli soldier holds the real gun, a loaded weapon[2] which can kill; but, through English, I can, and do, unload linguistic firepower which, in comparison, is harmless yet very effective as an instrument of situation management. By signalling in a polished form of English my inability to understand what the Israeli soldier demands of me in his less proficient English, I can ask questions, take turns, and use words which he does not know to unsettle him and to turn his attention away from the task at hand towards one of lexical retrieval and speech processing. This way, I can shift him out of his politically dominant position, enabling me to have enough elbow room to manoeuvre out of my subordinated position as a member of an oppressed people.

It may be said that my situation is not normal for most Palestinians living under Israeli occupation, even for those who have as good a command of English as I do. It would therefore be scientifically unsafe to use what may be an exception to draw a general observation about language, power and conflict. I think it is right to raise these issues; but the example I have just given is intended to show in a 'no bones' manner the dynamics of power negotiation in conflict situations, and how the symbolic power of language can be deployed to bring about a change in the balance of power between the interlocutors. The fact that I, a sociolinguist, am aware of this web of ingredients, and am able to put it to use to my advantage, does not invalidate the premise about language and power stated at the beginning of this section. On the contrary, it supports it by bringing it to light in a clear manner. The validity of my personal reflections in this and the following example is further justified by the fact that they are consistent with the insights generated on issues of language, power and identity in different cultural contexts (e.g. Calvet 1998; Edwards 1988; Fairclough 1989; Fishman 1972; Heller 1995; Mazrui and Mazrui 1998; Schmid 2001; Suleiman 1999a; Wardhaugh 1987). Let me exemplify this by referring to two such studies. In her study of the politics of language in North America, Schmid (2001: 42) observes that 'language is an especially salient symbolic issue because it links political claims with psychological feelings of group worth'. In a study of the politics of code-switching, a topic to be dealt with below, Heller (1995: 161) reaches a similar conclusion: 'Language practices are inherently political insofar

[2] The term is borrowed from Dwight Bolinger's (1980) *Language: The Loaded Weapon*. The phrase 'loaded weapon' provides an apt description of the language situation in the Middle East.

as they are among the ways individuals have at their disposal of gaining access to the production, distribution and consumption of symbolic and material resources, that is insofar as language forms part of processes of power.'

Let me pursue this theme by considering another example involving my elder son, who was seven years old at the time the situation I am about to describe took place. In 1995, my family and I spent two weeks in the Occupied Territories. We made East Jerusalem our base from which to visit Arab cities and towns inside Israel: Jaffa, Haifa, Acre, Nazareth and some villages in the Little Triangle. This meant that we had to walk from East to West Jerusalem (to reach the bus station) and back on many occasions. One day, as we were walking back from West to East Jerusalem, my son asked me in a matter-of-fact tone of voice: 'Dad! Can we speak Arabic now?' I thought that was a silly question. I told him: 'Of course you can! You can speak Arabic whenever you want and wherever you want!' Then it dawned on me that there was perhaps more to my son's question than I had initially discerned. I inquired of him why he had asked the question. He said: 'Dad, haven't you noticed that every time we reach this point we change from Arabic to English when going uphill [from Palestinian East Jerusalem to Israeli West Jerusalem], and that we change from English to Arabic when going downhill [from West to East Jerusalem]?'

I was stunned by my son's observation. First, what he had said must have been true, although I was not aware of it. Second, my son had intuitively identified a linguistic boundary which, to my astonishment, coincided with where the physical boundary between East and West Jerusalem had stood until 1967, when the Israelis occupied East Jerusalem and proceeded to annex it. The wall that stood between the two parts of the city, the Musrara wall, was pulled down, and roads linking East with West Jerusalem were built on what used to be the no man's land separating them. The wall, which by 1995 had long ceased to exist, was clearly inscribed in my mind as a mental boundary, but it had now translated itself from the memory of a physical boundary to a linguistic one.

The change from Arabic to English, which my son so perceptively observed and commented on, was a boundary-setting mechanism of which I was not aware in behavioural terms. Shifting between Arabic and English was my way of signalling where I was locating myself in identity terms. But it was also a method of negotiating my identity in what is one of the most conflict-ridden places on earth. By shifting from Arabic to English, I was resorting to a language of power to compensate for the power deficit which my Palestinian identity assigns to me in the Jewish environment of Hebrew-dominated West Jerusalem. On a different level, this language shift aimed to make me less visible as a Palestinian when interacting with Hebrew-speaking shopkeepers, bus drivers, restaurant proprietors and others. English therefore seemed to perform the double task of empowering me and masking my weakness at one and the same time. It also allowed me to express my 'Otherness' in a non-threatening way in an environment in which violent conflict can erupt without warning. On the psychological level, English offered me a safety valve. Having learnt it at school and university, and using it for teaching and research, English is first and foremost a language of thought, reflection and control for me. And since these are the very resources I need in an environment characterized by a simmering conflict, it is natural that I would shift to it in West Jerusalem.

The shift to Arabic in moving from West to East Jerusalem is not hard to explain. It served to assert my national identity as a Palestinian. It was also meant to express solidarity with other Palestinians. English is of little use in these domains. It is therefore natural that I would suppress it. But it was always there for activation when talking to or about Israeli soldiers or the police with my wife and two sons. On reflection, it is astonishing how much of this was done intuitively, and how quickly our two sons learned the rules of the game with virtually no explicit instruction.

The above examples suggest three important principles. First, the power–language relationship is an important aspect of ideological contestation, and of identity assertion and negotiation in inter- and intra-group interaction. The importance of this relationship increases in situations of conflict. While power may be allocated differentially between competing individuals and groups, it is nevertheless possible to achieve some reordering of this allocation by exploiting the linguistic resources available to speakers. This may require a shift to a language of power to compensate for the power differential between the interactants. My use of English in preference to Arabic with Israeli soldiers in the Occupied Territories illustrates this. By invoking power as a principle in my reflections on the above examples, I wish to draw attention to the *political* nature of language as cultural practice and as a site of ideological contestation (see Kramarae et al. 1984; Lakoff 1990).

Second, language is a marker of identity. In this function, language assumes greater importance than usual in situations of conflict. Language bonds its speakers internally and bounds them externally. In this respect, it acts as a boundary-setter between the in-group and the out-group. However, the negotiation of power relations between interactants in situations of conflict may lead to a temporary realignment of linguistic resources. My use of Arabic with Palestinians and the shift between Arabic and English in moving between East and West Jerusalem exemplify this principle.

Third, both the language–power relationship and the language–identity relationship operate at the communicative and the symbolic levels of signification. The communicative level allows us to study power and identity *in* discourse. Typical examples of this are the use of the active and passive in news reports, the ideologically loaded exploitation of lexical resources (particularly place-names), the use of personal pronouns in political discourse, and the structuring of role relationships between the interlocutors in interactions across group boundaries. On the symbolic level, language serves as the site of ideological contestation. This level of signification allows us to study the power *behind* discourse. Most of the arguments in this work will pertain to this level of language-related signification. What matters at this level is not so much what is being said, the communicative function of language, but the set of ideologically driven choices which the interlocutors bring to bear in communicating with each other or in reflecting on language and society. The way Arabic and English were deployed by the present writer in the examples above illustrates this point. Language attitudes – especially those that relate to national/ethnic identity formation – also belong to this level of symbolic signification. In studying these themes, I will deploy a variety of insights which conceptualize the link between language and society in a manner tending to give prominence to the latter (sociology of language)[3] over the former (sociolinguistics in its quantitatively driven mode).[4] The symbolic meaning of language-related discourse, in both its political and social settings, will therefore form a major part of this work (Bourdieu 1992). In this respect, the present study espouses a view of language akin to that proposed by Joshua Fishman in his study of the sociology of language (1997: 27):

> Language is not merely a *means* of interpersonal communication and influence. It is not merely a *carrier* of content, whether latent or manifest. Language itself *is* content, a referent for loyalties and animosities, an indicator of social statuses and personal relationships, a marker of situations and topics as well as of the societal goals and the large-scale value-laden arenas of interaction that typify every speech community. [original emphasis]

Language and conflict

Another premise underlying this study concerns the inevitability of conflict in human societies at the individual and group levels (Simmel 1955a, 1955b). Whether motivated by economic, social or political factors,

[3] See Fishman (1997) for the concept of 'sociology of language'.
[4] See Cameron (1997) for an excellent critique of sociolinguistics in its quantitative form.

conflict can occur within the group (intra-group conflict) or between groups (intergroup conflict). While the objective features of a situation may be considered a source of conflict, it is nevertheless individuals and groups, as actors, who determine whether or not conflict occurs. However, conflict is kept in check in normal circumstances by the multiplicity of criss-crossing associations and allegiances existing within and between groups. The existence of mechanisms for the expression, de-escalation and resolution of conflicts is also important for ensuring that intra- and intergroup conflicts do remain in check. When these mechanisms fail, conflicts intensify and may be translated into violence. In these situations, conflict becomes more tangible in the life of a community. Here, ideologized conflicts tend on the whole to be more intense than those driven by purely personal agendas. The role of the elites as active agents in formulating and forming these ideologies is crucial, especially in societies which value conformity over diversity. Thus the stronger that collective orientation is over self-orientation in a group, the greater the propensity for the ideologization of conflicts, and the greater the likelihood for the conflicts concerned, if left unchecked, to erupt into open violence.

The opposite of conflict is harmony and integration. The positive nature of these values should not, however, mask the equally positive contribution which conflict can make to group modernization at all levels: economic, political, social and cultural. Conflict can therefore be a force for change and modernization in society. Should conflict over resources and values, particularly the latter, cease to exist, then a society will start to ossify. Progress will slow down and the desire to innovate will be extinguished, leading to rigidity in social structures. The suppression of conflict is therefore as dangerous in the life of a community as is its unchecked escalation into violence.

How does the preceding sketch of conflict apply in the linguistic domain? Being an important resource in society, and the subject of competing values in the life of a community (El-Yasin and Mahadin 1996), it is inevitable that language is implicated in intergroup and intra-group conflicts. We may therefore talk about linguistic conflict as a phenomenon in its own right, and as one which is essential if the socio-political phenomena to which language relates are to undergo change and modernization in a group. However, this statement must be qualified in three ways. To begin with, linguistic conflict is not conflict between languages or language varieties per se, but between the speakers of a language, or those of different languages, who compete over resources and values in their physical and cultural milieux in inter- and intra-group situations. It is of course possible to talk about linguistic conflict within the individual, typically in bilingual situations; but this will not concern us here.

In addition, language is hardly ever the cause of conflict between speakers in intra-group or intergroup situations, but it serves as a most effective site for the expression and ideologization of other conflicts in and between groups. This is fully recognized in discussions of language planning, where the driving force behind such planning is not the recognition of linguistic problems per se, but such aims as 'national integration, political control, economic development, the creation of new elites and the maintenance of old ones, the pacification or cooption of minority groups, and mass mobilization of national and political movements' (Cooper 1989: 35). This same principle underlies Schmid's study of the politics of language in the USA (2001: 4): 'Language alone has rarely been the major source of conflict in American society; instead, it has been the proxy for other conditions that have challenged the power relations of the dominant group(s).' By discussing bilingualism at work and in school education in the USA, Schmid provides ample examples of the application of this principle. The same is true of a host of similar situations in other countries, including India (Das Gupta 1970), Canada, Belgium, France, Spain, Switzerland (Wardhaugh 1987) and Ireland (Ahlqvist 1993). The idea of linguistic conflict as a proxy for other more pervasive conflicts is important in this study because it orients us more towards society (and therefore the sociology of language) than towards language (and therefore sociolinguistics) in discussing language in society in the Middle East.

Finally, linguistic conflict involves both the communicative and the symbolic resources of language in asymmetrical power relations. Although the relationship between these two functions of language is not adequately understood, it is nevertheless the case that symbolism plays a more highly charged role than communication (instrumentality) in the articulation of linguistic conflicts. Questions of pride, loyalty and identity are anchored in the symbolic domain, and it is these that fuel linguistic conflicts. The fact that language is associated with education and employment, and that in some societies it is linked to religious belief and doctrine, adds to the potency of linguistic symbolism and, hence, to the force with which linguistic conflicts can be pursued.

Linguistic conflict is often designated by that name or as 'language conflict' in the titles of books and articles on the subject (e.g. Das Gupta 1970; Dua 1996; Inglehart and Woodward 1972; Jahr 1993; Laitin 1987). In some cases, the conflict involving languages is designated as 'war' (Calvet 1998; Lakoff 2000). Terms such as 'guerrilla warfare' and 'trench war' (Calvet 1998: 182, 193), 'language battles' and 'language peace' (Schmid 2001: 44, 61), and 'linguistic invasion' are employed in describing linguistic conflicts. For most writers, these terms are used metaphorically, but the relentless deployment of the 'war metaphor' in Calvet (1998) gives the impression that for this writer language wars transcend the metaphorical to the almost real. He comes close to expressing this view when he declares that 'the war of languages is nothing but the linguistic aspect of a wider war' (1998: 135). Instead of choosing between the two terms 'conflict' and 'war' in this work, I will reserve the latter to situations of linguistic conflict wherein open hostility and violence involving languages directly are present in intra- or intergroup relations. A language war in this sense may manifest itself in a series of linguistic skirmishes or battles which, as pointed out above, serve as a proxy for other conditions in society.

An example of this kind is the demonstrations that took place in 1913 in Palestine by the pro-Hebrew activists against the proposal to use German to teach science and technology in a tertiary-level institute of technology in Haifa. In the annals of Zionist ideology, this incident came to be known as the 'Language War' (Cohen 1918; Spolsky 1996; Spolsky and Shohamy 1999), which succeeded in defeating the proposal in favour of Hebrew. The fact that Jewish pupils from the German-run schools took part in these demonstrations indicates the degree of mobilization which the pro-Hebrew Zionist movement had achieved among the Jews in Palestine at the turn of the twentieth century. Furthermore, this incident provides an example of violent linguistic conflict, hence the acceptance of the established term 'linguistic war' to designate it. The intra-communal nature of this conflict illustrates how intra-group tensions can exploit language as a proxy for articulating national identity in the Zionist project in Palestine. In the following section, I will give more examples of linguistic conflict in the Middle East as a basis for generating further insights on the subject for reference later in this work.

Language and political conflict: Turkish in the fray

Let us consider a set of linguistic conflicts in which Turkish acts as the linchpin. The first such conflict involves Arabic in the second half of the nineteenth century and the first two decades of the twentieth. I have dealt with the underlying foundations of this conflict at some length in *The Arabic Language and National Identity: A Study in Ideology* (2003: 70–96). I will therefore restrict myself here to providing a brief outline of this conflict.

The increasing Turkification of the Ottoman Empire in the administrative and cultural domains during this period culminated in the promotion of linguistic Turkification of the various groups in the state as a policy instrument by the Young Turks upon their effective ascendance to power in 1909. From the perspective of the present research, cultural

Turkification proceeded on two fronts, which fed off each other. First, the rising interest among Turkish nationalists in Turkish as an instrument of nation formation was accompanied by an attempt to purify the language of most of the lexical and grammatical material borrowed from Arabic. This attempt was accompanied by a vision of the national self in which religion did not play as commanding a role as language. It was also consistent with a stereotypical view of the Arabs as inferior to the Turks. Turkification may therefore be regarded as a self-reflexive policy in which the first task was to Turkify the Turks by loosening the ties they had with the ethnically non-Turkish elements in the empire. Being the largest non-Turkish group in the empire, and the target of ethnic slurs by Turks, the Arabs responded by asserting their distinctive, linguistically based national identity. Claims that Arabic was superior to Turkish were promoted to endow the Arabs with a strong sense of self-esteem. This was not difficult to accomplish owing to the status of Arabic as the primary language of Islam, doctrinally and intellectually, and to its status as a donor language for Turkish. As a result, Turkish was projected as an impoverished language, which needed Arabic borrowings to function properly. With its large input from Persian and Arabic, Turkish was also described as a 'mongrel' language. Within the moral scheme of things in the Muslim milieu of the time, this description amounted to accusing Turkish of being a 'bastard' language, or at least one which lacked authenticity and pure pedigree.

Second, active Turkification by the Young Turks sought as a matter of policy to impose Turkish as the language of the administration, of the courts and of public education in the Arabic-speaking parts of the empire. Arabic was suppressed in these domains. In the few secondary schools that existed in Damascus in the period under consideration, Turkish teachers were hired to replace Arab teachers to teach Arabic to Arabic-speaking students. Arabic was effectively taught as a foreign language to these students, using the same books as the administration prepared for the teaching of Arabic in the Turkish schools. Students who were caught speaking Arabic were punished and humiliated. The Ottoman postal services were run through the medium of Turkish. Turkish administrators and members of the Ottoman parliament lamented the fact that the Arabs were not proficient in Turkish. The net result of these policies, whether officially promulgated or unofficially applied, was to set Arabic and Turkish against each other in a linguistic conflict in which the politically less powerful party, the Arabic speakers, had to engage in various acts of cultural resistance in defence of their language. I will outline some of these acts below to show the variety of mechanisms which the Arabs applied in defence of their tongue against Turkish.

In a series of placards published in 1880 and 1881 in Beirut, Damascus, Sidon and Tripoli, the demand was made to recognize Arabic as an official language in all parts of the Ottoman Empire in which the majority population was Arab, including the administration, the courts, the state schools and the postal services. The activists also demanded that the authorities post Arabic-speaking army officers in areas with an Arab majority. These demands were coupled with the call to grant these parts autonomy in running their own internal affairs in a decentralized system of government. The Turks were described as *'ulūj* in some of these placards, an abusive term which designates the notions of being a 'bully', 'unbeliever' or 'a person who does not speak Arabic or speaks it with a foreign accent'. Arab newspapers responded to the attacks on the Arabs and their language in the Turkish newspapers. Cultural and literary clubs were established, among other things, to instil pride in the language among its speakers and to defend it against the Turkification policies of the Young Turks. Poetry was composed to extol the superior virtues of the Arabs and Arabic over those of the Turks and Turkish. In some literary clubs, Standard Arabic was used in place of the Arabic colloquials in normal conversations. In some cases, acts of linguistic purification were carried out to rid Arabic of interference from other languages (see Kia 1998). Sometimes, members of these clubs denied charity to those who begged using the colloquial.

By attacking Arabic and by seeking to replace it with Turkish in conducting the affairs of the state, the Turkifiers were accused of harming the cause of Islam. This was a strong theme in the Arab counter-attack against Turkification, owing to the close connection between Arabic and Islam. The linguistic chauvinism exhibited by the Turkifiers elicited counter-chauvinism on the Arab side. Also, the Turkifiers' replacement of religion by language as the linchpin of national identity was met by a similar measure among the proponents of Arabic. Arabic was now projected not just as the language of Islam and as a source of affiliation among Muslims, but also as an instrument for uniting all those who spoke it, regardless of their religious affiliation. To gauge the strength of this transformation among Arabic speakers, I will quote Muhammad Rashid Rida (1865–1935), a Muslim cleric from Lebanon, who had strongly defended Arabic against Turkish before and after the effective dissolution of the Ottoman Empire in 1923. In conceptualizing his sense of his own identity, Rida wrote (quoted in Hourani 1983: 301): 'I am an Arab Muslim and a Muslim Arab . . . My Islam is the same in date as my being Arab . . . I say, I am an Arab Muslim and I am brother in religion to thousands upon thousands of Muslims, Arabs and non-Arabs, and brother in race to thousands upon thousands of Arabs, Muslims and non-Muslims.' The fact that a famous Muslim cleric can speak in this way reveals the transformation in identity conceptualization among Arab intellectuals in the period under consideration in this section. There is no doubt that the linguistic conflict between Arabic and Turkish during this period acted as a catalyst, directly or indirectly, in bringing about this change in self-definition.

Let us now consider the linguistic conflict between Kurdish and Turkish in present-day Turkey. I will occasionally refer to Arabic in Turkey in this context for comparative purposes. In terms of power relations, the Kurdish–Turkish conflict is an asymmetrical one in which Turkish exercises substantial hegemony over Kurdish in all spheres of public life. This hegemony is enshrined in constitutional provisions and penal codes which ensure that the state can act against Kurdish with impunity. As the following discussion will show, the onslaught on Kurdish in Turkey is a form of active linguicide. The situation is different in Iraq owing to the cultural autonomy the Kurds have traditionally assumed since Iraqi independence (1932), including the use of Kurdish in education and in the media in areas where the Kurds are the majority.[5] To illustrate how Kurdish linguicide is practised in Turkey, I will give the following moving account from the testimony of Esref Okumus, a Kurdish journalist, to the Conference on Minority Rights, Policies and Practice in South East Europe (cited in Skutnabb-Kangas and Bucak 1994: 347–8):

> As a Kurd in Turkey you are born in a village or town the name of which is not valid, because [the] names of nearly all Kurdish villages and towns I know are today changed into Turkish.
>
> If your parents wish to give you a Kurdish name, your name will not be registered by the authorities. It will be changed into Turkish. If your parents still insist to keep your Kurdish name, they will be prosecuted and forced by a court to change your name into a non-Kurdish name.
>
> When you, seven years old, go to school, you won't be able to communicate with your teachers. At least if you, just like me, have parents who do not speak Turkish. It will take 4 or 5 years before you at all can speak with your teachers.
>
> When you have become an adult, you must be aware of all the laws which prevent you from keeping your Kurdish identity.
>
> First of all, you are not allowed to claim that your mother tongue is Kurdish. The third section of law no. 2932 tells you what your mother tongue is: 'The mother tongue of all Turkish citizens is Turkish.' You are not allowed to speak Kurdish in public spaces (citations from law 2923) . . . If you, in spite of all this, speak Kurdish, you can be sentenced to a maximum of 2 years of imprisonment according to section 4 of the same law.

[5] See May (2001) for a wide-ranging study of the politics of language, ethnicity and nationalism and how these relate to minority rights. The excellent bibliography in this work provides a good starting point for both the specialist and the non-specialist.

All this means that you, as a member of the Kurdish minority in Turkey, are deprived of all the fruits of your culture. I want to emphasize this: ALL fruits of your culture. If you don't want to accept this, and clearly show your disapproval by, for instance, writing to a newspaper, then you can be prosecuted for 'weakening of national feelings', according to section 143 of the Penal Codes.

You can be sentenced to a maximum of 10 years' imprisonment. If you, as a Kurd in Turkey, 'build or attempt to build an association' to maintain your culture and language, you can be sentenced to a maximum of 15 years of imprisonment, according to section 1141 of the Penal Code.

Thousands of Kurds have been sentenced according to these laws. If you try to explain this situation abroad, exactly as I am doing at this moment, you can be sentenced to 10 years of imprisonment for 'damaging' the reputation of the Turkish state.[6]

[6] The conference was held in Copenhagen between 30 March and 1 April 1990, under the auspices of the Danish Helsinki Committee and the Minority Rights Group, London.

The following report in *The Times Higher Education Supplement*, 8 February 2002, deals with some of the issues raised in this testimony. The report appears under the headline 'Turks crack down on Kurd campaign', below a photograph of a Turkish police officer with a sub-machine gun. The caption for this picture reads: 'Language difficulty: riot police officer monitors a demonstration by pro-Kurdish protesters at Istanbul University'. The report refers to the linguistic factor in the Kurdish problem. It describes the ban on Kurdish, its use as a proxy in the conflict between the Kurds and the Turks, and the arguments used by each party to discredit the position of the other. I will give the report in full because of the interest it may hold for the reader:

> Demonstrations demanding that Kurdish be used in Turkish universities have triggered a crackdown and numerous arrests. According to the main Kurdish party, Hadep, more than 5,000 people have been detained and 300 arrested in January alone. Kurds have been collecting signatures calling on the government to give students the option to study in Kurdish. The campaign started in November [2001] and rapidly spread. The constitution stipulates that only Turkish can be used as a medium of instruction, with exceptions for Greek and Armenian minorities. Although a fifth of the 65 million population is of Kurdish origin, Turkey steadfastly refuses to recognize Kurds as a minority.
>
> Prime minister Bulent Ecevit defended the crackdown, saying that 'no concessions are possible on [Kurdish] education'. He accused the campaigners of being linked to the Kurdish separatist group PKK, which fought a 15-year war with the Turkish state that claimed over 30,000 lives.
>
> Kemal Guruz, head of the higher education authority, told *The THES* that students could face severe sanctions for signing the petition. 'Those who insist will be punished – we have just come out of a war, which we won. The PKK [Kurdish Workers' Party] tried with guerrilla terrorist tactics and failed. They know that it is never going to work. So now they've changed their tactics and this is the first step, *destroying* the very basic tenet of the republic.'
>
> *Dr Guruz denied that Kurdish existed.* 'People in this part of the world [Turkish Kurdistan] speak various dialects – there is no single language in the technical sense that can be called Kurdish. There are many dialects. They cannot even communicate among themselves, from one village to the next. There is very little written material.'
>
> Murat Bozlak, head of Hadep, maintained that the Kurdish language had existed for centuries and he denied that the campaign threatened the integrity of the country. 'In the Breton region of France and in Corsica people use languages other than French in education and there is no threat to the integrity of the country. In Turkey, it can be the same.' [emphasis added]

Language policy in Turkey is subject to article 3 of the constitution (1982): 'The Turkish State, with its territory and nation, is an indivisible entity. Its language is Turkish.' Article 4 of the constitution states that 'the provisions of article 3 shall not be amended, nor shall their amendment be proposed'.[7] Article 3 in earlier versions of the constitution states this relationship in a stronger fashion, declaring that the 'mother tongue of Turkish citizens is Turkish' (cited in Smith-Kocamahhul 2001: 46), thus denying that a Turkish citizen does have or can have a *mother* tongue other than Turkish. These two articles inscribe an indissoluble link between territory, nation and language, and they serve as the basis for extensive legislation, of the kind mentioned in the above testimony, restricting the use of other languages in Turkey outside the private domain. This applies to Arabic in Hatay (south-west corner of the country), although attention in the international arena – particularly in the European Union in the context of Turkey's attempts to join this organization – has traditionally focused on the ban on Kurdish only. Reporting on the situation of Arabic in Hatay, Smith-Kocamahhul says (2001: 47): 'When Hatay residents became Turkish citizens [in 1938], they were required to take . . . Turkish surnames [that] were sometimes assigned arbitrarily, with little regard to existing Arabic family names. Officials assaulted Arabic monolinguals for not speaking Turkish, as they assaulted Kurds in Kurdish areas. Turkish laws prohibited provisions for Arabic education.' Arabic-speaking Turks wishing to study Arabic at university level cannot do so at Mustafa Kemal University in Hatay, their local university. They must instead attend one of the universities in Ankara or Istanbul.[8]

The ban on languages other than Turkish contravenes the obligations placed on Turkey by the 1924 Treaty of Lausanne, which contains clauses safeguarding the linguistic rights of all Turkish citizens, regardless of their ethnic or religious backgrounds.[9] Thus, article 39.4 of the treaty states: 'No restrictions shall be imposed on the free use by any Turkish national of any language in private intercourse, in commerce, in the press, or in publications of any kind or at public meetings.' Article 39.5 of the same treaty

[7] For the Turkish constitution in English, see the home page of the Turkish Embassy in Washington, DC: www.turkey.org.

[8] Arnold (2002: 163) describes the precarious position of Arabic in Turkey as follows:

> [Arabic] is completely banished from public life and, therefore, the teaching of Arabic, the singing of Arabic songs, and the use of Arabic personal names are forbidden. A few people have learned, with difficulty and through a sheikh, to decipher the Arabic letters. Others have tried to learn Standard Arabic by themselves, with little success. Most of the Arabs in Hatay [south-west Turkey] today are illiterate in Arabic. Only the sheikhs and [the] priests have [some] knowledge of Classical Arabic.

[9] See www.lib.byu.edu/-rdh/wwi/1918p.html for the Lausanne Treaty.

stipulates: 'Notwithstanding the existence of the official language, adequate facilities shall be given to Turkish nationals of non-Turkish speech for the oral use of their own language before the courts.' The fact that Turkey acts against these provisions in the treaty signals the strength of the tripartite link between territory, nation and language in the ideology that drives nation-state building in this country. It is this attitude that generates the linguistic conflict between Turkish and Kurdish in Turkey (see Saatci 2002). There is a sense in which it can be said that the linguistic policy of the Turkish Republic, established in 1924, represents a continuation of the Turkification policies of the Young Turks in the dying years of the Ottoman Empire.

In spite of the massive onslaught against it, Kurdish has survived in Turkey, but not as an instrument of high culture in the arts or through education. Resistance to the ban on Kurdish is clear from the references in the above testimony to the sentences imposed by the Turkish authorities on non-compliant Kurds. Kurds have also been able to enjoy satellite broadcasting beamed from abroad, or from across the border in Iraq. The fact that the Kurds live in large and often isolated communities in south-east Turkey has afforded them a measure of protection by default. This is not true of the Arab minority in Hatay, whose dire condition is exacerbated by their religious and sectarian divisions into Sunnis, Alevis and Christians. The fact that Arabic is a majority language in the Middle East makes it difficult to draw attention to the plight of Arabic-speaking Turks in their attempt to defend their language against the onslaught of Turkish. There is in fact very little knowledge of this situation in the Arabic-speaking countries themselves (see La'ibi 2001), except perhaps in Syria which continues to articulate its territorial claim over Hatay, what used to be called the Sanjak of Alexandretta before its annexation by Turkey in 1938.

The policy of enforced linguistic and ethnic assimilation in Turkey is similar to the situation of Turkish in Bulgaria between 1984 and 1990. A wave of chauvinistic Bulgarian nationalism gripped the country during this period, leading to the imposition of policies which infringed the human and linguistic rights of Turkish Bulgarians (Rudin and Eminov 1990). The purification of Bulgarian from Turkish words continued a process in progress since before the end of the Second World War, but it was now formalized by drawing up lists of banned Turkish words. This mirrored similar policies in Turkey. Those falling foul of the restriction against using such words were punished or censored, replicating similar practices in Turkey against those using proscribed Arabic and Persian words. The use of Turkish in public places was prohibited, reproducing the practice in Turkey of banning Kurdish and Arabic in public places.

The Turkish pages of bilingual Bulgarian–Turkish newspapers ceased to exist, even in areas of Bulgaria with majority Turks, creating a situation of media void in the ethnic language similar to the situation for Kurdish and Arabic in Turkey. Bulgaria was declared to be ethnically Bulgarian, thus denying Bulgarian Turks their ethnic identity in exactly the same way as Turkey has behaved towards its Kurdish and Arab populations. Bulgarian Turks ceased to exist officially, in exactly the same way as the Kurds and the Arabs do not exist officially in Turkey. Bulgarian Turks were instructed to adopt Bulgarian family names, mirroring the policy the Turks imposed on the Kurds and the Arabs in Turkey. The Bulgarian policy of cultural and linguistic cleansing against the Turkish minority extended to ordering the removal of Turkish and Arabic inscriptions on tombstones, prohibiting the wearing of the *shalvari* (the traditional baggy trousers worn by Turkish women) and the practice of male circumcision, and punishing those Bulgarian Turks who wrote to their relatives in Turkey to complain about their treatment by the authorities (Eminov 1997). These policies were discontinued in Bulgaria after 1990. The situation in Turkey remains substantially unchanged.

The above examples of linguistic conflict illustrate a number of points of a general nature. To begin with, linguistic conflict is a part of wider ideological conflicts related to nation and state building or, viewed from the opposite direction, the enforced assimilation of a minority group into the majority. The Young Turks instituted their conflictual policy of Turkification as an instrument for fashioning a new Ottoman Empire in which different linguistically based ethnicities would be assimilated into a Turkish-dominated Ottomanism. The response of the Arabic-speaking elites was one of resisting this policy, and intensifying the demands for recognizing Arabic as an official language in the Arab provinces of the empire. Rather than weakening Arab ethnic identity, Turkification produced the opposite effect. The ban on Turkish in Bulgaria elicited a similar response. It strengthened the sense of Turkish identity among the Bulgarian Turks. Rudin and Eminov sum this up as follows (1990: 161):

> Speaking and writing Turkish became acts of political defiance. When speaking Turkish in public became an offence punishable by fines or imprisonment, parents were motivated to make the effort to teach their children to read and write the language, and children themselves became conscious of its importance to their cultural identity. Many people seem to have become more militantly Turkish than they had been before.

In a similar fashion, the ban on Kurdish in Turkey strengthened Kurdish ethnic identity and turned the language into the symbol par excellence of resisting assimilation by the Turks. The key word in the preceding sentence is 'symbol'. For even when a Kurd had lost his communicative facility in the language owing to enforced assimilation, he would nevertheless continue to hold to its symbolic role in fashioning Kurdish identity. A good example of this is Abdullah Ocalan, the (currently) imprisoned Kurdish leader, who cannot speak Kurdish, but whose pronouncements on Kurdish national identity display a strong awareness of the symbolic role of the language in protecting Kurdish ethnic identity.

In addition, the mechanisms of exercising linguistic hegemony by the majority group are more or less the same in at least two of the linguistic conflicts described above. Language bans, coupled with enforced name changes and various forms of arbitrary punishment, are instituted in penal codes in both Turkey and Bulgaria (the latter between 1984 and 1990). In Turkey, however, the legal validity of these measures is enshrined in the constitution. This method of prosecuting a linguistic conflict wields a heavy stick. Other forms of prosecuting linguistic conflicts are persuasion, inducement and segregation. I will present examples of these methods later in this work.

Furthermore, the status of a language as a majority or minority one is fluid in the Middle East, depending on the situation of the language concerned and the attitude of its speakers. Thus while Arabic is the majority language of the Middle East, it is a minority language in Turkey. By the same token, while Turkish is the majority language in Turkey and most of Central Asia, it is a minority language in Bulgaria. Kurdish is a minority language in Turkey, but it is the majority language spoken in those areas of south-east Turkey where a majority Kurdish population live. The oral supremacy of Kurdish in these areas is, however, functionally circumscribed in terms of the domains the language serves. In the written medium, Turkish dominates in these areas, turning Kurdish into a minority language in this functional domain. It is, however, true that what makes a language a minority language is the attitude of its speakers. A group which feels that the way society is structured denies it its just entitlement in the distribution of resources is bound to be a minority group. The language or dialect of such a group is therefore likely to be viewed as a minority language. These variations in the status of languages and dialects must be taken into account in discussing linguistic rights in conflict situations (Coulombe 1993).

Finally, acts of linguistic resistance are motivated by a sense of external danger which manifests itself on the linguistic front. This is true of all the linguistic conflicts I have discussed in this section. The attacks on one's language are seen as attacks on the integrity of one's group and as an infringement of its boundary. Although criss-crossing ties of association and allegiance may exist between groups, language can serve as a primary symbol of association that overrides other intergroup ties in affiliative terms – for example, religion. Thus although the ethnic Turks and the Kurds are united by religion – both are, in the main, Sunni Muslims – they are nevertheless divided by language. The same was true of the Turks and the Arabs in the Ottoman Empire. The situation of the Turks in Bulgaria is different. Turkish ethnic identity here implies a difference in both language and religion from the majority Bulgarian identity. However, the conflation of these two identity ingredients does not seem to translate into an ethnic vitality that is, in practice, stronger than that based on language alone.

Language and social conflict: Arabic in the fray

Let us now consider a series of conflicts involving Arabic in the social arena. For the purposes of this study, the term 'social' will be taken to include issues of culture in the widest sense. I will concentrate on Arabic here because the bulk of this work concerns this language in situations of political and social conflict. My aim in this section is to outline a number of socio-cultural factors that lie behind some of the linguistic conflicts of the Middle East in the nineteenth and twentieth centuries. To carry out this task, I will examine three sites of conflict instigated by different interpretations of aspects of the linguistic behaviour of Arabic speakers. Language, per se, is a neutral factor here; what matters therefore are the varying interpretations of language in use in the community of speakers.

Shop signs The first example involves the mixing of Arabic and English in shop signs in Arabic-speaking countries where the use of established borrowings (for example, the Arabized forms of *supermarket* and *cafeteria*) is not the issue. Three studies of shop signs in Jordan deal with various aspects of this phenomenon (Salih and El-Yasin 1994; El-Yasin and Mahadin 1996; Zughoul 1988). Recognition is given by El-Yasin and Mahadin to the pragmatics of shop signs in the city of Irbid, in the north of the country. The authors thus treat the use of English in shop signs as a means of persuading potential customers that the name-bearer provides quality goods and services, the underlying assumption here being one that associates quality and high prices with foreignness. The mixing of English and Arabic in shop signs of this type answers to what Eastman and Stein (1993) call 'language display', the aim of which is to allocate to the self some of the positively evaluated attributes that are associated with an outside group. Eastman and Stein (1993: 188) state that the 'purpose [of such display] is not to communicate linguistically across [ethnic] boundaries but to impress socially within one's linguistic territory'. Salih and El-Yasin (1994) investigate the attitudes of speakers to these signs in Jordan, pointing out that they serve to signal quality and modernity. Abdul-Fattah and Zoghoul (1996) present similar findings; they point out that the aim of foreign shop signs is to 'promote an image of modernity, good quality [of the goods], efficiency, utility and other Western values' (1996: 84).[10] However, these authors interpret the use of foreign shop signs as an indication of a feeling of 'cultural alienation' in Jordanian society (see Zughoul 1988), which may in fact induce negative feelings in the young towards their language.

This interpretation builds on a trend in the Arabic-speaking world, beginning in the nineteenth century (Sa'id 1964: 90–3), which interprets the introduction of foreign languages in education, commerce, the media and social life generally as a form of 'cultural invasion' (al-Safti 1982). For some writers, for example Khalidi and Farrukh (1982), the roots of this invasion go back to the educational work of the missionaries in the nineteenth century in the Levant. According to Nu'man (1992), the 'invasion' of the national language is the first step in the invasion of the recipient culture in all spheres, including those of political organization and practice. Taking the concept of invasion (*ghazw*) as an organizing principle of his argument, this author structures his discussion of the invasion of Arabic by foreign languages (for which read English and French) around the following headings: (1) the reasons behind the invasion; (2) the aims of the invasion; (3) the means of invasion; (4) the results of the invasion; (5) the types of invader and invasion; and (6) resisting the invasion. These headings make it clear that Nu'man's use of the term 'linguistic invasion' of Arabic is more than just a metaphor: it is regarded as being as real as a military invasion and, being less visible, may even be more dangerous. It has 'reasons', 'aims', and 'means' to achieve specific 'results'; it can be of various kinds, involving the machinating outsider and the unscrupulous insider.

On a more general level, linguistic invasion is viewed as part of a more pervasive condition of Arab cultural subordination (*tabi'iyya thaqāfiyya*) to the West in the arts, literature, education and culture, let alone in the fields of science and technology (see Rashid 1999). This view underlies the call made by the Iraqi educator and one-time Iraqi Prime Minister (in the 1950s) Fadil al-Jamali for the replacement of foreign materials by Arab names in public signs in the Arabic-speaking countries. The same view underlies a similar call made by the Iraqi scholar and statesman Abd

[10] The use of foreign languages in shop signs tends to be associated with cosmetics, fashion, clothing, tourism, medical services and business.

al-Rahman al-Bazzaz (in 1956), who deplored the use of foreign names in shop signs (including cinemas, theatres, hotels etc.) in cities such as Cairo, Baghdad and Beirut. Discussions of this condition of subordination have recently conceptualized globalization in the context of the GAT agreements with Arab countries as a form of violence against Arab culture (Abd al-Ghani 1999). In some cases, the use of foreign languages in shop signs is viewed as a mutilation (*tashwīh*) of the national language and as a form of linguistic hegemony (*haymana*) over it (al-Bahrawi 1997). It is no accident therefore that al-Bahrawi's paper on this topic is part of a volume entitled *Our Language in the Battle of Civilizations*.

Language mixing in shop signs has also been viewed as a partner of a host of corrosive socio-political forces at work in society. An example of this is the reading al-Bahrawi (1997) provides of the following shop sign which appeared in Heliopolis, a middle-class suburb of Cairo, towards the end of the 1970s: *al-Salām Shopping Centre li-l-Muḥajjabāt* (The peace shopping centre for veiled women). The term *al-salām* (peace) in the title is said to reflect President Sadat's policy of pursuing a unilateral peace treaty with Israel in March 1979. The English term 'shopping centre' is taken to signal the emergence of a group of Egyptian middlemen who sought to establish 'shady' deals with foreign partners, the aim being to import consumer goods into Egypt for quick profit, instead of investing in the productive side of the national economy. The fact that the shopping centre in question was no more than a small outlet, not indeed a shopping centre in the full commercial sense, is taken to indicate the strength of the Western-oriented consumerism of the Egyptian middle classes at the time, as well as the association between quality and foreignness – as in Jordan – in the popular mind. The term *al-muḥajjabāt* (veiled women) in the sign is taken to indicate the rise of Islamic fundamentalism in Egypt as a result of the following factors: (1) the defeat of Egypt at the hands of Israel in the 1967 war; (2) the influence of the more conservative culture of the Arabian Peninsula with which the Egyptians came into contact through labour migration; (3) the encouragement given to Muslim groups by the Sadat regime to counter the influence of other political forces in society; and (4) the belief in some circles in Egypt that the Muslim dress code can eliminate the visibility of socio-economic disparities between the rich and the poor in society. The fact that Heliopolis is not a poor part of Cairo but a wealthy suburb of the city indicates the depth of the Islamic impulse in Egypt at the time.

Al-Bahrawi's analysis seems convincing. However, the textual coexistence of the three components of the sign is no more than a posture of aspirational harmony in socio-political terms. In fact, it masks the ideological incompatibility of the forces these terms designate in the socio-political sphere: peace with Israel, Islamic fundamentalism, the rise of Western-oriented consumerism and social equality. It is as though, by seeking to marry these forces textually, the shop sign in fact exposes their antagonistic relations with each other. Witness the fact that Sadat's policy of peace with Israel, economic and Western-style liberalization, and encouraging Islamic groups to counter-balance other political forces in society created the very conditions that led to his assassination in October 1981. It is the collision of these forces in society that al-Bahrawi injects into his analysis of the above shop sign and the language mixing it incorporates.

Code-switching The second site of conflictual interpretation of linguistic behaviour concerns the phenomenon of code-switching involving Arabic and foreign languages. Code-switching refers to the 'use of more than one language in the course of a single communicative episode' (Heller 1988: 1). Being different from borrowing, the aim of which is to elaborate the lexicon, code-switching may be considered as a form of language mixing or, alternatively, as a form of behaviour resulting from the contact between two or more languages. In the modern period, Arabic came into contact with English and French in indigenous and diaspora settings, and it is with these two languages that code-switching is most associated – although local variations, as among the Palestinians in Israel, do exist (here Hebrew is involved). Defined by the colonialist and post-colonialist experience, this contact has taken place in a context of asymmetrical power relations on the political and social fronts. Interpretations of code-switching in the Arab discourse are therefore implicated in ideological constructions of these relations that seek to display them in conflictual and hegemonic terms. The fact that code-switching – whose roots go back to the nineteenth century (see Sa'id 1964: 82) – is emerging as a mode of linguistic behaviour for some speakers in the Arabic-speaking countries does not preclude its interpretation in conflictual terms by Arab intellectuals and Arabic speakers, including those who routinely practise this mode of behaviour.[11] In her study of the language situation in Jordan, Kamhawi (2000) elicited the responses of 149 male and female students at Amman Baccalaureate School about code-switching. Kamhawi's sample consisted of 74 males and 75 females between the ages of 13 and 17. The female student responses to the question 'Do you code-switch between Arabic and English?' are set out in table 2.1. The male student responses to the same question are set out in table 2.2.

[11] Code-switching is a feature of Arabic speech in the diaspora, but this will not concern us here (see Barhoum 1994; Safi 1992; Wernberg-Møller 1994, 1999).

Table 2.1 *Female code-switching at Amman Baccalaureate School*

	13–14 years	15 years	16–17 years	Average total
Always	29%	58%	72%	58%
Sometimes	64%	35%	28%	38%
Never	7%	7%	0%	4%

Table 2.2 *Male code-switching at Amman Baccalaureate School*

	13–14 years	15 years	16–17 years	Average total
Always	6%	21%	48%	28%
Sometimes	75%	58%	52%	60%
Never	19%	21%	0%	12%

Let me exemplify the antagonistic response to code-switching by considering the reactions to the widespread occurrence of this phenomenon in the countries of North Africa.[12] In his study of the language situation in Morocco, Bentahila (1983) comments on the routine occurrence of code-switching as a style of speaking among Arabic–French bilinguals. This situation is true of Tunisia and Algeria. It is also true of Lebanon, where English and French are partners to Arabic in code-switching. In other Arabic-speaking countries – for example, Egypt and Jordan – code-switching occurs, but mainly with English and in a more limited way. In most cases, the foreign language is mixed with colloquial Arabic in code-switches. There is also evidence that code-switching is more prevalent in female than male speech (see Kamhawi 2000), and that its occurrence is conditioned by the social background of the speaker and the salient properties of the situation. Code-switching thus tends to occur in courtship between young males and females with competence in a foreign language. It is not surprising that females, who are traditionally more prestige-conscious than males, do resort to code-switching. The fact that English and French are considered languages that convey sophistication, elegance, beauty, modernity and social liberation in the Arabic-speaking countries must also be a factor in their deployment in female Arabic speech through code-switching. As a form of language display, code-switching of this kind is an attempt at identity negotiation whereby the

[12] Although the scope of this book is the Middle East, this is one of the few places in this work where the language situation in North Africa will be discussed at some length.

speaker seeks symbolically to ascribe to the self some of the attributes associated with a more prestigious group.

Bentahila (1983) observes that code-switching is associated with colonialism in the North African experience, and that this experience conditions the negative views associated with it in Arab culture. He also reports that some North African writers conceptualize code-switching as a 'bastard' mode of speaking, brought about by Arabic–French bilingualism. To establish the extent to which these negative views are held by speakers, Bentahila elicited the responses of 109 Arabic–French Moroccan bilinguals. A vast majority of the respondents, 75.22 per cent, expressed disapproval of code-switching 'ranging from pity to disgust' (1983: 37). Some of the comments offered by the respondents were as follows: '[code-switchers] are to be pitied, like me'; '[code-switching] is a disgrace'; '[code-switching] is a bad habit which should be corrected'; and '[code-switchers] are ridiculous [and] worthless'. One respondent is reported to have said that he did not consider the code-switchers to be Moroccans. Code-switching was considered as a 'sign of ignorance' by 27.52 per cent of the respondents (1983: 37). A group of respondents, constituting some 9.25 per cent of the sample, thought the code-switchers suffered from 'psychological problems of some kind, that they lacked confidence, [or] had no sense of identity' (1983: 38). The last comment about identity was reiterated by 14.81 per cent of the respondents, who believed that the code-switchers 'fail to show a proper pride in their nationality and their national language' (1983: 38). Only 9.17 per cent of Bentahila's sample expressed no objection to code-switching, and only 4.63 per cent admitted to being code-switchers themselves. The last percentage is interesting because it shows the denial by Moroccan bilinguals of what is a widespread linguistic phenomenon in which they themselves partake. This reflects the strong awareness on their part of the negative evaluation of code-switching in Moroccan society. But it also shows the discrepancy between belief and practice in this society. What Moroccan bilinguals do and what they believe are inconsistent with each other. This fact must, however, be set against the positive evaluation Moroccan French speakers receive in comparison with their Arabic-speaking counterparts (1983: 120). If this is the case, then Arabic–French Moroccan bilinguals do not object to the use of the foreign language in its 'unadulterated' form, but to the mixing of French with Arabic in a way which creates the linguistic equivalent of moral or cultural 'bastardization'. I believe that questions of 'purism' lie at the heart of this reaction, and that it is considerations of this kind that inform the evaluation of code-switching above (see Thomas 1991). I will touch on this topic later in this chapter.

Code-switching in North Africa was the subject of a series of studies by the Tunisian sociologist of language al-Dhwadi (1981, 1983, 1986, 1988, 1996). Calling this phenomenon *franco-arab*, al-Dhwadi observes that its occurrence cannot be ascribed to language contact per se between Arabic and French speakers owing to its unidirectional nature. Thus it is invariably Arabic speakers who are competent in French – rather than French speakers who know Arabic – who code-switch between the two languages. Al-Dhwadi captures this linguistic asymmetry by pointing to the non-existence of an *arabo-franc* phenomenon to counterbalance the existence of *franco-arab*. Although al-Dhwadi does not offer any empirical evidence to support this claim, his observation receives indirect support from the directionality of Arabic–English code-switching in Jordan. A study by Bader and Mahadin (1996) of code-switching to Arabic by English speakers in Jordan shows the limited nature of this phenomenon. These two authors conclude that code-switching by English speakers (1996: 51) 'mostly occurred with words/phrases related to greetings and expressions pertaining to health'. The nature of these code-switches must therefore indicate that it is a fossilized or restricted property of English speakers' speech, being in this respect different from the open-ended and productive nature of the code-switches to English by Arabic speakers. The closed and frozen nature of English to Arabic code-switches may therefore be taken to indicate the occurrence of borrowing rather than code-switching per se. Moreover, the fact that English to Arabic code-switches are used mainly for 'referential' (naming) and 'directive' (commanding and requesting) functions, in addition to phaticity (greetings and 'small talk'), indicates the frozen nature of English to Arabic code-switching.

Although al-Dhwadi concentrates on code-switching in female speech in North Africa, his interpretation of it as a form of 'inferiority complex' (*shu'ūr bi-l-naqṣ*) is intended to apply to this phenomenon in all its manifestations in this socio-cultural milieu. Al-Dhwadi locates the roots of this complex in the colonialist experience in North Africa, when the French militarily occupied this part of the Arabic-speaking world and came to dominate it politically and culturally. The subordination of North Africa culturally to the French is said to have continued after the independence of Tunisia (1956), Morocco (1956) and Algeria (1962) under the guise of what is now called *francophonie* (see Bourhis 1997; Rukaybi 1992). It is this fact, and not the existence of bilingualism per se, that explains the occurrence of code-switching in North Africa. Invoking the dictum of Ibn Khaldun (1332–82) that the vanquished emulate the victor, al-Dhwadi now interprets code-switching in North Africa as an 'aping process' brought about by a historical encounter in which a situation of asymmetrical power relations existed. Hence al-Dhwadi's reference to the North African as the 'vanquished' party (*maghlūb*) in the context of code-switching, and to this phenomenon as a whole as a form of 'cultural colonialism' (*isti'mār thaqāfī*, 1981: 127). Al-Dhwadi shows his disapproval of this phenomenon by describing it as a form of 'deviant behaviour' (1981: 128, 132) and as an expression of a 'cultural illness' (1981: 129) that requires treatment. Thus he calls for waging a 'liberation battle' (1981: 134) to 'cleanse' (1981: 133) Arabic from the demeaning influence and corrosive impact of code-switching: hence the reference to purism earlier.

A similar interpretation of code-switching is given by Fadil al-Jamali (1996), who believes that code-switching is a form of cultural subordination (*tabi'iyya thaqāfiyya*) to the colonizers. For al-Jamali, code-switching is a form of cultural invasion, and the code-switchers are an advance party for this invasion into their nation. Bereft of self-respect, the code-switchers are said to be addicted to the humiliation their code-switching represents; in this respect, they are similar to an alcoholic who no longer cares about what is sacred in his society or its moral order (1996: 36). This interpretation of code-switching is not restricted to the academy.

In a recent article in the newspaper *Asharq al-Awsat* (13 August 2001), Sawsan al-Abtah describes code-switching and other forms of linguistic affectation in derogatory terms as *tabarruj lughawī*, i.e. an ostentatious make-over or linguistic 'tarting up' whose aim is to mask the inferiorities of the speaker and to inflate the esteem with which he is to be held by his interlocutors. Linguistic affectation for her extends beyond code-switching to include the depalatalization of such emphatic sounds as *[ṭ]* in Arabic to produce *batātā*, *battīkh* and *battāniyye* instead of *baṭāṭā* (potatoes), *baṭṭīkh* (water-melon) and *baṭṭāniyye* (blanket). Al-Abtah describes code-switching as linguistic poison (*tasammum lughawī*), and those who practise it as people who stab the language in the back. Rather than as a highway towards a bright future, as those who practise code-switching believe, al-Abtah describes this phenomenon as the quickest way to an abyss (*hāwiya*) of bastard speech (*lisān hajīn*) that fails to signify loyalty (*intimā'*) to the nation or mark its identity (*huwiyya*). In this scheme of things, code-switching is declared to be an enemy of the national self, which must be eradicated to endow Arabic speakers with self-confidence and pride in their language and culture. With this new concept of the self in place, national development can be launched without the stigma of inferiority which thus far has characterized the Arab linguistic and cultural scene.

So far, al-Dhwadi's interpretation of code-switching is primarily political in nature. It sees this phenomenon as an expression of the colonialist and post-colonialist experience in North Africa. However, al-Dhwadi posits a strong social dimension to this style of speaking in female speech. On the one hand, he sees it as a reflection of the concern with social prestige and status that is traditionally judged to be stronger in women than men in the sociolinguistic literature. By mixing elements of the highly regarded foreign language with the colloquial, females are said to enhance the social value of their speech and, therefore, their own standing in society. On the other hand, al-Dhwadi considers code-switching to be an instrument of social liberation by North African women, in that it allows them to express non-conformity to the native style of speaking with its male-dominated ethos. Furthermore, code-switching is said to allow North African women to attribute to themselves symbolically some of the social attributes that are associated with the more liberated French women.

Thus, while expressing cultural subordination for both male and female speakers on the political front, code-switching represents a form of liberation for female speakers on the social front. It enables them to escape in symbolic terms from their subordination to patriarchy. True cultural liberation in North Africa would therefore deliver the double function of (1) liberating both males and females from the political domination of the West and (2) liberating women socially in a way that eliminates the need to resort to code-switching as a means of acquiring symbolic power in the struggle against patriarchy. The fact that code-switching might disappear as a style of speaking if cultural liberation in its political and social dimensions were to be achieved is a moot point. What matters for our purposes here is al-Dhwadi's reading of code-switching as a site of political-cum-social conflict in North Africa. In particular, I am interested in this reading because of its direct reference to the differential allocation of political and social power in the North African context. Although such a reading has not been proposed for code-switching in the Arabic-speaking countries of the Middle East, there is no doubt that it can be easily transposed to this context. This is why I have dwelt on it at some length here.

Gulf Pidgin Arabic Let us now consider the third example in which language in the Middle East is viewed as a site of socio-cultural conflict. This is the type of Arabic called Gulf Pidgin by Smart (1990), whose work forms the basis of the following observations. In terms of provenance, Gulf Pidgin is used in 'slightly varying forms along the eastern seaboard [of the Arabian Gulf] from Kuwait to Oman, and also inland in Saudi Arabia itself' (Smart 1990: 83). Gulf Pidgin is used mainly in interaction between native Arabic speakers in the Gulf and immigrant workers from the Indian subcontinent in 'low-level discourse' (1990: 85).

The fact that Gulf Pidgin appears as a genre in the press for humorous writings and in cartoons testifies to its relative stability.[13] Smart's description of aspects of Gulf Pidgin shows that it has a set of fairly recurrent properties. Its existence is attested, albeit in an impressionistic manner only, by Birks (1988) and Seccombe (1988). The following examples, taken from Smart (1990), give an indication of this variety of Arabic (the fact that all these examples are culled from written sources shows the extent to which this variety has penetrated the linguistic behaviour of Gulf Arabs):

madrasa ʿarabī kabīr	the big Arab school
nafarāt yamanī	Yemeni People
jadīd jawāz	new passport
ana kallim inta sīda	I address you directly
ana awwal sūg taxi	I used to drive a taxi
bannid hādha kalām	Stop this (kind of) talk
yaman janūbī seem seem lubnān	South Yemen is the same as Lebanon
lāzim fī kansal hādha ḥarb	This war should be stopped
kamsa shahr	five months

The existence of Gulf Pidgin in speech and in writing, and, in the United Arab Emirates, the dominance of English in the commercial and financial sectors, have been seen as a threat to the position and role of Arabic in that country. This situation is described using the rhetoric of conflict (al-Bayyari 2001). Gulf intellectuals thus talk about how Arabic is under attack, how it is in grave danger of being overrun by other languages on its home ground, and how it is under siege and abandoned by its native sons and daughters who seem to prefer the lure of other tongues, mainly English. The position of Arabic in the UAE is likened to that of a small island that is in danger of being submerged under a foreign linguistic flood. The importation of foreign child-minders and other categories of domestic staff who speak Gulf Pidgin is held responsible for the inability of many Gulf children to speak Arabic properly. Children who spend long hours in the care of such staff have been observed to have a deficient command of the language.

This situation at home is continued in the pre-school nurseries. A recent survey of a number of private nurseries in the UAE established that out of 515 teachers in these nurseries only 95 were Arabic speakers, although the percentage of Arab schoolchildren in these nurseries was

[13] A Kuwaiti television comedy (November/December 2002) called *ʿAshshūg* is based around the issue of linguistic purity, code-switching and Gulf Pidgin. The thirty-episode comedy pokes fun at the linguistic situation in the Gulf region.

32 per cent. Describing this as a 'tragic' situation, some researchers have also observed that 90 per cent of the Arab children attending these nursery schools experience difficulties in articulating Arabic sounds, and that 95 per cent have a deficient lexicon in comparison with children of the same age attending all Arabic nursery schools (al-Bayyari 2001). These difficulties continue into primary school. A recent study revealed how, out of 10,665 pupils moving from Primary 3 to Primary 4 in the state schools, only 58 per cent were able to pass a standard language test for the year in question. In some schools the failure rate is much higher, in spite of the fact that the state schools enjoy first-class facilities and have excellent staff–student ratios. In the private sector, which caters mainly for the children of expatriate workers, English is the dominant language. This reflects the high status that English enjoys internationally. But it is also said to reflect an attitude towards Arabic which equates it with 'backwardness', so much so that weakness in Arabic is sometimes publicly paraded as a positive attribute to nurture and display high self-esteem.

The 'plight' of Arabic in UAE is the result of a complex web of factors. The international prestige of English, Arabic speakers' attitudes towards their language, the existence of Gulf Pidgin as a result of the high percentage of non-Arabic speakers in the workforce and new patterns in child-rearing and school education have all contributed to this situation. Seen as a threat to the identity of the country in socio-cultural and geopolitical terms, this situation has impelled some Gulf nationals to call for defending Arabic against other languages. For this purpose, a Society for the Protection of Arabic was established in 1999, with its headquarters in Sharjah, whose ruler is a staunch supporter of the language. The aim of this society is to counter (1) the decline in the positive evaluation of Arabic among its speakers; (2) the deterioration of standards in the language in schools and in public life generally; and (3) the subordination of the language to English in the commercial and financial sectors. A number of directive and voluntary measures are proposed by this society. While it is not certain that these measures will succeed, it is important to note that the relationship between Arabic and other languages in the UAE is represented in conflictual terms, with the metaphor of the attack and the counter-attack dominating the interpretations of the rhetorical arena of linguistic contact.

The above examples highlight a number of general observations about language and conflict in the Middle East. In the first place, the arena of linguistic conflict incorporates the spoken and the written word, the latter in an enhanced sense of textuality encompassing such phenomena as shop signs and, as we shall see later (chapter 5), other forms of public sign. Conflicts in this arena can tap into a set of values with provenance in politics, the political economy and some deep-rooted socio-religious beliefs and convictions. All three value strands are represented in the Heliopolis shop sign *al-Salām Shopping Centre li-l-Muḥajjabāt* described earlier. The textual fixity and stability of this sign on the graphemic front belies the potential for violent conflict in society between the competing ideological forces it signifies. The assassination of Sadat of Egypt in 1981 may therefore be seen as the result of the failure to manage, let alone resolve, the conflicts between the forces tethered precariously to each other in this sign.

Furthermore, the onset of colonialism in the Arabic-speaking countries gave rise to modes of linguistic behaviour reflecting the asymmetrical power relations between the West and the Arabs. Arabic–French code-switching is one such form of linguistic behaviour with a distinct political flavour. However, the subordination of Arabic to English in commerce, in the financial markets and in school education in the UAE seems to be more immediately related to the socio-political culture of the place than to any active modalities in its political practice. These two modes of linguistic behaviour are instructive because they remind us of the importance of avoiding artificially demarcating the political from the socio-cultural in conceptualizing linguistic conflicts. Thus, while the onset of code-switching may have been politically induced by the colonial experience, its continuation in post-independence Arabic-speaking countries seems to be more socially driven. This fact justifies treating code-switching as a style of speaking in the repertoire of verbal styles available to Arabic speakers. However, the negative view of this style of speaking described above, even by those who resort to it in practice, indicates a duality of the Arab self in which the *ideal* speaker censures the *actual* performer.

Finally, questions of national identity are central to the discussion of linguistic conflict. The call by al-Dhwadi to rid North African speakers of the 'scourge' of code-switching is motivated by a vision of the national self that is culturally free and historically rooted in its own authentic traditions. The establishment of the Society for the Protection of Arabic in the UAE is motivated by a similar conception of the national self. This is also true of the negative reading of the mixed shop signs in Jordan. The rhetoric of material conflict is injected into this construction of the self to promote task orientation and collective motivation. Moral considerations of purity and wholesomeness are also pressed into service. The language is projected as under attack not just from the outside but also from the inside, and not only by a stronger group but also by one that occupies a low position in society. In the UAE, the distinction between the outsider and the insider becomes less relevant than usual. The indigenous national, the expatriate Arabic speaker and the expatriate non-Arabic speaker all participate in the onslaught on Arabic. The danger to Arabic can come as much from English as an international language as from Gulf Pidgin, which is not even a fully fledged language in terms of the linguistic resources it has or the range of functional domains it serves. This and the other general observations in this section will be pursued later in this work.

Arabic and national identity: the clash of ideologies

So far, I have dealt with socio-political conflicts involving Arabic and other languages. In this and the following section, I will deal with conflicts of this kind concerning Arabic on its own. One of these conflicts pertains to the competing constructions of national identity in the Arab Middle East. I have dealt with this topic at length in a series of publications (1994, 1996b, 1997, 1999a, 1999b), culminating in *The Arabic Language and National Identity: A Study in Ideology* (2003). I will therefore restrict myself to a broad characterization of this topic here.

The role of language as a marker of national or ethnic identity is well attested in many cultures and at different times in history. Arabic has been deployed in this capacity in a variety of ideological articulations in the twentieth century, including (pan-)Arab nationalism, territorial nationalism and what may be called Islamic nationalism. Although these nationalisms are sometimes articulated in isolation from each other, they are usually set against each other, whether implicitly or explicitly. There is therefore a strong sense in which these nationalist ideologies can be said to compete with each other, and this competition sometimes takes the form of open conflict and hostility in the socio-political arena. Many of the attempted coups, actual coups or counter-coups in such countries as Jordan, Syria and Iraq in the twentieth century involved expressions of ideological conflicts concerning national identity. Let us deal with these ideologies below.

Arab nationalism in its classical form is of the cultural type. Although the ingredients that make up the Arab nation may vary from one ideologue of nationalism to another, there is almost universal agreement that language is a primary, if not the primary, ingredient in defining this nation. For some, it is the only ingredient. This is the case for the Syrian al-Arsuzi, a staunch primordialist, who bases his entire ideology of the revival (*ba'th*) of the Arab nation in the modern period on the ability of the Arabs to cull the set of original meanings preserved in the root structure of the lexical stock of the language.[14] For al-Arsuzi, the genius of the Arab

[14] As set out by al-Husri (see Suleiman 2003: 126–46), Arab nationalism is ethno-symbolist in character. See Smith (2001) for ethno-symbolism and primordialism in the study of nationalism.

nation lies in the genius of its language in its pristine, pre-Islamic and early Islamic condition (see Suleiman 2003: 146–58). Although al-Husri, the greatest ideologue of Arab nationalism, did not share al-Arsuzi's romantic and metaphysical infatuation with Arabic, he was no less adamant that it constituted, with history, the backbone of Arab national identity. Being an Arab, for al-Husri, thus came to be more or less synonymous with being an Arabic speaker. Both writers thus defended Arabic against its detractors: those who sought to negate its role in defining the Arab nation, or those who sought to undermine this role by promoting the colloquial as a badge of identity. The often acrimonious debates which al-Husri had with Antun Saʿada, the leader of the Syrian Socialist National Party, for his denial of the role of Arabic as a marker of a pan-Arab national identity, provide ample evidence of the ideological contestation involving the language in the Middle East.

Territorial nationalisms in the Middle East deny that Arabic can form the basis of a national identity encompassing all those who share it as a common language. This amounts to denying the validity of Arab nationalism. Examples of this are Egyptian nationalism and Lebanese nationalism (Suleiman 2003: 162–233). Environmental factors are given prominence as formative impulses of national identity here, the intention being to locate the nation in a territory that has shaped the character of those who inhabit it. The role of the state as an indispensable force in nation building is also emphasized, particularly in Lebanese nationalism. Nevertheless, the role of Arabic in these nationalisms is acknowledged, although in a form that is different from its role in Arab nationalism. For some, for example Taha Husayn in Egypt and Kamal Yusuf al-Hajj in Lebanon, Arabic in its standard form was an important ingredient of Egyptian and Lebanese national identity. For others, Arabic serves in this capacity in its colloquial form only. Intellectuals of this ideological persuasion, for example the Egyptian Salama Musa and the Lebanese Saʿid Aql, therefore sought to undermine Standard Arabic, describing it as a backward and fossilized language that is unfit to express the needs of Arabic speakers in the modern world. In its place, they called for promoting the colloquial. Saʿid Aql demonstrated his commitment to this enterprise by publishing a newspaper in the colloquial using the Roman alphabet. I will deal with the conflict between the standard and colloquial forms of Arabic at length in the next chapter.[15]

Both in principle and in practice, Islamic nationalism opposes all other forms of national-identity construction involving Muslims in which Islam

[15] See Gully (1997) for a discussion of these issues in the late nineteenth and early twentieth centuries.

is not regarded as the binding principle par excellence. Islamic nationalism, the roots of which go back to the nineteenth century, thus opposes Arab nationalism and all territorial nationalisms in the lands of Islam. Arab nationalism in particular came under attack because of the attempt by some of its proponents to allocate matters of religious belief to the private domain (Suleiman 2003: 140–2), summed up in the slogan 'Religion belongs to God, the homeland belongs to all' (*al-dīn li-llāh wa-l-waṭan li-l-jamī'*). Territorial nationalisms came under attack for the same reason. Attempts to treat Islam as a civilization that belongs to Muslim and non-Muslim Arabs in constructing the national self, at the pan-Arab or nation-state level, were also attacked. These attacks extended to all attempts which sought to sever or weaken the ideological links between Arabic and Islam (Attar 1966; al-Ghazali 1998; Husayn n.d., 1979; al-Jundi 1982; al-Nahawi 1998). Islamic nationalists launched a number of arguments in defence of Arabic, including: (1) as the language of God's revelation to the Prophet verbatim, Arabic is inextricably linked with Islam doctrinally; (2) the Qur'an and the Prophetic traditions (*ḥadīth* literature) are unequivocal about this link and the inseparability of the language from the religion; (3) the position of Arabic in the world derives its currency in historical terms from its association with Islam; thus (4) Arabic without Islam is like a body without a soul. Islamic nationalists therefore concluded that the involvement of Arabic in non-Islamic nationalisms is intellectually and historically bogus and must as a result be rejected, except in those cases where a nationalism sees itself as a step on the way to realizing the brotherhood of faith in Islamic nationalism.

Although Arab nationalism, territorial nationalisms and Islamic nationalism coalesce around the Arabic language, they do so in a conflictual manner. Both Arab nationalism and Islamic nationalism reject any association with the colloquial, but they differ from each other in that whereas the latter places Arabic within Islam completely, the former does not. In so doing, Arab nationalism recognizes that the Arab nation includes non-Muslims who nevertheless feel that Arabic is as much their language as it is the language of their fellow Arab Muslims. Territorial nationalisms share with Arab nationalism its avoidance of casting Arabic in an Islamic context ideologically, but they differ from it in the recognition they give to the effect of the environment and the state in shaping the national character, including the role of the language in forming it. Whether resort is made to Standard Arabic or to the colloquial, territorial nationalisms make the claim that each such nationalism has its own subtly and uniquely flavoured Arabic, often produced by the deep and long-lasting influence of the linguistic substratum. Ancient Egyptian and Coptic constitute this substratum in some articulations of Egyptian nationalism, whereas Phoenician is said to play this role in Lebanese nationalism. Arabic is caught up in the conflicts of identity construction involving these nationalisms. Considering its position in Islam and Arab culture, the role of Arabic as a proxy in these conflicts is understandable.

Arabic and modernity: the clash of tradition and change

The active promotion of modernity in the Arabic-speaking countries of the Middle East has traditionally been associated with the Napoleonic invasion of Egypt in 1798 and the rise of Muhammad Ali as the effective ruler of this part of the Ottoman Empire in 1805. Contact with the West intensified during this period through the many educational missions to France, the modernization of the military, the setting up of educational institutions and the establishment of a nascent bureaucracy to serve the state-building project inaugurated by Muhammad Ali and continued by members of his dynasty after his death in 1849. In the Levant, contact with the West began even earlier, but it did intensify during the nineteenth century owing mainly to the work of missionaries in the educational and social spheres. In the nineteenth century, the Ottoman Empire sought to modernize the institutions of the state in a programme of administrative reforms known as the Tanzimat (see Davison 1963), the aim of which was to put the empire on an equal footing with its European rivals in the military and political spheres. The coalescence of these developments had the effect of increasing literacy and the rise of a print culture – including the development of journalism and the promotion of translation from the European languages – to cater for the needs of a nascent middle class. The *nahḍa*, the modern Arab literary renaissance, had its roots in these developments.

On the linguistic front, Arabic had to serve as the medium of this new modernity with its emphasis on scientific thinking, instrumental rationality, social mobility and state building. In the process, Arabic itself became the subject of these new modernizing impulses. Broadly speaking, the argument was made that modernization cannot proceed in an effective manner without modernizing the language itself. The modernization of Arabic was therefore established as a material condition for the success of the modernization project in the socio-political sphere. This is one aspect of Arab modernity in the linguistic domain. The other aspect turned the modernization of the language into a symbolic motif for the modernization project itself. In this respect, the modernization of Arabic served as a proxy for a host of debates which directly or indirectly touched on issues of great sensitivity in Arab culture, particularly those belonging to the religious sphere. Conflicts over the modernization of Arabic may therefore be read as indices through which other conflicts were waged between different interest groups in society who, for the purposes of this study, may be broadly classified into the modernizers and the language-defenders (see al-Jabiri 1991). The fact that these two groups are not monolithic ideologically and in terms of the positions they have adopted vis-à-vis the reform of the language will not detain us here.

Some of the modernizers believed that Arabic was unfit for teaching the modern sciences; they argued that the delivery of this teaching ought to be entrusted to one of the European languages in schools, with English emerging as the prime candidate for this role. In a debate launched by the Lebanese weekly *al-Nashra al-usbūʿiyya* in 1881, the Lebanese educator Khalil Abu Saʿd argued that there was a pressing need for speedy modernization in the Arab lands, and that this would only be delivered by English, owing to the following factors (in Khuri 1991: 10–12): (1) the abundance of scientific works in the language; (2) as a result, the language can induce a genuine modernization in Arab society, rather than a counterfeit one constructed around Arabic and motivated by a sense of false piety (*ḍarb min al-taqwā*); (3) English is an easy language to learn; (4) it is used in many parts of the world; (5) it does not suffer from the diglossia characterizing Arabic; and (6) it facilitates trade between nations. Abu Saʿd finished his article by exhorting his compatriots to adopt English instead of Arabic in teaching the sciences 'to replace their humiliation by glory, their ignorance by scientific knowledge, and their backwardness by modernity and social progress' (Khuri 1991: 12). This position received support from another Lebanese, Ibrahim Katbe (Khuri 1991: 14–16), who declared that Arabic was rooted in a desert culture, so much so in fact that the Arabic lexicon deserves to be called *The Book of the Camel*, since (he claims) hardly any word in it falls outside the set of meanings designating this animal. Ibrahim Katbe ended this derogatory view of Arabic by stating that those who wish to enter the 'paradise of science and technology must do so from its proper gate as represented by . . . English' (Khuri 1991: 16). By so doing, he continued, the Arabs will be able to escape from 'the stain of oppression, the vice of confusion, and the depth of poverty which the speakers of Arabic inherit from their language' (Khuri 1991: 16).

It is clear that both Khalil Abu Saʿd and (especially) Ibrahim Katbe posit a positive link between Arabic and underdevelopment, not just in the field of material progress, but also in the social and cultural spheres. For these two writers, Arabic and modernization are not compatible with each other. Arabic thus emerges as an obstacle to modernization rather than as a vehicle that can deliver it. Other authors who entered the debate rejected this analysis. The educator Abdu Kahil pointed out that Arabic is a rich language lexically and morphologically (Khuri 1991: 7–10); it is also a language with 'a noble pedigree' which must be protected at all costs (Khuri 1991: 8). Fadlalla Arbili took the view that any attempt to restrict the functional domains served by Arabic is tantamount to reducing its affiliative role as 'the national language' in shaping group identity (Khuri 1991: 20). He accused the opponents of Arabic of being short-sighted and of pursuing change for its own sake. The educator Ilyas al-Rishani defended Arabic as a rich language and as the only sure way of rooting modernization in the Arab soil (Khuri 1991: 24–6). He acknowledged that Arabic is in need of modernization, but he added that pride in it as the national language demands giving it the support it needs and deserves, not abandoning it (see Safi 1992). Appealing to the Arab code of honour, he reminds his readers that abandoning one's language because of any temporary deficiency it may have is similar to abandoning one's mother because of her ragged clothes. Both are shameful acts. And in so far as the latter is regarded as morally reprehensible behaviour in Arab culture, the former must be viewed in the same manner.

Most of the attacks on Arabic in the quest for modernity fell short of calling openly for it to be replaced by a foreign language in most school subjects. However, one of the fiercest attacks on the language in the twentieth century came from the Egyptian writer Salama Musa (1887–1958). In his book *al-Balāgha al-ʿaṣriyya wa-l-lugha al-ʿarabiyya* (Modern Eloquence/Rhetoric and the Arabic Language, 1964), Musa reiterated the view that Arabic was steeped in the desert ethos and the outdated value system this engenders (Suleiman 2003). He therefore considered the language to be responsible for many of the uncivilized practices found in Egyptian society, including the so-called 'honour killings' of women for pre-marital sex or for having sex outside wedlock. The existence of diglossia in Arabic is said to create a kind of linguistic schizophrenia, whereby Arabic speakers think in one medium (the colloquial) and encode their thoughts in another (the standard). The pursuit of ornate style in Arabic is said to encourage excellence in form at the expense of excellence in content. Being difficult to learn, Arabic grammar diverts teaching and learning in and outside the school away from other worthwhile pedagogic objectives. The Arabic script is said to be economically (in printing terms) and pedagogically wasteful of much-needed resources. For all of these reasons, Musa concluded that Arabic could not serve the modernization project in Egypt without subjecting it to major modernization itself.

Musa therefore demanded (1) the simplification of Arabic grammar; (2) the adoption of the Roman alphabet; (3) the modification of Arabic style; (4) the culling of vocabularies which impel the Egyptian to behave in an uncivilized manner; (5) the adoption of foreign words and phrases to fill the gaps in the Arabic lexicon; and (6) the bridging of the gap between the standard and the colloquial by bringing the former as close to the latter as possible. Other modernizers proposed similar measures in the nineteenth and twentieth centuries (see Gully 1997). What distinguishes Musa, however, is his uncompromising attacks on Arabic in language that is at the same time accessible and full of vitriol. Thus he derided Arabic for being anti-modernization in the social arena and anti-democracy in the political sphere. He likened Arabic rhetoric to a drug to which its speakers have been dangerously addicted. Thus many of the crimes committed in Egypt are in Musa's view first and foremost linguistic crimes motivated by a fossilized language serving a fossilized religion. It is this condemnatory attitude towards Arabic and its associated culture that turned Musa into the target of some of the most virulent attacks by the language-defenders, as we shall see below.[16]

The calls to reform the language were not always cast in this antagonistic manner. More often than not, they were presented in a matter-of-fact way, for example in the calls to reform Arabic grammar made by the Egyptian Ibrahim Mustafa (1959) and the Lebanese Anis Frayha (1955, 1956, 1959, 1966). This is also true of some of the proposals to reform the Arabic script, including the proposal submitted by Abd al-Aziz Fahmi to the Arabic Language Academy in Cairo in the 1940s to adopt the Roman alphabet in place of the Arabic script (see Makdisi 1955; Musa 1955; al-Toma 1961; 'Umar 1987). The Egyptian educator and statesman Ahmad Lutfi al-Sayyid (1872–1963) adopted the same matter-of-fact approach at the beginning of the twentieth century when he called for bringing the standard and the colloquial forms of the language closer to each other (1945). The fact that these and other calls and proposals for language reforms were presented in a rational and balanced way did not spare

[16] Although rare, this attitude towards Arabic and its culture is expressed by a variety of writers from time to time. The Palestinian writer Fawaz Turki provides a recent example of this attitude (1999: 200):

> I grew up in a society that in fact socializes the individual to fear any form of originality. We are socialized to look upon the authority figure as someone to fear. This notion of socialization is reflected in the way we speak our language. *Arabic is a language that is not suitable for logical thinking. Arabic is probably the most degraded and dehumanized language in the entire world. It blocks us from being part of the global dialogue of culture.* Why is that? Because language is culture. We come from a culture that is repressive; the language we speak is equally repressive. So we have a problem on two levels: the problem is to liberate ourselves from occupation and on the other level to liberate ourselves, to have an Intifada, directed against our home. [emphasis added]

However, unlike Musa, Turki seems to think that all forms of Arabic, the standard and the colloquials, are repressive. See Suleiman (2000) for a critical discussion of similar views of the link between language and culture in the Arabic-speaking world.

their authors some of the vitriol which the language-defenders deployed in their attacks on the modernizers, as I will explain below.

One of the best statements on the modernization of the language is by Gibran Khalil Gibran (1883–1931). In his essay 'Lakum lughatukum wa-liya lughatī' (You have your language, and I have my language), Gibran proposes what may be regarded as the manifesto of linguistic modernization (see Ya'qub 1985: 258–62 for the full text of this essay). Gibran's essay produces in a style not lacking in poetic flavour many of the arguments concerning the modernization of the language discussed above, but it does so in a way that is full of sarcasm and ridicule of the opposite party. A dichotomy is created between the modernizers, in whose name Gibran speaks, and the defenders of the status quo on the linguistic scene. The former are projected as committed to a living and a free language. The latter are said to be slaves to a dead and enslaving language. The modernizers are anchored to the present and to the future; the language-defenders are anchored to the past. The modernizers shun the deadly boring and constricting theorization of the Arab grammarians; the language-defenders worship at their feet. The modernizers cull their vocabularies from the language of the ordinary people in normal and everyday situations; the language-defenders dig theirs out of dead lexica and dictionaries. The modernizers create their own poetic rhythms and themes; the language-defenders follow the rhythms and themes of an ossified past. The modernizers treat language as a means to something else; the language-defenders treat it as an end in itself. The modernizers are in contact with nature and real life; the language-defenders are in contact with inscriptions of the past. The modernizers pay attention to content; the language-defenders pay attention to form. Modernization is correlated with strength and the truth; the linguistic status quo is correlated with weakness and falsehood. By wedding themselves to the past and its stylistic and grammatical conventions, the language-defenders are said to consign their language to an early death, a death befitting an old and handicapped woman. In contrast, the modernizers' language is said to be young and full of life. To drive these points home, Gibran exploits the powers of intertextuality to full effect. The title of his essay, 'Lakum lughatukum wa-liya lughatī', which he repeats six times, echoes the final verse in chapter 109 of the Qur'an. Here, Prophet Muhammad addresses the unbelievers, telling them *lakum dīnukum wa-liya dīni* (You have your faith, and I have my faith). The whole chapter reads as follows: 'Proclaim: Hearken you who disbelieve! I do not worship what you worship, nor do you worship what I worship. I do not worship those that you worship, nor do you worship Him Whom I worship. You have your faith, and I have my faith.'

By adopting as the title for his creed of modernization a formula that recalls a verse in the Qur'an, Gibran likens the modernization of the language to the one and true religion in Islamic terms, declaring those who oppose this creed as unbelievers. Gibran – well known as the author of *The Prophet* – and his fellow modernizers are likened to the Prophet Muhammad and his followers in relation to those who oppose them. In the same way that Muhammad and his followers were totally separate from the unbelievers, Gibran and the modernizers are totally separate from those who oppose modernization. In the same way that Muhammad and his followers refused to worship the idols of pre-Islamic Arabia, the *jāhiliyya*, Gibran and the modernizers refuse to worship the idols of those who belong to the opposite camp, including Sibawayh, who is the acknowledged father of Arabic grammar. The fact that Arabic is the subject of this conflict of linguistic faiths between the modernizers and their opponents injects additional metaphorical power into the animosity between them. By placing the modernizers on the side of those who proclaim the truth in Islamic terms, Gibran projects the proponents of this linguistic creed as the true protectors of the language of the Qur'an, God's revealed word verbatim. In this way, he denies the traditionalists the right to project themselves as the party that can protect God's language – for how could those who proclaim linguistic falsehood be the protectors of the linguistic medium that encapsulates God's truth? These remarks reveal the cultural depth of the battle between the modernizers and their opponents. They also show that this battle is fought using discursive ammunition, what I shall call below the rhetoric of linguistic conflict. To illustrate how this discursive battle is joined, I will examine the rhetoric of the language-defenders below.

As a first indication of this rhetoric, we may refer to the titles of some of the books, special issues of journals, and newspaper and electronic articles that deal with the Arabic language in the modern world. An example of the first category is *al-Zaḥf ʿalā lughat al-Qurʾān* (The March against the Language of the Qur'an) in which the author, the Saudi journalist Ahmad Abd al-Ghafur Attar (1966), describes the proposals of the modernizers as the equivalent of a military march – hence the term *zaḥf* – whose aim is to destroy the Arabic language, thereby destroying Islam. Another example is a book by the Egyptian academic Muhammad Muhammad Husayn (n.d.) entitled *Ḥuṣūnunā muhaddada min dākhilihā* (Our Fortresses are Threatened from Within) in which he describes the efforts of the 'enemy within' to destroy Arabic and Islam as the sources of power and cohesion among the Arabs and the Muslims. A recent special issue of the Egyptian journal *Qaḍāyā fikriyya* carries the title *Lughatunā fī maʿrakat al-ḥaḍāra* (Our language in the battle of civilizations, 1997). This special issue carries a variety of articles describing the dire situation of the Arabic language. The tone for some of these articles is set in the preface in which the editor, the highly respected Egyptian journalist Mahmud Amin al-Alim, describes the present state of Arabic, using an abundance of military metaphors. I will return to this preface below. The title of an article in the newspaper *Asharq al-Awsat* (7 March 1995) accuses the colonialists and post-colonialists of restricting the functional domains Arabic serves in the modern world (Amamra 1995). As we have seen in the discussion of code-switching above (pp. 29–34), and as we shall see below, this is a recurrent theme in discussions of what is considered to be the 'plight' of the Arabic language in the modern world. A recent article on the web (14 May 2001) carries the title 'al-Lugha al-ʿarabiyya fī miḥna wa-lā budda min inqādhihā' (The Arabic language is in a crisis: we must rescue it!). This and the preceding examples are part of a growing genre of titles whose aim is to instil in the reader a sense of urgency about the dangers facing Arabic from the inside and the outside. The fact that these dangers are considered to be real, rather than imagined, is a defining property of the rhetoric of linguistic conflict in Arabic discourse. This observation will be elaborated further when we consider other examples of this rhetoric.

For this purpose, let us consider a set of items consisting of two dedications, a preface and a conclusion that have appeared in some books and essays dealing with aspects of the linguistic conflict in the Arab arena in the nineteenth and twentieth centuries. The Egyptian journal *al-Muqtaṭaf* sponsored a debate in 1882 to discuss the relationship between Arabic diglossia and modernization; in particular, it raised the question as to whether the Arabs should abandon Standard Arabic in favour of the colloquials (see Khuri 1991: 35–65). One of the participants in this debate was the Christian Lebanese educator and writer Asʿad Daghir (d. 1935), who eloquently argued in favour of the standard as the language of modernization. In the conclusion to his essay (Khuri 1991: 47–50), Daghir employs the rhetoric of the military encounter, no doubt for affective reasons. He writes (Khuri 1991: 50):

Who will give me friends, supporters and patrons . . . who will respect the sanctity of the pure Arabic language? [Who will give me friends, supporters and patrons] in whose fortified places I can take refuge and to whose leather stirrups I can attach myself, so that together we can embark on defending the honour of this noble language, guard its sacred turf, safeguard its rights, and protect the sanctity of its literatures? [Who will give me friends, supporters and patrons] who will serve Arabic for its own sake? [Who will give me friends, supporters and patrons] with keen desire [to perform this task], and who will not take to heart the reproaches of the fault-finders?

The Arabic term I rendered into English as the composite 'friends, supporters and patrons' is *anṣār*. This is an interesting term in Arabic, because it is the name of the followers of the Prophet in Medina who granted him refuge from his enemies in Mecca in AD 622. By using this term, Daghir invokes this experience for motivational effect in the defence of the Arabic language against its enemies. The fact that he, a Christian, does this is significant because it signals to his readers that the defence of their language is almost akin to a religious duty, and that this duty knows no religious boundaries. By a stroke of lexical luck, the word *anṣār* also conjures up the name of the Christians in Arabic, *naṣārā*, which signifies the giving of support to Jesus in his mission. This etymology gives further support to the idea that the defence of Arabic is akin to a religious duty that knows no faith boundaries in the Arabic-speaking world. This clever use of intertextuality is a recurring rhetorical strategy in the discourse of linguistic conflict in the Arabic arena, as we have seen in the discussion of Gibran earlier in this section. Daghir exploits this strategy to full effect through the Arabic expression *ghayr khāshīn lawmat lā'im*, which I have translated as 'who will not take to heart the reproaches of the fault-finders' above. This expression recalls part of verse 54 of chapter 5 in the Qur'an, in which God threatens those who renounce Islam with humiliation. By invoking this verse, Daghir seeks to imply that support for the colloquial against the standard is in moral terms equivalent to the renouncing of one's true religion, and that this act will bring humiliation to the linguistic apostates as apostasy in the early period of Islamic history had done to those who proclaimed it. I will give this verse in full below to help the reader make this comparison directly (Qur'an 5: 54):

> O you who believe, whosoever from among you turns back from his religion let him remember that in his stead God will soon bring a people whom He will love and who will love Him, who will be kind and considerate towards the believers and firm and unyielding towards the disbelievers. They will strive hard in the cause of God and *will not at all take to heart the reproaches of the fault-finders* (*wa-lā yakhāfūn lawmata lā'im*). That is God's grace; He bestows it upon whosoever He pleases. God is the Lord of vast-bounty, All-Knowing.

Let us pursue aspects of this rhetoric of linguistic conflict in the Arabic arena by considering the dedication to *al-Qawmiyya al-fuṣḥā* by Umar Farrukh (1961). This book considers some of the modernizing trends in Arabic and their negative impact on the integrity of the language in its role as a marker of Arab national identity. The title of the book signifies the indissoluble link between the language and national identity by conflating the name for Arab nationalism, *al-qawmiyya al-'arabiyya*, and the name of the language, *al-'arabiyya al-fuṣḥā* (pure Arabic), to create an amalgam of both: *al-qawmiyya al-fuṣḥā* (pure-Arabic nationalism). This amalgamation is carried through the dedication which, as can be expected, employs the rhetoric of the battlefield with full Islamic connotations (Farrukh 1961: 5–6):

> To the *garrisoned troops* (*murābiṭūn*, 3: 200) who know that they are members of the home front!
>
> To the first generation of *holy warriors* (*mujāhidūn*, 95: 4) who stood together shoulder to shoulder (*marṣūṣ*, 4: 61)!
>
> To those who carried the burning flame of pure Arabism and pure Arabic to the four corners of the universe in storm-swept conditions!
>
> To those who stood their ground in the heat of the battle!
>
> To those who put the confidence back in the hearts of the Arabs *after their eyes had become distracted and their hearts had risen up to their throats* (*zāghat al-abṣār wa-balaghat al-qulūb al-ḥanājir*, 10: 33)
>
> To all of these I dedicate this book in admiration of the past glories, appreciation of the present effort, and out of confidence in the future!

The numbers next to the texts in brackets indicate intertextual references to the Qur'an that specify chapter and verse. The military nature of these references in the dedication is not accidental: it is intended to cast the defence of Arabic against the modernizers as a fierce battle between the forces of good and evil, right and wrong, truth and falsehood. The message conveyed by the dedication is pretty clear: the defenders of Arabic will emerge victorious as the believers before them had done. The battle in defence of Arabic is further imagined as a holy war, a kind of *jihad* in which the glories of the past serve as harbingers of things to come. The future of Arabic is therefore assured. The modernizers will be vanquished, and the language-defenders will triumph.

Let us now examine the dedication by Attar to his book *al-Zaḥf ʿalā lughat al-Qurʾān*. I have chosen this book because of its strong Islamic orientation. This will enable us to show how the rhetoric of language-defence applies in Islamic discourse in a manner that strongly resembles its application in the discourse of Arab nationalism (Farrukh) and its precursors (Daghir). Another reason for choosing this book is the wide-ranging nature of its attack on linguistic modernization, including the proposals to reform the script or to replace it by the Roman alphabet, the calls to simplify Arabic grammar, and the attempts to encourage the use of the colloquial in literature. Attar writes in the dedication (1966: 5):

> To the friends, supporters and patrons (*anṣār*) of the pure Arabic language (*fuṣḥā*) who are waging a true holy war (*yujāhidūn fī Allah ḥaqq al-jihād*) by aiding the language of the Qur'an, its literatures and sciences. [To those] who defend the language and fight the proponents of the creeds of destruction and sabotage (*hadm wa-takhrīb*) whose aim is to destroy the Qur'an, sabotage the Prophetic

Traditions (*ḥadīth*), exterminate Islam, and demolish Arabic with its grammar, literatures, sciences and arts by aiding and establishing the colloquial and by making it triumph over the pure Arabic language. [To these friends, supporters and patrons I dedicate this book.]

Like Daghir before him, Attar uses the term *anṣār* to refer to the defenders of Standard Arabic, thus exploiting the religious and historical significance of this term for motivational effect. And like Farrukh, who was writing a few years before him, Attar describes the fight against the modernizers as a holy war against the forces of evil which want to fight Islam by fighting the language of the Qur'an. The defence of Arabic now emerges as the front-line battle in the defence of Islam. The loss of this battle would therefore presage the destruction of Islam. This is why it behoves those Muslims who care about their religion to engage fully and completely in a linguistic holy war in defence of Arabic. This message runs through the entire book, which refers to some of the modernizers I have mentioned above by name, including Salama Musa, Anis Frayha, Ibrahim Mustafa and Abd al-Aziz Fahmi.

Let us now consider the preface by Mahmud Amin al-Alim to the special volume of *Qaḍāyā fikriyya*: *Lughatunā al-ʿarabiyya fī maʿrakat al-ḥaḍāra* (1997). I have chosen this preface to show the continuity of the warfare metaphor in the Arabic rhetoric of linguistic conflict. This metaphor is signalled in the title of the preface: 'In defence of linguistic particularity' ('Difāʾ ʿan al-khuṣūṣiyya al-lughawiyya', al-Alim 1997: 9). The main point in this preface is an attack against the impact of globalization on the Arabic language, rather than the defence of Arabic in its capacity as the language of the Qur'an. Witness the fact that the words 'Qur'an' and 'Islam' do not occur once in this preface. Also, the fact that this preface is preceded by an excerpt from Gibran's essay 'You have your language, and I have my language' signals some sympathy on the part of al-Alim to aspects of the modernization programme. Nevertheless, this author attacks intrusions into Arabic from the European languages through lexical and grammatical interference, which he says 'eat away at the language by marginalizing and culturally impoverishing it, and by causing cracks to appear on its surface' (al-Alim 1997: 11). He declares that 'Arabic is in danger', and that this danger of external interference can, if left unchecked, bring about a situation of political and cultural subordination to outside powers. Arabic therefore is not only engaged in a linguistic battle, but in one involving a clash of civilizations (*maʿraka ḥaḍāriyya*, al-Alim 1997: 10). Al-Alim expands on the military nature of this metaphor in the following terms (1997: 10): 'The language regiment (*katībat al-lugha*) is the vanguard of the regiments fighting the political and economic battles between . . . nationalities, civilizations and cultures.' The defence of the national language is therefore a defence of one's nationality, civilization and culture.

In the rhetoric of linguistic conflict in the Arabic arena, the enemies of the language are mostly insiders who, wittingly or unwittingly, act as the vanguard of an externally constituted invader. Farrukh states this as follows (1961: 18):

> The battle between the colloquial and the standard is not the first battle to be waged against the Arab nationalist idea, and it will not be the last battle from which this idea will emerge victorious. We are confident of victory because we know that the battle is fought on Arab land, but that its General Staff (*arkān ḥarbihā*) sit in the capitals of the imperial powers: Washington, London and Paris.

The modernizers are regarded as part of this invasion, hence the use of the term *ghazw* (invasion) to describe the work of some of the proponents of modernization. I have given an example of this invasion metaphor on p. 29. Al-Jamali applies the same metaphor to describe the conflict between Arabic and the European languages. He describes the aim of the linguistic invaders as one of wanting 'to destroy Arabic from its very roots by claiming that it is a barren language and that it is unfit for modern life' (1996: 32). These invaders and saboteurs are drawn from the sons and daughters of the language itself, and they fall into four categories: (1) those who advocate the use of the colloquial and the Roman script; (2) those who call for using the European languages in teaching the modern sciences; (3) those who use the foreign languages in speech as a sign of high culture; and (4) those who employ code-switching in their speech.

The invasion metaphor was also used by al-Jundi (1982: 117), who attacked the modernizers as people who peddle in heresies and whose aim is to incite discord (*fitna*) among the Arabs and the Muslims. Among these he counted Gibran, Salama Musa, Ahmad Lutfi al-Sayyid and Taha Husayn. Al-Jundi believed that the battles fought against Arabic by these and other enemies of the language are part of a carefully planned war, what he dubbed the Arabic Language War (*ḥarb al-lugha al-ʿarabiyya*, 1982: 172). A similar attack against the modernizers was launched by the Syro-Egyptian scholar Mustafa Sadiq al-Rafiʿi (1881–1937). He accused them of waging a crusade against Arabic for the benefit of the colonizers (see al-Shakʿa 1970: 33). The Egyptian academic Muhammad Husayn deployed the metaphor of 'the invasion from within' in his attack against the modernizers (n.d.: 165). He referred to the modernizers as 'the enemies of Islam, the advocates of enslavement, the mouthpiece of the missionaries, and the agents of Zionism' (n.d.: 165). He gave particular attention to the proposal to simplify Arabic grammar put forward by Ibrahim Mustafa, describing it as an attempt to destroy the language and to spread poison in it. Husayn extended this attack to the applications of modern linguistic theory to Arabic, describing these applications as heresies and corruptions (n.d.: 190), before correlating them with social practices that are foreign to Egyptian society, including (1) discarding the turban and the fez in favour of European-style hats; and (2) the taking of European wives among the elite (n.d.: 191).

The rhetoric of the language-defenders conceives of translators and journalists as potential enemies of the language. The Lebanese writer Muhammad Abd al-Rahman Marhaba considered translation responsible for many of the grammatical and stylistic mutilations (*tashwīhāt*, 1990: 69) visited on Arabic under the influence of foreign languages. He therefore called for fortifying (*taḥṣīn*) the language against this new invasion (*al-ghazw al-jadīd*), which has spread in it like a deadly epidemic (*wabā' qātil*, 1990: 69). The Iraqi linguist Ibrahim al-Samirra'i (1979) shares this analysis in reflecting on the impact of journalism on Arabic. The introduction of modernity into Arab life and its impact on Arabic are described by another writer as 'the latest conspiracy of wanton and wilful destruction' against the language (Qassab 1994: 201). This writer described the modernists and the modernizers as a gang (*'iṣābat al-ḥadātha*, 1994: 225) who, by showing disregard for the language and by destroying its grammar, aim to destroy the very concept of Arabic as a language in its own right (1994: 204).

In the same way that Gibran's essay 'You have your language, and I have my language' may be said to constitute the manifesto of the modernizers, Hafiz Ibrahim's poem 'Shakwā al-lugha al-'arabiyya' (Complaint of the Arabic language, 1903) may be considered the rallying cry of the language-defenders. First, this is a poem in the name of the Arabic language about the Arabic language. The use of a first-person poetic voice turns the language into a living being that can address its users directly. It rejects the charges of lexical deficiency that are levelled against it, putting itself in the position of the prosecutor rather than that of the defendant. Second, it reminds its users of its past glories and its associations with Islam, telling them that it can respond to the needs of modern life. The fault therefore lies not in it but in them. Third, it mourns the fact that its own people have succumbed to the influence and machinations of the Europeans who are intent on destroying it. It reminds them that the strength of a people derives from the strength of their language. Fourth, it mourns the linguistic interferences that have found their way into it from the European languages. As a result, it tells its users that it has lost its purity. Fifth, it mourns the fact that its own people seem to be abandoning it in favour of the tattered patchwork of the colloquial. Sixth, writers therefore have a responsibility towards the language. They must either ensure its survival as a living and flourishing organism, or bring about its demise once and for all. The language-defenders agree on all these points. This is why parts of this poem find their way into their discourse (see al-Alim 1997: 11; al-Jamali 1996: 19) and why it may be said to constitute their rallying cry.

The conflict between the modernizers and the language-defenders may be viewed as one between change and tradition (see Vikør 1993). To some extent this is true. It must, however, be recognized that both parties acknowledge both the need for change and the importance of the continuity of tradition, except for those who have advocated the wholesale replacement of the Arabic script by the Roman alphabet; for these radical modernizers, change implies a complete break with the past, or at least some aspects of it. The conflict between the modernizers and the language-defenders may therefore be conceptualized as a power struggle over who has the right to decide on the mixture between change and tradition in the language, and what the exact makeup of this mixture should be. The modernizers favour change over tradition. The language-defenders favour tradition over change. Both parties, however, are aware of the socio-political nature of their linguistic agendas. In particular, they understand that their conflict over language is a struggle over the kind of community they wish to construct afresh or preserve. Should it be a modern community that is more oriented towards the future than the past? Or should it be a community that sees in the blueprint of its future the defining outlines of its past?

The conflict between the modernizers and the language-defenders is conducted by the latter via the rhetoric of military warfare. The language and its associated sciences and literature are said to be in danger of being overwhelmed by the modernizers, who act in partnership with outside powers that harbour deep-seated enmity towards the Arabs and Islam. Hence the references in the discourse of the language-defenders to invasion, the crusades, colonialism, imperialism and Orientalism (see Samʿan 1967, 1968). In this discourse, the enemy outside and the enemy within are presented as working in concert to destabilize Arabic for extra-linguistic (political) purposes. Their ultimate aims may not be the same, but the means with which they set out to achieve them are. The outsiders aim to subordinate the Arabs and the Muslims to Western hegemony in the service of its political and economic interests. The insiders are projected as a group wishing to change the fundamental character of society in the name of a false modernity characterized by scant respect for the Arab and Muslim traditions.

The polarization of the debate between the two groups reflects the belief that the conflict between them is a real one over values and, ultimately, who holds authority over language as a power resource in society. In pressing their case, both parties invoke the legitimizing impulses of the Islamic experience, although the language-defenders are more adept at exploiting these than the modernizers. Intertextuality is one of the means through which this is achieved. Christian and Muslim writers, whether on the side of the modernizers or the language-defenders, employ this discursive strategy. Echoes of the Qur'an and the messages it contains are used to claim that this or that group will have the upper hand. The affective power of this strategy is exploited in prose and in poetry, the latter mainly by the language-defenders. Although Hafiz Ibrahim's poem is the best-known example in this genre, other poems extolling the virtues of the language and its role in Arab and Muslim society exist (see al-Athari 1984; al-Dibl 1997; Hasan 1979; al-Jarim 1935; Khamis 1984; Mahfuz 1990; al-Qurashi 1990; al-Samirra'i 1990; al-Tayyib 1984); but they will not be dealt with here.

Awareness of the rhetoric of language conflict seems to have succeeded in putting some modernizers on the defensive. Anis Frayha (1959) signalled this when he hinted that the restricted nature of his call to reform Arabic grammar was motivated by the strong attitudes towards the language in the Arabic-speaking countries in the first half of the twentieth century (the 1950s were the heyday of Arab nationalism, with its strong support for Standard Arabic and Arab political unity in the wake of the Suez crisis in 1956). Awareness of the stiff resistance put up by the language-defenders seems to have been present in Ibrahim Mustafa's thinking when he came to write the introduction to his book *Iḥyā' al-naḥw* (Reviving Arabic grammar) towards the end of the 1930s. This is clear from his attempt to forestall their criticism by describing his work using the language of asceticism (*i'tikāf*). More specifically, Mustafa signals the ascetic religiosity behind this project in three ways: (1) by exploiting the mystical connotations of the number seven in Arab culture in specifying the number of years he spent preparing the book; (2) by suggesting that his devotion to the book led him to neglect his religiously inscribed duty of caring for his family and of ensuring his own physical well-being; and (3) by describing the effort that went into finishing the project as an act of martyrdom in the cause of Arabic (*fidan li-l-'arabiyya*). In spite of this, Mustafa was the subject of virulent attacks by the language-defenders, as indicated earlier in this section. His conciliatory words were viewed with suspicion because, it was believed, they set out to hide his real anti-Arabic position (Husayn n.d.).

Conclusion

The above discussion provides a general outline of some of the major ideas that guide this work. In setting out these ideas I have tried to offer a dual perspective in which empiricism and theoretical insight play a part. I have also tried to utilize a variety of Arabic sources to highlight the centrality of language in the Arab intellectual tradition. The references to newspaper articles serve to suggest that the issues dealt with in this work are alive and of interest to a wide-ranging public in the Arabic-speaking world. The utilization of poetry serves two objectives. On the one hand, it highlights the esteem in which the language – the subject of the poem – is held in Arab society, owing to the position of poetry as the Arab literary genre par excellence. On the other hand, it suggests that poetry can form part of the data on issues of language, identity and conflict. In this respect, the discussion of Arabic and socio-political conflict may offer a new dimension to our understanding of how linguistic conflicts are articulated in different cultures. However, it may be helpful at this stage to set out some of the most important principles upon which this study is based.

First, this study is rooted in an understanding of linguistic conflict in which the concept of power plays an important part. As applied here, power involves both the symbolic and communicative functions of the language, although I am mainly interested in the latter in this study. Also, I deal mostly with the political and social aspects of power. Linguistic conflicts become salient when power is allocated differentially between groups. This is true of all the linguistic conflicts I have discussed above. By linking language to the socio-political dimensions of linguistic conflict, this study veers more towards the sociology of language than quantitative sociolinguistics in disciplinary terms.

Second, linguistic conflicts do not take place between languages or language varieties per se, but between their speakers. The term 'linguistic conflict' is therefore no more than a short cut to a more complex phenomenon involving standard and non-standard language varieties and their speakers acting individually or in groups. Linguistic conflicts are therefore more dependent on how the speakers interpret the facts of their situation than on the objective reality of these facts. This does not, however, mean that linguistic conflicts can be fabricated out of nothing; they must always relate to an objective reality that resonates with the speakers. More often than not, linguistic conflicts are no more than a proxy for other conflicts between groups. The intensity of these conflicts varies from situation to situation, depending on the intensity of the extra-linguistic conflicts animating them and the density and extensiveness of the criss-crossing associations and allegiances in and between groups. With these provisos in mind, we may classify linguistic conflicts for the purposes of this research into three categories (see Janicki 1993): (1) conflicts between a language and one of its varieties or a generic form of a group of its varieties, for example the so-called colloquial in Arabic; (2) conflicts between two non-standard varieties of the same language; and (3) conflict between two languages. According to this typology, linguistic conflicts may take place between members of the same nation (intra-group conflicts) or between members of different groups (inter-group conflicts). I will deal with these three types of conflict in this study. Each will be examined at length in a separate chapter.

Third, linguistic conflicts are strongly associated with the nation- or state-building project in the Middle East. Broadly speaking, this project is intolerant of political expressions of linguistic diversity within the nascent nation-state. This is also true of the nation in its cultural guise which, additionally, seeks to promote a unitary ideological interpretation of its language to the exclusion of other competing interpretations. Having real power at its disposal, the state can institute a variety of legal instruments to suppress competing languages; this may have the opposite effect of turning language into an active entitlement issue that can galvanize hitherto dormant forces in society and the international arena. In situations of this kind, linguistic conflicts have the potential of getting entangled in issues of human rights and inter-state relations. The position of Kurdish in Turkey illustrates this mode of managing linguistic conflicts within the nation-state-building project. The situation in Turkey and Bulgaria also illustrates the inadequacy of classifying languages into majority and minority languages in an invariant manner, particularly in the context of linguistic conflicts.

Fourth, linguistic conflicts engage the impulses of change and tradition in society. The drive to modernize requires a commitment to change as a precondition for achieving future objectives. The fact that change is often accompanied by social dislocation, a challenge to the existing power structures and a rupture with the past often generates resistance from those who represent the status quo. Authenticity and continuity are engaged as instruments of validation and mobilization by those who set out to resist change in the linguistic arena as a means of thwarting the extra-linguistic objectives of their opponents. To achieve this, the past is excavated and turned into ideological ammunition in the fight with the enemy. The proponents of change may have access to this past, but being more future-oriented than backward-looking they are often less successful in exploiting it than are the language-defenders. When this happens, the proponents of change become more radical in their calls to modernize the language, which in turn generates stronger calls by the language-defenders to offer more stiff resistance to the modernizers. The references to Islam in the Arab rhetoric of linguistic conflict illustrate this return to the past for motivational effect.

Fifth, linguistic conflicts are waged using military rhetoric. It may, however, be said that these conflicts are more fiercely fought on the battlefield of discourse than in the spheres of political and social contestation in real-life situations. In waging linguistic battles, the combatants employ the full paraphernalia of lexical ammunition and the massive firepower of the culturally loaded metaphor. This fact explains the use of such terms as 'invasion', 'regiment', 'general staff', 'war', 'battle' and many others to characterize the conduct of the conflictual engagement in the linguistic battlefield. Hence also the talk about the 'enemy within' conspiring with the 'outside enemy' in fighting linguistic wars against the nation. The fact that these modes of characterizing linguistic conflicts are a shorthand for other conditions in society will become clear in the following chapters. Suffice it to say here that the application of military rhetoric to characterize linguistic conflicts is not restricted to Arabic or Arab discourse; it exists in other intellectual traditions and in different parts of the world, as the examples I have given on pp. 14–26 show. The Arabic rhetoric of linguistic conflict is part of a universal phenomenon, rather than the expression of a particularism or exceptionalism that sets the Arabs apart from other groups.

3 When language and dialects collide: Standard Arabic and its 'opponents'

Introduction

In chapter 2, we dealt with a set of linguistic phenomena to highlight the principles at play in intra- and intergroup conflict in situations of asymmetrical power relations. Placing these phenomena in their socio-political context, we were able to establish aspects of their symbolic meanings by invoking the concepts of identity, tradition and modernization. The role of language as a value-laden resource in society was given as the reason for its ability to act as a proxy for the prosecution of extra-linguistic conflicts of various kinds (see Cameron 1995; Heller 1999; Laforest 1999; Rickford 1999). By examining the discursive practices and lexical choices involved in articulating linguistic conflicts pertaining to Arabic, we were able to highlight the rhetorical import they have – vis-à-vis affect and task orientation – in their socio-cultural milieu. The present chapter will explore these themes further by analysing a number of debates involving Standard Arabic (SA) in the past two centuries, particularly the competition between this variety of the language and the dialects. Some of these debates will be familiar to specialists in Arabic language and culture. This chapter is intended for readers from outside this constituency, who are its primary audience.[1]

To help establish the parameters of this chapter, I will offer the following preliminary remarks. As used in this work, SA designates the literary form of the language in its modern and pre-modern manifestations, what is called *fuṣḥā* in Arabic, although the main emphasis will be on the former. The term *fuṣḥā* is derived from the root *f-ṣ-ḥ* in Arabic, which designates the ideas of purity, clarity, eloquence, chastity and freedom from speech impediments. As we shall see later, the moral dimension of these terms will be invoked in evaluating aspects of the conflict between SA and

[1] See Crowley (1989), Joseph (1987) and Milroy and Milroy (1999) for the meaning of 'standard' in English. In this work, the use of this term to describe the 'formal' level of Arabic reflects its general usage in Western studies to refer to what is called the *fuṣḥā* in the native tradition.

the dialects. In the modern period, SA is used in literature, journalism, discursive works on culture and science, school textbooks, newsbroadcasts, sermons and other public speeches. This is not an exhaustive list. Nor are these domains the exclusive arena of SA. The dialects are used alongside SA in these and other domains for a variety of purposes, including providing interpretations in the former of what has been encoded in the latter.

This exegetical relationship between the two forms of the language is a hallmark of the linguistic performance of the late Egyptian scholar Sheikh Muhammad Mutawalli Shaʿrawi. In a typical religious lesson on TV, he would read an extract from one of the exegetical works on the meaning of the Qur'an before proceeding to give, in his Egyptian dialect, a second-order exegesis of the original exegesis. On some occasions, he would provide a third-order exegesis by glossing parts of his own Egyptian Arabic, using another Arabic variety whose selection was determined by the dialect background of his audience. A similar mixing of SA and Egyptian Arabic occurs in the speeches of the late Egyptian President Gamal Abdul-Nasir (d. 1970), although the switch from SA to Egyptian Arabic in some of these speeches was motivated by reasons of affect more than exegesis (Holes 1993). These two functions of the dialect, the exegetical and the affective, are mixed in the speeches of Hasan al-Banna (1906–49), the founder of the Muslim Brothers party in Egypt, in spite of the fact that the third commandment of the party enjoins its members to use SA in its capacity as one of the distinguishing markers of Islam.[2]

This mixing of varieties in discourse is characteristic of the diglossic nature of the Arabic language situation. However, it is not the aim of this chapter to delve into the meaning of Arabic diglossia, whose interpretation has been the subject of extensive elaboration and debate since the publication of Ferguson's seminal paper on the subject in 1959 (Badawi 1973; Ferguson 1990, 1996; Fernandez 1993; Hary 1996; Holes 1995; Hudson 1992; Hussein 1980; Kaye 1972, 1994, 2001).[3] The above

[2] See al-Musa (1987: 156–7).

[3] In his 1959 paper, Ferguson defined diglossia as follows (p. 336):

> A relatively stable language situation in which, in addition to the primary dialects of the language (which may include a standard or regional standards), there is a very divergent, highly codified (often grammatically more complex) superposed variety, the vehicle of a large and respected body of written literature, either of an earlier period or in another speech community, which is learned largely by formal education and is used for most written or formal spoken purposes, but is not used by any sector of the community for ordinary conversation.

He adds (at p. 327): 'Diglossia differs from the widespread standard-language-with-dialects in that no segment of the speech community in diglossia regularly uses H [the literary form] as a medium of ordinary conversation, and any attempt to do so is felt to be either pedantic or artificial.'

remarks are merely intended to signal to the target readers the complexity of the Arabic language situation. They are also meant to indicate that SA and its associated dialects normally exist non-competitively in the linguistic behaviour of most speakers. Competition and conflict between SA and the dialects normally belong to a metalinguistic discourse in which these two forms of the language are the topic of contention between parties with irreconcilable ideological differences. The data for this chapter are therefore culled from this metalinguistic discourse rather than from the Arabic language per se. These data will be subjected to content analysis to isolate some of the themes that pervade them, and to highlight the ideological impulses on which they are based. My approach here is consistent with the view, referred to earlier (pp. 1–14), which conceptualizes language as 'a referent for loyalties and animosities, an indicator of social statuses and personal relationships, a marker of situations and topics as well as of the societal goals and the large-scale value-laden arenas of interaction that typify every speech community' (Fishman 1997: 27).

The data of this chapter justify treating it as a contribution to ethnolinguistics, dubbed 'folk linguistics' by Niedzielski and Preston (2000).[4] Giving credence to non-specialist views about language is anathema to most professional linguists working within the norms of modern linguistic theory.[5] For example, the folk belief in some literate cultures in the inequality of languages is inconsistent with the view in linguistics that all languages and language varieties are structurally equal. A similar clash pertains to folk views which treat the non-standard varieties of a language as an aberration or deviation from the standard, as we shall see later.[6] The elite in many societies in fact hold folk views of this kind, and they do so passionately. This phenomenon explains Niedzielski and Preston's refusal to use the term 'folk' to refer to 'rustic, ignorant, uneducated, backward, primitive, minority, isolated, marginalized, or lower status groups or individuals' (2000: viii). It further explains their insistence that 'folk belief

[4] See Bauer and Trudgill (1998) for a range of views, called myths, which fall under this heading.

[5] Niedzielski and Preston (2000: vii) tell us that Leonard Bloomfield's family used the term *stankos* to designate 'the language beliefs of nonlinguists'. The two authors point out that this term 'looks like a noun form of *stank*, for Bloomfield held the opinion of nonlinguists in low regard'; they point out further that 'many linguists have shared and continue to share that opinion'. Bloomfield was one of the most influential linguists in the twentieth century.

[6] Linguists reject this view, as may be exemplified by the following statement by Bourhis (1997: 306): 'Social psychological research has . . . shown that a prestige standard form of a language has no *inherent* aesthetic or linguistic advantage over non-standard varieties of this or other languages. Rather, the prestige ascribed to the standard form of a language is usually the product of culture-bound stereotypes passed on from one generation of speakers to the other' (original emphasis).

is simply belief', and that its folk character provides 'no indication of its truth or falsity' (2000: viii). Although this is true, the immunity of folk belief from empirical or logical refutation derives first and foremost from its ideological nature. It is this link with ideology – as a set of beliefs about language shared by members of a community – that, in my view, renders folk views about language such an interesting topic to study.

On the ideological front, folk beliefs about language signal covert convictions and attitudes of an extra-linguistic kind. Views that may be considered prejudiced if expressed directly are often articulated in an unguarded way in relation to language. In the 1970s, a British TV comedy programme called *Mind Your Language* exploited foreign learners' errors and their native-language interferences in English to express British stereotypical views of the French, the Germans, the Japanese, the Indians and others.[7] Language as a proxy serves in this capacity for the proponents of the 'English Only' movement in the USA (Schmid 2001). Rickford (1999: 272) highlights the same principle when he says that language was not the issue in the debate over Ebonics (African American Vernacular English) in the USA in the 1990s: 'Ebonics had become a proxy for African Americans, and the most racist stereotypes were being promulgated.' The same principle applies to discussions of French in Canada (Heller 1999), Catalan in Spain (Laitin 1987) and Hebrew in Israel (Shohamy 1994). The study of folk-linguistic beliefs in these and other contexts can therefore link language to the structure of power in society in subtle and culturally determined ways. Furthermore, the fact that some folk beliefs about language are held passionately and genuinely across speech communities indicates that (1) ignoring them will not cause them to disappear, and (2) they must therefore constitute valid objects for analysis and comparative study. This conclusion is strengthened by the fact that such beliefs have withstood the onslaught by professional linguists who, following Saussure, believe that 'no other subject has spawned more absurd ideas, more prejudices, more illusions or more myths' than language (cited in Aitcheson 2001: 614).[8] The continuation and relative fixity of these beliefs cross-culturally therefore represents a phenomenon worthy of study. The present chapter is a contribution to this enterprise, which seems to have gathered momentum among sociolinguists

[7] The Kuwaiti TV comedy *'Ashshūg*, broadcast during Ramadan 2002 (November/December), belongs to this genre. See chapter 2, n. 13.

[8] The importance of ideology as a line of defence against this onslaught is recognized by James Milroy (2001a: 538): 'Some linguists have attempted to engage in debates about [language-related beliefs], usually pointing out that they have not always fully understood the power of the ideologies of language that drive public opinion on these topics.' Jean Aitcheson (2001: 617) points out that 'linguists have generally pooh-poohed views of the general public on language' but to no avail.

over the past few years (see Aitcheson 2001; Cameron 1995; Garrett 2001; Johnson 2001; Milroy 2001b).

The title of this chapter needs some comment. First, the quotation marks around the word 'opponents' indicate that being one is a matter of construction, although in a few cases some writers have identified themselves openly as ideological opponents of SA – for example, the Lebanese writer Sa'id Aql. The fact that this construction of reality is both cultural and ideological makes it unavailable to empirical or logical refutation. Second, the status of being an opponent is ascribed to a given position, group or individual by the proponents of SA, who feel empowered to do so owing to the dominance of the standard-language ideology in society. Third, the linear ordering of the two constituents in the title confers on SA an ontological primacy over its opponents. This ordering is not arbitrary; it reflects the fact that most of the discursive space on the topic is claimed by the supporters of SA, whose overarching rhetorical trope consists of extolling the virtues of this variety and downgrading the status of the dialects. Fourth, this oppositional ordering of the relationship between SA and its associated dialects is consistent with how the relationship between the standard and the dialects is conceptualized in other cultures in folk linguistics. Witness in this connection the title of John Honey's controversial book *Language is Power: The Story of Standard English and its Enemies* (1997). Although this book has generated many critical responses from professional linguists (Crowley 1989), especially from those who hold different political views, it is still the case that its title reflects a general view among the non-specialist elite that Standard English is the *standard* – the measure of uniformity and excellence – by which other dialects are judged. This title also reflects the belief that Standard English is under attack.

The external front: Orientalism and the colonial encounter

In modern Arab thought, the dialects are sometimes constructed as the greatest opponent, even the enemy, to SA (Attar 1964, 1966, 1979, 1982; al-Barazi 1989; Farrukh 1961; Husayn n.d.; al-Jundi 1982, n.d.; Sa'id 1964). This is particularly the case when support for the dialects is allied to the promotion of nation-state ideologies that are opposed to pan-Arab nationalism, or when this support disallows the association of group identity through the language with Islam. It is also the case when this support is aimed at supplanting SA as the language of literary expression and culture. In the discourse of the language-defenders, the responsibility for this anti-SA attitude is attributed to a set of sources, including interference by external actors, who are charged with leading the attack on Arabic from their positions as colonialists or as Orientalists acting in the service of the European domination of the Arabic-speaking lands.[9] This is one of the major themes in Naffusa Zakariyya Sa'id's well-known study *Tārīkh al-da'wa ilā al-'āmmiyya wa-āthāruhā fī miṣr* (The history of the call to adopt the colloquial and its impact in Egypt, 1964). Sa'id was not a professional linguist but a kind of cultural historian with an interest in language-related matters. This makes the views she expresses in her *History* a contribution to folk linguistics in the sense outlined above. The fact that Sa'id does not link her defence of SA, against the attempts to promote Egyptian Arabic, to any *overt* political ideology – for example, to Arab nationalism or Egyptian nationalism – supports my decision to treat this work as an exercise in ethnolinguistic historicization. The book, however, is not devoid of ideology; it is in fact driven by a commitment to the standard-language ideology which is at play in most cultures with a long recorded history and a strong literary tradition. Furthermore, the book is a product of its time, a time in which an external Other is projected as the source of all kinds of machination against the native culture, including the socio-political resonance its language has for those who share it as a common code.

Sa'id's main thesis is a simple one: the promotion of Egyptian Arabic, and the call for it to replace SA in some domains of written discourse, is the work of Europeans who pursued this agenda for political ends. Although the active promotion of this 'scheme', in the negative sense of the term, coincided with the British occupation of Egypt in 1882, Sa'id believed that the way for it was prepared by the prior interest in the Arabic dialects in some European universities. Sa'id's thesis rests on the assumption that the study of the dialects in these universities was not motivated by purely linguistic ends that conform to the well-known maxim in modern linguistics of studying language for its own sake, but that it was carried out as a means to 'a more sinister' something else. The fact that Sa'id's position is expressed in an exaggerated manner, and that she does not offer any evidence in support of this assumption, is a weakness in her study. But this is hardly the point. It is of course possible to provide some substantiation for her views by drawing on Edward Said's (1978) analysis of Orientalism as a discourse of power, definition and domination. Circumstantial evidence of various kinds may also be adduced to support her thesis – for example, the fact that some Orientalists offered their services to the European colonial powers in the nineteenth century

[9] It would be wrong to assume that all Orientalists have consciously or unconsciously put themselves at the service of the political establishment.

in the pursuit of openly political objectives. It is, however, more plausible to suggest that Saʿid may have in fact felt that her 'assumption' is self-evident and that, therefore, it is not in need of substantiation.

It is likely that this indeed was the case. Saʿid was writing at a time (the 1960s), and reflecting on a period in modern Egyptian history (*c.*1850–1950), when the belief in foreign conspiracies against Egypt and her culture had common currency among Arab readers, as it still has now. The fact that conspiracies against Egypt did exist, as in the Suez crisis in 1956, lent credence to this belief and turned it into a 'given' of socio-political interpretation in Arab culture. If we accept this, then we must concede that (1) Saʿid's construction of the European scholarship on the Arabic dialects in the nineteenth century is embedded in a local hegemonic ideology; and (2) this ideology assumes the status of common sense for those who subscribe to it under the influence of the institutional (education, administration, the military) and semi-institutional (the media, the arts, literature) channels of cultural production and reproduction in society. According to this ideology, the promotion of Egyptian Arabic is part of the paraphernalia of the European war against Egypt in the political, economic and cultural spheres. This explains Saʿid's conceptualization of the promotion of Egyptian Arabic as, in effect, a colonial war against SA in which the dialect is used for spying and for establishing relations with the ordinary people for sinister reasons (Saʿid 1964: 9, n. 1).

There is in fact direct evidence to support Saʿid's thesis of the link between the Orientalists' interest in language-related matters and the pursuit of political and other objectives on the part of the European powers. In *Handbook of Modern Arabic: Consisting of Practical Grammar with Numerous Examples, Dialogues, and Newspaper Extracts in a European Type* (1895), Francis W. Newman – who was a fellow of Balliol College, Oxford, before becoming a professor at University College, London in the nineteenth century – admits such a link in the context of his call to use the Roman alphabet to record Arabic, Ottoman Turkish and Persian. The penultimate paragraph in this preface, which I will quote in full because of its relevance to the issue in hand, makes this point succinctly (1895: xv–xvi):

> And this seduces me into a political remark. England at vast expenses sustains an embassy in Constantinople, and a fleet in the Mediterranean, for the sake (it is said) of *English interests* in the East [original emphasis]. When we inquire what interests are intended, nothing else is discoverable but that we desire to maintain in Turkey 'good will to our commerce, our religion, and our communications with India'. Men not the least acute in the English Parliament have avowed their belief that our diplomacy and our fleets have no tendency to promote this 'good will', but rather the contrary. Without venturing on so large a question, one may

be permitted to assert, that if half the expense of our Mediterranean fleet were retrenched, and the money spent under the direction of our CONSULS in free schools for the native population of Turkey, – to instruct them in Geography and the elementary knowledge to which it is the key, by the intervention of the European character [alphabet] and European maps; it would do more in fifteen years to promote the intelligence and prosperity of Turkey, *and with it all the solid and legitimate interests of England, than ambassadors and fleets can do in five hundred years.* [emphasis added]

The reference to geography in the above quotation may strike the reader as out of place in a handbook on modern Arabic. The following quotation, earlier in the same preface, sets out this link clearly (Newman 1895: xiii–xiv):

A sound knowledge of geography lies at the basis of modern culture, and for it MAPS are necessary. Without this knowledge the Orientals must remain as children, with weak, empty and delusive ideas concerning other nations; incapable of receiving instruction by books or newspapers. But who will engrave maps for Turks, Arabs and Persians in the type of their native MSS? What publisher in Paternoster Row or New York will undertake the speculations? And if such maps existed, what native seeking information would be able to read them, traversed by dots innumerable in irregular directions? . . . The Arab vowel points, utterly insufficient as they are to express foreign names, would entangle the problem worse than ever; for, the objections to using them and to dispensing with them are alike powerful.

Newman starts by linking the use of the Roman alphabet to the dissemination of geographical knowledge, which he, rather condescendingly, considers to be necessary for the advancement of the 'Orientals', be they Arab, Persian or Turk. His choice of geography is not accidental: it allows him to assert that maps using the Arabic script are bound to be 'cluttered' and 'unintelligible'. Towards the end of his preface, however, he reveals his hand by linking his call to use the Roman alphabet to the task of furthering and underpinning English imperial interests in the lands of the Ottoman Empire.

Here we have an example which displays openly what is normally camouflaged by reference to language in its capacity as a proxy for the expression of extralinguistic concerns in society. Although Sa'id does not refer to Newman in her study, we can safely assume that ideas of the kind expressed by him were part of the structure of knowledge that underlay her analysis. We can also assume that suspicion of foreign scholars was an important factor in the reluctance of some Egyptians to act as informants for European folklorists. Sa'id refers to this in her study (1964: 46), pointing out how, in a field trip he conducted in Egypt in 1900, the French scholar Maspero was frustrated in his attempts to collect Egyptian folk songs. The reasons for this are unlikely to be directly related to the dialectal nature of these songs, but they point to the fact that the ordinary Egyptian regarded the European scholar as a cultural intruder who could not be trusted to act in a socio-politically honest manner.

This is indeed the prevailing attitude, in the language-related Arab discourse, towards William Willcocks, one of the most 'reviled' figures in the history of the call to use Egyptian Arabic in writing. Willcocks spent most of his career working as an agricultural engineer in Cairo, but he took an active interest in the linguistic life of Egypt. In 1893, he acquired a stake in the monthly magazine *al-Azhar*, which he soon turned into a platform for publicizing his views on Arabic. In the January issue of that year, he published an essay calling on the Egyptians to use their dialect in writing. Entitled 'Lima lam tūjad quwwat al-ikhtirāʿ ladā al-miṣriyyīn al-ān?' (Why are the Egyptians deprived of the power of invention now?), the essay ascribes the absence of the creative impulse among the Egyptians to the fact that they think and speak in one language, but write in another. The essay sparked a huge debate in the monthly Egyptian magazines *al-Muqtaṭaf* and *al-Hilāl*, and we often find references to it in modern works on the relationship between SA and the dialects in contemporary Arab discourse. This being the case, I will give a brief analysis of this essay below. The following reconstruction does not follow the order in which Willcocks presented his ideas in answering the question he poses in the title of his essay.

The word 'now' in the title suggests that there was a time in the past when the Egyptians possessed the 'power of invention'. By pointing this out, and by associating this past principally with ancient Egypt, Willcocks uses history for affect to give the Egyptians confidence in themselves. However, this validating role of a pre-Islamic past is consistent with the dominant nationalist ideology at the time, which sought to carve for Egypt an identity separate from those of other Arabic-speaking countries (Gershoni and Jankowski 1986; Suleiman 1996b, 2003). Locking indirectly into the debate on the 'veil' in the second half of the nineteenth century in Egypt – which the Egyptian writer Qasim Amin (1863–1908) pursued in his two books *Taḥrīr al-mar'a* (Women's liberation) and *al-Mar'a al-jadīda* (The new woman) – Willcocks likens the commitment to SA and its use in writing to a veil which prevents the Egyptians from seeing clearly and, therefore, achieving that of which they are capable. In pursuing this predictable analogy, Willcocks wishes to suggest that the Egyptian woman, and the Egyptians as a group, cannot achieve total liberation without casting off all manners of veil in their lives, whether in attire or in language. Social liberation and linguistic liberation must therefore go together.

However, being aware that the Egyptians were not politically free, and responding to their wish to rid themselves of British colonial domination, Willcocks tells his readers that the most assured route to political liberation is the rekindling and full activation of the 'power of invention' among them. By premising the revival of their creativity on the realization of political freedom, Willcocks implies that the Egyptians are, effectively, 'barking up the wrong tree'. To drive this point home, he tells his readers that the English nation advanced technologically in spite of the fact that the English were not socially free. This was possible because the English abandoned Latin and elevated English to the status of a national tongue for use in all functional domains. Herein lies the path of progress for the Egyptians: they must get rid of SA and replace it by Egyptian Arabic if they are to restore the 'power of invention' which they once had and which made them the envy of other nations in the past. As a dead language, SA consigns everything inscribed in it to certain death. In comparison, Egyptian Arabic is a living and vibrant language. This behoves the Egyptian elites to adopt it as the medium of writing to release their latent 'power of invention' and to communicate the results of this power to ordinary Egyptians. Willcocks warns that failure to do so may force the Egyptians to adopt a foreign language to release their creativity; but, he adds, this would have the drawback of excluding many Egyptians from participating in building their country.

The preceding analysis of Willcocks' essay, regardless of his real intentions, shows how deeply rooted in ideology his views about Arabic were. The references to the past as a source of validation, the equation of social with linguistic liberation and the suggestion that a weak nation can progress only by re-enacting the trajectory of a more powerful one are, unquestionably, covert ideological positions. The linking of the linguistic matter of which variety to use in writing to the extra-linguistic objective of material progress is another ideological assumption. The fact that all of these positions can be invoked in discussing a language-related matter shows how value-laden language can be. In addition, the whole essay is based on an ideology of power. Willcocks is no ordinary agricultural engineer. He is a member of an occupying power, and he speaks from that position. The tone of his essay is in fact condescending (*wa-aqūl lakum ayyuhā al-miṣriyyūn*: 'Egyptians! Let me tell you', 1893: 4); and, although he tries to project an image of someone who cares deeply about Egypt and its destiny, he nevertheless adopts the idiom of 'us versus them' (*anā wa-antum muttafiqūn*:'I and you are agreed', 1893: 4).

There is, however, no doubt about his determination to promote the dialect in writing. There are glimpses of this in his essay. Although the bulk of the essay is closer to SA grammatically and stylistically than to Egyptian

Arabic, still there are examples where the sentence structure is modelled on the syntax of the colloquial. In a few cases, lexical colloquialisms are used. However, Willcocks' commitment to Egyptian Arabic is given full expression in his translation of the Gospel. The same commitment is evident in his translation of extracts from Shakespeare. His book *al-Akl wa-l-īmān* (Food and faith) combines his commitment to the colloquial and his proselytizing tendencies (see Saʿid 1964; Abd al-Rahman 1969). It is perhaps the combination of these two impulses in his career that made Willcocks a 'hate figure' in the language-related discourse in modern Arab culture.

Willcocks' ideas met with stiff resistance from the Egyptian elite. They soon established a scientific journal, *al-Muhandis* (The engineer), in which all the articles were written in Standard Arabic to rebut his claim. Abdalla al-Nadim (1845–96) – who used the colloquial for pragmatic reasons in his writings to educate the Egyptian people – attacked Willcocks for meddling in Egyptian affairs and for championing the colloquial for ulterior motives. Instead of writing in the colloquial, the Egyptian elite started to send Willcocks articles in the standard. Initially, he published these articles, but expressed his hope that their authors would soon turn to writing in the colloquial for the benefit of their compatriots. When this did not materialize, Willcocks decided to close *al-Azhar* in October 1893 (see Abd al-Rahman 1969). In the final issue, he expressed his consternation at the fact that the Egyptian elite continued in their old ways of writing in the standard, and that they were unable to show the necessary courage to adopt the colloquial as the medium through which the benefits of modern science could be made available to their own people. Willcocks indirectly blamed this on the rigidity of Muslim belief, saying that God had destined that the old linguistic norms would persist, in spite of their limited usefulness in achieving the scientific development Egypt so desperately needed. And, in a condescending tone of voice, Willcocks declared that the Egyptian elites failed to make it worth his while to continue to commit his resources to pursuing their advancement.

The call to use Egyptian Arabic and the Roman alphabet in writing was pursued by Willmore in his book *The Spoken Arabic of Egypt* (1901). In the introduction to this book, Sayce declared that the Arabic script 'belongs to a pre-scientific age and people, and is wholly unfitted to represent the living sounds of a modern Arabic language [i.e. Egyptian Arabic]. For this we must have recourse to some modifications of the Latin alphabet' (Willmore 1901: vi). According to this view, modernity is incompatible with the Arabic script. That such a view can be expressed as a statement of fact is indicative of the 'naturalness' it had for its author and his target readers. As far as Sayce and Willmore were concerned, this view is a self-evident truth. Its 'common-sense' nature is not in question, although it is ideologically loaded. Commenting on this property of folk-linguistic views, Milroy (2001a: 536) says that to confer the status of 'common-sense' on a given view 'implies that any debate on the matter is superfluous: everyone must surely know that the view expressed is the correct – responsible, decent, moral – view. Those who might disagree cannot be taken seriously: they are likely to be eccentric, irresponsible or, perhaps, dishonest'. Milroy is interested in folk-linguistic views in intra-linguistic settings, but his comments apply with equal force to interlinguistic situations of the kind under consideration here. What we have in cases of the latter kind is a clash of ideologically held positions that are characterized by naturalness, self-evidence and common sense for those who believe in them. Thus, when Saʿid and other Arab intellectuals reject what Willcocks, Willmore and others say about Arabic, they do so from a position of equal naturalness, self-evidence and common sense. It is precisely this fact that makes folk-linguistic views unavailable for empirical refutation, rendering them almost an article of faith.

In the preface to his book, Willmore applies a range of arguments aimed at legitimizing the dialect. This attempt at legitimization suggests that, although he was writing in English, Willmore seems to have been addressing the Egyptians who – rather than his English readers – needed to be convinced of the legitimacy of their dialect as a medium of writing. This interest in legitimization is an important element in folk linguistics. It is often practised covertly and with little reflection. It would therefore be interesting to examine an attempt at legitimization which, on this occasion, is advanced deliberately.

The first argument by Willmore consists of ascribing *antiquity* and *pedigree* to Egyptian Arabic. According to this argument, Egyptian Arabic is closer than the Arabic of Quraysh, the Prophet's variety, to Hebrew. The fact that the comparison had to be made to Hebrew is itself an ideological position based on considerations of doctrine and the primacy of the written record in the reconstruction of linguistic genealogy. Second, although Egyptian Arabic contains borrowings from a number of languages, it is characterized by a *purity* that is unavailable to other varieties within the Semitic family of languages. Third, unlike SA, Egyptian Arabic is a *living* language. For all these reasons, the dialect is worthy of codification and use as a medium of writing. It is also worthy of professional study and institutional cultivation. This explains why Willmore found it 'startling to learn from a professor of Semitic languages at one of the English universities that he excluded the living Arabic dialects from his studies' (1901: xiii, n. 2). By pointing out these properties of Egyptian Arabic, Willmore hoped to counter the image of the dialect for its speakers as 'vulgar', 'unclean' or 'broken'. If Egyptian Arabic is vulgar, he tells his readers, it is so in the 'sense that it is popular and universal' (1901: x). In a telling footnote, Willmore further contrasts Egyptian Arabic rather favourably to SA, which, in the lexicon of the 'lower classes', is called *naḥwī*. This is how Willmore describes SA in this footnote (1901: xi n. 3): '*Naḥwī* means literally *grammatical* [original emphasis], and is commonly applied to the *mongrel* language employed in official correspondence. It is the "classical" language *artificially* adapted to modern wants' (emphasis added). The ascription of hybridity and artificiality to SA constitutes, albeit indirectly, a fourth validating argument in favour of the dialect. The aim of this argument is to downgrade SA to create the intellectual space for assessing Egyptian Arabic positively.

Willmore uses the above arguments to conclude that Egyptian Arabic is no less worthy of being used as a medium of writing than SA. He further argues that its deployment in this functional domain will lead to developing a 'real literature' from which ordinary Egyptians will benefit. As the mother tongue of the Egyptians, the use of the dialect in education will aid in the spread of literacy, modern knowledge and material progress. And, to show that he is not alone in thinking this, Willmore gives a long quotation (three pages) from a paper by an unnamed American philologist – 'who takes a deep interest in the welfare of the Egyptian people' (1901: xiii) – according to whom it is the duty of the British rulers of Egypt to codify the dialect and to use it in writing in the Roman alphabet for, ultimately, spiritual purposes (1901: xvi):

> Why cannot the men who have been the potent factor in bringing about [the] beneficent material revolution [in Egypt] now open the gate, as well, to the spiritual development of the people they rule so ably and so honestly? There is but one path that passes through that gate, and that path can be traversed only by a nation educated in the language it understands. That language is already the daily speech of social intercourse, of the family, the shop, and the farm.

By repeating these arguments, Willmore gives tacit approval to the idea that the British 'civilizing mission' in Egypt is dependent on two kinds of conversion: a linguistic conversion from SA to the colloquial, and a spiritual one – it is safe to assume – from Islam to Christianity. And as the quotation makes clear, Willmore seems to accept that the second conversion can be accomplished only if the former conversion takes place first since, presumably, it will weaken the connection of Muslim Egyptians to their religion. Under this interpretation, Willmore's grammar of Egyptian Arabic is not so innocent or academically neutral after all. It is indeed a grammar whose intention contravenes the principle in modern linguistics of studying language for its own sake, rather than as a means to something else.[10] In this sense, it is a document in the exercise of socio-political power, whose context on the ground is British colonial rule over Egypt. The ideological nature of this grammar does not challenge its academic validity as a philological piece of work, but it enables us to link grammar making to extra-linguistic aims and objectives. Furthermore, by noting this link, we can give credence to the charge made by Saʿid and other Arab intellectuals that the European interest in the colloquials is ideologically loaded, although we must be careful not to generalize this in a blind or overenthusiastic way.

Willmore's arguments provide a clear example of an interventionist attempt to create what may be called a state standard for Egypt, based around the dialect of Cairo. In this respect, Willmore belongs to a group of European scholars who include Willcocks, Newman, O'Leary (1872) and Vollers (1895). Although Willmore was a philologist, not a sociolinguist in the modern mould, his advocacy of Egyptian Arabic reveals a deep understanding of language planning as an exercise in linguistic empowerment. For example, he shows clear awareness that for the codification of a spoken dialect to succeed in a standard-language-dominated culture, this codification must be associated with an attitudinal change towards the dialect in question by its speakers. This explains his ascription of antiquity, pedigree, purity and vitality to Egyptian Arabic, as it does his description of SA as mongrel and artificial. Using Galtung's (1980) tripartite categorization of power, we may interpret this attempt by Willmore as an exercise in making overtly manifest what he regarded as the innate power of Egyptian Arabic. Considered from the perspective of language planning as empowerment, Willmore's grammar and advocacy of the Roman alphabet may be regarded as an attempt at endowing the dialect with resource power, which, in a more fully fledged context, would additionally include dictionaries, textbooks, electronic materials, trained teachers and examination boards. Finally, Willmore's call for Egyptian Arabic to be used in writing for literary and other purposes was aimed at endowing the dialect with structural power. Willmore was aware that the more functional domains a dialect acquires for itself, the greater its structural power will be in society. That this will enhance the power of the dialect overall is not in doubt.

Judged against the analysis given above, Saʿid's (1964) conspiracy-oriented reading of the call by some European scholars to promote Egyptian Arabic in writing cannot be dismissed as an act of paranoia.

[10] The use of linguistics for proselytizing purposes is not unknown in modern history. Linguistics was used to generate transcription systems for oral languages as a first step towards producing translations of the Bible in these languages. Within this framework, translation is treated as a neighbouring discipline of linguistics.

Her charge that this call represents an attack against SA has substance, in spite of the fact that she presses this charge more in the court of rhetorical appeal than in that of the factually based argument and counter-argument. I tried to explain this earlier by invoking the 'naturalness' and 'common sense' that characterize folk-linguistic views, hers included. For this reason, Sa'id felt justified in describing the promotion of Egyptian Arabic in writing as a 'war' against SA, and as the most dangerous 'crisis' in its history. She used expressions such as 'battle', 'conflict', 'struggle', 'campaign' and 'colonial machinations' to describe aspects of this crisis. The proponents of the dialect, be they external 'provocateurs' or 'internal agents', are therefore declared to be the 'enemies' of SA.[11] It is to the latter category that I will turn next. The discussion of this topic will encompass data from outside Egypt. It will also encompass material post-dating Sa'id's discussion of the debate over SA and the dialects.

The internal front: between the past and the present

In this section, I will highlight some of the recurring elements in the debate over SA and the dialects in modern Arab discourse. To begin with, most of this debate concerns the use of the dialect in writing in what may be called an operation of 'cultural trespassing' into a domain that is traditionally reserved for SA. The call to use, or the actual use of, the dialect in writing is resisted because it breaks what is in effect a 'cultural taboo' whose ideological validity is sanctioned by tradition and historical practice. How else can we reconcile the positive evaluation of the Arabic dialects by their speakers (Ferguson 1972; Ibrahim 2000) with their general resistance to having them used in writing? Other reasons have been adduced to explain this resistance, as we shall see later, but I contend that at its most basic or visceral this phenomenon is rooted in impulses about taboo in society. Under this interpretation, the resistance to orthographizing the dialects is an exercise in 'verbal hygiene', to use a term made popular by Cameron (1995); its aim is to protect SA against 'contamination' from the dialects. In moral terms, for the debate is sometimes conducted along these lines, this is equivalent to enjoining the good and forbidding the evil (*al-amr bi-l-ma'rūf wa-l-nahy 'an al-munkar*). Being norm-related, this resistance is relevant to questions of value in society, to what is right and what is wrong. This concern with taboo, norm and value is characteristic of folk views about language.

Furthermore, the language-defenders do not condemn all examples of the dialect in writing. Sa'id (1964) excludes Rifa'a Rafi'al-Tahtawi (1801–73), Abdalla al-Nadim (1845–96) and Muhammad al-Najjar

[11] See al-Tawil (1986) for an uncompromising statement of this accusation.

(d. 1911) from her attack on the proponents of Egyptian Arabic, because their intention was to educate the masses in matters of everyday life at a time when knowledge of SA was limited to the elite. Use of the dialect by these writers was also accompanied by strong support for SA as the national language of Egypt, and as the language of Islam and high culture. In some cases, this support was accompanied by criticisms of the dialect as a mongrel variety and as the object of ridicule (Saʿid 1964: 92). In Lebanon, Marun Abbud (1886–1962) adopted a similar attitude. He expressed his admiration for Lebanese vernacular poetry, which uses colloquialisms, but, at the same time, he expressed his opposition to the use of the dialects in writing. He articulates this attitude in an uncompromising manner in his book *al-Shiʿr al-ʿāmmī* (Vernacular poetry, 1968: 39): 'I was, I am and I always will be an enemy to two kinds of individual: anyone who calls for replacing SA by the colloquial, and anyone who advocates the use of the Roman alphabet in Arabic writing.'

Finally, there is a tendency to attribute the backing for the dialects by some Arab writers in the nineteenth century to a misguided support for the Orientalists.[12] Arabs working in European universities in this period are often said to have written about the dialects for reasons of professional advancement, or on the instruction *(bi-īʿāz min)* of 'the foreigners' *(al-ajānib)* who are the enemies of SA (Saʿid 1964: 17). This is an ideologically loaded reason. In folk-linguistic terms, it suggests that an Arab would not of his own free will commit an act of linguistic 'treason' against SA by supporting the dialect. According to this, the norm in an Arab's relationship with SA is one of loyalty. Support for the dialect is therefore a deviation from this norm in which the 'external provocateur' – the fifth column – and the 'internal agent' fight on the same side, but from different positions: the former by design, the latter by accident. Research in social psychology provides some support for this interpretation. If we accept the assumption in pro-SA discourse that the writing of dialectal grammars is a 'malicious' act, we may then evaluate the above differential reaction to these grammars as an expression of the way in which the in-group and the out-group are conceptualized in socio-psychological terms: 'When a malicious act [is] performed by an in-group member it [is] attributed to external pressures in the situation, whereas it [is] attributed to an underlying (negative) disposition when performed by an out-group member' (Giles and Powesland 1975: 166).

Support for the dialects from Arab intellectuals in the twentieth century tends to be assessed differently. It is assumed that some had taken it upon themselves to continue what the Orientalists and colonialists had begun.

[12] 'A'isha Abd al-Rahman (1969) does not believe that this interpretation applies in all cases.

In some cases, this accusation is linked to the religious or political background of the dialect-supporter or of anyone who is imagined to have pro-dialect sympathies. Umar Farrukh (1961) from Lebanon provides ample evidence of this tendency. He attributes Sa'id Aql's support for the Lebanese dialect to his Christian Maronite background. The same is true of his attack on the Lebanese linguist Anis Frayha (1902–93) – onetime Professor of Arabic at the American University of Beirut – whom he accused of dialect sympathies because of his call to simplify Arabic pedagogic grammar in several of his books (1955, 1956, 1959). Farrukh's defence of SA against the dialects knew no bounds. He even suspected Satiʿ al-Husri (1880–1968), the greatest thinker on Arab nationalism and one of the most ardent supporters of SA, of pro-dialect sympathies, attributing this to the lingering Ottoman leanings of his youth; and all because al-Husri invited Frayha to give a course of lectures on the Arabic language at the Cairo-based Institute of Advanced Arab Studies, which was sponsored by the Arab League at the time (1950s). Aql and Frayha were the subject of attacks by other language-defenders; but I have chosen to refer to Farrukh in particular because of his high standing among his peers, and also because he dared say overtly what others were prepared to hint at only.

Doctrine, linguistic tradition and history

The war against the proponents of the dialects on the internal front is fought on the battlefield of doctrine, linguistic tradition and history. It will therefore be necessary to set out aspects of this conflict from these three perspectives, particularly for those readers who are not familiar with Islam and Arab cultural history. On the doctrinal front, the support for the dialects is interpreted as an attempt to weaken the link between SA and Islam by putting sufficient 'linguistic distance' between the Arabs and the Qur'an, their founding linguistic document. The core of this argument is that the espousal of the dialects in writing will eventually lead to rendering the Qur'an, as well as the extensive body of texts in SA, unintelligible to Muslim Arabs. The fact that some supporters of the dialects called for the use of the Roman alphabet in recording them made this fear more believable for the language-defenders.

The fear, under this scenario, of losing Arab cultural continuity was very tangible for those who had knowledge of the situation in Turkey in the wake of the Romanization of the alphabet in 1928. In a short period of time, ordinary Turks lost direct access to their written heritage in Ottoman Turkish. To the Arabic language-defenders, this would be unthinkable because of the special relationship between the Arabs and Islam. The miraculous nature of the Qur'an, its inimitability (*iʿjāz*), is located in its medium, the pre-modern form of SA (the *fuṣḥā*). The Arabs' role in history (for which read Muslim Arabs) is to bear witness to this inimitability, for no matter how hard they may try they will not be able to emulate the linguistic uniqueness of the Qur'an (see Suleiman 2002). To give up SA in favour of the dialects would therefore represent more than a cultural rupture for the Arabs: it would be tantamount to the renunciation of a covenant which binds them to God, for in principle their role in history consists of continuing to show that the Qur'an is truly inimitable. Future Arab generations would have to have the text of the Qur'an translated for them into the dialects. This would lead to their contracting a new relationship with the Qur'an, and to the loss of their status as God's 'linguistically chosen' people. It would also make the Arabs *'ajam* (non-Arabs), which is a contradiction in terms. Attar draws this conclusion (1966, 1982), and he describes the proponents of the dialects as 'unbelieving communists', 'modern-day crusaders', 'apostates' and 'infidels'. These are highly charged terms in Arab culture; their deployment in this context indicates the strength of the anti-dialect feeling among the doctrinally committed language-defenders. Attar is not the only member of this group; it also includes such figures as al-Jundi (1982), Husayn (1979) and al-Rafi'i (1974) and al-Shak'a (1970).

Let us now examine the role of the linguistic tradition in forming the anti-dialect attitude among the language-defenders. A major argument in the armoury of this group consists of linking the modern dialects directly to the phenomenon of solecism (*laḥn*, linguistic corruption) in the Arab intellectual tradition (see Suleiman 2003: 49–55). According to this tradition, solecism appeared as early as the beginning of Islam itself in the seventh century. The Prophet is reported to have likened solecism to deviation from the true path. Some early caliphs and Muslim scholars considered solecism, particularly in reciting the Qur'an, to be a punishable offence. Arabic grammar owes its beginnings to the desire to stem the onset of solecism in the text of the Qur'an, although the literature contains stories about the occurrence of this phenomenon in the speech of some famous grammarians. Solecism for some scholars is said to create a linguistic 'stench' that resembles the smell of rotting flesh. Such expressions of moral and social disapproval of solecism did not, however, stem its progress in society. Contact between Arabs and non-Arabs after the success of the early Islamic conquests accelerated the progress of solecism to the extent that it became a feature of the linguistic performance of the elite in society.[13] The expansion of solecism in fact gave rise to a

[13] This is noted by Ibn Khaldun (1332– 82) in his *Muqaddimah* (vol. III), although this thinker takes a view of this matter that is remarkably similar to the principle in modern linguistics which decrees that all language varieties are bound by their own grammatical rules.

tradition of grammatical writing (*laḥn al-ʿāmma*) whose primary aim was to correct the deviations from the linguistic norms of SA.

This tradition continues to this day among the language-defenders (Dayf 1994; Hamadi 1981). According to these defenders, the modern dialects are the repositories of all kinds of linguistic corruption and deviation from the norms of SA. They constitute a state of decay in the linguistic fabric of the Arabic language. Instead of nurturing them, as the proponents of the dialects argue, they must be subjected to the same kind of purification and linguistic culls that the Arab grammarians proposed for the phenomenon of solecism in the past. History must not be aborted, but respected and re-enacted to legitimize the present. Thus, some anti-dialect treatises in modern Arab thought make a point of listing the major works on solecism, or refer to them indirectly (Saʿid 1964; Id 1980; Matar 1966). This attitude towards the dialects as departures from the standard is prevalent in many literate cultures, which tend to treat them as 'performance deviations from competence, not alternative competencies' (Niedzielski and Preston 2000: 22). Support for the dialects is therefore interpreted as support for the forces of decay and corruption in society, in linguistic and moral terms. SA must therefore be protected from any attempt to codify the dialects or to legitimize them by giving them orthographic visibility and fixity.

This concern with purity, correctness and legitimacy animates what is called the 'complaint tradition' in folk linguistics, whereby readers write to newspapers to complain about what they regard as deviations from the standard. In modern Arab thought, the whole tradition of *qul wa lā taqul* (Say this but not that!) is an example of this phenomenon (Hamadi 1981; Suleiman 1996a). It exploits the power of grammar as a metaphor which can express extra-grammatical symbolic meanings (Cameron 1995).[14] As a discipline-inducing activity, grammar is used to drill the learners into accepting order, conformity and authority in society.[15] And since grammar is a property of SA, but not of the dialects, in Arab folk linguistics, support for the latter is interpreted as a defiance of the values the

[14] Cameron and Bourne (1988: 149– 50) express this view in discussing the position of grammar in British socio-political life:

> To understand the peculiarly violent responses that grammar inspires we need to examine its social significance in our culture. Arguably, grammar is an innocuous concept in itself, but has become inextricably linked with less innocuous concepts such as authority, hierarchy, tradition, order and rules. Attitudes to grammar are connected with attitudes to authority; anxieties about grammar are at some deeper level anxieties about the breakdown of order and tradition, not just in language but in society at large.

[15] See Eisele (2001) for a discussion of these and similar points using Bourdieu's notion of *habitus* as an overarching concept.

grammar of the former represents.[16] Vigilance is therefore required in the defence of SA against the dialects, for although the core of this variety is fixed, its status as a standard means that it is 'always in the process of being maintained' (Milroy 2001a: 542). What is in flux is therefore systematized by reference to what is fixed, using analogy as an instrument of inducing conformity with a standard that belongs to the past. This is why the link between the past and the present is so important in the thinking of the language-defenders in modern Arab thought.

There is another aspect of the link between SA and grammar which the support for the dialects can undermine in Arab culture. Although this point is not explicitly or systematically worked out in what the language-defenders write, it is nevertheless implied in some of their pronouncements on the unique qualities of SA. These qualities include the highly systematic or logical structure of this variety.[17] I have tried to argue elsewhere that a connection is established between this and other qualities of SA, and the belief in the qualities of the Arabs as a unique nation among the peoples of the world (Suleiman 1999c, 2003). The Arab grammarians sum this link up in what they call the 'wisdom of the Arabs' principle (*ḥikmat al-ʿarab*). By challenging SA and seeking to replace it with the 'grammarless' dialects, the proponents of the latter can therefore be charged with (unknowingly) destroying the basis upon which the Arabs may establish their ethnic/national pre-eminence in the world. As another example of the value-laden nature of language in society, and of its use as a proxy to express extra-linguistic ideas, this argument locks into the concept of linguistic nationalism that is so prevalent in modern Arab thought. The connection between SA and an all-encompassing national identity for its speakers is a recurring theme in the discourse of the language-defenders. Support for the dialects, as we shall see later, challenges this concept of identity. As a result, their proponents are accused

[16] This is why the debate over the teaching of grammar in schools in Britain in the late 1980s acted as a barometer for a host of political and ideological views within the ruling Conservative Party at the time (Cameron 1995).

[17] The Arabs are not unique in this respect. A similar view exists among the French. Anthony Lodge (1998: 30) describes this situation as follows:

> Since the French language is the language of reason and logic, any French person who uses it improperly must be cognitively defective, irrational, even mad. Since the French language is . . . the symbol of the nation, failure to use the national language and even failure to use it 'properly' makes you a traitor to the national cause. Indeed, it is still widely believed that to speak French badly, to break the rules of French grammar or to make frequent use of foreign words is to be in some way unpatriotic. In 1980 the politician Raymond Barre is reported to have said, 'The first of the fundamental values of our civilization is the correct usage of our language. There is among young people a moral and a civic virtue in the loyal practice of French.'

of harbouring schismatic tendencies which can only harm the position of the Arabs in the world (see Abd al-Mawla 1980; Sha'ban 1994).

Let us now turn to the way in which cultural history is deployed in the fight against the dialects. The main argument in this connection is the well-known theme of *shu'ūbiyya*, the anti-Arab feeling among non-Arabs in early Muslim society (Anis 1970; Gibb 1962; Goldziher 1966; Norris 1990; Qaddura 1972).[18] *Shu'ūbiyya* is a complex socio-political phenomenon with a strong language-related dimension in which SA (in its pre-modern form) is the subject of attack.[19] In an apocryphal tradition of the Prophet, it is claimed that 'if God intends a matter which demands tenderness he reveals it to the ministering angels in . . . Persian, but if He wishes for something demanding strictness He uses Arabic' (Goldziher 1966, I: 157). In another version of this tradition, tenderness and strictness are replaced by pleasure and anger respectively (Goldziher 1966, I: 157). This aspect of *shu'ūbiyya* has caused Goldziher to dub it 'linguistic *shu'ūbiyya*' (1966, I: 192). For Anis (1970) the whole edifice of *shu'ūbiyya* is based on a linguistic conflict involving attacks by the *'ajam* (non-Arabs, but mainly the Persians) against their Arab co-religionists. It is therefore not surprising that some of the best-known linguistic treatises in the Arab grammatical tradition are motivated by the desire to defend Arabic against the *shu'ūbiyya* attacks.[20]

The language-defenders exploit this history to describe their opponents as the 'descendants' of this early *shu'ūbiyya*. By so doing, they turn these opponents into cultural renegades or self-hating Arabs. This in fact is the attitude towards Sa'id Aql and Anis Frayha in Lebanon (see pp. 72–4). It is also the attitude towards Salama Musa and Luwis Awad in Egypt. In his book *al-Balāgha al-'aṣriyya wa-l-lugha al-'arabiyya* (Modern rhetoric/eloquence and the Arabic language, 1964), Musa launches a bitter attack against SA. He accuses it of being an ossified language that is unfit for the needs of a modern and a modernizing Egypt. As the determinant of thought, SA is accused of leading Egyptians into practices – for example, honour killings – which are at variance with the civilized values of the modern world. He therefore urges that SA be reformed in the direction of Egyptian Arabic, the genuine mother tongue of all Egyptians.

18 *Shu'ūbiyya* is more complex than this description implies. I have highlighted this aspect of its meaning here because it is the most prevalent in the discourse of the language-defenders.

19 See al-Duri (1960) and Agius (1980) for discussions of *shu'ūbiyya* in nationalist historiography and in the literary field.

20 Examples of works in this mould are: al-Anbari's (327/938) *Kitāb al-aḍdād* (1987), Ibn Durayd's (321/933) *al-Ishtiqāq* (1958), Ibn Faris' (395/1004) *al-Ṣāḥibī fī fiqh al-lugha wa-masā'ilihā wa-sunan al-'arab fī kalāmihā* (1993) and al-Zamakhshari's (538/1143) *al-Mufaṣṣal fī al-naḥw* (1840).

He further advocates the use of the Roman alphabet in writing this new hybrid language. In setting out his views on these topics, he refers to Willcocks approvingly, declaring that he had the best interests of Egypt at heart when he advocated using the dialect in writing. Awad was equally daring in his attack on SA and in his support for the colloquial. In his book *Plutoland wa-qaṣā'id ukhrā* (Plutoland and other poems 1947), Awad declares that SA is foreign to Egypt and that it represents the language of the Arab/Muslim occupation of his country. This, in his view, explains the inability of the Egyptians to produce great poetry in the language. To rectify this situation, he promises never to write in SA, a promise he honoured only in his book *Mudhakkirāt ṭālib ba'tha* (The memoirs of a scholarship student, 1965). Awad was aware of the connection between SA and Islam, and in *Plutoland* he expresses the hope that his call to use the dialect in writing would be championed by a Muslim writer whose enthusiasm for it cannot be dismissed on grounds of religious affiliation.

The language-defenders subjected Musa and Awad to ferocious attacks. Their Coptic background was used as a stick with which to beat them. They were dismissed as enemies of Islam and the Qur'an, and as the champions of a modern form of the despised *shu'ūbiyya*. Epithets such as crusaders, communists and lackeys of the colonialists were applied to them. The Egyptian writer al-Aqqad (1889–1964) opposed Musa's nomination as a member of the Arabic Language Academy in Cairo, pointing out that it would be unforgivable to elect him because of his anti-SA views. Awad was subjected to similar attacks. The Egyptian writer Mahmud Muhammad Shakir (1972) described him as an 'evil charlatan' (*sharrlatān*), 'impostor' (*da'iyy*), 'transgressor' (*mujtarri'*), 'puppet' (*dumya*), 'trash' (*lā khayr minh*), 'insane' (*muḍṭarib al-dhihn jiddan*), 'rotten' (*tālif*), 'depraved' (*ghabiyy*), 'full of hate' (*ḥāqid*), 'that useless thing' (*shay'*) and 'missionary errand boy' ([*aḥad*] *ṣibyān al-mubashshirīn*). Attar refers to Awad as a 'Christian and communist zealot' who is an 'enemy of Islam, the Qur'an, Islamic culture and heritage, and the Arabic language and literature'. He further describes him as an 'atheist Marxist Leninist Stalinist radical communist leftie' (*yasārī mutaṭarrif mārksī līnīnī stālīnī* (Suleiman 1997: 130)). In a culture where hate mail is not a phenomenon (see Rickford 1999), these attacks are its equivalent in a public sphere where legal action against slander is not the norm.

The combined force of the sanctity of doctrine, the authority of the linguistic tradition and the legitimizing contribution of cultural history constitute a powerful instrument in the armoury of the language-defenders. As forces of cultural defence or coercion, depending on one's point of view, these factors are deployed to intimidate their targets in the court of public opinion. By locking into a host of symbolic meanings, the debate over SA and the dialects acquires a resonance in a society in which the past and the present are brought into communion with each other. It is also used to define the dividing line between cultural loyalty and treason, or between members of the in-group and the out-group intra-nationally. In the discourse of the language-defenders, Musa and Awad are the vanguard of a 'fifth column' consisting of a group of intellectuals who, by aligning themselves with the colonialists, have committed an act of cultural treason for which they must be punished. Punishment may consist of the withholding of privilege, as when Musa was denied membership of the Arabic Language Academy in Cairo; or it may involve legal sanction and censorship, as happened with Awad's *Muqaddima fī fiqh al-lugha al-'arabiyya* (1980). Although this book is silent on the debate over SA and the dialects, there is no doubt that the trial that resulted in its banning from circulation had in it an element of the settling of old scores (Mijli 1995; Zahran 1985).[21]

The battle of national identities

A prominent theme in the discourse of the language-defenders concerns the danger the dialects pose to the association between SA and national identity on the pan-Arab level. In its most comprehensive form, Arab national identity is based on language as the criterion that binds the Arabs culturally; it further acts as a force in the drive to achieve the political unity of which the nationalists dream. SA is impregnated with these symbolic meanings in all the ideological pronouncements on the topic (Suleiman 2003). The smallest whiff of interest in the dialects is therefore likely to be interpreted as an attempt to undermine this role of the language and as playing into the hands of those who aim to make the fragmentation of the Arabs a (more) permanent feature of the political scene. This sensitivity among the language-defenders sometimes amounts to paranoia. An example of this is the accusation that Ahmad Lutfi al-Sayyid (1872–1963), one of Egypt's most respected figures in the nineteenth and twentieth centuries, was a supporter of Egyptian Arabic in spite of the fact that he opposed its use in writing and for the stage.[22]

[21] Joseph (1987) reports how a Greek professor was stripped of his chair and accused of 'communist sympathies' because he wrote in a low variety of Greek. Violent demonstration followed the publication of his work and led to loss of life.

[22] The following quotation from an article by Ahmad Lutfi al-Sayyid is cited by Wendell (1972: 280); it shows his views of the dialects:

> I saw this on the stage of the Abbas Theatre when the Abyad troupe presented four plays which had been translated into poetry in the colloquial tongue by the late Uthman Bey Jalal. I saw the great crush of people, the enthusiastic applause, and the tremendous

Three factors gave credence to this accusation, which lingers to this day: (1) al-Sayyid sought to effect a rapprochement between SA and the dialects in the direction of the former; (2) he referred to this kind of Arabic as the Egyptian language (*al-lugha al-miṣriyya*) in several of his articles in the newspaper *al-Jarīda*, of which he was editor; and (3) he treated this form of Arabic as the language of a separately constituted national identity for Egypt. It is interesting to note in this connection the existence of a tendency in the discourse of the language-defenders which refuses to acknowledge that support for SA can be allied to state nationalism, in spite of the fact that such an association does exist in some ideological pronouncements on Egyptian, Lebanese and Tunisian nationalism (Suleiman 2003). This tendency is indicative of the strength of the language (SA) and national-identity association in Arab political discourse.

The accusation that support for the dialects may in fact be symptomatic of support for territorial nationalism is, however, not unwarranted (Faysal 1989; al-Musa 1987). This is particularly true of Lebanon and Egypt. In the latter, the drive – in the first three decades of the twentieth century – to forge a national identity for Egypt that was specifically Egyptian went together with the call to raise the spoken dialect to the status of a national language (Suleiman 1996b, 2003). A host of arguments were offered to support this nationalist enterprise. SA was said by some nationalists to be a foreign language which came to Egypt with the Arab 'occupation/invasion' of the country in the seventh century. Some nationalists argued that Egyptian Arabic is distinct from other Arabic dialects and SA because of the influence of the Coptic linguistic substratum on it. A group of nationalists based their ideology on the view that the environment is the key factor in national-identity formation. Applying this principle to Egypt, they argued that the environmental conditions of the Nile valley stamped the Egyptians, their language and their culture with an identity that is peculiarly Egyptian. Identifying this language mostly with the dialect, nationalists of this persuasion called for using it in all functional domains, to enable the Egyptians to describe their own reality in a medium that is uniquely suited for the task. For this group, literature was the primary arena for the implementation of this nationalist ideal, owing to its function as the 'emblem' and 'nectar' of a nation's civilization.

acclaim which greeted these popular plays. I saw everyone [so transported] except for myself and a few of my friends who were of the same mind; who felt depressed by the spectacle of [this sick language gaining in strength], jostling the literary language, and forcing it out of the stage; and who were oppressed having to listen to solecisms [affecting the ends of words].

See Irsan (1992) for a discussion of the use of SA and the dialects in the theatre.

Thus they argued very strongly for the use of the dialect in writing. It was believed that, by acting in this way, the Egyptians could distance themselves from other Arabic-speaking peoples in forming their national identity. Tawfiq Awwan, a radical member of this group, expressed this constellation of views and attitudes as follows (cited in Gershoni and Jankowski 1986: 220):

> Egypt has an Egyptian language; Lebanon has a Lebanese language; the Hijaz [in Saudi Arabia] has an Hijazi language; and so forth – and all of these languages are by no means Arabic languages. Each of our countries has a language which is its own possession: so why do we not write as we converse in it? For the language in which the people speak is the language in which they also write.

Views of this kind were anathema to the language-defenders. Support for the dialects was in their view tantamount to undermining the chances of Arab unity and, therefore, to consigning the Arabs to a position of political weakness in the world. Doctrinally minded language-defenders treated the views noted above as an attack against Islam and the Qur'an. The Egyptian nationalists were accused of self-delusion because they refused to acknowledge that the ties of language link the Egyptians with other Arabs synchronically and with Arab and Islamic history diachronically. Finding themselves between the rock of doctrinal dogma and the hard place of Arab nationalist aspirations, the Egyptian nationalists started to turn their faces in an Arabist direction in the 1930s. This, however, did not end the aspirations of some Egyptian nationalists, for example Musa and Awad, for an Egyptian Egypt. Nor did it stop the use of the dialect in writing, particularly in literature (Abbas 1967; Abdel-Malek 1972; Berg 1996; Cachia 1990; Holes 1995; Munif 1994). The controversy over the latter appeared in different guises and in different places. I will deal with one such example in the next section.

Saudi Arabia: a case study

Although Egypt and Lebanon have traditionally constituted the socio-political spheres in which the major debates over SA and the dialects have taken place in the twentieth century, Saudi Arabia provides another interesting example of this debate towards the close of this period. Sometimes acrimonious, this debate was initially conducted in the press, mainly in *al-Jazīra* newspaper, in the context of the controversy over the legitimacy of vernacular poetry, *al-Shiʿr al-nabaṭī*, in modern Saudi culture.[23]

[23] Sowayan (1985: 1) defines *nabaṭī* poetry as the 'popular vernacular poetry of Arabia'. The term 'vernacular' is misleading. It suggests that it is composed/written in a language

Articles from this debate were later collected by Wahba (1983) in a book entitled *al-Shiʿr al-shaʿbī* (Vernacular poetry).[24] Three years later, Ibn Tinbak, another Saudi writer, brought out a study that was very critical of vernacular poetry and the support it lent to the dialectal form of the language. A second edition of this book was published in 1988, reflecting its popularity and the fact that it was awarded the Gulf Cooperation Council Prize for the best book in Arabic studies published that year. However, this book was not the last word on the subject. Al-Suwayyan (2000), a Saudi folklorist, brought out a study in support of vernacular poetry in which he discussed the SA versus the dialect issue.[25] The length of the period over which this debate took place testifies to the importance of the language issue in Saudi culture.

The timing of this debate is also significant. It coincided with the oil boom in Saudi Arabia, and the attendant fear that the traditional values of Saudi society were coming under attack from the forces of modernization and globalization. It is ironic that both parties to the debate, those in favour and those against vernacular poetry, used the rising popularity of this genre to opposite ends. The former argued that vernacular poetry and its language constituted the best defence of the traditional values of Saudi society against the unwanted aspects of modernization and the rolling menace of globalization. Part of their argument revolved around the inroads made by the European languages, mainly English and French, into SA in areas of terminology. The popularity of foreign languages in the Arabic-speaking countries, and the Western literary influences on Arab letters, made vernacular poetry look like the final bastion against these externally induced challenges to Arab cultural authenticity. Opponents of vernacular poetry argued that the support it gives to the dialects was bound to weaken SA and to make it less able to withstand the onslaught of the languages of wider communication in an increasingly globalizing world culture. Although many of the debates about SA and the dialects in Saudi Arabia and elsewhere in the Arabic-speaking world are cast in

which stands in a daughter relationship to SA similar to that between, say, French and Latin. This is not the case. It would therefore have been better to replace 'vernacular' in this definition by 'dialectal' or 'colloquial'. However, I will continue to use the term 'vernacular' because of its widespread use in the literature.

[24] The view that vernacular poetry disregards the rules of grammar is an ideological assertion that lacks empirical validity. Bamia advances this view in her study of Algerian vernacular poetry (2001). The fact that vernacular poetry does not follow the stipulations of SA does not mean that it is ungrammatical. For this reason, we cannot accept the assertion by Bamia that the 'freedom to distort the language grammatically and phonetically . . . provided the masses with a deep psychological boost, a liberating feeling, freeing them from formal Arabic's linguistic restrictions' (2001: 23–4).

[25] The English study by al-Suwayyan (Sowayan 1985) is not relevant in this context because it excludes the language issue in vernacular poetry in Saudi Arabia.

more or less the same intellectual mould, there are three features of the Saudi debate that make it worthy of special mention.

These features coalesce around one issue: the identity of Saudi Arabia as a Muslim and Arab country. First, the language-defenders reject vernacular poetry and its dialectal medium because of the challenge they pose to the identity of the country as the guardian of Islam in the modern world. Supporting the dialects, directly or indirectly, is seen as tantamount to undermining the link between the Qur'an and SA. This association between scripture and SA is not unique to Arabic; it existed in eighteenth-century England, where the King James translation of the Bible acted as the defender of both linguistic standards and religious faith.[26] Thus, in symbolic terms, support for the dialects in Saudi Arabia was regarded as a rejection of, or a diminution of, the special place of the country inside and, to a lesser extent, outside the Muslim world. In this respect, Saudi Arabia, the birthplace of Islam, is said to have a unique mission that no other Muslim or Arabic-speaking country has. Support for the dialects in, say, Egypt or Lebanon cannot therefore be endowed with the same negative meanings that would accrue to it in Saudi Arabia.

Furthermore, the language-defenders reject the argument of the supporters of vernacular poetry to the effect that, by undertaking to preserve the linguistic integrity of the Qur'an (chapter 15, verse 9), God has guaranteed the survival of SA. They point out that God's guarantee is restricted to the text of the Qur'an per se, and that it excludes SA as its medium. It would therefore be possible for the text of the Qur'an to survive irrespective of what might happen to SA. For the language-defenders, the popularity of vernacular poetry, and the tendency to collect and catalogue it, endow the dialect with resource power which can erode the place of SA in society. This power is said to be enhanced by the burgeoning interest in organizing festivals, convening conferences, forming societies, instituting prizes and launching specialized journals in the Arab Gulf countries to promote vernacular poetry. The call to devise a writing system, based on the Arabic script, to record this genre is regarded as another manoeuvre in endowing the dialect with legitimacy. These publicly supported activities acquire a heightened socio-political meaning when correlated with the rise in the number of young people composing

[26] Writing in 1864, the nineteenth-century educator E. Hagginson expressed the linguistic role of the King James translation as follows (cited in Crowley 1989: 94): 'The English Bible is practically the standard of our language. It has been, more than any other influence, the means of teaching the English language, and maintaining it comparatively unchanged for 250 years. No academy or authoritative dictionary or grammar could have produced so general a standard of appeal, or given such uniform instruction throughout the nation.' These claims are similar to what is universally claimed for the Qur'an in Arab ethnolinguistics.

vernacular poetry, and with the competition between private collectors in acquiring manuscripts in this genre. Noting the young age profile of the majority of those composing vernacular poetry, it is possible to say that this poetry is seen as a voice of the youth.

As far as the language-defenders are concerned, the challenge to SA from vernacular poetry is a real one which, they believe, must be met with determined resistance in defence of Islam and the special place Saudi Arabia has in the modern world. This helps explain the rhetorical force of Ibn Tinbak's (1988) attack against this genre. He delivers this by deploying a discourse which invokes the war metaphor that characterizes discussions of linguistic conflict; hence the references in his book to the 'ferocious campaigns', 'intrigue', 'conspiracies', 'insurrections', 'disturbances' and 'destruction' waged against SA. Hence also the charge of conspiracy against those who call for an Arabic-based writing system to record vernacular poetry. To the language-defenders, this call is a continuation of the Romanization proposals under a different guise.

The second feature concerns the duality of the impulses at work in the construction of national identity in Saudi Arabia. The language-defenders treat the support for vernacular poetry and its linguistic medium as a proxy for promoting a specifically Saudi state-nationalist ideology. This is reflected in the claim of the defenders of vernacular poetry and its lexicon that poetry and lexicon preserve a cultural and linguistic heritage that is specific to Saudi Arabia. The language-defenders acknowledge the local value of this heritage and its political implications, but they argue that these factors work against the attempts to promote a nationalist ideology encompassing all the Arabic-speaking countries. However, support for this pan-Arab ideology tends to be hedged by references to Islam and to the traditional norms of society to avoid inciting the full force of the official state-nationalist ideology. Fear of this backlash explains the flattering references to patronage from members of the Saudi royal family as a protective cover in the advocacy of supra-state Saudi national identity. Some of the articles in Wahba's collection bear witness to this debating strategy.

The third feature pertains to the struggle between elite and vernacular cultures in forming the identity of Saudi Arabia. The language-defenders espouse the former, with its reliance on SA, as the only valid source for weaving a historically sanctioned identity for the country. This is seen to be consistent with the attempt to form a supra-tribal identity for the tribally disparate Saudis. The fact that Saudi Arabia was built on shifting and bloody tribal alliances, whose memory is still alive and is recorded in vernacular poetry, injects a sense of urgency into this enterprise. Elite culture is also considered consistent with the SA-oriented Muslim identity of the country, since Islam is the bedrock of Arab elite culture and the source of its inspiration. This explains the rejection by the language-defenders of those aspects of this poetry which they take to promote social values that are inconsistent with the spirit and doctrine of Islam, notwithstanding the fact that this criticism applies with equal force to some poetry and prose works in SA.

As a sign of moral decay in society, the content of this poetry is said to accord with the decay of the linguistic medium expressing it. It is therefore imperative, according to the language-defenders, that the vernacular poetry of Saudi Arabia is deprived of any resource power that may lead to its legitimization in the eyes of the people. However, these defenders know that they must tread carefully in their critique of vernacular poetry because of its association with the state-oriented nationalist ideology. To this effect, they argue that whereas older examples of this genre were composed by people with sound linguistic intuitions that broadly conform to the norms of SA, modern examples of it veer from these norms because of the loss of those intuitions, in the modern generation of vernacular poets, under the onslaught of urbanization, dialect mixing and external linguistic interferences. Applying the metaphor of linguistic and moral decay, it becomes possible to accept some examples of vernacular poetry and to reject others. Those belonging to an imagined pristine past, or golden age, are accepted; those that do not are rejected. The fact that this is an arbitrary temporal division is not the issue here.

The debate over vernacular poetry in Saudi Arabia provides another example of the use of language as a proxy to discuss issues of national and state identity construction. On one level, vernacular poetry and its language are taken to undermine the formation of a pan-Arab national identity. On a different level, vernacular poetry and its language are espoused as a means of establishing a state identity that is specifically Saudi. In this tug of war between national and state identities, Islam is invoked as an important legitimizing principle, whose association with SA strengthens its position against the dialect. This support does not translate into a strengthening of the national over the state-oriented in identity construction. Its main function is in fact to invoke a concept of identity that is rhetorically equidistant from the other two forms of identity construction. In this respect, Islam mediates between the supra-tribal state identity and the supra-state nationalist ideology. Language is part of this contestation and mediation, although in this case the immediate concern is with vernacular poetry.[27] However, unlike the SA versus dialect debate in, say,

[27] The debate over the position of the dialects in Saudi Arabia was the subject of critical comment by the conservative Egyptian academic Muhammad Muhammad Husayn (nd.). Reminding his readers of Saudi Arabia's position as the birthplace of Islam, and

Egypt or Lebanon, the Saudi debate is pursued in a low-key ideological idiom. In tone, this idiom is consistent with the socio-political realities of a nascent, centralizing and consolidating nation-state, whose identity demands that a socio-political equilibrium is maintained between the three pillars of its self-definition: Saudi-ness, Arabism and Islam.

Conflict resolution: from *Sesame Street* to *Iftaḥ Yā Simsim*

For the language-defenders, the main priority is protecting SA against the dialects on the ideological battlefield. The major flashpoint in the conflict between these two varieties is the call to render the dialects in writing, either by means of the Roman alphabet or by devising a system based on the Arabic script. The scholarly interest in the dialects represents another, less intense flashpoint. For some language-defenders, the ultimate requirement to resolve this conflict is defeating these and other modes of validating and expanding the functional domain of the dialects. As Bakhtin (1981: 270) states, a 'unitary language is not something given . . . but is always in essence posited . . . and at every moment of its linguistic life it is opposed to the realities of heteroglossia', in this case the dialects. In this 'zero-sum' game, no compromise is countenanced with the dialects as expressions of a degenerate heteroglossia in society. To these language-defenders, the security of SA cannot be guaranteed until the dialects are completely defeated. They argue that the spread of literacy and active language planning in the socio-political arena can help in achieving this objective (see al-Musa 1987). In some cases, violence and repression may have to be practised and given justification by appealing to a great moral good: the preservation of the purity of the language as a mirror of the purity of the nation and its culture.

In pursuing this ideological orientation, the language-defenders point to the revival of Hebrew in Palestine in the twentieth century as an example of how language planning – underpinned by acts of linguistic repression from time to time – can work by breathing life into what was a dead

as the guardian of the link between this faith and SA, Husayn expressed his surprise that the University of Riyadh was in 1975 building a language laboratory in which the dialects would be studied. Husayn tried to discredit this project by linking it to the external enemies of Islam and SA, who impress their will on Saudis graduating from Western universities and use them as recruits for the dissemination of a linguistics that does not recognize the uniqueness of SA. Husayn believed that general linguistics and phonetics were developed in Europe to study the European languages. In his view these two disciplines are therefore unsuitable for describing Arabic, which is linguistically and culturally different and which has its own, historically sanctioned, native linguistic tradition. In a memorandum he sent to the Saudi Minister of Higher Education, Husayn called this foreign orientation in the study of Arabic a 'harmful corruption and a distortion of the established order' (n.d.: 205).

language in the oral domain (see al-Musa 1987). By invoking this example, this group of language-defenders aims to activate the political will of Arabic speakers to emulate the experience of the Jews in Palestine who inflicted many defeats upon them on the military battlefield. This argument, however, suffers from underestimating the vast objective differences between the Hebrew revival movement in Palestine and the call to turn SA into the language of daily speech. These differences, which will be left out of consideration for reasons of space, create a differential in the pertinence of linguistic politics in the two speech communities which, on the Arab side, cannot be bridged by rhetorical power.

A second group of language-defenders believes that the conflict between SA and the dialects can be resolved if the latter are restricted to the verbal domain only. Language-defenders of this persuasion point out that the diglossic nature of the Arabic language situation dictates that this be the case.[28] They also point to the existence of the formal versus informal levels of language, which they equate with SA and the dialects respectively, as a universal feature in all speech communities. According to this position, the domain specialization of SA and the dialects is not an aberration, but a reflection of a universal phenomenon in which formality is characteristically associated with writing and informality with speech. This is a misleading argument because it wrongly generalizes diglossia into a universal feature by associating it analogously with register distinctions in language. Suffice it to say here that formality and informality apply in speech and writing, and that they cut across the standard versus dialect divide that is the *sine qua non* of all living language situations. The force of this counter-argument should not, however, obscure the fact that the present group of language-defenders uses diglossia as a means of sanctioning the use of the dialects in speech by the SA supporters, and the utilization of SA in writing by the proponents of the dialects, although the logic of the two groups would demand otherwise. On the moral level of linguistic politics, this recognition eliminates the charge of hypocrisy which each party levels against the other because it deviates from what it linguistically preaches.

As a means of resolving the conflict between SA and the dialects, the acceptance of diglossia in Arabic is given a philosophical interpretation by the Lebanese scholar Kamal Yusuf al-Hajj (1917–76). According to this

[28] In fact, SA and the dialects are usually mixed in cross-dialectal situations, or in situations demanding a high level of spoken and impromptu formality, to produce what has been dubbed Educated Spoken Arabic in the literature (see El-Hassan 1977, 1978; Mitchell 1978, 1986; Sallam 1979, 1980). However, this form of Arabic has not been the subject of ideological discussions among Arab intellectuals. This is why I have not discussed it in this work.

interpretation, the distinction between SA and the (colloquial) dialects is an expression of a fundamental difference between sense and mind in man: sense is related to feelings and sensibility, while the mind is related to the intellect and rationality (al-Hajj 1978). Furthermore, while sense is raw and spontaneous, the mind is reflective, deliberate and calculating. These characteristic differences between sense and the mind are said to require different modes of expression which, in the Arabic language situation, are correlated with the dialects and SA respectively. The dialects, by virtue of being colloquial and informal, are characterized by false starts, digressions and loose ends. In this respect, they accord with the spontaneous and impulsive nature of sense. By contrast, SA is controlled and regulated. In this respect it accords with the measured and methodical workings of the mind. Diglossia therefore is not a linguistic aberration, but a fact of language which reflects the constitutional duality of man into mind and sense. There is therefore no need to argue in favour of SA against the dialects or vice versa in Arab culture. One form of the language is the philosophical and psychological counterpart of the other in a relationship of mutual implication. Each serves a particular function in society and responds to a different set of needs in the speakers. It is therefore unwarranted to try to eliminate the dialects by expanding the domain of SA to include speech. It is equally unwarranted to eliminate SA by expanding the domain of the dialects to include writing. For, even if it was possible for the one variety of the language to eliminate the other, it is inevitable that the standard versus dialect divide would re-emerge in whatever language situation emerges, whether it is dominated by the standard or the dialects. By accepting this fact, the language-defenders and their dialectal opponents can replace their conflict-ridden ideologies by a consociational perspective that is accommodating of both.

A third group of language-defenders accepts the SA versus dialects divide, but they seek to reduce the gap between them by corpus-planning measures. Corpus planning refers to the 'creation of new forms, the modification of old ones, or the selection from alternative forms in a spoken or written code' (Cooper 1989: 31). Broadly speaking, two modes of corpus planning are proposed by this group. The first consists of levelling up by injecting SA elements into the dialects, mainly in the lexical domain. The second mode consists of simplifying or reforming pedagogic grammar to enhance the learners' mastery of SA.[29] This mode reflects the belief that Arabic grammar in its traditional form is pedagogically unwieldy. Several attempts were made to convert this measure into a practical objective

[29] See Dayf (1986a, 1986b, 1990), al-Jawari (1984), Khalifa (1986), Omran (1991) and Suleiman (1996a) for a discussion of the grammar-reform proposals.

in the educational systems of various Arabic-speaking countries. New grammar books were composed for this purpose, but it seems that they had little impact on the learners' ability to master SA effectively (al-Musa 1990). Members of this group came under attack from the first group of language-defenders, who considered any attempt to simplify or reform Arabic grammar as a distortion of SA and all it stands for – on the religious and national fronts – in the life of its speakers. For example, al-Jundi (1982: 147) called the reform movement in all its manifestations *bid'a*, a doctrinally loaded term in Arabic which signifies anything between heresy and unwarranted innovations in matters of faith and that can lead to consigning those who propagate it to hellfire.[30]

An interesting example of corpus planning of the type advocated by the third group is provided by the children's TV programme *Iftaḥ Yā Simsim* (Open sesame), the Arabic version of *Sesame Street* (Abu-Absi 1990, 1991; Alosh 1984; Palmer 1979).[31] In preparing the materials of this programme, three options were considered: (1) using Egyptian Arabic in its capacity as the most widespread dialectal variety in the Arabic-speaking countries; (2) producing four versions of the programme in the four major dialectal varieties of Arabic: Arabian, Egyptian, Levantine and Maghrabi (North African); and (3) utilizing a lexically and grammatically simplified form of SA. The first two options were rejected for pedagogical and extralinguistic reasons. On the pedagogical front, these options were judged to present the viewer with varieties of the language which are not used in instruction in schools. From the extralinguistic point of view, the use of these varieties was judged to undermine the role of SA as a medium of high culture and as a factor in the definition of national identity. In opting for a simplified form of SA, the programme's producers encouraged the use of all grammatical and lexical features shared by SA and the dialects.

As far as unshared features are concerned, three categories of SA materials were established: (1) those that should be used regularly – for example, the dual; (2) those that should be used sparingly – for example, the

[30] This is expressed by the expression *kull bid'a ḍalāla, wa-kull ḍalāla fī al-nār* (every heresy/unwarranted innovation is an error, and every error leads whoever propagates it to hellfire).

[31] This series was produced by the [Arab] Gulf States Joint Programme Production Institution in cooperation with the Children's Television Workshop of New York, the originators of 'Sesame Street'. This two-part series consists of 260 half-hour programmes which have been aired and rerun by several television stations throughout the Arab world. Part I, which was first televised in September 1979, was intended for children between the ages of three and six. Part II, with a target audience of children between the ages of seven and nine, was first broadcast in October 1983. The content of IYS represents original materials written in Arabic, with only about fifteen hours of Part I and ten hours of Part II being translated or adapted from 'Sesame Street' materials. (Abu-Absi 1991: 111)

passive form of the verb; and (3) those that should be avoided – for example, the superlative form of the adjective. The aim of these stipulations was to produce a simple form of SA which could be easily understood by children, in addition to its being characterized by naturalness in its spoken mode.[32] Preliminary testing in Amman, Kuwait, Cairo and Tunis, and post-programme parents' and teachers' reports (Alosh 1984), indicated that these two objectives were met. The programme was hailed as a great success and as a pioneering experiment in how the gap between SA and the dialects can be closed in favour of the former. This experiment became a trend-setter in another sphere: the dubbing of foreign children's programmes into Arabic, where aiming at an approximation of SA tends to be a linguistic objective. This is particularly true of programmes dubbed in Jordan, where the lead has been taken in this area of (unconscious) corpus planning.

The above solutions to the conflict between SA and the dialects are grounded in ideology. The first group of language-defenders, the hardliners, sees the battle between the two forms of the language as one between the grammatical and the ungrammatical, the pure and the contaminated. Members of this group tend to be of an Islamist political persuasion. Their aim is to protect SA, in its capacity as the medium of the Qur'an and the Islamic sciences, against the corruption of the dialects. The fact that this group upholds the ideal of linguistic purity, although it is rarely realized in linguistic practice, is not the issue here, since what matters in ideological terms is the attitudinal orientation of these defenders rather than their linguistic behaviour. Members of the second group, the realists, know that eradicating the dialects is not an option. They are aware of the limitations of language planning in achieving any such result, particularly in view of the absence of a strong political and popular will to do so. Accepting the dialects is, *ipso facto*, recognition of the status quo in the Arabic language situation. Members of the third group, the reformers, adopt a middle position. They believe that the dialects can be dissolved by language-planning measures whose aim is to encourage the use of SA in speech. The fact that SA and the dialects interact in a different way in actual linguistic performance is of little concern to these language-defenders. This is not surprising, because their primary interest is in the ideology of language use rather than in language use per se. Using the 'war metaphor' as an organizing principle, we may characterize the conflict-resolution strategies of the three groups of language-defenders (towards the dialects) as 'confrontation and hegemony', 'disengagement

[32] A similar solution was adopted by the Egyptian playwright Tawfiq al-Hakim in his play *al-Ṣafqa* (1956). See Holes (1995: 304–5) for a discussion of this issue.

and truce' and 'détente and disempowerment' respectively. However, in none of these strategies do the language-defenders relinquish the option of discursive power as a means of conflict resolution.

The existence of different opinions about the dialects among the language-defenders is characteristic of language–ideological debates. As Blommaert (1999: 11) reminds us, 'the hegemony of one [language] ideology does not necessarily imply total consensus or total homogeneity. On the contrary, ambiguity and contradiction may be key features of every ideology, and subjects' adherence to one ideology or another is often inconsistent or ambivalent.' There must, however, exist a core of commonality among those who subscribe to an ideology for them to be considered partners in it. More often than not, this commonality is one of attitudes and shared values, consisting in the case under consideration of the belief in the superiority of SA over the dialects and of the imperative of defending the former against the corrosive influences of the latter. These attitudes and values tap into cultural societal currents whose legitimacy is not the subject of major popular dispute. These currents include the belief that undermining the standard is tantamount to subverting the existing social order in society. Involved in this is an attitude in literate societies which views the 'spoken language as ephemeral, an epiphenomenon, a wavering and imperfect reflection of what we believe to be the true, real, ideal forms embedded in the written language' (Cooper 1989: 137). This attitude is promoted by the elite through a variety of institutional and semi-institutional channels of communication and opinion formation.

Conclusion

The belief that SA is under attack from external provocateurs and internal agents is a common feature of the debate over language in the Arabic-speaking world. This is reflected in the use of variations on the war metaphor to describe the conflict between SA and its 'enemies'. Linguistically, the dialects represent the main enemy, especially when calls to expand their structural power into writing are issued. As a local source of destabilization, the dialects are said to be championed by external provocateurs – in the guise of the colonial administrator and the Orientalist scholar – and internal agents who work for the same objective of weakening the role of SA in collective self-identification on the national and doctrinal fronts. Acting as a fifth column, the internal agents are imagined to be in collusion with the external provocateurs who are at the citadel gates. In setting out these themes, the language-defenders point to other dangers facing SA from the outside, including the media and translation, which act as infiltration channels for 'subverting' influences from foreign languages. The title of an article by the well-known Iraqi linguist Ibrahim al-Samirra'i (1979), 'The Arabic language and the media: translation or linguistic infection?', and another by the Lebanese linguist Muhammad Abd al-Rahman Marhaba (1990), 'The Arabic language and the distortions visited upon it by translation', highlight this theme in the armoury of the language-defenders. This 'us versus them' construction of the Arabic language situation is an important mobilization strategy in the ideology of the language-defenders. The fact that these defenders do not, most of the time, feel the need to justify their ideology is indicative of its normalization and hegemonic power in society. As far as they are concerned, the view that SA is under attack is a self-evident article of faith whose truth is not in doubt. As a cultural 'given', this view is sanctioned historically; it is seen as a continuation in the present of the socio-political agenda of the *shu'ūbiyya* of the past. It is also a most useful tool of cultural mobilization.

Gramsci (1985: 183) writes that 'every time the question of language surfaces, in one way or another, it means that a series of other problems is coming to the fore'. This is true of the language debate dealt with in this chapter. Acting as a proxy for extralinguistic issues, the SA versus dialects debate is used to signal metonymically the concern with identity, modernization, tradition, change and globalization. State and pan-national identities are set out in relation to this debate. The same is true of the role of Islam in the conceptualization of state identity, as we have seen in the case of Saudi Arabia. The widespread belief that the dialects are a degenerate and ungrammatical form of Arabic is taken to indicate the existence of moral and cultural decay in society, and the state of impotence in the socio-political arena. This correlation of the state of the language with the moral standing of the nation is found in other cultures. In England, this view was expressed by John Rae, ex-headmaster of Westminster (an exclusive, fee-paying school), in a letter to the weekly newspaper the *Observer* published on 7 February 1982 (quoted in Cameron 1995: 94): 'The overthrow of grammar coincided with the acceptance of the equivalent of creative writing in social behaviour. As nice points of grammar were mockingly dismissed as pedantic and irrelevant, so was punctiliousness in such matters as honesty, responsibility, property, gratitude, apology and so on.'

The view that grammatical errors in linguistic performance represent a moral blemish is signalled by a tradition of Prophet Muhammad according to which solecism is treated as a deviation from the true path of Islam.

This theme is articulated in different forms and at different times in Arab culture (Suleiman 2003). The presumed ungrammaticality of the dialects therefore provides a linguistic arena in which this moral judgement can be writ large. If so, the defence of SA is a defence of the values society ascribes to it. The use of *jihad* (holy war) by some language-defenders to describe the defence of SA reflects this concern with morality, with what is right and what is wrong in society. Part of this war consists of fighting any attempt to legitimize the dialects by codifying them, or by endowing them with resource power in the form of textbooks or dictionaries.

In his study of the politics of Standard English in British culture, Crowley writes (1989: 258): 'Language becomes a crucial focus of tension and debate at critical historical moments, serving as the site upon which political positions are contested.' He illustrates this with the debate over grammar in Britain in the 1980s. Applying this generally held principle in the study of language debates to the SA versus dialects conflict, we can point to its coincidence in the twentieth century with the rise of nationalism in the Arab Middle East, the end of colonialism, the struggle for Arab political unity, the promotion of territorial national identities, the interest in modernization and the dislocation this brought about, the reassertion of Islam as a political ideology, the perceived threat of globalization, and the political economy of print culture in a linguistically unified area. Most of these points have been highlighted at different places in this chapter. Two factors, however, need some comment: globalization and the political economy of print culture. By activating tradition as a mode of resistance, globalization strengthens the standard language ideology as a bastion against external encroachments; it does so by virtue of the organic link between SA and the elite tradition in Arab culture. As far as print culture is concerned, the preservation of a linguistically homogeneous cultural market favours the standard language ideology: it enables a book in SA printed in Morocco to be read in Oman. Linguistic fragmentation along dialectal lines would lead to the fragmentation of this market as a single unit of economic activity.

On the rhetorical front, the SA versus dialects debate is a form of 'discursive struggle and contestation' (Blommaert 1999: 8). By taking part in this debate, participants act as ideology brokers in a conflict of texts and counter-texts for which they can claim a degree of authorship. The fact that the main arguments in these texts tend to be repeated *ad nauseam* in each generation and, in the same generation, in different locations testifies to the perennial nature of the issues that animate them (see Daniels 2002). Here, every act of textualization becomes one of retextualization in which society and culture share the right of authorship. It is, however, possible to give this fact of discursive repetition a more sympathetic reading. Like Kelloggs or Colgate adverts, the arguments in these texts are meant to maintain the visibility of the issues they enunciate in their target audience. Remove this visibility, and the brand name will wither and die. And so it is with the SA versus dialects debate: stop repeating the arguments in favour of the former, and you risk losing its commanding position in the cultural marketplace. If so, the feeling of intellectual déjà vu is not a terrible price to pay after all.

4 When dialects collide: language and conflict in Jordan

Introduction

In chapter 3, we dealt with a series of debates involving SA and the dialects to highlight the role of language as a proxy in articulating ideological conflicts of low political intensity. The value-laden nature of the Arabic language was related to issues of external threat and internal collaboration as factors in the SA versus dialect conflict. The colonial and post-colonial experience was treated as the defining context for this interpretation of the conflict. Issues of religious doctrine, linguistic heritage, ethnic identity, and nation and state building were established as major driving forces in this situation. Some of the participants in this conflict saw it as a zero-sum contest between the defenders of SA and their opponents. Their aim was to eliminate the dialects from the Arab linguistic scene, unrealistic though this was, so as to protect and to promote the set of values SA embodies on the cultural and political fronts. Others sought to define the conflict in a way that allows a rapprochement to take place between SA and the dialects. Unlike the maximalists on the SA side, this group did not treat diglossia in Arabic as a case of linguistic corruption or as a moral aberration, but as a fact that needs to be recognized and managed through grammatical reforms, lexical modernization and improvements in pedagogy.

The present chapter will build on some of the issues raised in chapter 3, in particular the role of ethnic/national identity and nation-state building as drivers of interdialectal conflicts. The role of dialect as a boundary-setter will be invoked, as will the linguistic attitudes towards competing dialects in the socio-political arena. The notion of power, which was discussed in chapter 2, will be used to help explain conflicts of this kind. The language situation in Jordan will serve as the case study for this chapter. Emphasis will be placed on the socio-political meanings of this situation by utilizing the concepts of code-switching, dialect convergence, dialect shift and dialect maintenance in relation to the symbolic function of language in society. Dialect variation and speech accommodation will therefore form the sociolinguistic context of this study, as will nation-state building on the socio-political front.[1]

The present chapter will utilize the findings of two earlier studies by the present author (Suleiman 1993, 1999a). It will, however, present new evidence and offer new arguments in support of the set of theses it will advance. The chapter will also draw on my extensive knowledge of the language situation in Jordan, emanating from my role as an 'eyewitness' to some of the most dramatic changes that took place in the country in the wake of the bloody confrontation between the Palestinian guerrilla movement and the Jordanian army in 1970–1. The publication of Adnan Abu-Odeh's *Jordanians, Palestinians and the Hashemite Kingdom in the Middle East Peace Process* (1999) provides an informative statement of the socio-political impact of this confrontation that corroborates the findings of this study. Abu-Odeh is a Jordanian of Palestinian origin. He served in a number of ministerial posts, was Chief of the Royal Court to King Hussein (d. 1999), and later acted as a political adviser to King Hussein and to his successor, King Abdullah II. He therefore writes from the position of one who had an important part to play in the recent history of Jordan, and as one with an intimate knowledge of the events he describes and analyses. Furthermore, his position in Jordan has given him official protection, thus enabling him to say what others have tried to ignore for a long time, although his narrative could have been more daring in what it reveals and in its formulation. Finally, the present chapter will utilize materials that have come to my attention since the publication of my two earlier studies. These materials will provide the quantitative data for this chapter.

[1] We must treat the concept of the nation-state with caution. Very few examples of this kind of political community exist in the modern world. For this reason some scholars have suggested the term 'national state' instead. Anthony Smith (2001: 123) sets out the thinking behind this suggested change in nomenclature:

> A nation-state can be said to exist only where more or less the whole population of a state belongs to a single ethno-national group and where the boundaries of the group and those of the state are co-extensive. Only then do 'nation' and 'state' coincide. But such coincidence is extremely rare, particularly in today's world of migration and cultural mingling. Instead, we have the much more common type of political community known as the 'national state', that is, a state where the great majority of the population belong to a single or dominant ethno-national group, even though other small ethnic groups are found within the state's borders, and where the political community is legitimated in terms of tenets of nationalist ideology.

I believe this description applies to Jordan, which forms the target of this study. I will, however, continue to use the term 'nation-state' in this work because of its currency in the literature.

The variable (Q) as a sociolinguistic marker

The main aim of this chapter is to investigate the socio-political meanings of interdialectal shift and speech accommodation patterns in Jordan involving the variable (Q). There are four principal realizations, called variants, of this variable in Jordan: [q], voiceless uvular plosive; [?], voiceless glottal plosive; [g], voiced velar plosive; and [k], voiceless velar plosive. Although the first variant is a native feature in the speech of a small number of Jordanians (Sawaie 1994), it belongs to Standard Arabic. The remaining variants are dialectal. Each one of these variants has its socio-political connotations by virtue of correlating with a set of demographic factors, as shall be explained later. The status of the variable (Q) as a sociolinguistic marker in Jordan derives from the emblematic role of its variants as stereotypical features of the speech styles and speech communities in which they exist.[2] Broadly speaking, [q] is associated with SA, and [?], [g] and [k] are associated with what in folk-linguistic terms are called Madani (urban), Bedouin or rural pastoralists and Fallahi (rural) dialects respectively (see Cadora 1970, 1992). The fact that linguistically untutored speakers can make these identifications in a fairly consistent manner, as demonstrated by Shorrab in his study of Palestinian speakers (1981), implies that these categories of classification are grounded in some socio-psychological reality. Identifications of this kind are recorded by al-Wer in her study of phonological variation in the speech of women in Jordan (1991). Al-Wer points out that people in Jordan (1991: 58) 'define their own as well as others' linguistic behaviour by a variant of (Q)'. She adds: 'The most common way of describing somebody's speech, or the speech of a certain social group is by referring to them as speakers of [g], speakers of [?] or speakers of [q].' In some cases, speakers attach ethnic labels to these markers. Al-Wer reports that some of her informants associated the variant [q] with the small communities of Druze and Syriacs in Jordan.

Although I have always been aware of this feature of the sociolinguistic competence of speakers in Jordan, I was most struck by it recently when my two sons, who were born and brought up in Scotland, were able to utilize it in their word play in a rather unusual manner. I once heard them discuss whether to call one of their schoolfriends – a boy called Ian – Qian, Gian, or Kian when speaking about him in code in the presence of their friends. When I inquired of them as to why they modified Ian's name in this way, they both replied that they were copying what people in Jordan

[2] See Trudgill (1986) for the notion 'marker'. See also al-Wer (1991: 59–63) for a discussion of this notion in relation to the variable (Q).

do. And when I pressed them further, they said that if Ian were living in Jordan he would be called all four names depending on the speaker. The fact that my two sons – who were twelve and nine at the time and spent only their summer holidays in Jordan – were able to exploit the (Q)-variation as they did suggests that these variants are characterized by a high degree of salience for speakers. My two sons were unable to attach any ecological labels (urban, Bedouin or rural) to the variants they 'played with', but they could make relevant observations as to who used which variant in Jordan. For example, they pointed out that women would use *Ian* most, that men would use *Gian* most and that older people would use *Kian* most. Although these observations are not entirely correct, they nevertheless contain a high degree of empirical validity, as will become clear later.

The choice of (Q) as a sociolinguistic marker in Jordan is supported by a set of observations that endow this variable with this role in Arabic speech communities throughout history. In the fourteenth century, the famous scholar Ibn Khaldun offered a set of observations concerning the variable (Q). First, he pointed out that this variable was rendered as [g] in the speech of Bedouin speakers in his day 'wherever they may live' (1958, III: 348). Second, he considered this variant of (Q) as a 'distinguishing mark' of the speech of the Bedouin Arabs that 'no one else shares with them' (1958, III: 348). Ibn Khaldun expanded his understanding of this property of Bedouin speech by saying that those who wished to associate themselves with the Bedouin Arabs must accommodate to this variant. Third, he set out two contradictory attitudes towards this variant. On the one hand, this variant is said to have been held in high esteem because it represented a continuity with the pure speech of the early Arabs – as reflected in Sibawayh's canonical description of Arabic phonology in the eighth century – and that of the Prophet himself (according to the Shi'ite tradition). On the other hand, Ibn Khaldun tells us that the Arab philologists later 'denounced [g] as an ugly, un-Arabic sound' (1958, III: 350). Fourth, although Ibn Khaldun does not specify which variant of (Q) was used among the sedentary population in his day, it is clear that [g] cannot be one of them. Ibn Khaldun talks about an articulation range for this variable extending between [q] and [k]. It may therefore be the case that these two variants were characteristic of sedentary speech in Ibn Khaldun's day. There is no mention of [ʔ] as a variant of (Q) in Ibn Khaldun.

The function of (Q) as a group boundary-setter is exhibited in various speech communities in the modern period. This is attested in a large number of studies, not all of which will be utilized here (Abdel-Jawad 1981; al-Amadidhi 1985; Blanc 1964; Cleveland 1963; Holes

1983, 1987; Hussein 1980; Hussein and El-Ali 1988; Jabeur 1987; Jassem 1993; al-Khatib 1988; Sallam 1980; Sawaie 1986, 1994; Shorrab 1981; Suleiman 1985). Blanc (1964) reports that the communal dialects of Baghdad are marked by the prestigious variant [g] in the speech of the Muslims and by the stigmatized [q] in that of the Christians and Jews (see also Kattan 1976). This pattern of communally based linguistic variation is found in Bahrain. Holes (1983) reports that the prestigious variant [g] is a marker of the speech of the Sunnis in Bahrain, while the stigmatized variant [q] characterizes the speech of the Shi'ites. In Tunis, the prestigious variant [q] is a marker of urban speech, while the stigmatized variant [g] is a marker of the rural or semi-nomadic communities (Jabeur 1987). These, and the other studies listed above, generate four observations:

(1) The variable (Q) serves as a marker of group membership. These groups may be communally defined, as in Baghdad and Bahrain, or ecologically designated, as in Tunisia and in Ibn Khaldun's study.
(2) The prestige or stigma associated with a variable is contextually defined. Thus while [g] is the prestige variant in Baghdad and Bahrain, it is not in Tunis.
(3) The prestige of a particular variant may change in time. Ibn Khaldun's observation about the variant [g] exemplifies this phenomenon.
(4) Whenever dialect shift takes place it tends to move in the direction of the prestigious variant in a speech community.

All four observations are relevant to my analysis of the language situation in Jordan, as shall be shown later.

The language situation in Jordan: an overview

Before giving an overview of the dialect situation in Jordan, it would be helpful to provide an outline of the main events which shaped the history of the country, with special reference to those that are relevant to this study. Transjordan was created by the British in 1921 and assigned to Emir Abdullah as ruler (assassinated in Jerusalem in 1951). At the time, Transjordan had a population of about 225,000. Half of the population were nomadic tribesmen, and the inhabitants of Amman, the present capital, numbered no more than 2,500 people (Sluglett and Farouk-Sluglett 1996). Owing to the high level of illiteracy in the country, most of the officials of the new emirate were drawn from Palestine and Syria. It is estimated that 8,000–10,000 people from these two backgrounds came to live in the country soon after its creation. In 1946, Transjordan gained its formal independence from Britain, Emir Abdullah was declared monarch and the country changed its name to the Hashemite Kingdom. It is estimated that the country had a population of 435,000 at the time, and that the population of Amman rose from about 10,000 in 1930 to 60,000 in 1947. Following the creation of Israel in 1948 and the influx of Palestinian refugees into the kingdom, the population of Jordan more than doubled. The population of Amman rose to an estimated 110,000 as a result of the influx of Palestinian refugees to the city in 1948. The 'annexation' of what later came to be known as the West Bank to Jordan in April 1950 increased the number of Palestinians under Hashemite rule to about 1.5 million. The new expanded country was renamed the Hashemite Kingdom of Jordan, with King Abdullah as its monarch, Amman as its capital, and all its people as Jordanian citizens.

Between 1950 and 1967, more Palestinians moved from the West Bank to Amman in search of employment in the public and commercial sectors. Their number increased dramatically after the Israeli occupation of the West Bank in 1967. According to official figures, about 450,000 Jordanians of Palestinian origin had entered the East Bank of Jordan by 15 June 1968. It is very likely that the figure is higher, since some people failed to register with the authorities as 'refugees'. Most of the Palestinians lived in and around Amman, which in 1970 had a population of about 550,000. The 1967 defeat enabled members of the Palestinian guerrilla movement to enter Jordan to use it as a staging post for mounting attacks against the Israeli forces occupying Palestinian lands. This led to clashes between the Jordanian army and the Palestinian guerrillas towards the end of the 1960s. The situation worsened in 1970, culminating, in September that year, in bloody confrontations between the Jordanian army and the Palestinians. The latter were defeated and forced to leave Amman for a designated area in the northern part of the country. It is reported that some 3,000 Palestinians lost their lives in the September 1970 clashes (Sluglett and Farouk-Sluglett 1996), which came to be known as the civil war in Jordan.[3] In July 1971, the Jordanian army attacked the Palestinian guerrillas in their new location and forced them to leave the country completely; most went to Lebanon. On 31 July 1987, King Hussein announced his decision to start 'administrative and legal disengagement from the West Bank'. Territorially, as of this date Jordan encompassed what before 1946 had been called Transjordan. Demographically, however, the majority of the population are of Palestinian origin.[4] The term

[3] Abu-Odeh (1999) rejects this term and disputes the figure of 3,000 casualties cited by some historians of modern Jordan.

[4] The government of Jordan has recently declared that Palestinian Jordanians constitute 43 per cent of its 5.3 million citizens (see *The Economist*, 7–13 December 2002 issue: 66). Many people in Jordan do not believe this figure. Some say that the reason behind this declaration is to allay the fears of East Jordanians who believe that the Palestinians are the majority, and that the government must act to reduce their number. *The Economist*

'Jordan' is used in this chapter to refer to this entity, but it is used in its pre-1967 sense whenever necessary.

The bloody clashes between the Jordanian army and the Palestinian guerrillas between 1968 and 1971 had a lasting effect on the history of the country. To begin with, they pitted the two segments of the population, the East Jordanians (Jordanians) and the Palestinians, against each other. The tensions created by this event in the history of the country constitute an active undercurrent in the socio-political arena to this day. Furthermore, these events helped create a vociferous Jordanian nationalist movement, which argued for the de-Palestinianization of Jordan (Abu-Odeh 1999). On the Palestinian side, a feeling was created that they are somehow less Jordanian than the East Jordanians. Although East Jordanians and Palestinian-Jordanians are Jordanian citizens, there is no doubt that the majority in each group conceptualize themselves as belonging to distinct ethnic/national identities. However, while East Jordanians, henceforth Jordanians, locate their national identity in Jordan in territorial terms, the Palestinians continue to treat historical Palestine, or any part thereof, as the territorial locus of their national identity and nation-state aspirations (see Reiter 2002).

Let us now consider the language situation in Jordan in broad outline. Jordan is no exception to the diglossia that characterizes all Arabic-speaking countries (see pp. 58–62). However, since the main interest in this chapter is the local dialects or varieties, I will leave SA out of consideration.[5] Therefore, the three varieties I will deal with are: (1) the Madani variety with its emblematic [ʔ]; (2) the Bedouin variety with its emblematic [g]; and (3) the Fallahi variety with its emblematic [k]. Before the influx of Palestinian refugees into Jordan in 1948 and 1967, the Bedouin variety was the main variety in the country, which hardly had any urban centre to speak of. The Madani variety was present among Palestinians and Syrians who came to Jordan in the 1920s and early 1930s (Sawaie 1994), but the number of speakers from this background was too small to challenge the numerical dominance of the Bedouin variety. The same is true of the Fallahi variety, the presence of which in Jordan is directly linked to the forced mass movement of Palestinians into the country after the 1948 and 1967 wars with Israel. It would therefore be true to say

article deals with equality between men and women in a new decree about nationality rights, sponsored by Queen Rania of Jordan (of Palestinian origin). The article states: 'In their battle to keep their supremacy, Jordan's indigenous minority of East bankers have launched a successful counter-attack against last month's decree by Rania, their Palestinian-born queen, that mothers as well as fathers can pass their nationality on to their children.'

[5] This will skew the percentages in some of the tables I will give later, but it will not affect the general orientation of the arguments to be set out below.

that the presence of both the Madani and, especially, the Fallahi dialects in Jordan is directly related to the way in which the Palestine problem unfolded on the political scene over the past six decades. This explains why (East) Jordanian nationalists refer to these two dialects – with their emblematic [?] and [k] – as 'alien', and why, by the same token, they refer to the Bedouin dialect – with its emblematic [g] – as 'indigenous' (al-Wer 1991: 75). In presenting the attitudes towards these dialects below, I am aware that the situation is far more complex and fluid than my discussion will suggest.

The Madani variety is spoken mainly in the big urban centres in Jordan, particularly among women. According to al-Wer (1991), this dialect distribution does not seem to apply to smaller cities – for example, Karak in the south and Ajloun in the north – although the fact that the researcher in this study is a staunch [g] speaker may have discouraged code-switching by members of her all-female sample. Linguistic attitudes towards this variety declare it as 'soft' and 'pretty' in comparison with the other two dialects. In his study of the linguistic attitudes of a sample of 233 speakers in Irbid, north of Amman, Sawaie found that the Madani variety had the highest scores for 'beauty' and 'high social status'. In fact, it is likely that the scores for the Madani variety would have been much higher if the study had been conducted in Amman, the biggest urban centre in Jordan and where a majority of [?] speakers and Palestinians live. The 'softness' and 'beauty' of the Madani dialect are part of the attitude towards this variety as 'effeminate', at least in comparison with the Bedouin variety. Sawaie (1994: 82) notes that 'men using [?] . . . in the regions where this variant is not spoken indigenously are generally viewed on the positive side as urban, and on the negative side as sissy, effeminate and "city-slick" '.

The effeminateness of [?] speakers is part of the traditional view among both Jordanians and Palestinians that city-dwellers (proper) are lacking in manly qualities, particularly bravery and generosity. This attitude is extended by [g] speakers to the Fallahis (Shryock 1997). This judgement of the sedentary population, particularly the city-dwellers, echoes some of the views expressed by Ibn Khaldun in his *Muqaddimah* (1958, I: 257):

> [The] Sedentary people have become used to laziness and ease. They have sunk in well-being and luxury . . . They find full assurance of safety in the walls that surround them . . . [They] have ceased to carry weapons. Successive generations have grown up in this way of life. They have become like women and children, who depend upon the master of the house. Eventually, this has come to be a quality of character that replaces natural (disposition).

The high social status of the Madani variety results from the position of the city as the seat of government (national or regional), and as the

Table 4.1 *Dialect attitudes in percentages for the three varieties*

	[ʔ] Speaker	[g] Speaker	[k] Speaker
The most beautiful speech is uttered by	27.8	15.7	9.9
The speech that shows a high social status is uttered by	44.4	5.4	3.1
Speaker speaks in a way that reveals effeminate characteristics	49	.9	4.9

Source: Sawaie (1986), tables 4 and 8 (scores in the bottom row are the totals of the 'strongly agree' and 'agree' percentage scores).[6]

centre for commerce, higher education, medical services, communication, transport, culture, sport and entertainment. This dimension of the Madani variety will not concern us in this chapter.

The Bedouin dialect is the indigenous variety of most Jordanians. However, as used in this context, the term 'Bedouin' does not mean that the speakers of this variety lead a nomadic, or even semi-nomadic, existence. The vast majority of Jordanians live in settled communities: in villages, towns and cities. Those in the north of the country – the Houranis, for example (see al-Khatib 1988) – have been leading a sedentary life for a long time. This is also true of the settled communities in the south of the country, around the city of Karak, and of those in the central region around Amman, known as Balga (Shryock 1997). Although al-Wer (1991) objects to the use of the term 'Bedouin' to designate the speech of these communities because of the sedentary mode of their life, this term is nevertheless an appropriate label, for three reasons. For a start, as Shryock (1997) and Layne (1994) demonstrate, tribalism and memories of Bedouin life still play an important role in constructing group identity for many segments of the Jordanian population. This is also true of the communities Shryock and Layne did not study (Peake 1958). Abdel-Jawad makes a similar observation in his study of linguistic variation in Amman (1981: 68–9):

> It can be assumed that the majority of villages on the East Bank of the Jordan developed from . . . tribal settlements . . . [The] people in such villages still consider themselves tribes. There are many cases where settlers in Amman are still loyal to the tribe and to the head of the tribe who might be living in another village or outside Amman itself.

6 Some of the percentage scores would have been higher had Sawaie not included the SA variant [q] in his study.

Furthermore, the term 'Bedouin' has some folk-linguistic validity. It is used widely in the Levant, and in Jordan itself, to designate [g] speech in the region as a whole. Furthermore, Ibn Khaldun considered this variant as emblematic of the speech of the Bedouins, as we have seen above. Finally, most of the claims that are made to explain the loyalty of Jordanians to their variety are echoes of arguments that were adduced in the Arabic linguistic tradition in favour of the 'pristine' nature of the speech of the Bedouins in the past. Ibn Khaldun (1958, III: 351) commented that the speech of the Bedouins in his day (fourteenth century) was less remote than that of the sedentary population from the 'original Arabic language'. As a participant observer, I have sometimes heard Jordanians invoke the role of the Bedouins in the past as arbiters in linguistic disputes among the grammarians, as evidence of the closeness of their variety to SA. The fact that this is a 'linguistic myth' does not challenge its rhetorical function as a discursive strategy in the formation of folk-linguistic beliefs in Jordan. For all of these reasons I believe that the term 'Bedouin' is an appropriate label to describe the speech of 'indigenous' Jordanians.

Two further attitudes of importance to this study characterize the Bedouin dialect. On the one hand, this variety is judged to be the most 'masculine' of all three dialectal varieties. This is confirmed by Abdel-Jawad's study of Amman (1981), al-Khatib's study of Irbid (1988), Hussein's study of triglossia in Jordanian Arabic (1980) and al-Wer's study of the towns of Karak, Ajloun and Sult (1991). The general orientation of Ibn Khaldun's discussion of Bedouin speech is consistent with this linguistic attitude towards the dialect. On the other hand, the Bedouin dialect is viewed as the indigenous variety of the Jordanians, in spite of the fact that it is also native to some Palestinians – for example, those who originated from the Negev area or the villages around Hebron in the Israeli-occupied West Bank (Shorrab 1981). This is a major premise in al-Wer's study (1991), although it is foreshadowed by Sawaie (1986) and Hussein (1980) who refer to it, but without giving it the same explanatory function in their work. Relying on Sawaie (1986), we may reconstruct the above attitudes to the Bedouin variety in table 4.2.

The Fallahi dialect was introduced into Jordan as a result of the influx of Palestinian refugees into the country after the wars of 1948 and 1967. Although the speakers of this variety used to live in the rural areas in Palestine north of Hebron, they now reside in the big urban centres in Jordan, mainly in Amman, Zerqa and, to a lesser extent, Irbid. Two attitudes towards this variety are relevant in this study. On the one hand, the Fallahi dialect is the most stigmatized variety in Jordan (Abdel-Jawad

Table 4.2 *Dialect attitudes in percentages for the three varieties*

	[?] Speaker	[g] Speaker	[k] Speaker
Speaker's dialect is closest to SA	2.6	16.6	9.4
The speech that reveals the most masculine characteristics is that uttered by	2.7	36.8	8.1
Speaker is from Jordan	27.8[7]	81.6	2.7

Source: Sawaie (1986), tables 9 (first row), 9 (second row), 5A (third row); scores for the first two rows are the totals of the 'strongly agree' and 'agree' percentage scores.[8]

1981; al-Khatib 1988).[9] In many ways, this is a carry-over of the attitude towards this variety, in comparison with Madani speech, in its native milieu in Palestine (Shorrab 1981; Spolsky et al. n.d.). This attitude is reflected in the percentage scores for 'dialect beauty' allocated to this variety by the subjects in Sawaie's study (1986). On the other hand, there is general agreement in all the studies I have consulted that the variant [k] is a Palestinian feature. Table 4.3, based on Sawaie 1986, sets out the percentage scores for these two attitudes.

The appeal to attitudes in discussing the three dialectal varieties above springs from three considerations. First, these attitudes reflect folk-linguistic beliefs about dialects in the speech communities in Jordan. They are therefore endowed with some socio-psychological validity that has empirical meaning for the speakers, thus allowing bridges to be established between theory and social practice. Second, as Baker (1992: 9) points out, the concept of attitude 'is not a jargon word invented by

[7] This score, when compared with its counterpart for Palestine in table 4.3, is intriguing in view of the fact that the Madani variety is generally acknowledged to be (1) non-indigenous in Jordan, and (2) more characteristic of Palestinian city-dwellers' speech (see Sawaie 1994: 82). We may interpret this score as an indication that [?] is in the process of indigenization in Jordan. The fact that [?] is the urban variant par excellence in the Levant and Egypt may have reduced its visibility as a Palestinian variant for the subjects in Sawaie's study.

[8] See note 6.

[9] In a previous study (Suleiman 1993), I attributed this attitude to the negative view of agriculture (*filāḥa*) in Arab life. Ibn Khaldun comments on this mode of life as one that is characterized by 'meekness'. He then quotes a tradition of the Prophet (1958, I: 289–90): 'When [Prophet Muhammad] saw a ploughshare in one of the houses of the Ansar [his protectors and followers in Medina, present-day Saudi Arabia], he said: "Such a thing never entered anyone's house save accompanied by humbleness".' Badawi (1985: 28) reiterates this point in the literary domain: 'Agriculture . . . was definitely considered one of the lowliest occupations, suitable only for the meanest type of human being'. He adds: 'It was the beauty of nature, and not the beauty of the *fellah* who lived in close proximity with nature, that was the object of the poet's praise. Likewise, it was the garden, not the gardener, which elicited a positive response from the numerous poets who composed countless descriptive poems about gardens in Islamic Arabic poetry.'

Table 4.3 *Dialect attitudes in percentages for the three varieties*

	[?] Speaker	[g] Speaker	[k] Speaker
The most beautiful speech is uttered by	27.8	15.7	9.9
Speaker is from Palestine	22.9	8.5	96.4

Source: Sawaie (1986), tables 4 (first row) and 5A (second row).

specialized psychologists that has narrow utility within a small group of people'. As a result, the value of attitudes extends beyond their most immediate domain. They may therefore be used to link issues of language to politics and intergroup relations. Third, by adopting a concept of attitude in this study that consists of cognition, affect and the readiness to act (Baker 1992: 13), we may be able to interpret what people declare to be their attitude towards a given variety and the way in which they act, or do not act, towards it in empirical situations. This may be most clearly explained by reference to SA. The belief that SA is the medium par excellence of cultural expression and continuity among speakers in Jordan (cognition) is usually associated with feelings of high esteem for this variety (affect). However, the congruence of cognition and affect in this case may not be translated into the 'readiness to act' by using it as the language of instruction for all subjects at school or university levels. Similarly, the expression of pride in the Fallahi dialect by some of the subjects in Shorrab's study (1981) does not prevent these subjects from code-switching to the Madani variety in interdialectal group settings.

The introduction of the Madani and Fallahi dialects into Jordan is bound up with the intractable politics of the Middle East. The Arab–Israeli wars in 1948 and 1967 led to an influx of Palestinian speakers from these two backgrounds into Jordan, most of whom migrated out of necessity rather than free choice. In turn, this led to the introduction of the dialects of these two groups of speakers into the country, thus challenging its mono-dialectalism as expressed through the variant [g]. This is a very clear example of how conflict in the Middle East can alter the linguistic map of a country and the dynamics of its socio-political evolution. It would, however, be interesting to speculate as to how the language situation may have developed in Jordan if the Palestinian problem had been solved in favour of the Palestinians in 1948, thus stemming the influx of Palestinians into the country. It is likely that [g] would have continued to assume an emblematic role in marking Jordanians against others in the Levant (Lebanon, Syria and Palestine) – where [?] is socio-politically dominant – at the level of nation-state politics. But it is also likely that new markers would have emerged as stereotypes for different groups of Jordanians – for example, those from the north, the central belt and the south. Whether this would have extended to sociolinguistic differentiation along gender lines is harder to guess. It is, however, possible that [?], as the prestige female norm in the Levant countries, might have made some inroads into Jordan as a marker of high status.

Code-switching and dialect shift: sex and interdialectal variation

As used in this study, code-switching refers to the incorporation of linguistic material from one or more of the above dialects into another. Code-switching can take place in the phonological, grammatical or lexical domains. My main interest in this study is phonological code-switching in so far as it affects the interdialectal deployment of the variants [?], [g] and [k]. Code-switching is a patterned phenomenon whose realization in speech co-varies with such sociolinguistic variables as (1) the education, sex, age group and ethnic/national background of the speaker and the hearer; (2) the topic of conversation; (3) the setting (where and under what conditions the conversation takes place); and (4) speech style (along the formal versus informal continuum). Not all of these sociolinguistic variables will be utilized in this study. Emphasis will be placed on how the above dialectal variables correlate with the sex/gender and ethnic/national background of the speaker. Reference will be made to education and age group from time to time to contextualize the point being made. Finally, code-switching can lead to dialect shift when interdialectal variation achieves a degree of stability and permanence.

There are two patterns of interdialectal code-switching in Jordan. The first involves female code-switching from the Bedouin [g] and the Fallahi [k] to the Madani variant [?].[10] This pattern is confirmed for Amman, as table 4.4, based on Abdel-Jawad's findings, sets out.

The general explanation for this phenomenon invokes three factors. The first concerns the attitude towards the Madani variety, with its emblematic [?], as 'soft' and 'feminine'. Although Abdel-Jawad (1981) calls this phenomenon linguistic urbanization, which is an appropriate term, we may also refer to it as speech feminization. As a matter of fact, the latter term may be more appropriate because many of the female [g] and [k] code-switchers already live in the major urban centres in

[10] Code-switching by Madani speakers is exclusively in the direction of the SA variant [q]. Abdel-Jawad (1981: 321) gives the following percentages for the distribution of the (Q) variable among female Madani speakers: [q]: 23 per cent, [?]: 77 per cent.

Table 4.4 *Distribution of (Q) variants for the three speaker categories (females)*

	[?]	[g]	[k]
Madani speakers	77	0	0
Bedouin speakers	46	30	0
Fallahi speakers	26	0	46

Source: Abdel-Jawad (1981), tables 6.15, 6.16 and 6.17.

Jordan. Some moved to the big centres decades ago. Furthermore, code-switching to [?] by female speakers takes place in non-urban environments when certain conditions obtain. The second factor involves the high prestige of the Madani variety in Jordan and in the Levant countries as a whole. This is reflected in code-switching to [?] from other local varieties in these countries and in Egypt (Sallam 1980). Spolsky et al. (n.d.) show that this is the case in Bethlehem in Palestine, which, until recently, was dominated by the Fallahi variant [k]. Jassem (1993: 130–92) shows that Syrian refugees from the Golan Heights switch from [g] to [?] in interdialectal settings involving Damascene speakers. He also shows that the rate of conversion increases as the setting moves from the sub-urban areas around Damascus to the urban areas where the refugees live. Abu-Melhim (1991) shows that Jordanian [g] speakers, including males, code-switch to [?] when speaking with Egyptians for whom [?] is a salient marker. The third factor invokes the observation, generated by many sociolinguistic studies in various parts of the world, that women are more prestige conscious than men. Although this is true for Jordan, this observation must be modified in two important ways. On the one hand, the prestige norm for women in speech is not the standard (SA), as is assumed in the literature on English and other languages, but the Madani variety with its connotations of 'femininity' (Ibrahim 1986). I believe that the diglossic language situation in Arabic is responsible for this deviation from the general rule, which assigns prestige exclusively to the standard form of the language. On the other hand, it is not true that men are less conscious of prestige in language than women. As shall be shown later, males are also prestige-conscious, but they express this through a different pattern of interdialectal code-switching in Jordan.

Female code-switching from [g] and [k] to [?] is not distributed uniformly for all speakers. It varies with education and age. This is shown to be the case for the city of Irbid by al-Khatib (1988), who sets out co-variation patterns for these two sociolinguistic variables.

Table 4.5 *Distribution of [g], [?] and [k] among females of [g] and [k] backgrounds*

	Speakers of [g] background		Speakers of [k] background		
	[g]	[?]	[g]	[?]	[k]
Highly educated	29	26	10	39	0
Middle educated	58	2	1	20	53
Non-educated	92	0	0	0	98

Source: al-Khatib (1988), based on tables 9.12 and 9.16.

Table 4.6 *Distribution of [g], [?] and [k] among females of [g] and [k] backgrounds*

	Speakers of [g] background		Speakers of [k] background		
	[g]	[?]	[g]	[?]	[k]
Young age group (14–29 years)	70	1	6	47	0
Middle age group (30–44 years)	49	17	3	7	71
Old age group (45 years and older)	95	0	0	0	94

Source: al-Khatib (1988), based on tables 9.13 and 9.17.

Table 4.5 shows that the rate of code-switching to [?] is higher among more educated women than among less educated ones. Bedouin women exhibit a greater degree of loyalty to their variety than Fallahi women. We can gauge the extent to which the Fallahi dialect is stigmatized by tracing the decrease in percentage scores for the variant [k] from 98 per cent to 0 per cent across the three education categories, although this change is exhibited in apparent rather than real time. The fact that this variant is not used by Bedouin women explains its absence from their repertoire in the table.

Table 4.6 shows that code-switching to [?] is higher among the two younger age groups than the older age group for both [g] and [k] speakers. It is, however, interesting to note that the middle age group is leading the way in code-switching to [?] among Bedouin speakers, and that the younger age group is playing this role among Fallahi speakers. Although these discrepancies call for an explanation, what matters for our purposes here is the fact that [?] is gaining at the expense of the other two dialects among female speakers.

Although the above pattern obtains for the big urban centres in Jordan, where the three dialects exist in a contact situation, the same phenomenon does not seem to apply in smaller urban centres. Al-Wer (1991, 1999) has shown this for the towns of Ajloun (6,000) in the north, Sult (33,000) in the central region and Karak (16,000) in the south. Al-Wer attributes the dominance of [g] among female speakers from these three towns to three factors. First, she points out that the high salience of [?] as an 'alien' (out-group) variant, coupled with the equally high salience of [g] as the indigenous marker, motivate the speakers to remain loyal to their local dialect. I think al-Wer is right in invoking salience as a factor in dialect maintenance among her subjects, although this salience works in the opposite direction with respect to the stigmatized Fallahi variant [k]. She is also right in claiming that this is motivated by issues of national identity, as we shall see later, although we must read this non-switching as an act of symbolic practice if we are to reconcile it with code-switching to other Madani features by her subjects. Second, the absence of dialect contact and the density of the social networks in the three towns motivate dialect maintenance. Third, the geographical distance of the three towns from Amman, where code-switching to [?] is most prominent, plays a role in [g] maintenance in the three towns. Thus, Sult (29 km from Amman) shows more examples of code-switching to [?] than Ajloun (73 km) and Karak (124 km). However, al-Wer's findings are not significant enough, in numerical terms, to challenge the validity of the code-switching trend from [g] to [?] among female speakers of the Bedouin variety. The fact that this code-switching is implanted as a permanent or semi-permanent feature among [g] and [k] speakers in Jordan implies that a degree of dialect shift has taken place for some of these speakers.

Interdialectal code-switching for men tends to move in the opposite direction. This is shown to be the case in Abdel-Jawad's study of Amman (1981). The pattern established in this study will, I am sure, have accelerated over the past twenty-five years.

Table 4.7 shows that (1) no code-switching takes place to the Fallahi variant; (2) interdialectal code-switching from the Fallahi and Madani varieties is in the direction of the Bedouin variant [g]; and (3) although Abdel-Jawad does not comment on the reasons behind code-switching to [?] by Bedouin speakers, it is likely that this pattern is less pronounced in present-day Amman speech. The standard explanation for the [g] code-switching phenomenon is the masculinity connotations of the Bedouin variety. This explanation is a 'given' in all the studies on variation in Jordan (Abdel-Jawad 1981; Hussein 1980; al-Khatib 1988; Sawaie 1986, 1994).

Table 4.7 *Distribution of (Q) variants for the three speaker categories (males)*

	[?]	[g]	[k]
Madani speakers	46	9	0
Bedouin speakers	4	61	0
Fallahi speakers	1	11	29

Source: Abdel-Jawad (1981), tables 6.15, 6.16 and 6.17.

Table 4.8 *Distribution of [g], [?] and [k] among males of [g] and [k] backgrounds*

	Speakers of [g] background		Speakers of [k] background		
	[g]	[?]	[g]	[?]	[k]
Highly educated	37	1	37	1	0
Middle educated	76	0	51	2	1
Non-educated	85	1	78	0	0

Source: al-Khatib (1988), based on tables 9.12 and 9.16.

As with the code-switching to [?] among females, the code-switching to [g] among males is shown by al-Khatib, in his study of Irbid, to co-vary with the level of education and age group of the speaker. Table 4.8 shows that [g] maintenance among the Bedouin group co-varies inversely with the increase in the level of education of the speaker. This decrease in the maintenance rate is caused by the increase in code-switching to the SA variant [q], which stands at the following rates for the three categories of education: Highly educated (62 per cent), Middle Educated (46 per cent) and Non-educated (22).

According to table 4.9 [g] speakers display a high rate of dialect maintenance. The level of this maintenance co-varies inversely with age. This is explained by the fact that the majority of highly educated speakers, who code-switch to the SA variant [q], belong to this age group. The table also shows that Fallahi code-switching is in the direction of [g], and that the code-switching to [?] among Bedouin and Fallahi speakers is negligible. These two observations are related to the stigmatization of the Fallahi variety in Jordan and to the status of [g] as the target of code-switching for male speakers. The extent and stability of this code-switching among

Table 4.9 *Distribution of [g], [?] and [k] among females of [g] and [k] backgrounds*

	Speakers of [g] background		Speakers of [k] background		
	[g]	[?]	[g]	[?]	[k]
Young age group (14–29 years)	51	2	38	1	2
Middle age group (30–44 years)	49	0	37	3	0
Old age group (45 years and older)	95	0	64	1	0

Source: al-Khatib (1988), based on tables 9.13 and 9.17.

Fallahi male speakers indicates that a dialect shift has taken place in the community. Commenting on his own linguistic behaviour, al-Khatib reports (1988: 316): 'At home in intimate communications with family members, the variant which prevails in my speech is . . . [k] . . . whereas outside home, even with friends of all three local groups, the colloquial variant that I use exclusively is . . . [g], although in alternation with the SA variant [q].' Al-Khatib's analysis of his own speech with [g] speakers during his field research in fact shows that he used the [g] variant more (72 per cent) than these speakers had done. The same analysis shows that [k] was completely absent from the researcher's speech in the same setting, confirming the argument that a dialect shift is taking place in male speech in Jordan. It is clear that the social values of [k] for al-Khatib pertain to intimacy and loyalty, while [g] expresses his solidarity with the non-family group.

The above data suggest that interdialectal variation in Jordan is characterized by polarization, with females pulling in one direction and males pulling in the other (see al-Wer 1999). It seems reasonable to assume that this polarization reflects the social segregation of males and females in traditional Arab society, or the existence of two social spheres along gender lines. As I have said earlier, the standard explanation for this interdialectal variation is the double trajectory of the femininity of the Madani variety and the masculinity of its Bedouin counterpart. The Fallahi variety is squeezed between these two antithetical linguistic forces in Jordanian society, losing its female speakers to the Madani variety and its male speakers to the Bedouin variety. Female code-switching from this dialect to the Madani variety is in fact a continuation of an older trend among Palestinians on the West Bank. However, before 1967, code-switching to

[g] hardly occurred for men on the West Bank. I recall how, as a schoolboy in Jerusalem before 1967, [g] was a butt of jokes for us as an 'uncouth' and 'ugly' variant. The full force of this became apparent to me on one of those rare occasions when a schoolboy from this background, an East Jordanian, joined our school. It is therefore understandable that when a Fallahi male wished to divest himself of the stigma of his variety he would code-switch to [?] or to standard [q], but never to [g]. In its re-orientation towards [g] in Jordan, code-switching for Fallahi males took a different twist to express a new socio-political meaning, as I will argue below. What is, however, more significant is the code-switching to [g] by Madani males who, on the West Bank, would avoid this mode of interdialectal variation beyond its most instrumental and utilitarian function – for example, in market interactions.

The sex-based explanation of interdialectal variation in Jordan yields interesting quantitative correlations. It establishes patterns of co-variation between phonological variants and demographic factors, including the level of education and the age group of the speakers. But it hardly advances our understanding of this variation beyond this limit. To do so, we must appeal to complementary data which situate interdialectal variation within its socio-political context. Power and conflict will be shown to be important factors in understanding this context and, by implication, of variation itself. For this purpose, I will devote most of the following discussion to the male code-switching from Madani [?] and Fallahi [k] to Bedouin [g], what Abdel-Jawad (1981: 323) calls the process of speech Bedouinization in Jordan. Reference will be made to female code-switching to [?] to advance the argument made whenever necessary.

The sex-based explanation: a critique

There are a number of reasons why the sex-based explanation, in spite of its statistical usefulness, is inadequate. First, the sex-based account fails to explain the onset of code-switching in male speech in Jordan as a significant sociolinguistic phenomenon. As an observer, I remember how this shift coincided, for young males, with the conclusion of the September 1970 confrontations – called Black September by the Palestinians – between the Jordanian army and the Palestinian guerrillas in favour of the former who, together with the police and the intelligence service (*mukhābarāt*), consisted mainly of [g] speakers. As a student at the University of Jordan at the time, I recall how some of my Palestinian male friends started to use [g] in speaking with Jordanians. This was particularly noticeable in routine exchanges between the Fallahi students and the soldiers who operated the Sports City (*al-Madīna al-Riyāḍiyya*) checkpoint between the town centre and the university.

For almost a year (if not actually longer) after the start of the academic session in October 1970, an identity-card check was carried out on every single bus entering the city from the university, so I had ample opportunity to observe this code-switching. Although I was not one of the code-switchers, we all used to joke at this momentary shift from [k] and, to a lesser extent, [?] to [g]. One soldier in particular (I can still picture his face) used to joke about this with us, for he could tell from the name, the place of birth on the card, and the poor rendition of Bedouin speech that the 'gifted' switcher (*mawhūb*, as he used to call them) was not an indigenous [g] speaker. I can also report from the same period how one of my brothers, who was eleven years old in 1970 and went to a school with a majority of Palestinian children, suddenly started to use [g] in public, something he still does now after over thirty years although [g] was never part of the family speech repertoire.

These observations (I can actually give more) cannot be explained in a satisfactory manner by invoking the masculinity of [g]. If this variant is indeed characterized by masculinity, and was branded as such by Ibn Khaldun six centuries ago, why was it that Palestinian males started to code-switch to [g] in 1970, and not before? Is it that, all of a sudden, they started to realize that [g] was masculine? And why did Madani males, whose variety was held in high esteem before 1970, start to code-switch to [g] in the same period? Was it that they were unaware before that date of the femininity connotations of their variety or the masculinity meaning of the Bedouin variety? Although we have no information on interdialectal variation before this period, I am inclined to agree with Sawaie (1994) when he speculates that, if anything, the Palestinian dialects had a greater impact on Transjordanian speech than vice versa in the early period of dialect contact between them (before 1967). Sawaie's view is based on sociolinguistic findings elsewhere in the world which privilege education and institutional power as factors in conditioning the direction of code-switching and dialect shift, things which the Palestinians had before 1967. I will quote Sawaie, who is of East Jordanian origin, in full to convey the basis of his view (1994: 14):

> *First*, Palestinians at the time of taking their refuge in Trans-jordan in and after 1948 enjoyed a higher rate of education than Trans-jordanians . . . Consequently, Palestinians occupied major governmental positions in the early 1950s and 1960s, especially in the educational sectors in the newly-expanded kingdom of Jordan. As might be expected, Palestinians, especially those who came from the cities such as Haifa, Jaffa, Jerusalem, etc. formed an 'elite' group, perhaps to be emulated by the less 'privileged'. If this claim is acceptable, one expects that the language

varieties of this new social class may have become a 'model' to be emulated by others. *Second,* and this follows from the first observation, there was a rather significant expansion in the number of schools and educational institutions in Trans-jordan, partly as a result of the Palestinian exodus in the early 1950s and early 1960s. Most teachers in these schools were Palestinians because of their higher level of education . . . The dialectal influences of Palestinian teachers are likely to have had some effect on their Trans-jordanian pupils.

As a functionalist (as opposed to symbolic) explanation of interdialectal variation, the gender-based account fails to capture the emergence of discursive and symbolic practices in post-1970 Jordan, lending support to the hypothesis that factors other than masculinity are involved in [g] code-switching. I will start by giving one example to illustrate this point. It concerns the use of the ethnolinguistic label *beljīk* (s. *beljīkī*) to refer to the Palestinians in Jordan. This label, the literal meaning of which is 'Belgians', is closely associated with the 1970 confrontations between the Jordanian army and the Palestinian guerrilla movement. In a paper on the topic, Lalor (1997: 3) wrote: 'The vast majority of people I spoke with [in my fieldwork in Jordan in 1987] were certain that the term originated in the period leading up to what the Palestinians call Black September [1970] . . . These people were also sure that the term did not exist prior to this time.'[11] The appearance and speedy currency of this label at this period in Jordan's history was not fortuitous. Labels of this kind are often coined for a purpose and under specific conditions. There is a vast body of literature on the use and function of ethnolinguistic labels in different parts of the world that can help us explain the situation in Jordan (Allen 1983; Barth 1969; Benson 2001; Douglas 1966; Goffman 1959; Paxman 1999; Wilson 2002). However, I will rely on two summary points made by Khleif (1979: 160) of aspects of this research to explain the functions of the ethnolinguistic label *beljīkī* in Jordan:

1. Ethnolinguistic labels are . . . stereotypes deliberately manufactured to enhance a sense of collective identity, to express stratification, to support an ideology that buttresses socioeconomic and socio-political interests, to signal identity and membership, to exorcise the group – so to speak – from an assumed filth or pollution, to prevent boundary transgression.
2. Ethnolinguistic labels are a special form of 'restricted code' in that they condense communication and force it into unbridgeable dichotomy; . . . they refer directly to position and hierarchy; . . . they make their meaning richly implicit; they reaffirm unquestioned boundaries and psychologically link the speaker to his kin and community, giving him personal and social integration at the same time.

[11] See Massad (2001: 253) for similar views.

In researching aspects of *beljīkī* in Jordan, Lalor (1997: 3) unearthed folk-linguistic explanations of the term which resonate with many of the points summarized in Khleif. I list some of these below for comparative purposes:

1. The Palestinians are not originally from the region and came from places like Bosnia, Crete and Belgium . . . Others will talk about Palestinians being a legacy of the Crusades.
2. The Belgians are a mix of many races, German, French and Dutch, like the Palestinians. The implication here is that Palestinians are 'mongrels'.
3. Like the Belgians in the First and Second World Wars, the Palestinians became refugees as a result of Arab–Israeli wars in 1948 and 1967.
4. The French look down on the Belgians the way the Jordanians look down on the Palestinians.
5. *Beljīkī* is a corruption of Bolshevik, a term used against [some Palestinian guerrilla groups] in government propaganda in 1970–1, for instance in the army newspaper, *al-Aqsa* which began publication in mid 1969.
6. *Beljīkī* is derived from the acronyms BLJ, in turn derived from the Arabic *min barra li-juwwa*, meaning 'from outside to inside'.
7. *Beljīkī* was coined by Muhammad Rasoul Kaylani, Head of the Jordanian *mukhābarāt* [Intelligence service] at the time, who wished to avoid alerting Palestinians to the fact that he was speaking about them.

These folk-linguistic explanations are consistent with many of the points made by Khleif (1979). *Beljīkī* is a stereotype used by the indigenous Jordanians, the insiders, to label the Palestinians as non-indigenous and as outsiders.[12] It is a boundary-setting label, demarcating the Jordanians, the in-group, from the Palestinians, the out-group. *Beljīkī* therefore is an identity-laden label based on 'an unbridgeable dichotomy' that signals 'position and hierarchy'. The two groups involved in this dichotomy are envisaged as having an unequal share of power in the body politic of the state, at least in terms of symbolic resources. Later, disparities started to emerge between the two groups in the allocation of employment opportunities in the various branches of the government, in the armed forces

12 The symbolic meaning of this stereotype has undergone some subtle changes over the past few decades. When Palestinians in Jordan refer to themselves as *beljīk* they now take the term to imply a higher socio-cultural status than that of East Jordanian. I have also heard the term used with this implication by East Jordanian academics, some of them sociolinguists. After all, the Belgians, after whom the Palestinians are made, are more advanced than the Jordanians. Lalor's (1997) data actually confirm this. This mutation in symbolic meaning is in line with the findings of anthropologists for communities in comparable situations, in what is called the 'ritual of reversal'. Anthony Cohen (2000: 60) explains the use of this strategy in the symbolic construction of communities in the following way: 'A more recent strategy observed among ethnic and other disadvantaged groups has been to "honour" the stigma, to render it as a positive value, and, thereby, to destigmatize it. Perhaps the most powerful and innovative use of this tactic lay in the assertion by black militants in the United States in the late 1960s, that "Black is Beautiful!" '

and the security services and in the allocation of seats in the parliament (see Abu-Odeh 1999). These disparities in institutional power relations justify calling the Palestinians the subordinate group and the Jordanians the superordinate group.

The fact that the Palestinians lacked an ethnic label by which to brand the Jordanians in reply is another indication of the imbalance in power distribution between the two groups. I was told recently, however, that some Palestinians used the term *garādina* (folk neologism from Bedouin *gird*, lit. ape or monkey) to refer to the Jordanians in private at the time. If this is true, this label never caught on, thus giving further evidence of the imbalance in power relations between the two groups. It is, however, an interesting label in code-switching terms. In Arabic, Jordan is called *ʔurdun*. The failed label thus replaces what is projected to be the Palestinian phoneme [ʔ], in the name of the country, by the Bedouin [g] in *garādina* as though to inverse the Jordanian view of who is 'original' and who is not (although this phonological coincidence is fortuitous). However, as we shall see below, the difference in symbolic resources between the two groups later translated into an ideology which demanded that the Jordanians be given a larger share than the Palestinians in the 'socio-political and socioeconomic' stakes of the state. As a stereotype, *beljīkī* was used to denigrate the Palestinians as a group that is politically inferior to the Jordanians. This term is still operative in the socio-political discourse in Jordan. Lalor (1997) tells us of a joke that was 'doing the rounds' in Amman in the wake of the Oslo Accords between the Palestinians and the Israelis in 1993; this joke plays on the lingering status of the Palestinians as outsiders in Jordan: 'The day after the Oslo agreement the Head of the *mukhābarāt* came into his office in an angry mood. He summoned an underling and said, "You told me these people were *Beljīkiyyūn*. Well, it is clear that you are wrong. They are Norwegians!"' These functions of the label *Beljīkī* are recognized by Adnan Abu-Odeh who, until recently, was part of the state structure at the highest level. Abu-Odeh comments (1999: 255):

> As of the early 1970s, the Palestinians began to be stereotyped [in Jordan]. Transjordanians started to refer to Palestinian-Jordanians as *Beljīk* (Belgians). The term was used first among Transjordanians in reference to Palestinian-Jordanians, but it gradually came to be used in front of Palestinian-Jordanians in a light-spirited manner. In the beginning, Palestinian-Jordanians did not feel insulted by this stereotyping. They were even flattered by it, understanding [it] as an implicit recognition of their sophistication. Belgians are a sophisticated European people in comparison with Arab Jordanians. But when the term persisted alongside discriminating practices against them, Palestinian-Jordanians began to resent it; they realized then that the term *Beljīk* implied that they did not belong to Jordan and

that this justified the discrimination. In attempting to discover the source of this odd term for Palestinian-Jordanians, I heard a myriad of interpretations ranging from the most insulting to the most flattering. I believe, though, that *Beljīk* is just a label for the Transjordanian nationalists' definition of 'the other' – namely, the Palestinian-Jordanian.

I have given an extensive discussion of the ethnolinguistic label *beljīk* for two reasons. On the one hand, I want to suggest that the onset of [g] code-switching as a significant sociolinguistic phenomenon in Jordan coincided with the emergence of a label that was intended to accentuate group boundaries between Jordanians and Palestinians, in their capacity as the in-group and the out-group respectively. This interpretation is consistent with research on code-switching in other parts of the world (see Heller 1988). All the evidence so far suggests that [g] code-switching as a significant phenomenon dates back to 1970, and that this coincides with the political and military conflict between the political establishment in Jordan and the Palestinian guerrilla organizations. According to this interpretation, [g] code-switching is generated more by conflict than by the masculinity of this variant. It may, however, be possible to reconcile these two interpretations if we read the masculinity of [g] in a symbolic or metaphorical way. I believe that this can be done by interpreting 'masculinity' as a social trope, metaphor or motif for the power and domination of one group, the victorious Jordanians, over the Palestinians, who emerged as the defeated party in 1970; hence the reference to these groups earlier as the superordinate and subordinate groups respectively. If we accept this, then we must treat the sex-based explanation as an inadequate mutation of a more inclusive gender-based one. This change in labels highlights the socially constructed nature of [g] code-switching and its ability to signal symbolic meanings beyond itself. On the other hand, the emergence of the label *beljīk* in 1970 shows how military and political conflict is responsible for some of the discursive practices in Jordan. Ethnolinguistic labelling is often read as a practice whose meaning lies outside language itself. But this should not obscure the fact that it is in the first place a linguistic practice whose genesis lies outside language, in this case intergroup conflict.

The 1970–1 clashes in Jordan also coincided with the utilization of the red-chequered *kufiyya* as a symbol of a Jordanian identity that excludes the Palestinians. As a witness to events of this kind at the time, I can report how some Jordanian male students at the University of Jordan started to wear this head cover in an ostentatious display of their Jordanian identity and anti-Palestinian credentials. Most of these students were suspected of being members of the *mukhābarāt*; others, who were not, never tried to dispel this image. Palestinians who, before 1970, would sometimes wear the black-chequered *kufiyya* (imitating Yasser Arafat) stopped doing so. The two head covers suddenly became symptomatic of two identities, one Jordanian and the other Palestinian, although the origins of this practice seem to go back to the early 1950s, after the absorption of the West Bank into Jordan. In his book *Memories of Revolt: The 1936–1939 Rebellion and the Palestinian National Past*, Swedenburg (1995: 35) states that 'the origins of the black-and-white checkered *kufiyya* as the distinctive Palestinian headscarf apparently date to the early 1950s. Glubb Pasha, the English Commander of Jordan's armed forces, distinguished his Palestinian soldiers from his Jordanian ones by outfitting West Bank Palestinians in black-and-white *kufiyyat* and East Jordanians in red-and-white ones.'

Massad (2001: 250–1) explains the use of the chequered *kufiyya* in framing national identity in Jordan along East Jordanian and Palestinian lines after the events of 1970 in a way which lends support to the main argument of this chapter:

> Transjordanian [East Jordanian] urban male youth began to assert their Jordanianness sartorially. They started to wear the red-and-white *shmagh* or *hatta* as a winter scarf around their necks as an assertion of national pride. Palestinian Jordanians followed suit by wearing the black-and-white *hatta*. The urban youth's donning of the red-and-white *hatta* was, in fact, following in King Hussein's footsteps, as he had begun to wear it as a head-gear much more frequently after 1970, especially when [he] addressed tribal leaders or the military, or when on trips to the Arab Gulf states. Moreover, the king's picture wearing the *shmagh* appeared on Jordanian currency bills and on Jordanian postage stamps.

It is unlikely that those who gave the *kufiyya* its revived meaning in Jordan were aware of the earlier practice promulgated by Glubb.[13] There is, however, no doubt that they intended it to signal a new reality, one that separates the in-group, the indigenous Jordanians, from the out-group, the Palestinian *beljīk*. I believe that the coincidence of male [g] switching with this and other identity-promoting practices is not accidental, and that national identity considerations – arising out of a particular datable conflict – are important factors in motivating this switch.

The sex-based account also fails to explain why Palestinians in the Israeli-occupied West Bank (unlike Palestinian-Jordanians) did not code-switch to [g]. My observations of (male) West Bank Palestinians visiting Jordan reveal that, if any code-switching to [g] occurs in their speech, it is invariably of an exploratory nature to establish whether the interlocutor uses another – by elimination Palestinian – variant. If this is positively ascertained, [g] is more or less immediately dropped in favour of a

[13] See Massad (2001) for an interesting discussion of the creation and definition of modern Jordanian identity. Massad focuses on the law and the military, but his discussion contains interesting references to a host of other material.

Palestinian variant. It is also interesting to note how Palestinians who shifted to [g] in Jordan code-switch back to their indigenous variant, or SA [q], when they go back to visit members of their families in Palestine. None of these observations can be adequately explained under the sex-based view of [g] code-switching.

Nor would we be able to explain why [g]-speaking Syrians, from the areas bordering Jordan, code-switch to [?] in interacting with speakers from this background. This is true of the Golan Heights refugees in Syria too, as shown by Jassem (1993). The border between Jordan and Syria divides communities that are related to each other by descent. Members of the Zu'bi and Shar' tribes from this border area have held high-level government posts on both sides of the border. Listening to Farouk al-Shar', the present Foreign Minister of Syria, speaking in public, one cannot but notice (1) the interference of aspects of the [?]-marked Damascus variety in his speech; and (2) the absence of any traces of [g] in this speech. The speech of Sadiq al-Shar', one-time high-ranking army officer and government minister in Jordan, reveals the opposite pattern. Do we then conclude that one Shar' male has chosen to be more 'feminine' and the other has chosen to be more 'masculine'? This is a counter-intuitive conclusion, but it is the only one that is available to us under the sex-based explanation of code-switching. An alternative and, in my view, more adequate solution would ascribe the differences I have just noted to the existence of nationally defined prestige norms in Jordan and Syria. The emergence of [g] as that norm in Jordan is, in my view, related to the 1970 conflict and to considerations of state and national-identity building, as shall be explained later.

Both Abdel-Jawad (1981) and Hussein (1980) stick to the sex-based explanation, in spite of the fact that aspects of their research suggest that the ethnic/national background of the speaker is an operative factor in [g] code-switching. Abdel-Jawad (1981: 176) reports that one of his informants, a Palestinian head of an orphanage in Amman, explains her son's code-switching as follows: '[My son] uses [our] Urban variant [?] only at home with the family, but outside the home, with his friends, he uses the "Jordanian variant [g]" because he feels he is too feminine if he uses [?] with his friends.' This informant's report acknowledges the role of 'sex' in code-switching, but it also brands [g] as the 'Jordanian variant'. And, if the ethnic/national background of the speaker is not relevant in code-switching, as Abdel-Jawad's study suggests, why does he designate his informants in a way which indicates this background (1981, appendix A: 360–3)? In a similar vein, Hussein (1980: 75) tells us that 'it is not . . . unreasonable to designate the Fallahi and the Madani varieties as Palestinian Colloquial Arabic and . . . Bedouin Arabic as Jordanian Colloquial Arabic'. But he then goes on to ignore this observation.

So, what reasons do Abdel-Jawad and Hussein give for not using the ethnic/national background of their informants to explain interdialectal variation?

Hussein explains his decision as follows (1980: 75): 'Since the West Bank is here viewed in the context of the Jordanian kingdom, we will, at least for the purposes of this study, include the Fallahi, Madani and the Bedouin variety under the *rubric* of Jordanian colloquial Arabic' (emphasis added). Abdel-Jawad (1981: 64) gives a similar explanation: 'In this study nationality will not be considered because we are taking our data and informants from one country, namely Jordan. The origin of the speaker in this study is taken to mean his cultural/social background.' A similar explanation is adduced by al-Khatib (1988: 56) to explain his exclusion of ethnic/national background as a criterion in discussing interdialectal variation in Irbid: 'If we take Jordanian citizenship as a criterion, all people in Jordan at present, be they of Jordanian or Palestinian origin, are considered Jordanian.' This is rather surprising since Sawaie (1986), who conducted his study among university students in the same city, invokes ethnicity/nationality as a factor in his study of linguistic attitudes in Jordan.

There are two interpretations for this strategy of ethnicity/nationality avoidance on the part of these researchers. The first may be related to their failure to invoke the difference between ethnicity/nationality, on the one hand, and citizenship on the other. Applying this distinction to the above studies, it would be possible for a subject to identify himself as Jordanian by citizenship and Palestinian by ethnicity/nationality. This possibility of dual identification does exist in Israel. Thus, some Palestinians define themselves as Palestinians by nationality and Israelis by citizenship. I do not personally believe that the researchers were unable to see this distinction between nationality and citizenship. I therefore read the use of the term 'rubric' by Hussein as a distancing strategy, an attempt to signal a degree of doubt about what he says. Second, the identification of 'the origin of the speaker' as his 'cultural/social' background by Abdel-Jawad is bizarre, to say the least. In sociolinguistic research the social background of the speaker is usually his 'class', not his origin. As to 'cultural background', I am not sure what meaning one can give to it in sociolinguistic research. The possibility of linking it with education is not available to us here since Abdel-Jawad lists education separately as an independent social variable. Third, al-Khatib acknowledges that a primary meaning of 'origin' is 'Palestinian' or 'Jordanian', but he chooses to ignore this, opting for the terms 'Hourani' and 'Fallahi' in his research, although the former is the designation of a local identity and the latter of an ecological background. The explanation for these theoretical stances must therefore be sought elsewhere.

The three researchers share a common denominator: they are all Jordanians of Palestinian origin. I think their reluctance to invoke ethnicity/nationality as a sociolinguistic variable in their research is dictated by political considerations, as one of them in fact confessed to the present researcher. As members of the out-group in Jordan, these researchers could not afford to be seen to 'rock the boat' of inter-ethnic relations in a country that had suffered bloody civil strife only a decade or so before their studies were concluded. At the time, strict security measures were still being conducted as a precondition for employment in the country's universities where all three researchers ended up working. If this interpretation is true, then we have in front of us a case where a political conflict affects not only the course of interdialectal variation on the ground, but also the academic and scholarly engagement with it; in short, we have a case of academic self-censorship. If valid, this interpretation represents a significant finding of the present study. It shows that language is a loaded weapon, and that those who study it must make sure that it does not misfire. I will return to this issue in the next chapter.

So what evidence can we adduce to support this conclusion? As a starting point, I can report that, until now, I personally have been very reluctant to advance this explanation fully for exactly the reason I have attributed to Abdel-Jawad, Hussein and al-Khatib. This explains the truncated nature of my two earlier studies of code-switching in Jordan (Suleiman 1993, 1999a).[14] We all are children of the 1970s generation in Jordan, an experience that has left its indelible marks on our outlook on politics and intercommunity strife. At one point, I did think of conducting a controlled study of language and ethnicity in Jordan, following the framework used by Bourhis et al. (1979) for Flemish–French speech accommodation in Belgium, but I was advised that this would be politically sensitive.

Second, it is significant that the only researchers I know of who have been able to discuss the role of ethnicity/nationality in the sociolinguistic situation in Jordan are Jordanians – Sawaie (1986, 1994) and al-Wer (1991, 1999) – although the former did so only in passing, and the latter without relating it fully to its historical context. As members of the in-group, these researchers feel more empowered to discuss what the political establishment in Jordan regards to be divisive, although as Shryock (1997) shows, this taboo is being openly challenged by some Jordanians in present-day Jordan. One vocal critic of this taboo is Ahamd Uwaydi al-Abbadi, who served as a member of the Jordanian parliament a few years

[14] The publication of Abu-Odeh's book (1999), which deals with this topic openly for the first time, gave me the encouragement to provide in full my interpretation of code-switching in Jordan.

ago. I was told by several Palestinian-Jordanians that al-Abbadi led a small demonstration in Amman city centre calling for the de-Palestinianization of Jordan, shouting the slogan *bidnā niḥkī 'al-makshūf, falasṭīnī mā bidnā nshūf* (We want to declare it openly: We do not want to see any Palestinians [in Jordan]).

Third, even a figure as important and influential as Adnan Abu-Odeh was reluctant to publish his critique of Jordanian–Palestinian relations, as he explains in his book. When he did so in 1999, he was subjected to a vociferous campaign by East Jordanians who demanded retractions and apologies, or the dismissal and punishment of the ex-minister, ex-Chief of the Royal Court and political adviser to the late King Hussein (d. 1999) and King Abdullah II (see *Al-Quds al-Arabi* of 4, 7, 8 and 21 February 2000, 14, 28, 29 and 30 March 2000 and 1/2, 4, 6, 7 and 15/16 April 2000). Abu-Odeh was able to ride the storm for a little while before he was later 'released' from his duties by King Abdullah II. Abu-Odeh was bruised by the experience, hence his reluctance to allow the book to be translated and published in Arabic (al-Hamad 2001).

The preceding discussion provides evidence from a variety of perspectives to suggest that the sex-based explanation of [g] switching in Jordan is of limited validity. I have offered an alternative explanation, based on the notions of ethnic/national identity, which subsumes the earlier solution by re-designating it as a gender-based explanation. I have also tried to link this new explanation to the political conflict in Jordan in 1970–1. This has enabled me to generate two additional senses in which political conflict impacts on interdialectal variation. The first pertains to the emergence of ethnolinguistic labels and their deployment to highlight group boundary. The second relates to the constraints researchers impose on themselves in discussing the link between language and inter-ethnic/national conflict. Although language often serves as a proxy for alluding to, highlighting or debating extralinguistic issues in society, at times it is too hot a topic to be exploited in this way. Interdialectal variation in Jordan is an example of this situation. The socio-political meanings of this variation were given their high intensity by bloody conflict; hence the sensitivity with which this variation is studied in the literature.

Speech accommodation and code-switching

To gain an enhanced understanding of male code-switching in Jordan, I will invoke some of the findings of speech-accommodation theory (Bourhis 1979; Bourhis et al. 1979; Giles and Powesland 1975; Giles and Smith 1979; Giles et al. 1977). One of the distinguishing marks of this model is the insight it offers into variation by relating it to ethnic/national identity in intergroup relations. This is particularly applicable to Jordan, as we shall see later, although most of my comments will lack empirical support owing to the sensitivity of conducting research in Jordan that can yield evidence of this kind. The main categories in this model are: (1) speech convergence, which takes place when speakers bring their linguistic behaviour close to each other; (2) speech maintenance (non-convergence) which takes place when speakers maintain their own linguistic behaviour with other speakers; and (3) speech divergence, which obtains when speakers exaggerate the difference between their speech and that of their interlocutors.[15] Each one of these patterns of speech accommodation has its motivations, the establishment of which can help us advance our understanding of the dynamics of interdialectal variation in Jordan beyond the limits of the sex-based account outlined on pp. 108–24. Applying speech-accommodation theory to this account, we may categorize the phenomena we have observed so far as follows:

(1) Speech convergence: female code-switching to the Madani variety and male code-switching to the Bedouin variety.
(2) Speech non-convergence: non-switching by female Madani speakers and male Bedouin speakers.

Speech divergence may be said to occur if a speaker produces an emphatic [g] intentionally to distinguish himself from another [g] speaker, whether indigenous or not. To the best of my knowledge, studies on variation in Jordan have not dealt with speech divergence. Of the studies on Jordan I have considered so far, al-Khatib's (1988) is the only one that raises speech accommodation as an issue, but it does so in a manner that subverts the intentions of this model by reducing it to short-term accommodation, code-switching proper, and long-term accommodation, what I have chosen to characterize as dialect shift in this work. Although speech accommodation is related to variation in language, the two are different categories.

Standard accounts of speech accommodation consider as one motivation for convergence the desire on the part of the switcher to gain the social approval of an interlocutor.[16] Giles and Powesland (1975: 159) state that 'one effect of the convergence of speech patterns is that it

[15] Giles and Powesland (1975: 156) characterize speech convergence and divergence, by which they most probably mean speech maintenance or non-convergence, as follows: 'Speech convergence is a strategy of identification with the speech patterns of an individual *internal* to the social interaction, whereas speech divergence may be regarded as a strategy of identification with regard to the linguistic norms of some reference group *external* to the immediate situation' (emphasis in original).

[16] Giles and Smith (1979: 49) report that 'there is empirical evidence in a number of cultural contexts that supports the notion that people react favourably to those who converge towards them in terms of language, dialect or accent'. Giles and Powesland (1975: 159) also report that 'a person who exhibited response-matching in respect of the gestures and postures of the person with whom he was interacting was liked more than someone who did not behave in this manner'.

allows the sender to be perceived as more similar to the receiver than would have been the case had he not accommodated his style of speaking in this manner'. Under this interpretation, called the similarity-attraction model, the rate of convergence varies with the speaker's needs. The higher the need of the speaker for approval, the greater the rate of the convergence practised by him. Convergence of this kind must, however, reflect a perception of power difference, material or symbolic, between the speaker and the listener. Interdialectal [g] switching, as a form of speech convergence in Jordan, is rooted in perceptions of power difference between the Palestinians and the Jordanians, the out-group and the in-group respectively. Based on my observations in Jordan, I can report that convergence towards [g] speakers tends to increase when the interaction is with a member of the police, the armed forces, or the government departments.[17] One of the clues that invariably identify me 'as a Jordanian citizen living abroad' – *'il-akh 'āyish bi-l-khārij/barra?*' would be the usual remark – is the way I speak, including the use of the [?] variant with male [g] speakers, indigenous or not. Perhaps the fact that I do not need 'the social approval' of these speakers is a reason for this aspect of my linguistic behaviour.[18] I am also sure that other reasons exist, as I shall set out below.

Although speech convergence may have its rewards, utilitarian or otherwise, it does have its costs. Building on the insights of social-exchange theory, speech-accommodation theorists believe that speakers engage – consciously or unconsciously – in a kind of 'cost and benefit' assessment of the likely outcome of their speech convergence (or divergence, for that matter). Myers-Scotton (1993: 100) expresses this by saying that 'a major motivation for using one variety rather than another as a medium of interaction is the extent to which this choice minimizes costs and maximizes rewards for the speaker'. In Suleiman (1999a), I tried to explain speech accommodation in Jordan by applying Bourdieu's (1992) notion of the linguistic market, which is consistent in its broad outlines with the basic

[17] When I am in Jordan, I stay with my mother, who lives a few hundred metres to the west of the main passport office in Amman. I have, on several occasions, engaged passport applicants in conversation to establish whether they were indigenous [g] speakers or not. I then continued chatting to those (invariably Palestinians) who were not to activate their indigenous (Q) variant. I would then follow them inside the building to listen to them speaking to male members of the counter staff, including one gentleman who I know is a Palestinian. In most cases, young to middle-aged males would switch to [g] in a pre-emptive convergence to what they assumed to be the speech of the employee.

[18] A female [g] speaker told me at a conference at Yarmouk University in Irbid (14 April 1996), that I would have found it very difficult, if not actually impossible, to maintain [?] in my speech had I been living in Jordan, where my need for social approval would be infinitely greater. There may be some truth in this.

insights of social-exchange theory.[19] The explanation I offered may be summed up as follows: (1) speakers have a repertoire of speech styles; (2) they are aware of the value of these styles as cultural products; (3) they are able to make an assessment as to which style is likely to fetch the greatest benefit, or to incur the least cost, on the linguistic market; and (4) they deploy these styles/products accordingly. Social approval and solidarity with the in-group may be regarded as part of the benefits of convergence for members of the out-group. The desire to be integrated with the in-group may be the ultimate motivation for this kind of convergence. In some cases, the motivation may be of an instrumental kind, aiming at achieving a desired short-term objective (Lambert 1979). In either case, the success or failure of the convergence will depend on the motivation attributed by the listener to the speaker. On the cost side, a perceived loss of integrity or identity is often highlighted as part of what the speaker may have to incur for his convergence. Fear of this may cause some speakers to practise speech maintenance (non-convergence). It is very likely that this is one of the reasons why I do not code-switch to [g] with [g] speakers, indigenous or not. This fear may sometimes lead to speech divergence. Bourhis (1979) reports that a group of English-Canadian school pupils learning French were found to exaggerate their Anglicized accents as their exposure to, and proficiency in, the language increased.

To gain an enhanced understanding of the links between speech accommodation and power in Jordan I will consider [g] code-switching from the perspective of ethnolinguistic vitality, characterized by Giles et al. (1977: 308) as 'that which makes a [linguistic] group likely to behave as a distinctive and active collective entity in intergroup situations'. Giles and his associates classify this vitality under three headings: status variables, demography variables and institutional support variables. Not all of the variables listed in this classification apply to Jordan. I will therefore deal only with those that seem applicable. The general insight in this model is that the more well-endowed a variety is with respect to a set of variables, the greater its linguistic vitality and, by implication, the status and power of the group that speaks it. Ethnolinguistic vitality partakes of the power of the group and, in turn, adds to it. Giles et al. (1977: 309) schematize this model, which is reproduced in figure 4.1.

Of the status variables, socio-history and language are the most relevant factors, as it is not possible to make any meaningful generalizations about the other two. Since the mid-1970s, Jordan has been engaged in a vigorous project of nation-state building that includes historicizing the nation-state

[19] Haeri (1996) applies this notion in studying variation in relation to gender, class and education in Cairo.

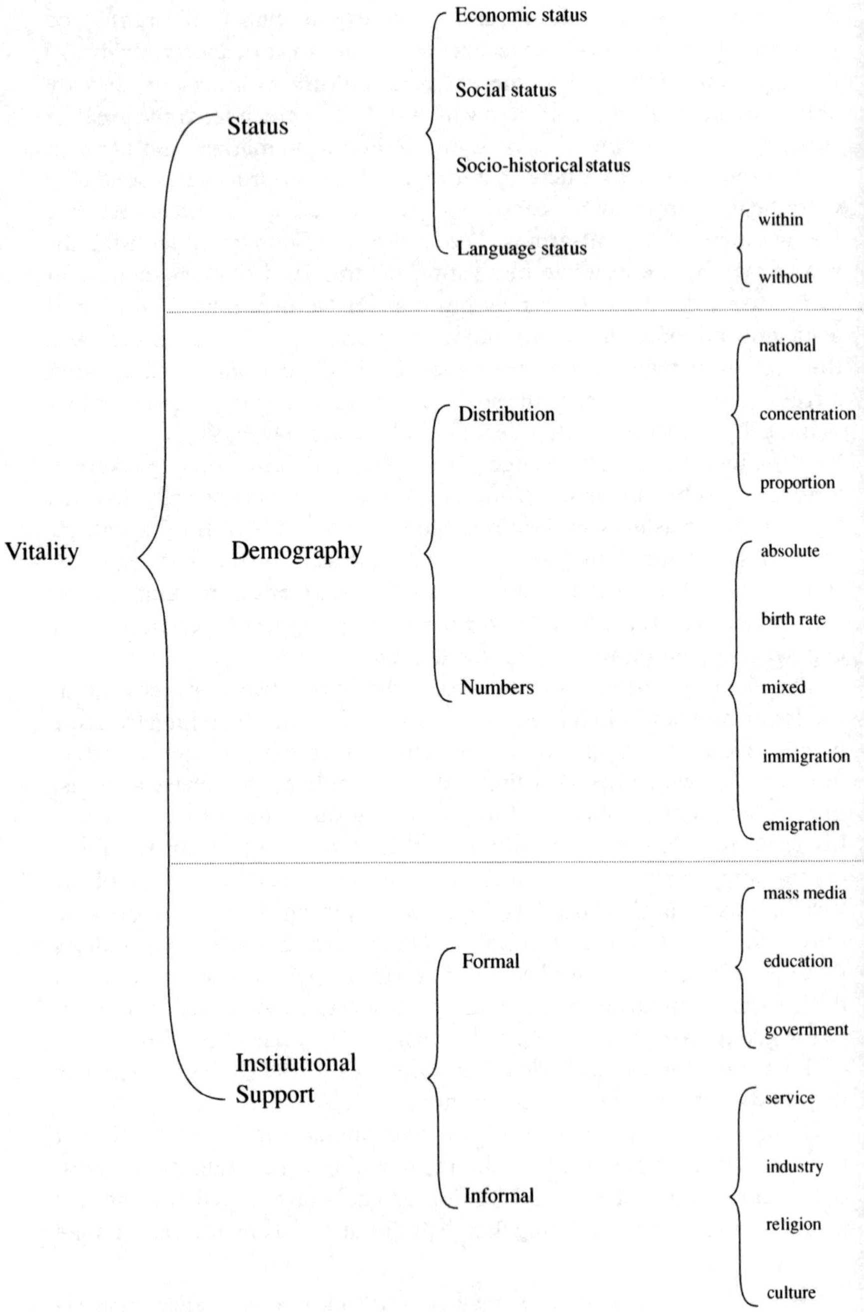

Figure 4.1 Variables in ethnolinguistic vitality

territory by (1) promoting such historical sites as Petra, Jerash and Amman's amphitheatre as symbols of national continuity (see Abu-Odeh 1999: 254); and (2) identifying the burial sites of early (Arab) Islamic military leaders as confirmation of the country's Arab heritage. The fact that all of these sites are in Jordan endows the indigenous Jordanians with a socio-historical status that is different from the status of the Palestinians, who continue to locate their national territory west of the River Jordan, at whose heart lies the symbolism of Jerusalem (see chapter 5). This in my view correlates with the emergence of [g] as the nation-state variable, and as that feature of speech that marks the in-group from the out-group. I will say more about this below.

As far as demography is concerned, the most important factor is the perception of Jordan as the national territory of the Jordanians, captured in the formula *iḥna abnā' al-balad* (We are the true sons of the country!), or 'Jordan for Jordanians' (Abu-Odeh 1999: 194, 231).[20] This perception has been strengthened over the past three decades as a result of the calls by some ultra-nationalist Israelis, including Ariel Sharon at one time, to turn Jordan into a substitute homeland for the Palestinians, what came to be known as *al-waṭan al-badīl* formula in Jordanian politics. Although the Palestinians, who are believed to be the majority in absolute numerical terms in Jordan, are as opposed to this idea as the staunchest Jordanian nationalists, this does not seem to allay the fears of some Jordanians, who continue to believe that regional and international imperatives may cause it to happen. This fear has led to an intense preoccupation among some Jordanian nationalists with Jordanizing Jordan by de-Palestinizing it (Abu-Odeh 1999). Some call on their Jordanian compatriots not to sell land or building-plots to the Palestinians (see Shryock 1997).

In the discourse on the national territory, the Palestinians are projected as outsiders, adding to their perception of themselves as the out-group in relation to whom the Jordanians define themselves as the in-group. The following example illustrates this point. In a speech on 30 November 1974, following the Arab Summit in Rabat, King Hussein described the Palestinians in Jordan as the *muhājirīn* (lit. immigrants) and the Jordanians as the *anṣār* (lit. those who give succour), in a clear reference to the early period in Islamic history when Muhammad's early Meccan followers sought refuge in Medina (see Abu-Odeh 1999: 211). These two terms are impregnated with positive symbolic meanings of brotherhood and solidarity. There is no doubt that the king wanted to deploy these

[20] Abu-Odeh (1999: 228) comments on a variant of this expression as follows: '[During the late 1980s] I became familiar with the Arabic expression *ana ibn al-balad* (I am a genuine Jordanian), used when a Transjordanian would call [on me] to ask for my help in getting a job, a scholarship, or medical treatment abroad. *Ana ibn al-balad* was supposed to strengthen the person's credentials.'

highly resonant meanings in Arab political culture to underpin Jordan's national unity, following the Rabat Summit's decision to declare the PLO 'the sole legitimate representative of the Palestinian people in any Palestinian territory that is liberated [from Israeli occupation in 1967]' (Abu-Odeh 1999: 210). However, Jordanian nationalists quickly seized on these terms and exploited them to brand the Palestinians as outsiders, in relation to whom they could be established as the insiders.

The institutional support factors play an important role in endowing the Bedouin variety with ethnolinguistic vitality. Although there is no dialect discrimination in the education system, government correspondence and declarations, high culture, the press or in religious discourse – diglossia takes care of that – institutional support is nevertheless given to the Bedouin variety in the electronic media and in the arts. For example, Jordan TV produces most of its community programmes in the Bedouin variety. Its most successful soap operas and comedies are also in this dialect; the former are mostly about desert life. The Jordanian song is invariably a [g]-dominated song, even when sung by women. It seems that the promotion of this variety is more than an expression of spontaneous [g] speech; it is also part of a language-engineering policy whose aim is to promote [g] as emblematic of Jordanian national identity. The Lebanese singer Samira Tawfiq, who is the best-known representative of what is called the 'Jordanian song', related to an MBC TV presenter a few years ago how she was trained 'to speak in the [g] variety' by Information Ministry officials as a prelude to launching her singing career as Jordan's first female voice in the early 1960s.[21]

The convergence of the above factors on the Bedouin variety endow it with an ethnolinguistic vitality which the Palestinian varieties cannot match, particularly the heavily stigmatized Fallahi dialect. As the dialect of the in- (and politically dominant) group, the Bedouin variety acts as the target of speech convergence for the Palestinians. This reflects the difference in power allocation between Palestinians and Jordanians at various levels, as will be explained in the next section. The causes of this lie in the turbulent history of the Middle East: the dismemberment of Palestine in 1948, the absorption of the West Bank into Jordan in 1950, the 1967 war and the bloody confrontations between the Jordanian government and the Palestinian movement in 1970–1. These events have left their indelible marks on the linguistic history of Jordan with its mixed Palestinian and Jordanian population.[22]

[21] See Massad (2001: 250) for the role of songs and soap operas about Jordanian, i.e. Bedouin, life in framing Jordanian national identity.

[22] Khalidi (1997) argues convincingly that the effect of the 1948 war on the Palestinians was to strengthen their sense of group identity. The same is true of the 1967 war and the 1970–1 events in Jordan. Khalidi writes (1997: 22):

The nation-state and code-switching

The preceding discussion suggests that male code-switching to [g] is related to the formation of the nation-state in Jordan, and to the attempts by this state to promote a national identity that is specifically Jordanian. This trend is part of a much wider phenomenon of nation-state building in the Arabic-speaking world. The early optimism of the Arab nationalists, of whom Satiʿ al-Husri was the leading figure (see Suleiman 2003, chapter 5), failed to undermine the nation-state as the primary principle of political organization in the area. Witness the fact that the Arab League, which was formed in 1945, is the League of the Arab *States*, and not that of the Arab Nation or Nations. At its formation, the League had seven members. It now has over twenty states, a phenomenon dubbed by George Tarabishi (1982: 81) as 'the inflation of the nation-state' in the Arab world (*taḍakhkhum al-dawla al-quṭriyya*). In some of these states Arabic is not even the dominant language of the local population – for example, Somalia and Djebouti. Attempts at political unity between some Arab states – for example, Egypt and Syria (1958–61) – failed to withstand the pressure of the nascent nation-state and its associated identity. The Arab nationalist claim that the nation-state was a temporary outcome of the colonial era proved to be false. Each nation-state has its national flag, national currency, national anthem, national days, national carrier, education system, stamps, passports, borders, capital,[23] armed forces, police force, *mukhābarāt*, TV and radio stations, legal system, economic plans, diplomatic representation abroad and its own system of government. In some countries, the parliament is called *Majlis al-umma* (lit. the council of the nation), as in Kuwait and Jordan. In others, it is called *Majlis al-shaʿb* (lit. the council of the people), as in Syria and Egypt. In some countries, Arabic is the official language, *al-lugha al-rasmiyya*, while in others it is the national language, *al-lugha al-waṭaniyya* (see Suleiman 1999b).

Arab cultural discourse is full of references to *Iraqi* poetry, the *Syrian* novel, the *Jordanian* short story, the *Egyptian* theatre, the *Lebanese* song

After 1948 the Palestinians in fact were to some degree integrated into the Arab host countries, whether socially, economically, or politically, as might be expected given the overlapping identities of the Palestinians with many of their neighbours. But instead of causing their absorption into these countries, the trauma of 1948 reinforced preexisting elements of identity, sustaining and strengthening a Palestinian self-definition that was already present. The shared events of 1948 thus brought the Palestinians closer together in terms of their collective consciousness, even as they were physically dispersed all over the Middle East and beyond.

23 In a play on the root meaning of the word for 'capital city' in Arabic, *ʿāṣima* (to defend, to protect), Tarabishi (1982: 102) coins the derisive phrase 'The [Arab] capitals defend the states of division [the nation-states] against Arab unity' (*ʿawāṣim taʿṣim duwal al-tajziʾa min al-waḥda*).

or cuisine, *Saudi* vernacular poetry, *Moroccan* music and the *Tunisian* character/mind, among other nationalist appellations. The headline of an article in *al-Quds al-Arabi* (26 April 2001) reads: 'The Egyptian "Prose Poem" Plunders (*mustaliba*) the Lebanese Poem, towards which it Feels Inferior.' Another article in the same newspaper (18 April 2000) complains that the literary press in Egypt does not give non-Egyptian Arab works the same visibility it affords Egyptian ones. A similar point is made by the Syrian writer George Tarabishi (1982), who provides a set of surveys of the tables of contents of leading magazines, journals and bibliographical dictionaries in Arabic to show the dominance of the nation-state in the cultural arena. The Iraqi poet Maʿruf al-Rusafi (1875–1945) complained about this bias in a poem he wrote in the first half of the twentieth century (2000: 239). In this respect, Egypt is not an exception to the nation-state rule. The same pattern applies in other Arab states which favour their own cultural products over those from other Arab countries, in the contest of identity formation. In response to this trend, some Arab nationalists have called for a fight against what they call 'nation-state culturalism' (*al-quṭriyya al-thaqāfiyya*, in *al-Quds al-Arabi*, 20 February 2001).

Language has not been immune to this trend of state-bound cultural nationalism. Al-Bashir bin Salama (1974), a Tunisian writer and one-time Minister of Education under Bourbougiba, claimed that SA in Tunisia has a specifically Tunisian character which makes it qualitatively different from the 'Arabics' of all other Arabic-speaking countries. This claim is not dissimilar to the views put forward in various territorial nationalisms in the Arabic-speaking world in the twentieth century (see Suleiman 2003, chapter 6). A few years ago, the Bahraini singer Ahlam accused the Syrian singer Asala of linguistic trespassing when the latter sang 'Gulf songs' in 'Gulf Arabic'. In an article in *al-Quds al-Arabi* (25 August 2000), the Palestinian writer Rashad Abu-Shawar mocked these trends of linguistic state nationalism and their manifestations in the electronic media. He gave as an example (most probably made up, but still very plausible) the case of a newsreader who rendered the expression of praise *kaththar Allāhu amthālakum* (May God increase the number of people like you!) as *kassar Allāhu amthālakum* (May God smash people like you!) owing to the dialectal interference of the newsreader's dialect into SA. Although interferences of these kinds are mostly unconscious, Abu-Shawar nevertheless criticizes the corporations employing these newsreaders for failing to eradicate these colloquialisms.[24]

[24] One of the games we play at home (as a family and with Arab friends) is guessing the nationality of a TV newsreader from the 'local colouration' of his or her speech. The most difficult ones to guess are those of Al-Jazeera TV.

In Jordan, the nation-state has been defined in increasingly Jordanian – by implication non-Palestinian – terms. Adnan Abu-Odeh (1999: 190–1) locates the roots of this mode of nation-building in the 1970s clashes in Jordan. He points out how these clashes led to a strengthening of both Palestinian and Jordanian nationalisms, reaching a point of polarization for some on both sides. He also points out (1999: 190) how the emerging 'hatred towards the state' among the Palestinians was accompanied on the Jordanian side with a feeling that the Palestinians 'constituted a threat to the [Jordanians'] very identity rather just to its regime' (1999: 191). A policy of removing Palestinians from the army, police and security services ensued, turning these institutions into symbols of Jordanian power. Abu-Odeh argues that, as a result, the 'monopoly on violence' within the state became the preserve of one group, causing the members of the dominated group to develop a 'sense of victimization' (1999: 197).[25] In the civil service, Abu-Odeh tells us (1999: 196), 'the majority of the people holding middle-management positions . . . are Transjordanians'. The dominance of members of this group in all institutions of the state means that Palestinians are excluded from the fringe benefits of government employment (1999: 198), including health care, social security and subsidized goods (food, clothes and appliances). We are also told that, to compensate for their lack of institutional power, the Palestinians – who dominate the private sector[26] – tend to employ Jordanian lawyers and other personnel to deal on their behalf with the Jordanian officials of the state. To show the discrepancy between Palestinians and Jordanians in the public sector, Abu-Odeh (1999: 231) gives the figures reproduced in table 4.10.

Returning to interdialectal variation, it would be very strange if the above discrepancies in power relations between the Jordanians and the Palestinians had no effect on the linguistic situation in the country. The linguistic feminization of the Palestinian through [?] and the linguistic masculinization of the Jordanian through [g] are in fact no more than metaphors for this asymmetry in power distribution in the country. Applying this metaphor further, we can say that the Palestinian is the equivalent of the marked category in grammatical terms, and the Jordanian is his

[25] Abu-Odeh goes even further (1999: 197): 'The dominated group members [i.e. the Palestinians] feel that they are in either a xenophobic country or one that is occupied by a foreign power.' In my experience, this is an exaggerated view. However, Abu-Odeh may be aiming at rhetorical impact (rather than absolute factual truth) in expressing this view.

[26] Abu-Odeh (1999: 196) refers to a study on capital participation in Jordan – carried out in 1996 by the Centre for Strategic Studies at the University of Jordan – which established that 'Palestinian participation amounted to 82.6 percent of the capital, while Transjordanian participation amounted to 11 percent'.

Table 4.10 *Palestinian Jordanians in positions of power, August 1997*

	Transjordanians	Palestinian Jordanians	% of Palestinian Jordanians
Cabinet ministers	18	6	25
Ambassadors	39	6	13.3
Key and senior posts	80	20	20
Members of parliament: lower house (elected)	67	13	16.25
Members of parliament: upper house (appointed)	33	7	17.5

unmarked equivalent, in the same way as 'prince' is the unmarked category in morphological derivation and 'princess' is the marked one. In the case of [k] and [g], the former is the stigmatized version of the latter. In Jordan, the tabloid *Shehan*, a weekly in the colloquial, is dominated in its dialectal component by a [g] linguistic ethos in male characters' speech, unless the other two variants are intended. In 1999 I conducted a little experiment to check that this is the case. My hypothesis that [g] is the unmarked dialectal variety for men, and that [?] and [k] are the marked ones, was confirmed. I asked five male speakers (university students in their early twenties) – two Jordanians and three Palestinians – to read a colloquial passage from the newspaper. It was immediately noticeable that most instances of [q] were realized as [g]. Deviations from this norm were in favour of SA [q], showing the interference of the standard and reflecting the fact that when the Madani and Fallahi variants of (Q) are intended they tend to be represented by the glottal stop, [?] and [k] respectively.

The above discussion is intended to suggest that [g] maintenance and code-switching in male speech is part of nation-state identity formation in Jordan, and that, on a different level, this is a manifestation of nation-state building in the Arabic-speaking world. Interdialectal code-switching in Jordan further reflects the distribution of institutional power within the civil and military-cum-security apparatus of the state. The fact that these – particularly the latter – are male dominated gives more weight to [g] code-switching than [?] code-switching in symbolic terms. If nation-state identity is related to power, and if [g] is emblematic of that power, it follows that [g] more than [?] is metaphorically symptomatic of that identity. In this respect, it is similar to the other symbolic accoutrements of the state. However, in putting forward this thesis, the point must be made that this nation-state identity is born out of conflict, and that it is to a great extent determined by the fact that Jordan before 1948 lacked a centre similar to Beirut, Damascus and Jerusalem to whose speech others must accommodate. Jordan was created by the British out of the spoils of the First World War. The emergence of [g] as a linguistic emblem of the country is bound up with this event, and with the series of wars and conflicts in which Palestine and the Palestinians were an important factor.[27]

Conclusion

My aim in the above discussion has been to show how interdialectal variation in Jordan is bound up with politics and conflict. Code-switching and dialect shift in male speech thus provide us with an opportunity to locate specific linguistic practices in relation to power, nation-state building, national identity and the competition over resources, whether symbolic or material, between groups of speakers. For these operative concepts to apply in a complementary fashion, it is essential that their coincidence is located at a specific historical moment (see Heller 1995), and that this moment is cataclysmic enough to create a rupture in the established socio-political order. Although the clashes between the Jordanian government and the Palestinian guerrilla movement in 1970–1 have been projected as this 'cataclysmic historical moment' in this study, it is nevertheless important to see this moment in relation to other defining or cataclysmic events that had preceded it: the establishment of Jordan in 1921 in the wake of the Ottoman defeat in the First World War, the dismemberment of Palestine in 1948 and the annexation of parts of it to Jordan, and the 1967 Arab–Israeli war which led to the loss of the West Bank and the influx of further refugees into the country.

Previous studies of the language situation in Jordan have generated valuable data on, and explanations of, code-switching which they (on the whole) sought to cast into a sex-based model. This model has been shown to be of limited validity. The present study provides a set of observations which this model cannot explain, or does so in a counter-intuitive manner. I have therefore sought to incorporate this model into a more comprehensive gender-based explanation, in which masculinity as a sociolinguistic variable is symptomatically read as a metaphor for the power and the dominance of the Jordanian male as a political actor in nation-state building. Looking at male code-switching from this perspective has enabled us to relate this linguistic practice to significant changes in the allocation of resources between Jordanians and Palestinians in Jordan.

[27] See Massad (2001: 251–2) for a global discussion on this point.

Adnan Abu-Odeh's study (1999) has proved crucial in providing the historical context for the main argument of this chapter. In particular, it enabled us to establish that the Jordanian and Palestinian varieties do not enjoy the same levels of ethnolinguistic vitality by virtue of their being the dialects of the in-group and out-group respectively.

Speakers are rational actors. It is therefore important to seek rational explanations for their code-switching and dialect shifts. I have done this by invoking the concept of social approval to explain what speech accommodationists call 'speech convergence'. Solidarity with the in-group, and the desire to integrate with it, or be assimilated in it, were cited as factors in male code-switching in Jordan. The same phenomenon may be explained by social-exchange theory, or the notion of the linguistic market. But these two constructs can also help us explain instances of speech non-convergence/maintenance, or even speech divergence. Issues of out-group identity and loyalty, which are often external to the linguistic interaction, were cited as part of the motivation for maintaining aspects of the linguistic repertoire of the out-group in interacting with members of the in-group. But there is more to code-switching than social approval, solidarity, integration, assimilation and loyalty. As a form of linguistic practice, it is used to alter the situation of the speaker and to provide him with a better opportunity of accessing the symbolic and material resources of the society. When used in an instrumental capacity, code-switching is a blatant form of camouflage, what Bourdieu (1992) calls euphemized speech. As a dissembling strategy and as an example of linguistic self-censorship, code-switching is a utility-driven style of speaking. In this respect, Heller (1995: 164) is right when she describes code-switching in the following terms: 'For the analyst, [code-switching] acts as a flag, it signals that here, in this interaction, people are drawing on their linguistic resources in some ways which [may] have an effect both on them and on others. They are using language to take action in a complex world, to react to their experience and to create it anew.' This applies to Jordan in two ways: (1) when male speakers switch to [g] in the public sphere and back to their native dialects in private settings; and (2) when those who have shifted to [g] on a more or less permanent basis switch back to their original variant or out of [g] into another variant, mostly SA [q].

5 When languages collide: language and conflict in Palestine and Israel

Introduction

In chapter 4, we discussed what happens when two dialects collide under conditions of intra-national conflict. Jordan served as the socio-political sphere for this study. Issues of ethnic/national identity and nation-state building were invoked to explain dialect shift and dialect maintenance in male and female speech. The view was put forward that female code-switching to the Madani variety was motivated by considerations of social prestige in a rapidly urbanizing/modernizing society. Male code-switching to the Bedouin variety was attributed to nation-state building in Jordan. Both phenomena, however, were linked to the demographic and political impact of the Arab–Israeli conflict on the history of Jordan. More specifically, the onset and accelerated development of male code-switching were ascribed to the clashes between the Jordanian government and the Palestinian guerrilla movement between 1970 and 1971. Evidence from a number of sociolinguistic studies on the language situation in Jordan was interpreted in terms of speech-accommodation theory and linked to Bourdieu's concept of the linguistic market to provide support for the above conclusions. In addition, considerations of differential power allocation in society were utilized to explain the direction of the dialect shift in male speech. This chapter will continue the discussion of language and socio-political conflict by considering the language situation in Israel/Palestine.

Nothing has affected the course of political events in the Middle East more than the Arab–Israeli conflict. The Zionist drive to establish a home for the Jews in Palestine culminated in 1948 in the dismemberment of the country and the establishment of the state of Israel. The events leading to this conclusion were characterized by political strife, military confrontations and demographic dislocation on a massive scale. Hundreds of thousands of Palestinians (estimated at around 700,000) were forced to leave their homes, to be replaced by waves of Jewish immigrants from all over the world. Some 150,000 Palestinians remained under Israeli rule. Almost overnight, the Palestinians in Israel lost their majority status and found themselves a minority in their own country. A high birth rate has, however, ensured that their proportion to the Jewish population has remained constant, ranging between 13 and 16 per cent over the past fifty years, in spite of massive Jewish immigration to the country.[1] The Israeli policy of separate educational provision for Israeli Jews and Palestinians, coupled with the geographic and social separation of the two communities, has helped the Palestinians in Israel maintain their national identity. Rather than weakening the sense of national identity among them, the Jewish and Hebrew domination of the state has strengthened this identity as a marker of group boundary. Israeli Jews and Israeli Palestinians share a common citizenship, but they are divided in nationality, as indeed their respective identity papers testify.

The Six Day War of 1967 ended in a crushing defeat for the Arabs. Israel occupied the West Bank and Gaza, adding more than 1.5 million Palestinians to its control. Soon after the war, Israel unilaterally annexed Arab East Jerusalem (including the Old City and the surrounding areas), declaring it, together with West Jerusalem, its 'eternal capital'.[2] Although this action is illegal under international law, Israelis have designated it a 'liberation' and 're-unification' of the city. One of the most important aspects of the Arab–Israeli conflict is the manipulation of terminology to create a *linguistic map* that conditions people's perceptions of the facts on the ground.[3] I will discuss this dimension of the Arab–Israeli conflict later, but it is worth saying at this stage that the Israelis have been more adept than the Arabs at associating linguistic deployment with military action and troop deployment. This awareness of the important role of language

[1] Israeli sources put this percentage at a higher level because they include the Palestinians in East Jerusalem within the total number of Palestinians in Israel. East Jerusalem was occupied in 1967. It is therefore not a part of Israel under international law and will, therefore, be treated accordingly in this study.

[2] This annexation was formally ratified by the Israeli Knesset in 1980.

[3] In a dispatch from the Middle East entitled 'Israel wins war of words', Brian Whitaker from *The Guardian* touches on this very issue. He illustrates it by the way the term 'response' is used in talking about the Israeli-Palestinian conflict (9 April 2001, http://www.guardian.co.uk/Archive/Article/0,4273,4167706,00.htm): 'A familiar tale from the Middle East: Palestinians launched three bombs overnight against the Eile Sinai settlement in the far north of the Gaza Strip. Israeli troops responded with tank shells, destroying a Palestinian border post and hitting two houses.'

This report, which happens to have come from the BBC, is familiar not only for the events it describes but also for the way it describes them: the Palestinians attack and the Israelis 'respond'.

Military actions by the Israelis are always a 'response' to something, even when they strike first. If they haven't actually been attacked, it's a 'response' to a security threat.

'Response' is a very useful word. It provides a ready-made reason for the Israelis' actions and neatly brushes off demands for further explanation. It says: 'Don't ask why we did it, ask the other side.'

in shaping the political perceptions of the international community – via translations from Hebrew into English, in most cases – is also evident in Israel's management of the peace negotiations with the Palestinians. Israel has been successful in depicting her offer to return occupied territory to the Palestinians as a 'concession', with all the false implications and presuppositions that this term carries by way of a legal entitlement. Talk about Israeli 'concessions' in return for Palestinian territorial compromises over the West Bank (including Arab East Jerusalem) has even entered the Arab political lexicon, which now demands that Israel offer *tanāzulāt* (concessions) in return for a peace treaty with the Palestinians and the normalization of relations with the rest of the Arab world. The fact that almost all of the 'concessions' are no more than retractions of deliberate violations of international law perpetrated by Israel does not seem to create any political or legal dissonance in the minds of those who routinely consume such terminology, including some Arab policy makers and media pundits. The same applies to the term 'compromise'; accordingly, the offer to dismantle some illegal Israeli settlements on the West Bank is depicted as a 'compromise' which demands a reciprocal move from the Palestinian side. In fact, it never ceases to amaze how bewildered people in the West feel when I tell them in public lectures that an Israeli withdrawal from the Old City of Jerusalem would not represent a 'concession' to the Palestinians, but an act of compliance with international law from which Israel is not legally exempted. The strength of their feelings and the intellectual resistance they show to this view of the conflict, when not ideologically driven, are both to some extent a reflection of the power of the linguistic map on people's conceptualization of political geography. Language does not just reflect reality; it also helps shape it. The Arab–Israeli conflict provides ample examples of this principle, as this chapter will show.

Arabic and Hebrew in the fray

The Arab–Israeli conflict has conditioned the linguistic attitudes towards Arabic and Hebrew on both sides of the Arab–Israeli divide (Ibrahim 1981). The Israeli Jews and the Arabs – excluding the Israeli Palestinians, who are in a special category (Amara 1999) – hold reciprocally antagonistic views of the language of the Other. Although there are some exceptions, both parties look at the language of the Other as the language of the 'enemy'. Referring to the situation before 1967, Fisherman and Fishman (1975: 513) comment that the Israelis felt that 'Arabic did not represent a developed culture and that it was a language of an enemy for whom there was little respect'. Recent studies indicate that this view of Arabic has persisted – if not actually intensified – in the last few years, among Israeli Jews. Kraemer and Olshtain (1989: 199) note that, for Israeli Jews, 'Arabic represents both the majority language of a predominantly hostile region and the language of a local growing minority which is highly identified ethnically, culturally and religiously with the broader regional majority'.[4] Lefkowitz (1993: 95) reports that 'many Jews in Haifa *derisively* [emphasis added] call the University of Haifa *Bir Zeit*, the name of a university on the West bank, because it "feels" to them like an Arab environment . . . a place where Arabic can be spoken freely'. Tabory (1981: 301) states: 'Since language constitutes one of the elements of national identity [for Israeli Jews and Israeli Palestinians], the tension of the national conflict may well affect the attitude of each nation toward the language of the other.' This feeling towards Arabic dominated the early discussions of the Language Council, the forerunner of the Hebrew Language Academy, some of whose members opposed the borrowing of lexical items from Arabic. A member of this council expressed the view that 'neologisms from Arabic . . . will prove how much [Hebrew] is not comfortable in welcoming Arabic influence' (Saulson 1979: 134). Jacob Fichman, a member of the Language Council, expressed the view in an article in 1910 that Hebrew 'will not digest the new names of plants, especially those which have been taken from the Arabic language', and that these borrowed names 'will always be like atrophied limbs' (Saulson 1979: 134). Fichman justified this position by declaring that 'despite the fact that the Arabic language is our sister language in the family of Semitic languages, it has no foundation in our psyche' (Saulson 1979: 134).

For ideological reasons, Fichman ignores the fact that Jewish philosophy in the Middle Ages – especially in Spain under Arab Muslim rule – flowered in Arabic, and that a high proportion of the Jews in the world

[4] A full, but circumspect, characterization of the view of Arabic among Israeli Jews is given by Spolsky and Shohamy (1999: 118):

> For most Israeli Jews, Arabic is first and foremost the language of the surrounding Arab states, many of which have been engaged in war with Israel since its establishment and which continue to be seen as threats to national survival. It is, second, the language of the Palestinians living in Gaza and the West Bank, the heirs and continuing supporters of a national liberation movement that has used terrorism to achieve its goals. It is, third, the language of a minority group within Israel, granted civil rights since the creation of the state, but feared as a potential fifth column in struggles either with the Palestinians or with other Arab states.

Ben-Rafael reiterates some of these points, but he also refers to the low prestige the language has in Israel (1994: 210): 'The concentration of the Arabs in lower social strata contributes to the lower linguistic status of their language in the eyes of the Jewish Israeli public.'

at the time had a form of Arabic as their mother tongue. This attitude towards Arabic signalled the close involvement of language in Zionist ideology in the pursuit of the nationalist project of establishing a home for the Jews in Palestine. Sometimes, the Arab–Israeli conflict manifests itself in practices that show the depth of the feeling between the two communities. It is said that the 'Egged Bus Company forbade its drivers to air Arabic radio programmes on its buses, even in Arab areas' (reported in Tabory 1981: 303), to the dismay of the Arabs in Israel. When an attempt was made to establish a mixed Israeli Palestinian and Israeli Jewish high school in Haifa in the 1960s, the Jewish parents objected very strongly and threatened to withdraw their children. The school remained 'mixed', but each group was taught separately. Spolsky and Shohamy (1999: 123) report that although mixed Palestinian and Jewish kindergartens exist in Jaffa, and that although the Palestinian children are given Hebrew names and are taught a Jewish Hebrew curriculum, the proposal to introduce bilingual and bicultural education failed 'when Jewish parents withdrew their children'.

Reactions like these recall earlier Jewish practices in Palestine during the mandate period. In 1921, Sir Ellis Kadouri set up an endowment to establish a joint Arab–Jewish agricultural school in which the teaching would be carried out in Arabic to Arab students and Hebrew to Jewish students in the first stages, followed by instruction in English in later stages. The British director of education in Palestine also proposed that all practical work, dining and sleeping facilities would be shared between the two groups. Under pressure from the Zionist Executive, who opposed the idea because the Jewish students were not going to be taught in Hebrew throughout the curriculum, the project had to be abandoned in favour of two separate schools (Tibawi 1956). Politics and ideology are important factors in all of the above incidents.

The Arabs, correspondingly, see Hebrew as the language of a foreign body that has been forcibly implanted in their midst, one that continues to occupy Arab lands. This view of the situation is articulated by Abd-el-Jawad and al-Haq (1997: 419), who chart the course of the linguistic conflict between Arabic and Hebrew in the following way:

> We have a linguistic situation where one native language [Arabic] was dominant in a society [Palestine], then another hostile language [Hebrew] with its speakers who are hostile and occupiers came into the picture and imposed themselves by force on the native land and language at the expense of the native population and their language, thus creating a deep-rooted and prolonged conflict.

This stark view of the linguistic conflict between Hebrew and Arabic is an extension of the Arab narrative of the Arab–Israeli conflict in its historical

Table 5.1 *Attitudes towards learning Hebrew among university students in Jordan*

	Yes %	No %	Don't Know
Hebrew is a beautiful language	27.4	49.5	23
I like studying Hebrew	24.6	65	9.5
Knowledge of Hebrew is a distinctive feature of an educated person	35	54.6	10.1
I want my children and siblings to study Hebrew at school	42.6	48.6	7.6
Learning Hebrew undermines my religious faith	7.6	76.3	14.8
I hate Hebrew, it is the language of the [Israeli] Jews	41.6	50.8	6.9
Learning Hebrew does not entail liking [Israeli] Jews	88	7.6	4.1

and political settings. In a recent study of the attitudes towards the study of Hebrew in Jordan, al-Haq (1999) reveals that his sample of university students identified the learning of Hebrew mainly with instrumental objectives. Outside this domain, a negative attitude towards the language was found to exist, as the responses in table 5.1 show (al Haqq 1999: 57).

Similar views towards Hebrew were expressed in Bethlehem after the Oslo Accords between Israel and the Palestinians (in 1993 and 1995), and the withdrawal of the former from the city (Spolsky et al. n.d.: 164–7). The views of the informants in this study are coloured by the experience of occupation ('It is bad that the [Israeli] Jews know Arabic because this means continuing their occupation and control of us') and the difference in power between the two parties ('It is normal that an [Israeli] Jew does not use Arabic, because the [Palestinian] mainly needs the [Israeli] Jew'), although there seems to be a greater appreciation than in the Jordan study of the non-instrumental value of learning the language of the Other among the Palestinians ('It is good to know each other's language to avoid falling in error, worry and evil').

These views motivate two contradictory attitudes among the Arabs and the Israeli Jews towards the language of the Other. They explain the reluctance to learn and seriously promote the language of the Other in their respective communities, with the exception of the Palestinians in Israel, who need Hebrew for instrumental and other reasons. This is evidenced by the low take-up rate of Arabic in Israeli schools, in spite of the fact that Arabic is an official language of the state of Israel and is, at least in theory, a semi-compulsory subject in high school in that a student is required to choose between it and French. On the Arab side, it is evident in the general lack of interest in learning Hebrew in the few centres that offer the language in Arab universities, in spite of the fact that both Egypt and Jordan have signed peace treaties with Israel, in 1979 and 1994 respectively. In an Arab Gulf university I visited in 1998, not a single student opted to study Hebrew, although the university in question went to huge expense to offer courses in the language. Studies of Hebrew language proficiency among Palestinians in the Occupied Territories have established that knowledge of the language is lowest among the educated segment of the society, and that it is highest among workers and Palestinian prisoners who come into contact with Israeli Jews on a regular basis (Amara and Spolsky 1996; Spolsky and Amara 1995; Spolsky and Cooper 1991; Spolsky et al. n.d.). The fact that Palestinian prisoners tend to be more proficient in Hebrew than their educated compatriots is in itself an indication of the conflictual and asymmetrical nature of the contact between the Palestinians and the Israeli Jews.

Furthermore, the fact that Hebrew and Arabic are treated as the languages of the enemy conditions a largely instrumental and security-driven motivation in learning them on the Israeli and Arab sides. This explains the strong interest in Arabic in the Israeli army and intelligence services. Lefkowitz (1993: 95) reflects this orientation when he says that the 'teaching of Arabic in [Israeli Jewish schools] is motivated more by concerns over security than over pluralism', and that 'many [Israeli] Jews who know Arabic learned it (or perfected) it in the army for use in intelligence work'.[5] A similar, but not so successful, interest in Hebrew is found among the less efficient Arab intelligence services. Statements to the effect that the 'study of Hebrew is a national duty' are often encountered in the press and among the elite (see Abd al-Latif n.d). This sentiment is often reflected in statements that deride the Arab countries for failing to pay attention to Hebrew, the language of the 'enemy' (Abd-el-Jawad and al-Haq 1997).[6] Owing to this, competence in the Other's language is sometimes interpreted negatively. Some of the views expressed by Bethlehemites about competence in Arabic among Israeli Jews are

[5] Rabinowitz (2002: 308) gives examples of how some Israeli anthropologists, Arabists and Middle Eastern specialists started their careers as part of the military/intelligence apparatus: '[The] shift from civil service jobs associated with state control of Palestinians to academic life was not unique to anthropologists. Israeli officers who relinquish jobs with the security establishment to pursue a career in university departments and research centres – particularly ones that specialize in Middle Eastern studies – are a common feature of Israeli academia today.'

[6] Ex-Prime Minister Abdul-Salam al-Majali, the head of the Jordanian team that negotiated the 1994 peace treaty with Israel, expressed a similar point when he noted that one of the serious difficulties his team faced was that 'no member of the delegation could speak Hebrew fluently', but that 'in contrast, most members of the Israeli team could speak Arabic' (Abd-el-Jawad and al-Haq 1997: 420).

related to this perception of language learning (Spolsky et al. n.d.: 164–7): 'I do not like the [Israeli] Jew who knows Arabic because he knows our secrets'; '[An Israeli] Jew who speaks Arabic does not necessarily want peace'; and '[An Israeli] Jew who knows Arabic is a bastard.' Arabs also report that they sometimes suppress their native language in public places because of fear. Lefkowitz (1993: 95) mentions that many Israeli Arabs censor their native language in public places because of fear, exemplifying this by a Palestinian woman who was surprised to find she was speaking in Hebrew to another Arab woman on a Tel Aviv bus. A Bethlehemite (Spolsky et al. n.d.: 167) makes a distinction concerning native-language suppression among Israeli Jews and Palestinians: 'Sometimes the Palestinian is forced to hide his knowledge of language because of fear, but the [Israeli] Jews do the same because they have dishonest motives.' What matters here is not the factual truth of this statement, but the fact that it imputes bad intentions to the other party in the conduct of its linguistic practices. It would be hard to explain this and similar reactions without placing them in the context of the Arab–Israeli conflict.

Before the formal institution of the British mandate in Palestine in 1922, the linguistic conflict in Zionist circles was between Hebrew and Yiddish. This intra-ethnic conflict was in the end resolved in favour of Hebrew, as will be explained later. In 1916, before the British government issued its Balfour Declaration (November 1917), in which it promised to establish a national home for the Jews in Palestine, Zionist leaders started to campaign for giving Hebrew 'equal rights with Arabic' (Fisherman and Fishman 1975: 500), the language of the vast majority in the country. These efforts succeeded in convincing the British government to recognize Hebrew as an official language in Palestine, alongside English and Arabic. The proclamation setting this out is incorporated in paragraph 82 of the Proclamation of the King at the Council on Palestine on 10 October 1922 (Fisherman and Fishman 1975: 499):

> All ordinances, official notices and official forms of the government and all official notices of the local authorities and municipalities in areas to be prescribed by order of the High Commissioner, shall be published in English, Arabic and Hebrew. The three languages may be used in debates and discussions in the Legislative Council, and subject to any regulations to be made from time to time, in the government offices in the Law Courts.

In addition to the above domains, Hebrew started to appear on postage stamps and coins. However, its use in the magistrates' courts was restricted (at an earlier period) to reflect the demographic constitution of the country, in which the vast majority were Arabic-speaking Palestinians. Thus statute 4 in the statutes regulating the languages of the courts allowed for the use of Hebrew in trilingual areas only, defined as those parts of Palestine in which the Jews constituted one-fifth of the population.[7] Reflecting the demographic composition of the country, rule 2 in this statute names the areas from which Hebrew is to be excluded (Fisherman and Fishman 1975: 499): 'In the magistrates' courts in Gaza, Hebron, Bethlehem, Ramleh, Beersheba, Tulkarem, Nablus, Jenin, Acre and Nazareth, Arabic shall be the language of pleading.' Rule 3 of the statute allowed for the use of English, but not Hebrew, in cases tried in district courts in these areas, or in the Court of Appeal dealing with a case tried in any of the places mentioned in rule 2. According to these rules Arabic, but not Hebrew, was available to be used throughout the whole country, since the Arabic-speaking Palestinians often represented the majority population in the remaining areas. The institution of Hebrew as an official language in Palestine must therefore be considered a victory for the language over Arabic. Zionist leaders, however, continued to fight for complete parity between Hebrew and Arabic at all levels, including the functional and symbolic domains. The focus in the latter domain was on replacing the vertical representation of the three languages on public notices – English first, followed by Arabic and Hebrew in that order – with a horizontal mode of representation whereby the three languages would appear on the same linear plane. The following extract from a memorandum sent by Eliezer Ben-Yehuda and David Yellin, two members of the Hebrew Language Seminar, to Herbert Samuel, the British High Commissioner, sets out their concerns (Fisherman and Fishman 1975: 501–2):

> We hope that the day is near when the Hebrew language will become one having equal rights with English and Arabic in the municipality and in the government offices from the highest to the lowest, on the trains and in the custom houses, in the post and telegraph, the police and the courts, in official orders and government announcements on ticket stubs and receipts, and on coins and stamps. The Hebrew Seminar considers it a *national insult to see our language in the position it is given in most instances of being beneath the other two languages* since the country was founded by international agreement as being a national home for the Jews. The Language Seminar considers the most fitting form to be that which was given to the three languages in the official sheet of the Royal Proclamation where the languages are not one under the other but side by side. [emphasis added]

[7] This position was set out in a statement by Herbert Samuel, the high commissioner, before the Mandate Committee on 30 October 1924 (Fisherman and Fishman 1975: 501): 'The Hebrew language serves the needs of the central administration, but is only used in the districts if the Jewish inhabitants of the area constitute any important factor in them. The actual number which serves as the criterion is a fifth of the residents, and any areas where the Jews are not a fifth of the population is not considered a tri-lingual area.'

The establishment of Israel in 1948 changed the balance of power between Arabic and Hebrew decisively in favour of the latter. Documents from the early days of the state refer to the revival of Hebrew as one of the achievements of the Jews in Palestine, before they go on to proclaim that the newly established state will guarantee freedom of language for all of its citizens. Unlike English, Arabic kept its official status, but this did not stop some members of the Israeli Knesset (parliament) from putting forward proposals to deprive it of this position. In response to one such proposal from MK Esther Raxiel-Naor in 1952, David Ben Gurion, the prime minister at the time, set out the views of his government on the language issue in the following terms: (1) Hebrew is the language of the state whose Jewish character it signals alongside the Law of Return;[8] (2) it is the policy of the state to impart knowledge of Hebrew to all its citizens irrespective of their national background; and (3) the Arab minority has the right to use its own language, including in the Knesset even though an Arab MK may know Hebrew. It is interesting to note here that Ben Gurion stopped short of declaring that Arabic was an official language of the state of Israel. Abdul Aziz al-Zu'bi, an Arab member of the Knesset, responded to the statement made by Ben Gurion, pointing out that it was 'open to many interpretations', and that 'it placed new doubts in [the] minds of the Arabs with regard to the future of their language' in Israel (Fisherman and Fishman 1975: 506).

When in 1952 a Jewish MK from the Communist Party asked for Arabic to be given parity with Hebrew as a condition for naturalization, a right-wing MK strongly opposed the idea, declaring that in 'the State of Israel only the Hebrew language will rule' (Fisherman and Fishman 1975: 507). Some Jewish MKs from outside the traditionally pro-Arab Israeli Communist Party thought that it was only fair that Arabic should be given the status of an official language.[9] The fact that views of this kind

[8] This law stipulates that any Jew anywhere in the world has the right to immigrate to Israel and to claim its citizenship upon satisfying some formal conditions.

[9] MK Elazar Globus expressed this view (Fisherman and Fishman 1975: 510):

> Fairness obligates us to recognize the Arabic language as official. From the time of the founding of the League of Nations we Jews requested and forcefully pleaded in all parliaments of eastern Europe for rights as a national minority and we even defended as much as possible the rights of other national minorities. Now that we have won a state of our own it is only just and fair that we grant the rights of a minority to the Arab people who dwell in our state.

This is an interesting statement because it depicts the linguistic rights of the Palestinians in Israel in relation to the Jewish experience in the Diaspora. It is also interesting because the Palestinians are treated as people who 'dwell in our state', rather than as an indigenous minority that lives on its land in a state that belongs to all its citizens regardless of their ethnic or religious background. It is the absence of this perspective that, in my view, informs Israeli Jewish conceptualizations of the status of Arabic in Israel.

were expressed in the early years of the state is indicative of the doubts that existed at the time concerning the status of Arabic as an official language in Israel.[10] These doubts continued to be voiced in the Knesset in later periods. Arab members asked questions about the teaching of Arabic in the Jewish schools; they also complained about the absence of the language from the public landscape. In one such complaint (16 February 1966), which I will quote at length to give the reader some of the feelings surrounding the language issue, Abdul Aziz al-Zu'bi declared (Fisherman and Fishman 1975: 514–15):[11]

We are concerned with one of the most important requests of all the Arabs in the State, whose number approaches 300,000, an issue which reflects the attitude of the State to these citizens and their language. All nations are proud of their language and love it and we also love our language and are proud of it and will not give it up. We must praise the government for its official attitude to our language, Arabic, in many areas, such as postage stamps, coins and currency and the register

[10] In a High Court case touching on the status of Arabic as an official language, the ruling of the chief justice implied that a change occurred 'in the official position of Arabic because the very creation of the State of Israel brought about a change in its official standing' (Fisherman and Fishman 1975: 520).

[11] Similar observations are made by a Canadian visitor to the Old City (Lehn 1980: 6):

On one occasion I was riding with a Palestinian journalist in his car. He is a resident of [Palestinian] East Jerusalem, and he was showing me around his city. At one point . . . he made a wrong turn. As soon as he had completed the turn, he realized that he was heading the wrong direction in a one-way street. He stopped immediately and started to back up, whereupon a traffic officer blew her whistle and he stopped. She came over to the car and spoke to him in Hebrew; he responded in English, apologizing for his inability to speak Hebrew . . . The officer then asked for the registration of the vehicle . . . She then told him that he had made a wrong turn. He responded that he realized he had and apologized for having done so, noting that the change to one-way had been made only a few days ago . . . and that the sign to this effect was in Hebrew only which he could not read. Her response was that Jerusalem is an Israeli city, and that Israelis speak Hebrew . . . Why had he not learned Hebrew? (I wondered if she knew that Arabic was also an official language in Israel and that, in any case, we were in occupied East Jerusalem).

David Grossman, a well-known Israeli writer, makes a similar point in his reflections on his travels among the Palestinians in Israel (1993: 197–8):

Without [Hebrew] how could I know how to find my way when, over the thousand kilometres I've burned these past months, I saw almost no important road sign written in Arabic . . . even though Arabic is an official language in Israel? At the grocery store, how would I be able to tell the difference between spaghetti and macaroni, between yoghurt and sour cream, if I didn't know how to read Hebrew? How would I know that I should keep my children away from poisonous cleaning fluids and pesticides? Could I tell the difference between aspirin and antibiotics if I couldn't read Hebrew and English? How could I understand that a sign says FALLING ROCKS, while another says CAUTION – HIGH TENSION WIRES? (At least I'd be spared the bumper stickers on the pickup trucks that read JEWISH LABOUR! and the placards pasted up by Meir Kahane's disciples that proclaim 'We propose five years' imprisonment . . . for every non-Jew who has sexual relations with a Jewish woman.')

of the members of parliament, all of which are published in Hebrew and Arabic. Every Arab can submit a legal claim and appear before the court at any level in Arabic; but for routine and practical purposes our language is disappearing from use, something which offends the honour and rights of these citizens and educates the Jewish citizens negatively and even negates the respect for Arabs among them, if some of this still remains. Honourable Knesset, why must an Arab citizen run from attendant to attendant in the central bus station in Tel-Aviv when thousands of Arab citizens pass through it each week, in order to find out where the bus to Nazareth or Ramla waits? Why is there not even one Arabic word in the Tel-Aviv train station, nor in Haifa either, to denote the timetable of the trains except for one sentence, which is also important, showing the way to the bathroom?

Why are all the signs which direct and show him [how] to behave in the Dan buses written in Hebrew and English only, except for one sign which is translated into Arabic, 'Beware of pickpockets'? Why can't an Arab send a telegram from the telegraph office in Tel-Aviv in Arabic, except in Hebrew or Latin letters, while it is possible to use Arabic letters in the Haifa telegraph office? More serious than all of this is the sad fact that the Arabic language is disappearing from the scene throughout the country from its highways and streets, and even at the entrance to Arab villages. Tens of approach roads which were paved to Arab villages bear no sign in Arabic. By the direction of an adviser a beautiful, large sign was set up at the entrance and exit of Nazareth with Hebrew and Latin letters. Members of the Knesset, this is a gross insult, whether intentional or not, to the feelings of honour and to the rights of the Arab citizens of the State. There is no doubt that this fact does not promote understanding between the two peoples.

One of the principles upon which the present study is based is the utilization of language as a proxy for voicing extralinguistic concerns in the cultural, economic, social and political spheres. In the Arab–Israeli conflict, the latter sphere matters most. Although the early demands of the Arab MKs to clarify the status of Arabic may have been most directly motivated by cultural and social concerns, they were no doubt related to political impulses of a nationalist kind. In his study of Hebrew and Arabic in Israel, Landau (1987: 129) rightly points out that 'politics is inescapable when discussing the language issue'. Landau was of the view that this is especially true of the Palestinian minority in Israel wherein the language domain, more than some other domains, serves to unite the 'moderates' and the 'radicals' in their dealings with the state. It may therefore be interesting to highlight some of the features in al-Zu'bi's speech which make it an excellent example of the use of language as a proxy in the domain of socio-political interaction between the minority and the majority in society.

Al-Zu'bi's use of the pronouns 'we' and 'our' indicates where he locates his identity and that of the group on whose behalf he is speaking. These pronouns create a linguistic boundary between the Arabs and the Jews as 'two peoples' in Israel. Although the request to make Arabic visible and usable in the public domain has a functional and utilitarian purpose, its force emerges from the symbolic value of the language as the emblem of an Arab national identity in Israel. The reference to the 'pride' of the Arabs in their language and to their 'love' for it can have meaning only at this level of symbolic enunciation. This is also true of the reference to the treatment of Arabic by the authorities as a 'gross insult . . . to the feelings of honour . . . of the Arab citizens' of Israel. It is interesting to note in this context the similarity between this formulation and that used by Ben-Yehuda and Yellin in their memorandum, quoted above, to the High Commissioner in Palestine. By reminding his audience that the Arabs are citizens in a state that consists of 'two peoples', al-Zuʿbi effectively claims that Israel is a binational state which must grant members of the minority group their full civic and national rights. The demand to give Arabic public visibility is further promoted as a measure which can induce the Israeli Jews to respect the Arabs, the implication being that such respect is not always present among members of the dominant group. In return, the promotion of Arabic in the public domain is presented as a measure which can increase the understanding between 'the two peoples'. The fact that this was judged to be a desirable outcome indicates that the level of understanding between the 'two peoples' at the time was not as positive as it might have been under different conditions. Finally, the reference to Arabic as 'disappearing from the scene' serves to remind the audience of the pre-state period when the language was dominant in Palestine. The feeling of nostalgia towards the past provides the speaker with an emotional charge. It additionally serves as an authenticating element in his demand for linguistic equality between Arabic and Hebrew.

Al-Zuʿbi's seemingly innocuous statement about the place of Arabic in the public domain in Israel turns out on close analysis to be full of socio-political meanings. It touches upon concepts that invoke the symbolic role of language as a marker of national identity. Commenting on this issue, Landau (1987: 128–9) says that the central role of language in Arab nationalism 'could serve to sharpen' such an identity among the Palestinians in Israel, and that this may have 'implications for the determination of ethnic frontiers' in historical Palestine. In a telling remark that reveals the 'fear' that linguistic conflicts can create in an ethnically structured society, Landau adds (1987: 129): 'Needless to say, Arab irredentism is totally unacceptable for all Jews in *tiny* Israel' (emphasis added). Landau explains the basis of this fear as follows (1987: 128):

> Israeli Jews fear that with the advent of universal literacy and growing political awareness among Israeli Arabs, a potentially centrifugal tendency may be fostered among the latter: language diversity, combined with other factors, could lead to

demands for frontier revisions. Actually, Israeli Arabs constitute demographic majorities in certain areas near the State's borders, such as parts of Galilee; a violent call for secession might be initiated by some of those Arabs, should they be so conditioned by their education. After all, the spread of Arabic accompanied the conquests of early Islam and served to outline the political frontiers of Arab rule. A careful sampling of public opinion among Israeli Arabs recently indicated that no fewer than 59% favoured a return to the 1947 frontiers . . . (a move that would deprive Israel of a sizeable part of its territory).

The 'fear of irredentism' that Landau talks about is beyond the realm of rationality if we consider the commanding military and political strength of the Israeli Jews and the weakness of the Palestinians in Israel. However, the fact that such a fear is expressed, and that it is linked to education, history and the formation of national identity in the linguistic domain, indicates the potency that can be ascribed to language in informing political conflicts and deciding their course. The paranoia and overstatement on both sides of the Arab–Israeli conflict are not restricted to politics. They also exist in the linguistic domain, as the preceding quotation illustrates.

The subordinate position of the Palestinians in Israel is signalled in the curricula for Arabic and Hebrew in Jewish and Arab schools. For students in the Arab schools, Hebrew is a compulsory subject from the third grade. Arabic is a 'semi-compulsory' subject in the Jewish schools. However, not all Jewish schools are required to offer it, and in the high schools where it is taught it tends to be offered to students with lower grades. Students in such schools can ask for an exemption from Arabic and can opt to study French instead. Mar'i (1978) highlights more important discrepancies between the two languages by investigating the goals for teaching language and literature in Arab and Jewish schools.[12] Whereas the teaching of Hebrew in the Jewish schools is linked to the cultural and ideological values of the Israeli Jews as a nation, the teaching of Arabic in the Arab schools tends to revolve around developing the linguistic competence of the students in grammar, rhetoric, composition and literary appreciation in isolation from the national and ideological values that envelop them.[13] The subordinate position of Arabic in the Arab schools may be further explicated by comparing it with that of Hebrew in the same schools. In the final four grades of high school, Hebrew language and literature are allocated 768 hours, whereas Arabic language and literature are allocated a slightly lower number of 732 hours. In addition,

[12] Although some of the goals and objectives of the curricula have been modified in the 1990s, al-Haj (1995) says that these changes have been of a marginal nature.

[13] See Mar'i (1989), Peres et al. (1970), Sarsour (1983) and Winter (1979) for information on Arab education in Israel. For the status of Arabic in Israel, see Koplewitz (1992), Landau (1970), Tabory (1981) and Talmon (2000).

whereas Hebrew literature is allocated two-thirds of the hours assigned to Hebrew-related subjects, Arabic literature is allocated half of the hours assigned to Arabic-related topics. Furthermore, whereas the curriculum for Hebrew in the Arab schools contains readings from the Bible, Mishnah and Agadah that take up half of the time allocated to the study of Hebrew literature, only a small proportion of the 22 per cent of the time allocated to the study of the history of literature in the Arabic curriculum deals with Islamic texts.[14]

These discrepancies reflect the nature of Israel as a Jewish state in which the Arab minority are thought to constitute an ever-present danger. Educating the Arab youth in Hebrew is therefore conceived as a means of imparting to them an understanding of the dominant culture and its national ideology, in so far as this revolves around Judaism as a religion and Zionism as a political movement. Instead of reducing the conflict between Jew and Palestinian in Israel, this policy antagonizes the Arab youth and causes them to look for alternative sources of information, outside the school environment, on aspects of their national culture. However, it may be judged that Israel cannot afford to act differently since the promotion of Arab national culture in the Arab schools would legitimize this culture politically and, without doubt, would unleash a Jewish backlash in defence of the Jewishness of the state. For the Israelis the Jewishness of the state rules supreme. Defending it is therefore a duty of the highest order.

The discussion in this section serves to highlight a number of points. First, although language is not the cause of the Arab–Israeli conflict, and although it is unlikely that language could by itself lead to the outbreak of hostilities between the two parties in this conflict, it is nevertheless true that there is a linguistic dimension to the Arab–Israeli struggle. Second, the linguistic conflict between the Israeli Jews and the Israeli Palestinians is contested more vigorously in the symbolic sphere than in the functional domain. The position of Arabic as the functional language of the Palestinians in Israel is not under threat, not least because the policy to preserve the Jewish nature of the state demands that Hebrew preserves its unique and exclusive link with the dominant ethnicity/nationality in society. Ben Gurion expressed this position when he declared in the Knesset

[14] Spolsky and Shohamy (1999: 113) note this point:

> One of the central issues in the teaching of Hebrew in Arab schools continues to be the amount of Jewish content. Jewish sacred and traditional texts (Bible and rabbinical writings) take a prominent part in the curriculum, and there is also a great deal of emphasis on the Jewish world . . . Arab pupils feel they spend more time learning Judaism than their own religion and traditions . . . The question is a basic and difficult one, related to fundamental issues about the place of the Arab minority in Israel.

in 1952 that the 'State of Israel is a Jewish state and [that] this is indicated by the Law of Return and by the Hebrew language' (Fisherman and Fishman 1975: 505). The fact that the Palestinians are not just outside the dominant ethnicity in Israel, but are to be excluded from it as a matter of policy, has endowed their language with such low prestige and negative connotations that it can, paradoxically speaking, continue to serve as a national language for them. Jewish uniqueness demands functional and symbolic exclusion on the ethnic and linguistic fronts, and it is this that guarantees Arabic its place as the national language of the indigenous minority. Ben-Rafael (1994: 210) had this in mind when he said that the 'low status' of Arabic means that the language 'is not coveted by privileged [Jewish] groupings' and, therefore, 'the Arabs face no difficulty in maintaining their control over the language [to] assert their own values, tenets and outlooks'.

Third, the exclusionary link between the Hebrew language and Jewish ethnicity in Israel conditions some of the reactions towards Hebrew language use by the Palestinians. David Grossman (1993: 55), an Israeli Jewish writer, highlights this fact when he declares that 'when [Israeli Palestinians] attack or despise me in Hebrew, there is something confusing and implausible about it'. Grossman believes that Hebrew can build bridges between the Palestinians and the Jews in Israel; but there is no reason why this should prevent the Palestinians from attacking the Jews in Hebrew, in the same way that Jewish speakers can use the language to attack each other. Grossman reacts in the way he does because the Palestinians, as non-Jewish Israelis, attack him using what he sees as a Jewish language; hence the confusion and the implausibility he talks about. This link between Hebrew and the Jewishness of the state in Israel was, in my view, a major factor in some of the antagonistic reactions to *Arabesques*, a novel in Hebrew by the Palestinian Israeli writer Anton Shammas. Brenner (1993: 434) refers to the 'readerly resistance' with which the novel was met by some Jewish Israeli critics. In Israel, Hebrew is often treated as a metaphor for the security of the nation. By writing in Hebrew, Shammas effectively carried out an act of subversion against the nation and its Jewish character.[15]

[15] Hever (1987: 49) reiterates this point in her analysis of Amos Oz's reaction to Shammas's *Arabesques*: 'The reaction of the Israeli Jewish writer Oz . . . is based in large measure on the historical fact that Hebrew is the language of Zionism, the national liberation movement of the Jewish minority which founded the state of Israel.' She adds (1987: 73):

> Shammas's *Arabesques* places Israeli Jews in an uneasy position. On the one hand, they cannot just dismiss him or ignore him as someone totally Other, especially in the light of his virtuoso command of Hebrew as a literary medium and his vigorous participation in the Israeli mass media as journalist, polemicist, and author. On the other hand,

Some critics attacked Shammas for having trespassed into the Jewish linguistic household, from which they sought to evict him because he dared to inscribe a Palestinian narrative in the in-group language (see Ghanayim 2001).[16] Brenner (1993: 436) articulates this point by saying that 'as Shammas internalizes the creative energy in Hebrew . . . he subversively uses the power gained to dismantle the dogmatic conceptualization of the "holy language"'. Summing these arguments up, Ami Elad-Bouskila (1999: 51), a Jewish Israeli specialist on Arabic literature, says that 'some [Israeli Jewish] critics suggest that by writing in Hebrew, Shammas [was] deliberately defying Israeli linguistic-cultural conventions and mounting a challenge to the dominant Zionist discourse to include Israeli-Arab culture within it'.

Fourth, the linguistic dimension of the Arab–Israeli conflict finds an expression in the educational domain. This is reflected in the differences between the goals of teaching Hebrew and Arabic in the Jewish and Arab schools, the contents of the curricula associated with these languages, the number of hours allocated to them and the proportion of literature to language for each of them in each type of school. Finally, 'peace' between the Arabs and Israel has generated an enhanced instrumental interest in the language of the Other. However, the two languages are still in a state of conflict. As long as this continues, it is unlikely that an integrative interest in the language of the Other will develop (see Abd-el-Jawad and al-Haq 1997; HaCohen 1997).

Arabic as a Jewish language in Israel

The position of Arabic in Israel is complicated by the fact that it is the language of hundreds of thousands of Oriental Jewish immigrants, called Mizrahim, who came to Israel after its establishment in 1948. In comparison with the Ashkenazi (European) Jews, the Mizrahim tend to congregate at the lower end of the socio-economic scale in Israeli society. Coupled with this, their cultural proximity to the Palestinians in Israel endows Arabic, the language of their pre-immigration days, with low social prestige. This has led Ben-Rafael (1994: 209) to characterize

> Shammas's violation of the accepted boundaries of Hebrew culture makes it difficult for Israeli Jews to identify easily with him or adopt him as one of their own . . . The very fact that a novel like *Arabesques* exists at all undermines seriously the traditional view of Hebrew literature as a *Jewish national* literature . . . [The] novel contributes to a process of deterritorialization, challenging the long-standing coincidence of the Hebrew language with its Jewish subject matter.

[16] Shammas (1991: 75) characterizes the relations between Hebrew and Arabic as a 'state of fierce war'.

Arabic as the 'language of the weak', reflecting its impoverished sociolinguistic status in Israeli Jewish society. In another study dealing with bilingualism, Ben-Rafael (2001) compares the positions of English, French, Yiddish and Arabic among Israeli Jews. He sums up the sociolinguistic status of each of these languages by correlating it with the social standing of the group that speaks it as a mother tongue. English is characterized as 'the prestigious language of the privileged', French as 'the prestigious language of the underprivileged', Yiddish as 'a non-prestigious language of a privileged category' and Arabic as the 'non-prestigious language of the underprivileged'.

The characterizations for French and Arabic are interesting in the way they apply to Jews of North African origin. Thus, whereas French is characterized as a prestigious language when correlated with this group, Arabic is described as non-prestigious. This indicates that the status of a language is not dependent on the status of the in-group who are traditionally associated with it. The same applies to Yiddish, but in the reverse order. It is certain that this disjunction between group and language reflects the political and ideological basis of the Israeli Jewish view of Arabic as the language of a backward and hostile enemy.[17] But it is also indicative of the dominant Ashkenazi-centric construction of Israeli Jewish identity. It is this fact that endows the Ashkenazi pronunciation of Hebrew with a higher sociolinguistic value than its Mizrahi counterpart, in spite of the fact that the standard form of Hebrew is based on the pronunciation of the latter for authentication purposes, not least because of the proximity of Hebrew to Arabic.[18] Among Mizrahi Jews, socio-economic advancement therefore tends to be associated with advancement up the sociolinguistic scale, leading to abandonment of the emblematic features of their Mizrahi speech in favour of the Ashkenazi variety. However, in certain situations – for example, during elections – a Mizrahi candidate may use his Mizrahi variety to appeal to voters from this background and, ambiguously at least, to be seen to uphold the standard variety in its capacity as a metaphor for the security of the state. Upholding the Mizrahi form of Hebrew may also be intended to signal to Ashkenazi Jews

[17] The following quotation, from *In the Name of Sorrow and Hope* by Yitzhak Rabin's granddaughter Noa Ben Artzi-Pelossof, explains how deep-rooted this picture is on the Israeli side (1996: 55–6): 'At primary school, we were given lessons to familiarize us with the Arab world – their countries, their mentality, their beliefs, their language and their way of life. It must have been difficult for our teachers to handle these topics objectively, because Arabs provoke such emotional reactions, for good or for bad, among Israelis, even children.'

[18] The extent to which modern Hebrew can be said to be a Semitic language is the subject of a 'revisionist' debate among Israeli linguists. See Kuzar (2001) and Wexler (1990) for this debate.

at such times that they lack the linguistic authenticity of their Oriental compatriots.

Arabic and Hebrew bilingualism among Israeli Jews is subject to the socio-political strains of the linguistic conflict between the two languages. In a study of Romema, a Moroccan Jewish settlement in the northern Negev, Bentolila (2001: 248) claims that members of the community suffer from a 'psychological state of *linguistic insecurity*' (original emphasis). Thus, whereas Hebrew in Romema is considered the language of the Jewish state to which the residents belong, and in which they can fully participate if and when they advance up the social ladder, it is nevertheless considered as the 'language of the rulers' (Ashkenazi Jews) to whom they relate as members of a 'subordinate' group (2001: 254). As far as the Romemites are concerned, Hebrew as *the* language of the state is a means of inclusion into the body of the nation, but it is also an instrument of ethnic exclusion in its dominant Ashkenazi form. This disjunction in the attitude towards Hebrew creates a third space into which Romemites inject Arabic as a 'secret language' of intra-Jewish ethnic exclusion. Bentolila (speaker A) gives the following interesting exchange he had with a sixteen-year-old youth (speaker B) from Romema to illustrate this point (2001: 249):

A: Who, for example, speaks Judeo-Arabic with you?
B: The lads, and also . . .
A: Of your age?
B: Yes, When we don't want that – when we don't want anybody to understand us, then we speak Judeo-Arabic . . . and also my mother . . .
A: That who won't understand?
B: Uhm . . . somebody . . . an Ashkenazi or . . . from another community
A: But among yourselves what do you speak?
B: Mostly Hebrew.

Ben-Rafael (1994) provides two anecdotal pieces of evidence in support of the position of Arabic as a language of intra-ethnic identification among Mizrahi Jews on the group and the individual levels. The first anecdote is related by a young Israeli Jew of Iraqi origin. She recounts how the 'ethnic unrest of the early 1970s [to protest] against the poverty of low-class neighbourhoods of Middle-Eastern Jews' was accompanied at home with an increased use of Arabic, the reappearance of Iraqi meals and an enhanced popularity of Jewish Iraqi music (1994: 85). Arabic in this example is deployed as a symbol of solidarity in a situation of intra-Jewish ethnic conflict. In the second story, a young English-speaking South African immigrant gives the following account of the pattern of code-switching in the home of her Jewish Tunisian boyfriend (1994: 83):

I always wondered why sometimes the parents would speak to the children in French and other times in Arabic. Especially with regard to my boyfriend, I found that the code-switching was phenomenal. In a situation where the mother, my boyfriend and myself were conversing, the mother would speak in Hebrew if she wanted me to understand, in French if she wanted to compliment me without my knowing about it, and in Arabic if she decided to insult me, without my knowing about it either. At first, I would ask my boyfriend what she had said. Now I no longer question what has been said as I judge for myself according to the language that is being spoken.

In this example, Arabic is used as a secret code to signal the status of a speaker as an outsider in an inter-family setting. It is, however, more interesting to note in this context that Arabic is reserved for a low social function, and one that involves disapproval and the expression of low-intensity aggression. Low social prestige and conflict are characteristic of this mode of interaction in which Arabic dominates. This is consistent with one of the findings for Romema in Bentolila's study. Commenting on the use of Arabic for 'swearing and other manifestations of anger', Bentolila writes (2001: 249): 'Expressions of strong emotions, especially of disdain, may bring forth the most vulgar linguistic variant . . . It is in . . . Judeo-Arabic that the adults of Romema insult each other, and these are probably the only conveyances of displeasure that the children of this community have heard since their earliest childhood.' The use of Arabic for swearing is not restricted to Mizrahi Jews. The language serves in this capacity among Ashkenazi Jews too. I once asked a leading Israeli sociolinguist why this was the case. His answer was very revealing. He told me that there were two reasons behind this phenomenon: (1) as a revived language, Hebrew is poor in swear words; and (2) swearing in Hebrew is felt to be taboo because of the 'holiness' attached to the language (*leshon hakodesh*). When I pointed out that similar claims of 'holiness' are made about Arabic in Islam, he was embarrassed and very quickly apologized.[19] The fact that this sociolinguist knew Arabic and wrote about it indicates the extent to which Israeli Jews are desensitized about the stigma attached to Arabic in their society.

The diffusion of Arabic in Jewish schools provides additional information concerning how the low status of the language is related to its socio-political context. Employing Bourdieu's work on the linguistic market,

[19] Commenting on the attitudes towards Arabic and Hebrew in their respective cultures, Patai (1977: 110) wrote:

> Compared to [the] veneration of and attachment to Arabic in the Muslim world, the Jewish position was always a much more flexible one. While the Jews considered Hebrew their Holy Tongue and referred to it as *l'shon haqodesh* (lit. 'language of holiness'), they never clung to it with anything comparable to the fervent, almost sensual, attachment the Arabs had for Arabic.

Ben-Rafael and Brosh (1991) refer to the low capital value of Arabic as a 'backward' and 'useless' language of speakers who are 'hostile towards the Jews'. One of the respondents in their study of a sample of 890 students in the metropolitan Tel Aviv area summed up a predominant attitude among the respondents saying (1991: 14), 'I will not go to an Arab doctor or an Arab tailor, and I won't buy anything in an Arab shop. Why, then, should I learn Arabic?' This negative attitude towards learning the language extends to the parents, the curriculum and the teachers of Arabic who are normally of Jewish background.[20] The study also reveals that many of the respondents opposed the idea of either meeting Arab children, or watching TV in Arabic, or investing personal time to improve their competence in the language. Instead of offering help to a student who is performing badly in Arabic, parents tend to seek an exemption from learning the language.

Teachers of Arabic in the study reported that very few parents ask about the performance of their children in Arabic during parents' evenings, preferring to spend the time standing in long queues to see the teachers of English, French or other school subjects. Students of Arabic and their parents tend to undervalue high performance in the language. Ben-Rafael and Brosh (1991: 14–15) mention how in a 'chat between students overheard after the distribution of report cards at the end of the school year, one of them told his peers about his high grades in English and in maths', but 'when asked about his results in Arabic, he said: "In Arabic I also got an A, but it is of no importance." ' The study also reveals that learning the language does not lead to improving the image of the Arabs among Jews. This is particularly true of Mizrahi respondents, who continue to hold more negative views of the Arabs than do their Ashkenazi counterparts.

This attitudinal difference may be explained by the need among Mizrahi students to distance themselves from the Arabs, who are close to them linguistically, culturally and socio-economically. Ashkenazi-dominated Israeli culture demands that Mizrahim are desocialized of their pre-state Arabic cultural heritage and resocialized by conforming to the norms of the dominant culture.[21] As a result, Arabic is not taught to

[20] See Kinberg and Talmon (1994) for the learning of Arabic by Israeli Jews and the use of Hebrew by the Palestinians in Israel.

[21] Shohat (1989: 116) highlights this feature of Ashkenazi-dominated Zionist ideology by quoting David Ben Gurion, the first prime minister of the Israeli state: 'We do not want Israelis to become Arabs. We are duty bound to fight against the spirit of the Levant, which corrupts individuals and societies, and preserve the authentic Jewish values as they crystallized in the Diaspora.' Abba Eban, one-time Israeli foreign minister, made the same point with greater clarity (Shohat 1989: 117): 'One of the great apprehensions which afflict us is the danger lest the predominance of immigrants [to Israel] of Oriental origin force Israel to equalize its cultural level with that of the neighbouring [Arab] world.'

the Mizrahi students as the language of their heritage, but as the language of the Other – the Arabs, whether inside or outside Israel. Arabic therefore is caught between the devil of an almost non-existent ethnic backing among the Mizrahim and the deep blue sea of the hostility that accrues to it in its capacity as the language of 'aliens' and 'enemies'. These two features of the Israeli setting highlight the conflict-driven view of the language in its socio-political context. Sasson Somekh (see Ghanayim 2001: 181), an Iraqi Jew and an Israeli professor of Arabic literature, sums this up by referring to competence in Arabic, or association with it, among Mizrahi Jews as a 'curse not a blessing' (*niqma lā ni'ma*).

Another interesting feature of this setting is the use of Arabic as a lower-order bond of affiliation among groups of Mizrahi Jews in situations of intra-Jewish ethnic conflict. In Romema, Arabic as a secret code is deployed for this purpose by the Mizrahim to set themselves apart from the Ashkenazi Jews. However, the role of the language in this capacity is subsumed within a domain of identification in which religion (Judaism), not language (Arabic), is the most important common denominator of group membership. The fact that some Jews and non-Jews in Israel share Arabic does not endow the language with the power to override the bond of religious identity among the Jews, particularly because Jews treat Hebrew as their national language and as the primary language of an exclusive religion to which they doctrinally or socially subscribe. Israel represents an almost unique case in the world where religion, language and national identity coincide. In the mind of the dominant group in society, being an Israeli implies being a Jew as well as being a Hebrew speaker. This, in my view, is how the idea arose that Anton Shammas 'transgressed'. By writing *Arabesques* in an excellent Hebrew to which many a Hebrew-speaking Israeli Jew would aspire, Shammas (an Arabic-speaking Palestinian Christian in Israel) did in effect pose a challenge to the triadic relationship between Israeli, Jew and Hebrew speaker.[22] The connection between the first and second categories, which invariably implies a connection to the third, is expressed succinctly in the following dialogue about self-definition by A. B. Yehoshua, one of Israel's most celebrated poets (cited in Rouhana 1997: 230):

- Who are you?
- I am an Israeli.
- No, what nationality? (*Leomiut*)

[22] Shammas declared that one of his aims in writing in Hebrew is to 'deterritorialize' or 'un-Jew' the Hebrew language (1991: 77): 'What I am trying to do is deterritoliaze the Hebrew language, or, more bluntly, to un-Jew the Hebrew language and make it a language of personal narrative discourse.'

– I am an Israeli.
– But also the Arab is an Israeli.
– I am an Israeli in my identity and not only my citizenship.
– But are you a Jew?
– Of course. I just told you that I am an Israeli.

The connection between Israeli and Jew is not part of the literary discourse only. It is also present in the discourse of the geographers. In an article on place names in Israel's ideological struggle over what they call the 'Administered Territories', Cohen and Kliot (1992: 656) wrote: 'For Israelis . . . a name offers instant symbolic meaning, for it evokes an image of the Israelite Kingdom. It is this past that is the idealized Jewish landscape of the Administered Territories.' I will deal with the issue of names in the next section. Suffice it to say here that it is not likely that the 'symbolic meaning' talked about by Cohen and Kliot would be the one that a place name would evoke in the Palestinian citizens of the state of Israel. Even if it does, it is likely that the interpretation or socio-political value given to it would be one that delegitimizes it as a hegemonic imposition from the outside. Such erasure of the Palestinians from academic discourse may not be intentional, but it signals their routine exclusion from the construction of national identity among Israeli Jews.[23]

Mapping the national self, unmapping the Other: the map as a cartographic text

Naming is a linguistic phenomenon in which the decision-making process, the product and its reception interact in a complex manner involving psychology, aesthetics, ideology, politics, history, culture and instrumentality. Although the primary function of a name is to designate a particular entity, human or non-human, its symbolic meaning is normally derived from the set of cultural and ideological values that are associated with it at the points of production and reception. However, discovering the real motivation behind a name is not an easy matter. The same is true of the interpretation given to the name by the receiver. But one thing is certain: the symbolic meaning of a name assumes greater importance in situations of conflict than in conditions of neutral interaction. This is true of place names in the Arab–Israeli conflict where ideological considerations rule supreme, particularly on the Israeli Jewish side, which has shown a remarkable awareness of the power of the map to 'draft a

[23] In cases where the Palestinian is not erased, he is typically constructed as the inferior Other in terms of which the Israeli Jew is defined. See Rabinowitz (2002) for an excellent discussion of this trope in Israeli anthropology. See also Abu El-Haj (2001) for a magisterial study of how this trope is applied in Israeli archaeology.

deed of Jewish ownership' to the land of historical Palestine (Benvenisti 2000: 12). The fact that most of the studies dealing with this topic are produced by Israeli Jews is a reflection of the salience of the map and its associated place names in the symbolic construction of the nation. Studies by Palestinian or Arab authors of maps and place names are very rare indeed. To some extent, this reflects the scarcity of studies that deal with the symbolic construction of Palestinian national identity in the literature (Azaryahu and Kook 2002; Bardenstein 1999).

Zionist understanding of the political power of the map as a model for the nation was apparent from the early days of the British mandate in Palestine. The main battleground was the names the mandate government allocated to places on the map. The two Jewish members on the Geographical Committee for Names in Palestine, which worked under the authority of the Royal Geographical Society, considered the use of the names 'Palestine' and 'Nablus' – instead of Eretz Israel and the biblical name Shechem respectively – as 'an act of discrimination and a searing defeat for Zionism' (Benvenisti 2000: 13), in spite of the fact that the Jews in Palestine at the time constituted only a small proportion of the population.[24] The Zionist opposition to the use of Arabic names on the maps produced by the Jewish National Fund, itself a Zionist organization, reflects the role of the map as a model *for*, rather than a model *of*, the landscape in Zionist ideology.[25] In 1941, before the establishment

[24] In 1931, the government of Palestine published its *Transliterated Lists of Personal and Geographical Names for Use in Palestine*, in which it adopted the Arab names as the norm for designating the landscape. The Zionists campaigned against the lists. In 1932, the Jewish Palestine Exploration Society published their own proposals on naming practices in Palestine, *Memorandum on Methods of Transliteration of Geographical and Personal Names*, intended as a rebuttal of the British proposals. This was accompanied by a political campaign to make the government change its mind. The introduction to the memorandum set out its position on the issue in the following terms (cited in Abu El-Haj 2001: 89):

> This strange tendency to Arabicize Hebrew names is prejudicial to scientific and historical accuracy. It amounts to an offensive distortion of the original forms of Hebrew names as fixed by usage in the Hebrew Scripture and in Talmudic literature, and at the same time it inflicts a gross injury upon the Hebrew language itself. All this is not only sure to outrage the feelings of the Jews of Palestine, but when the book comes to the notice of hundreds of thousands of Jews in the Diaspora, it will provoke them to a feeling of humiliation and distress.

[25] In its *Memorandum on Methods of Transliteration of Geographical and Personal Names* in Palestine, the Jewish Palestine Exploration Society put forward the following suggestions for allocating names to the landscape (cited in Abu El-Haj 2001: 89):

> (1) Each place with an historical name in Hebrew, whether occurring in the Bible or post-biblical literature (e.g. Apocryphal literature, the New Testament, Hellenistic literature, the Mishna, the Talmud, etc.), shall be known by its Hebrew name, even if its present Arabic appellation bears no resemblance to the original Hebrew. Thus, even as the Hebrew uses 'Shechem,' and not 'Nablus'; 'Hebron,' and not 'Khalil'; 'Jerusalem,' and

of the state of Israel, the Settlement Committees of the Hebrew-named Z'vulun Valley wrote to the Jewish National Fund to express this position (Benvenisti 2000: 30):

> The 1:5,000 scale site plan has come into our possession . . . In this plan such names as the following are displayed in all their glory: Karbassa, al-Sheikh Shamali, Abu Sursuq, Bustan al-Shamali – all of them names that the JNF has no interest in immortalizing in the Z'vulun Valley . . . We recommend to you that you send a circular letter to all of the settlements located on JNF land in the Z'vulun Valley and its immediate vicinity and warn them against continuing the above-mentioned practice [i.e. the use of] old maps that, from various points of view, are dangerous to use.

Soon after Israel occupied the Negev in 1949, Ben Gurion established a Negev Names Committee and charged it with the task of assigning 'Hebrew names to all the places – mountains, valleys, springs, roads and so on – in the [newly conquered] region' (Benvenisti 2000: 12). When differences between members of the committee arose concerning how many of the existing Arabic names to preserve for reasons of scientific research and as a democratic gesture towards the Arab population of the state, Ben Gurion wrote to the committee, instructing them: 'We are obliged to remove the Arabic names for reasons of state. Just as we do not recognize the Arabs' political proprietorship of the land, so also we do not recognize their spiritual proprietorship and their names' (Benvenisti 2000: 14). Most members of the committee agreed with him, pointing out that the Arabic names must be eradicated because 'they sound strange to our ears' and signal values at variance with the ethos of Zionist ideology: 'Many of the names are offensive in their gloomy and morose meanings, which reflect the powerlessness of the nomads and their self-denigration in the face of the harshness of nature' (cited in Benvenisti 2000: 17).

The irony is that 333 of the 533 names assigned by the Negev Names Committee were chosen on the basis of their phonetic similarity to the Arabic names they were intended to replace. The committee often justified this decision by arguing that the Arabic names were garbled versions of earlier Hebrew names. By assigning Hebrew names anew to places on the map, the committee was therefore 'redeeming' these places from the corrupt and 'alien' Arabic names that they acquired over the centuries.

not 'el-Quds'; so we should write 'Dor,' and not 'Tantura'; 'Adpraim,' and not 'Dura'; 'Egannim,' and not 'Jenin', etc.; (2) When the Arabic name of a place is derived from the Hebrew it should be written in Hebrew in its original Hebrew name, e.g. 'Ashkelon,' and not 'Asqalan' . . . 'Zippori,' and not 'Saffuriya' . . . 'Beth Degan,' and not 'Beit Dajan,' etc.; and (3) Names not occurring in Hebrew literature, which are adaptable to a Hebrew form with only a change in the vowels and with no change in consonants, should be used in the Hebrew form; e.g. instead of 'Dair Aiyub,' 'Deyr Job'.

The committee also argued that since the Bedouins of the Negev do not normally sink roots in any one place, it follows that the names they give to places should not be allowed to gain cartographic permanence. Zalman Lifshitz, chair of the committee, acknowledged the power of these arguments, but he declared that the whole project was motivated by the political imperatives of the state: 'The Hebraicization of the names has a political intent, and that is the direction in which our deliberations must be channelled. The task that has been laid upon us is fundamentally political. In truth, the whole question of Arabic place-names in the Negev has become irrelevant since there are almost no Bedouin there' (cited in Benvenisti 2000: 18).

The cartographic cleansing of the Negev map of Arabic place names and their replacement by Hebrew names is an enactment of the ethnic cleansing of the Palestinians from their homeland (Benvenisti 2000; HaCohen 1997). This is indirectly acknowledged by Lifshitz, chair of the Negev Names Committee. This policy was applied to the rest of the country later, but was done in such a way that a cartographic palimpsest was created. Two Israeli maps for civilian use were produced in 1956 and 1958; these maps were based on the mandatory map of 1946. The 1956 map inserted the names of the new Israeli settlements in Hebrew. Other features of the landscape were left on the new maps as they had existed before the establishment of the state in 1948. The Hebrew word *harus* (destroyed) was entered next to the names of more than 400 Arab villages that Israel had destroyed. However, all the English renderings in black, of the place names on the 1946 map, were overprinted with Hebrew renderings in violet. This map, with its English renderings of all Arab place names and its use of the Hebrew word *harus* for destroyed Palestinian villages, inadvertently inscribed a cartographic text that was to be lost forever in later Israeli maps. It served to record a narrative that acknowledged what the Palestinians called their *nakba* (catastrophe), the dismemberment of Palestine and the establishment of Israel on the largest part of the country in 1948. The Israeli maps of 1956 and 1958 are important because they represent 'slices through time' (Massey 1995) in which different narratives and histories are juxtaposed.

By removing most of the Arabic place names from the map, Israel did not just create a new map, it also inscribed a new reality in which Hebrew won the battle over Arabic, just as the early Zionists hoped it would in the cartographic domain. The elimination of Arabic place names from the map has also caused the loss of a set of meanings and traditions[26] that express the connection of the Palestinians to the land. Meron Benvenisti,

[26] See Benvenisti (2000: 50–1) for some of these traditions.

the son of a Zionist cartographer in the pre-state era and a deputy mayor of Jerusalem under Teddy Kolek after 1967, expresses this point with a tinge of sadness and guilt (2000: 49): 'The wealth of Arabic toponymy is astounding in its beauty, its sensitivity to the landscape, its delicacy of observation and choice of images. Its metaphors have a poetic quality; its humour is sometimes refined, sometimes sarcastic. The knowledge of the climate, the familiarity with nature and inanimate objects is absolute.'

The struggle over the map of Palestine since the early days of the British mandate represents the meeting point of the conflict between the Palestinians and the (Israeli) Jews in the political, ideological and linguistic arena (Azaryahu 1992; Azaryahu and Kook 2002; Bar-Gal 1989; Cohen and Kliot 1981, 1992). On the Israeli Jewish side the struggle over names is expressed in two ideologically driven tendencies: continuity and change. The former is signalled by the use of the lexical resources of biblical and post-biblical Hebrew to express the continuity of Israel with the mythic construction of its 'national' past. The use of these resources has the added value of signalling the revival of Hebrew in the land which Zionist ideology treats as the inalienable property of the Jewish people. Change is signalled in a number of naming strategies, including the commemorative use of the names of the heroes of the Zionist struggle to establish Israel, or in the use of the names of fauna and flora to express the connection of the Jewish people with the land and to signal a break with their urban nature in the Diaspora. In their study of place names for the settlements in the West Bank and Gaza, Cohen and Kliot (1992) have found that whereas names signalling continuity were more prevalent under Likud-led governments, names signalling change and the assertion of new Zionist values dominated under Labour governments.[27]

[27] Menachem Ussishkin – a member of the Union of Hebrew Teachers and a moving force behind the founding of the Hebrew University in Jerusalem as a 'new national Temple' – signalled the two tendencies of continuity and change in assigning place names to Jewish settlements in Palestine, called colonies in early Zionist literature, as follows (cited in Benvenisti 2000: 27):

> First of all, we must examine them [the names] from a Hebrew-historical point of view. The historical Hebrew names of places in Eretz Israel are the most reliable testimony that these places have been our patrimony from time immemorial and that our rightful claims to these places and to this land are historical and ancient. Therefore, if the [Jewish National Fund] Naming Committee is convinced that a new settlement is located near a place – a place where there was a Jewish settlement during one of the periods when the nation of Israel dwelt in Eretz Israel, but whose name was forgotten in the course of generations or was preserved in a different form by various conquerors, reaching us in its present form, embodied as an Arab village, the remains of a ruin, or an archaeological 'tel', or such like – the committee shall assign to the new or restored settlement the historical Hebrew name of the place in its original form. If the committee is not convinced that the new or restored settlement is located in the vicinity of a place where there was a

The elimination of Arabic names from the map is part of the political-cum-linguistic conflict between the Arabs and the Israeli Jews. The linguistic dimension of this conflict is sometimes manifested in the academic discourse on place names. Examining this meta-linguistic discourse may therefore give us valuable insight into how aspects of the naming process are manipulated to signal a political interpretation of the Arab–Israeli conflict. Since English is the language of wider diffusion through which this is done on the international scene, I will examine a number of works in this language.[28]

The first work is an article by Yoram Bar-Gal, of the University of Haifa, entitled 'Cultural–Geographical Aspects of Street Names in the Towns of Israel', published in the journal *Names* in 1989. Although this article deals with street names before 1948, the official term 'Palestine' is not used to refer to the name of the country in this period. On page 333, a map of the towns the author used in sampling street-name patterns is given; but this map fails to indicate where the borders of the state, the so-called green line, were before the Six Day War in 1967. It therefore gives the impression that the Occupied Territories were part of Israel. Jerusalem is indicated on the map, giving the impression that the city, including the part occupied in 1967, was part of Israel. On page 330, the author writes:

> Some of the Jewish towns, for example Jerusalem, Haifa, Akko and Tiberias have old quarters established before the renewed Jewish settlement of Israel in the late nineteenth century. Others, the veteran towns, were established in the period culminating in 1948 – the end of the British Mandate. Those established after 1948 in the process of population dispersal and the absorption of Jewish immigrants were called 'new' or 'development' towns (Efrat).

> Jewish settlement during a prior period in the history of Israel in its land – the committee shall assign it a name memorializing a personality or a symbolic name.

This is an interesting instruction in the way it sets about giving advice on the symbolic construction of Israel. There is first the view that Jews existed as a nation in pre-modern times. Second, the Palestinian Arabs are treated as conquerors, and therefore non-original inhabitants of the land. Third, Arabic village names act as a guide to the existence of Jewish settlements when they recall biblical and post-biblical Hebrew names. Fourth, these Arab names are distortions of the original Hebrew names. By restoring their correct antecedents, the committee is eliminating the linguistic corruption that the Arabic names represent.

[28] In his study of literature and partition in Ireland and Palestine/Israel, Joe Cleary (2002: 10) comments on the use of English in his field in ways that are applicable in the present context:

> It is also the case in Israel/Palestine, as in Ireland, that a considerable body of literary and intellectual work is written not only with domestic national audiences in mind but out of a concern to explicate the crises in these regions to wider Diaspora and international audiences. English is the medium through which much of this cultural traffic and exchange usually passes, and it is therefore a revealing medium in its own right.

These three sentences are informed by an ideological framework that colours their seemingly scholarly content. First, the first sentence gives the impression that the 'renewed Jewish settlement . . . in the late nineteenth century' took place into Israel, thus ignoring the fact that Israel was established only in 1948. Second, witness the fact that the term 'Palestine' is not used at all, in spite of the fact that this was the standard name of the country until 1948. Third, the first sentence fails to specify that the 'old quarters' in some of the cities it names were – and some still are, as in Acre – dominated by Arabic-speaking Palestinians. Fourth, the first sentence treats occupied East Jerusalem, in whose 'old quarter' the vast majority are still Arabs, as part of Israel. Fifth, the last sentence fails to mention the identity of those who were 'dispersed' in 1948. Furthermore, the term 'population dispersal' describes the depopulation of the Arabs from that part of Palestine on which Israel was established in 1948 in neutral terms. The fact that this narrative of the events leading to the creation of Israel is contested by the Palestinians – and by some Israeli historians – is not acknowledged.

These points show that what is intended to be a scholarly article is in fact steeped in a political ideology whose aim is to deny the existence of the Other by making it invisible. The conflict here is not between languages per se, but between ideologies that employ language – in this case English – for hegemonic purposes to paint a picture of the geographical, political and historical landscape that codifies one view and eliminates its rival. We may exemplify the success of this strategy by considering how Bar-Gal's ideological framework is unwittingly absorbed in a study of the interaction between politics and street names in an Andalusian town (Faraco and Murphy 1997). The authors of this study refer to Bar-Gal to support their own thesis (1997: 125): 'Bar-Gal (1989) reports the complete elimination of most of the English- and Arabic-language street names of Israeli communities following the war of Independence of 1948.' The fact that the Arabic street names in cities such as Haifa before 1948 were used in the Arab – not Jewish – areas of the town is rendered invisible by ascribing these names to 'Israeli communities'. In this formulation, 'Israeli communities' must refer to Jewish communities, for why would the Palestinians in Haifa eliminate the Arabic names of the streets of their own volition? Bar-Gal's ideologically driven study of street names telescopes history and casts it in a Zionist framework, and it is this that Faraco and Murphy unwittingly absorb and promote in their study of street names in a different context.

Let us pursue how place names are manipulated in academic discourse by considering another example: an article entitled 'Place-Names in Israel's Ideological Struggle over the Administered Territories' by

Saul Cohen and Nurit Kliot,[29] published in *Annals of the Association of American Geographers* in 1992. The use of 'Administered Territories' in the title, instead of the more correct term 'Occupied Territories', immediately announces the ideology underlying the 'scholarly' content of the article. However, although the label 'Administered Territories' dominates in this study, the authors use other terms to refer to these territories or parts thereof. The following is a set of the labels and convoluted descriptions used to refer to these territories: Administered Territories; the territories captured by Israel in the Six Day War of 1967; the territories conquered by Israel in June 1967; the Territories; the territories; the West Bank (Judea and Samaria); the West Bank; Judea and Samaria; Administered (Occupied) Territories; the Occupied Territories.[30] The latter term, which derives from the UN resolution 242, is used once only in spite of the fact that it is the only term that defines the legal status of the so-called 'Administered Territories'. The term 'Occupied' is used once and then only as a *gloss* for the term 'Administered', thus favouring the latter term over its former counterpart. The multiplicity of terminologies in the article is no doubt intended to satisfy different political and ideological imperatives, but it ultimately has the effect of making the Israeli occupation of the Occupied Territories almost invisible. As a matter of fact, quantitatively – in terms of frequency – the 'names/labels' in the article promote a view of the legality of occupation over its indisputable illegality.

This ideological position is signalled in other labels used by the authors. In discussing the place-name patterns in Palestine/Israel, the authors refer to three periods: the 'Pre-state' period before 1948, 'Old Israel' for Israel between 1948 and 1967, and 'Greater Israel' for Israel after 1967. This set of labels expresses a seamless transition between the second and third labels that defies international legality. In addition, the transition to the second period is from a 'nameless' pre-state period that

[29] Cohen's institutional affiliation is given as Hunter College, New York. Nurit Kliot is a geographer from Haifa University, Israel.

[30] See HaCohen (1997: 397) for the history and political ideologies associated with these terms. The general avoidance of 'occupation' in describing the West Bank and Gaza is part of an official policy which finds expression in the 1985 version of the Guidelines for Broadcasting News and Current Affairs, which, under a heading entitled 'The limits of objectivity', says the following: 'The territories in the west Land of Israel that have been under Israeli control since June 1967 are to be called Judea and Samaria. The terms "The Bank" and "The West Bank" are prohibited' (cited in HaCohen (1997: 400)). The term the 'Land of Israel' in this context does not refer to the state as such, but to the land of the Jews, whether they are Israeli citizens or not. The 1995 version of these guidelines reiterates the prohibition on the use of the term 'West Bank', which is described as 'an obsolete Jordanian term' (HaCohen 1997: 405). This view of the status of the West Bank in Israeli state ideology means that the Israeli army 'evacuation' from any part of the Occupied Territories cannot be described as 'withdrawal' but as 'deployment' or 'redeployment'.

eliminates Palestine to a named second period that inscribes Israel. Ironically, the only time the term 'Occupied Territories' is used in the article is in defining Greater Israel as consisting of Old Israel plus the 'Occupied Territories'. The fact that Arab East Jerusalem is part of the Occupied Territories is denied by the references to the city which make it part of Israel, although it is not clear which Israel it is a part of: Old or Greater Israel. Furthermore, by using the term 'settlement' in its standard geographical sense to refer to both the illegal Israeli Jewish settlements in the Occupied Territories and the indigenous Arab villages in these territories, the authors de-politicize the geography of the landscape by decanting it into neutral terminological receptacles. At best, the net effect of these terminological practices is to confuse the reader. At worst, they are intended to write the occupation out of the Occupied Territories. Either way, Cohen and Kliot's terminology is not free of ideological bias in spite of the 'scientific trappings' into which this terminology is embedded.

The idea that academic or scholarly discourse often reflects the ideological presuppositions and political convictions of the author, particularly in situations of conflict, is not new. In fact, the construction of the author's identity in academic writing is not an esoteric subject (see Ivanic 1997). What is interesting about the two examples I have dealt with, however, is their subject matter (place names) and the scholarly identity of the authors (political geographers). Within these constraints, one expects a greater awareness of the bias that ideology and politics may impart to scholarly discourse, particularly in the choice of names. This is clearly an unfulfilled expectation. To illustrate the extent to which ideology and politics interact with scholarly discourse, I will examine one study whose subject matter lies at the centre of the present work: *The Languages of Jerusalem* (1991) by Bernard Spolsky (Bar-Ilan University) and Robert Cooper (Hebrew University of Jerusalem), two leading scholars on various aspects of linguistic theory.[31]

The opening sentence on the front flap of the dust jacket sets the tone for the book: 'The locus of this study of language knowledge and use is the Old City of Jerusalem, a complex microcosm of Israeli Society and a focus of conflict of all known history.' Here the Old City is treated as part of Israel, although, as I have said earlier, its legal status under UN resolution 242 is that of an occupied city. It is also not true that the Old City is a microcosm of Israeli society, for if that were the case one would be entitled to conclude that Israel is a predominantly Arab country because of the demographic ascendance of the Palestinians in it (the Old City). This ideological way of speaking is reflected in two formulations the authors use to avoid referring to occupation: 'Politically, the Old City

[31] Some of the points made in this study are repeated in Spolsky (1993).

is part of Jerusalem; it was incorporated into Israel after 1967' (1991: 3); and 'After Israel captured East Jerusalem in 1967 . . .' (1991: 121). Most of the time, the Old City is treated as part of Israel in a matter-of-fact way. By choosing to present the political context of the sociolinguistic situation in the Old City in this fashion, the authors diminish the role of intergroup/nation conflict in explaining this situation.

In fact, it is not until page 114 of the book (out of 151 text pages) that intergroup/nation conflict is brought actively into the analytical framework of the book. For the most part, the sociolinguistic situation in the Old City is described in a manner which does not give full justice to the contemporary politics of the place. This situation is also described in terms of a structure, a para-text, which gives undue emphasis to Jews and Hebrew over Palestinians and Arabic, although the authors tell us in a few places in their book that Arabic was the majority language in the Old City in the nineteenth century, and that it is still the majority language now. An example of this hegemonic way of describing the language situation is the use of the Hebrew borrowed term *shuk* (1991: 8), instead of the Arabic *sūq* or the borrowed English term *souk* or *suq*, to describe the language of the marketplace in the Old City where Arabic is the native language par excellence.

Since Arabic is the language of the majority of the population of the Old City, as the authors themselves point out and as their data indicate, one would expect the book to take full account of this fact. Instead, the book proceeds in a way which gives prominence to Jews and Jewish languages over the Palestinians and the Arabic language. In the first chapter, entitled 'The socio-linguistics of the Old City in the 1980s', Arabic is said to be the 'most common language', followed by Hebrew and English (1991: 1). However, the description of the modern and Palestinian-dominated geography of the city defines it for the most part in terms of ancient Jewish features.[32] This is in effect an archaeological description of the city rather

[32] This is how Spolsky and Cooper describe the geography of the city (1991: 1):

> The line [of the Ottoman-built] walls includes the Temple Mount in the east, now under Muslim control; it excludes the original City of David (about 1000 BCE), now occupied by part of the village of Silwan in the South, and cuts Mount Zion in two. The Western Wall of the Old City is close to the Line of the original Herodian Wall (about 30 CE), and divides the Old City from the new Jewish city that arose in the nineteenth and twentieth centuries. The northern wall sets off the fourth side of the rough square, following a line that also dates from the Herodian period and that divides the Old City from the newer Arab central and suburban areas.

The references to the Temple Mount, City of David and Western Wall define the modern geography of the Old City archeologically by reference to Jewish landmarks in a way which erases the centuries of continued Arab and Muslim settlement in Jerusalem. Witness also the reference to the 'new Jewish city' which ignores its mixed Palestinian–Jewish makeup.

than a modern one that a person would be able to identify immediately on an ordinary map. This Jewish-dominated archaeological description sets the scene for what follows. It signals a mode of analysis in which particular features of the sociolinguistics of the city are privileged over more pervasive ones.

Chapter 2 (pp. 18–33) is entitled 'Jewish multilingualism'. The chapter describes the various languages used by Jewish communities in historical Palestine, not just Jerusalem, from 'two millenniums ago' (p. 18). The justification for this is that such information is necessary to 'understand the present socio-linguistic situation of Jerusalem in its fullest historical context' (p. 18). To say the least, this is a very spurious justification. It is not at all clear why a description of the presumed sociolinguistics of an ancient Jerusalem, that most probably is not geographically coterminus with the Old City of the 1980s, can be descriptively or analytically relevant. Surely one does not have to deal with the ancient past at such length to make the point that Jerusalem has throughout its history been multilingual. The languages dealt with in this chapter are Hebrew, Aramaic, Greek and Latin, the last three of which are largely irrelevant to understanding the sociolinguistics of the Old City in the present. Furthermore, the title of the chapter conflates the multilingualism of the Jews in the city 'two millenniums ago' with the multilingualism of the city itself. Was the city at the time totally Jewish? Were there non-Jews in the city, and in what proportions? These and other questions must be answered before one can confidently conflate the multilingualism of the Jews in Jerusalem with the multilingualism of the city itself.

Chapter 3 (pp. 34–48) carries the title 'The socio-linguistics of old Jerusalem: non-Jewish languages in the late nineteenth century'. The jump from 'two millenniums ago' to the late nineteenth century is a major leap in historical terms, but this is left unexplained. This is astonishing, considering the fact that we have ample records which can guide us in describing the language situation in the city in this intervening period of almost 2,000 years. The chapter deals with the following languages: spoken Arabic, Classical Arabic, Turkish, Greek, Latin, French, Armenian, English and German. By referring to these languages, including Arabic in spite of its being the majority language, as the 'non-Jewish' languages of old Jerusalem, the authors establish them as the marked or derived category, with the Jewish languages acting as the unmarked yardstick by which the identity of a language is defined. Jewishness is the principle of linguistic classification here. Witness also the fact that the authors' description of the Arabic language situation covers six pages only (middle of page 38 to middle of page 43), and that the focus in this description is on the use of the languages by the Jewish population in the city, some of whom must have used it natively[33] and may in fact have conceptualized their own identity in relation to it under specific situational triggers. The remaining languages had a small or formal presence in the city; for example, Greek and Latin were mainly liturgical languages. However, by putting these languages on a par with Arabic in the classificatory schema of the book, Arabic somehow participates in their marginality.

Chapter 4 (pp. 49–56) is entitled 'The socio-linguistics of old Jerusalem: Jewish languages in the late nineteenth century'. The languages dealt with in this chapter are Judezmo, Hebrew and Yiddish only. Although (Judaeo) Arabic was in fact the major Jewish language in the Old City in the nineteenth century (see Piamenta 1992), it is not treated as a Jewish language. Because Arabic in Palestine was the language of the Arabs, both Christians and Muslims, it is judged by the authors as a non-Jewish language against the fact that it was the universal language of the indigenous Palestinian Jewry.[34] Chapter 5 (pp. 57–73) is entitled: 'The revitalization and spread of Hebrew'. As its title indicates, the chapter deals with Hebrew and its battle for supremacy over the other languages

[33] There is ample evidence to support this interpretation of Jewish multilingualism in Jerusalem, even among Jews who, before the establishment of the state, lived outside the city wall. Witness the description of the multilingualism of one Yitshaq Aroh (1896–1972), recordings of whose speech (made in 1953) were analysed by the Israeli linguist Moshe Piamenta (1979: 263):

> [Yitshaq Aroh] was a cotton teaser by profession, an illiterate bi-cultured multilingual who resided in the Montefiore quarter of Jerusalem [outside the Old City's walls, off Jaffa Gate]. Like most inhabitants there, he spoke local Judeo-Espanol as home tongue, but prayed and conversed in Hebrew with Jews who spoke neither Judeo-Espanol nor Arabic, especially of the younger generation. With Arabs or Jews who spoke local or some other Arabic dialect he spoke Arabic fluently, missing dialectal features. He understood Yiddish, but did not speak it. His mother descended from a family that had emigrated from Damascus in the 19th century. This explains the tinge of Damascus Arabic in his speech . . . His substandard Jerusalem Arabic is typical of the final stages of native Arabic spoken by sectors of the Jewish community in Jerusalem.

This description makes it clear that: (1) Yitshaq Aroh was bilingual in Judeo-Espanol and Arabic; (2) he was less fluent in Hebrew, which he used for religious purposes and with Jews who could not speak either of his two dominant languages; and (3) that his Arabic repertoire extended beyond his native Jerusalem Arabic. In fact, the two texts analysed by Piamenta show clear examples of the Damascene dialect, which may indicate that this colloquial was Yitshaq Aroh's 'real' mother tongue in Arabic.

[34] Piamenta writes (1992: 81): 'Up to the 1880s the Sephardim were the dominant Jewish group in Jerusalem', and (1992: 83): 'Jerusalem Judaeo-Arabic was characteristic of the Jews of the city' for whom it was the 'lingua franca'. He also writes (1992: 82): '[Ashkenazi Jews in Jerusalem] were foreign nationals protected by the European powers which had established consular representation in [the city], viz., Russia, France, Great Britain, Germany, Austria-Hungary and Italy.'

which the Jews brought with them to Palestine.[35] The combined total of these two chapters is twenty-six pages, whereas Arabic thus far in the book is allocated six pages only, most of which are devoted to Judeo-Arabic. Although Arabic is given more space in the rest of the book, the emphasis on Hebrew continues to dominate.

This discrepancy between the space allocated to Arabic, the majority language in the Old City, and to the other languages, including Hebrew, can be explained only by reference to the ideological underpinnings that inform the researchers. I am not claiming that there is an intentional political bias in the book, but that a particular (Zionist) ideology dominates the structure of the research, its underlying plan, in such a way that Arabic as the majority language in the Old City is made to look like a minority language. This impression is consistent with the terminology the authors use to locate the Old City politically in Israel and to describe its geography in such a way that what is Palestinian and Arabic is suppressed in favour of what is Jewish and Hebrew.

The Languages of Jerusalem is an extremely interesting work, not just because it gives evidence that the academic lexicon in sociolinguistic research can be considered an ideological way of speaking, but also because the structure of the book itself, its para-text, enacts this way of speaking. *The Languages of Jerusalem* is doubly ideological, in both its content and its form. In spite of its scholarly achievements, the book provides an ideological way of looking at the language situation in the Old City of Jerusalem as part of the conflict between the Arabs/Palestinians and Israel on the political and linguistic fronts. The authors do not eliminate Arabic from the map of Jerusalem, but they certainly depress its importance relative to Hebrew and the other Jewish languages. The unwary reader could therefore be excused for thinking, after finishing the book, that the Old City of Jerusalem is a predominantly Jewish and Hebrew-speaking city, thus leaving the presence of Arabic and its mode of interaction with Hebrew not fully explained. One of the main insights of sociolinguistics is the treatment of language as a resource of political contestation. Here we have an extension of this principle whereby the academic study of languages in conflict situations itself becomes – whether intentionally or unintentionally is irrelevant – an instrument of political contestation. Further studies of sociolinguistics as a form of

[35] See Paulston et al. (1993) for a critique of the term 'revitalization' as it is applied to Hebrew in Spolsky and Cooper (1991). Paulston et al. distinguish between language revival, language revitalization and language reversal. Modern Hebrew is regarded as a paradigm case of revival.

scientific inquiry in practice are needed to yield more insights on how politics and ideology permeate what purports to be objective academic discourse.

Awareness of place names as linguistic artefacts with an ideological content, and the realization that the Arab–Israel conflict knows no linguistic frontiers, have made English, as the language of international communication and scholarship, a primary medium for pursuing this conflict. An example of this is the battle over names that accompanied the Israeli plans in 1998 to build an illegal settlement, to the south of the Old City, on a hilltop called Jabal Abu-Ghneim in Arabic (lit. Abu-Ghneim's mountain). The Israeli authorities called the settlement Har Homa, and it is this term that eventually won the battle of names in the international media. The project to build this settlement – called a 'neighbourhood' of Jerusalem by Netanyahu who served as Israel's prime minister at the time – came to the attention of the British and international media during a visit to the site by Robin Cook, the then foreign secretary in the Labour government in Britain.

In an article about Cook's visit in the Anglican newspaper *Church Times* (20 March 1998), Gerald Butt, BBC correspondent in Jerusalem, described the planned settlement as follows: 'Har Homa, a controversial new Jewish construction project in Arab East Jerusalem'; 'Har Homa – or Jabal Abu-Ghneim, as it is called by the Palestinians'; 'Jabal Abu-Ghneim/Har Homa'; and 'Jabal Abu-Ghneim'. The first three descriptions of the settlement project are used when Robin Cook or the Foreign Office is the originator of the sentence; the last term is used in a sentence whose author is a Palestinian Christian; it therefore has the status of a quotation. Butt performs a fine balancing act in which international legality is sacrificed in favour of political expediency. In the same issue of *Church Times*, Stephen Sizer – a British cleric and long-time campaigner on behalf of the Palestinians – contributed an article in which the following descriptions of the settlement site are used: 'Abu-Ghneim' (six tokens); 'Har Homa' (three tokens); 'Jabal Abu-Ghneim – or Har Homa, as the Israelis call it', which is the reverse of the first usage by Gerald Butt; and 'Jabal Abu-Ghneim/Har Homa'. It is unlikely that Sizer would have used Har Homa on its own to refer to the site. If this is the case, we must treat its use in his article as a balancing intervention by an editor.[36] Evidence for this, showing the political and ideological importance of naming practices in the Arab–Israeli conflict, is in fact found in the article itself:

[36] The caption under a picture of Robin Cook in the article refers to the settlement as 'Har Homa'.

Israeli Officials and newspapers now use only the Hebrew name of the site, Har Homa. This is more than simply a translation from Arabic into Hebrew. Like thousands of other locations in Israel and the Occupied Territories, the site will be cleansed of its former Arab associations and retain only an Israeli identity . . . This process may sound phoney, but it has proved highly successful. Hebrew's links to the Bible enable the Israelis to reconstruct history in accordance with Zionism. Christian Zionists naively equate contemporary Israel with biblical Israel. When Jabal Abu-Ghneim becomes Har Homa in the Israeli consciousness, it will also become part of the nation's inheritance to be defended at all costs. And the world will forget Jabal Abu-Ghneim soon enough.

Sizer's prediction in the last sentence came to pass sooner than expected. On 22 March 1998, I wrote to Robin Cook to support his courageous stand against the Jabal Abu-Ghneim settlement, which earned him the wrath of hardline Israelis (see appendix 1). In my letter, I used the Arabic name of the site once, but not the Hebrew term. However, the reply I received from the Foreign and Commonwealth Office, dated 2 April 1998 (appendix 2), eliminated all reference to Jabal Abu-Ghneim and used the Hebrew name Har Homa throughout (four times). The fact that the official who signed the letter has an Arab/Muslim name makes the response very interesting indeed. One would have expected a person with such a name to be particularly aware of the ideological dimension of the terminology of the Arab–Israeli conflict. The fact that this is not the case may be because the author of the letter was using Foreign Office-speak, hence official terminology, for the settlement site. The importance of names as an instrument of shaping the political agenda and the ideological landscape in the Arab–Israeli conflict has been commented on several times by the veteran Middle East correspondent Robert Fisk, who writes for the British newspaper *The Independent* (10 June 1998 and 4 August 2001). In another article published on 3 September 2001, Robert Fisk wrote:

Just as the BBC last month ordered its reporters to use the phrase 'targeted killings' for Israel's assassination of Palestinians, CNN – under constant attack from right-wing Jewish pro-settler lobby groups – has instructed its journalists to stop referring to Gilo [an illegal settlement in the occupied West Bank] as a 'Jewish Settlement' . . . The instruction from CNN's headquarters in Atlanta is straightforward. 'We refer to Gilo as "a Jewish neighbourhood on the outskirts of Jerusalem, built on land occupied by Israel in 1967".'[37]

The interest in names as ideologically loaded linguistic artefacts is an important feature in the Israeli Jewish milieu. The significance of this

[37] Even if we choose to ignore the fact that this description creates a false equation between the 'legal' and the 'illegal', its convoluted wording undermines the demand for brevity in news construction.

phenomenon is not restricted to place names. Mapping the nation by conferring Hebrew names on the landscape is mirrored in the personal domain by the act of giving the new immigrant to Israel a new name to signal a process of self-transformation and initiation into Israeli Hebrew culture. In her book on *dugri* (talking straight) speech in Israeli sabra culture, Tamar Katriel (1986: 19) refers to the adoption of the new name as a 'memorable moment' for the immigrant.[38] This interest in names makes Israeli Jews very aware of the ideological dimension of any perceived infringement of their own linguistic map.[39] The following two stories help explain this.

The *Jewish Chronicle* reported in its issue of 1 February 2002 that the communications giant Motorola had to apologize to Israel because it listed its contact number in Palestine but not in Israel. For this perceived infringement Motorola was accused of seeking to 'remove Israel from the world map'. The *Jewish Chronicle* issue of 19 July 2002 reports a similar incident. The 'offending' organization this time was Air France, whose pilot on a Paris-to-Tel Aviv flight announced that his plane was about to land in 'Israel/Palestine'. This announcement angered a number of Israeli companies, including Bezek (the state communication firm with a workforce of 8,500 people), which mounted a boycott of Air France and, in addition to an apology, demanded that the pilot be named and immediately sacked. These two incidents indicate the importance attached to names, on the Israeli Jewish side, in the execution of the Arab–Israeli conflict. In particular, they show the extent to which any 'infringement' of the linguistic-cum-ideological map of Israel as a Jewish nation will be resisted. And if that means denying the Palestinians any of the trappings of statehood at the linguistic level, then so be it.[40] We may therefore ask

[38] Katriel recalls this experience in her early childhood in moving terms (1986: 20):

> One of my own earliest memories is of the day when, as a five-year-old newcomer to Israel, I was told to choose between two Hebrew-sounding names to replace the Yiddish name I had been given at birth in memory of a grandmother I would never know. I can clearly remember the scene: I was standing in the hall of my aunt's small apartment, my back pressed against the rough surface of her wardrobe, encircled by the adults in the family, who were glaring down at me: 'What will it be, Tamar or Ruth?' I remember clumsily trying to roll the foreign sounds on my unaccustomed tongue, and, finally, exhausted by the piercing, expectant stares, I heard myself pronounce 'Tamar'.

[39] See Zerubavel (1991: 197) for an interesting discussion of the role of names in Israeli Zionist discourse.

[40] Examples of this occur in the Israeli Guidelines for Broadcasting News and Current Affairs (1985), including the prohibition on referring to the 'Heads of the PLO' as 'prominent persons' (Hebrew *ishim*) because of the 'connotations of honour and importance' this term has. This extends to using the 'PLO-flag' instead of the 'flag of Palestine' (see HaCohen 1997: 404). Even after the signing of the Oslo Accords with the Palestinians in 1993, the guidelines of 1995 contained instructions which demanded removing

whether this interest in names as artefacts of ideological contestation is reciprocated on the Arab and Palestinian side?

Every action has a reaction

Interest in the importance of language and its application in naming practices is evident among the Palestinians in Israel. Arabic newspapers in Israel report on name changes in the Occupied Territories and link their news stories to the ideological and political imperatives of the state. *Kul al-Arab*, a Nazareth-based newspaper, published a story in its issue of 16 April 1999 in which it reported the denunciation by the Higher Islamic Council in Jerusalem of the decision by the Israeli authorities to change the name of an Islamic building complex (Ribāṭ al-Kurd) to Hebrew. The report made a direct link between the name change and the policy of the government of Israel to Judaize Jerusalem institutionally and demographically by, among other things, closing down Palestinian quasi-national institutions and withdrawing the identity papers of native Palestinian residents of the city. In its issue of 28 May 1999, the newspaper published an article in which it rejected the use of the compound Hebrew–Arabic term 'Urshalim al-Quds' to refer to the whole of Jerusalem. The newspaper asked its readers sarcastically in the headline to the article: 'Have you heard of a city whose name is Urshalim-al-Quds?' The newspaper attacked the state-owned Arabic radio and TV service for using this and other place names – for example, Judea and Samaria – calling it a Hebrew-through-Arabic service because it diffuses Hebrew-based state ideology through the Arabic language. The highly respected Israeli Palestinian journalist Salman Natour carried out a similar attack on the name 'Urshalim al-Quds' in the 16 April 1999 issue of the Haifa-based *al-Ittihad* newspaper. Natour reminded his readers that names in Israel are ideologically loaded linguistic constructs whose purpose is to promote the politics of the state. He then called on the Palestinian Authority, as the representative of the Palestinians, to promote the name al-Quds in the international arena because the English name Jerusalem has now come to signify a unified city under Israeli authority.

The importance of names in the Arab–Israeli conflict, especially in Jerusalem, is recognized by Rashid Khalidi in his excellent book *Palestinian Identity: The Construction of Modern National Consciousness*

the term 'National' from the Palestinian National Authority (PNA) in Hebrew. In the same guidelines, ministers in the Palestinian Cabinet are not to be referred to by this term, but as 'holders of a portfolio in the Palestinian Authority', and the Palestinian flag may be referred to as the 'PLO flag' or the 'Palestinian flag' (*ha-degel ha-palestini*), but not as the 'flag of Palestine' (*degel palestin*). See HaCohen (1997: 407) for other examples.

(1997). Khalidi comments on the oppositional sets of names for the city and some of its most important landmarks between the Palestinians and the Israeli Jews: *Bayt al-Maqdis* (house of sanctity) and *al-Quds al-Sharif* (noble/holy sanctuary) *versus Yerushalaim* (city of peace); *al-Haram al-Sharif* (noble sanctuary) *versus Temple Mount*; *al-Buraq Wall* versus the *Wailing* or *Western Wall*. This conflict extends to the names *Filastin* (Palestine) *versus Israel* as designations for the country which each group sees as its homeland. Khalidi (1997: 14) is right when he declares that 'although such measures may seem petty, they are related to the significant process of attempting to signal control by imposing place names'. As I have pointed out earlier, these names are ideological ways of speaking whose purpose is to press a territorial and political claim by linguistically mapping the national self on the landscape and unmapping the Other. As means of symbolic enunciation, these names are more than labels with a utilitarian and instrumental function: they are the substance from which the national self is inscribed on the grids of the map as a text of the nation.

We may exemplify this in relation to the plan by the Israeli-controlled municipality of Jerusalem to give street names to parts of East Jerusalem. The Israeli authorities expanded the limits of the occupied city after 1967 to include some of the nearby Palestinian villages and suburbs. One such suburb was Beit Hanina to the north, on the way to Ramalla. The director of the Beit Hanina 'neighbourhood council' in the mid-1980s was Ziyad Darwish, a Palestinian Israeli from the Galilee who had recently moved to the area. The municipality contacted him to ask for a list of names to be considered for use in Beit Hanina. Here is how Cheshin et al.[41] (1999: 146–7) tell the rest of the story:

It was several weeks before the list was sent to the city. As municipal officials reviewed the list, they slowly began to understand its significance. All the names were of Arab villages that had existed before 1948 but were destroyed by Israel during the [1948] war: Umm Rashrash, Banias, Majdal, Askalan, Yaffa, Pluga and others. The municipality contacted Darwish, and he unabashedly explained the neighbourhood council's idea: 'We see the map of Beit Hanina as representing that of all Palestine,' Darwish said: 'In the north of Beit Hanina, we will give the streets names of the villages that once stood in northern Palestine, in the west of the neighbourhood, the roads will have the names of the villages that once stood in the west of Palestine and so on.' Darwish was told to try again. The municipality would not accept such an expression of Palestinian nationalism on the streets of the city. 'You'd be better off choosing names of flowers and trees,' Darwish was told. 'You can also include great Arab figures, but stick to poets and writers, not conquerors. Do us a favour and include a short biography with each figure chosen. It would be good if you mentioned if he had any connection to Jerusalem.' The municipality had a names Committee that had the final say on such matters

[41] Amir Cheshin is a retired Israeli army colonel who served as senior adviser on Arab community affairs and assistant to former Jerusalem mayor Teddy Kolek.

as new street names. In those years [the mid-1980s], committee members were known to be on the whole from right-wing parties that were suspicious about any Arab names and would want to know details about the candidate's relation to the Jews. Darwish got the picture of what he was up against. He followed the new orders to the letter, and the second list of flowers and trees and Arab poets he presented to city hall was approved by the names Committee with hardly a peep.

This is a fascinating story. It stands as a superb act of cartographic *re*-membering, and this is why I quoted it in full. It clearly shows the power of the symbolic meaning of street and place names in situations of political conflict. The attempt by the Beit Hanina community council to inscribe a map of Palestine on their streets represents a bold attempt at challenging the hegemonic ideology of the state and its narrative of the modern history of Palestine. The suggested list constitutes a map of history and, as such, it is intended to give cartographic expression to the collective memory of the Palestinians. The fact that it was spearheaded by an Israeli Palestinian in the part of Palestine that was occupied after 1967 signals the unity of the Palestinians as a people. These meanings were not lost on the names committee, which insisted on a different list. The Beit Hanina community council must have been aware that their list would be rejected, but it is reasonable to assume that their aim in suggesting the list was to make a point: to remind the Israeli authorities, as represented by the municipality, that the past is not forgotten and that Beit Hanina is imagined as a microcosm of the whole of Palestine. The Beit Hanina council was effectively saying to the city authorities that the state can destroy their towns and villages but it cannot eliminate the memory of these places and the mental map on which they are indelibly inscribed.

Cheshin et al. give another example which shows the importance of street names as the carriers of politically impregnated meanings. The example relates to the Palestinian village of Beit Safafa (on the outskirts of Jerusalem), which in 1948 was divided in half between Israel and Jordan. Relying on municipality records, Cheshin et al. tell the following story (1999: 147):

Israel learned the hard way that it could not unilaterally choose a name for a road in East Jerusalem without consulting the residents, or at least looking for a name that would appeal to them. For example, city hall decided that the road running where a fence once divided east and west Beit Safafa between 1948 and 1967 should be named the Unification of the City Street. Residents, who rejected the 'unification' of Jerusalem under Israeli authority, strongly opposed the street name. When the municipality put up a Unification of the City Street sign, it was ripped down by residents. Not to be bullied, the city authorities reposted the sign, at which point demonstrations broke out in Beit Safafa and the sign was pulled down and set on fire. At that point municipal officials decided to reconsider the name, and instead of doing it unilaterally, they consulted with village leaders. An agreement was reached. The road would be called Unification of the Village

Street instead of Unification of the City [Street]. That Beit Safafa was no longer divided in two by a fence was a good thing, both the city authorities and the residents agreed. A new street sign was put up, at a small ceremony attended by city officials and village leaders.

Here we have an excellent example of how street names can serve as a site for challenging the power of the state and its hegemonic ideology. The contest over the name of the street in Beit Safafa is a proxy for a larger struggle between two conflicting national ideologies and two competing narratives of the recent history of Jerusalem. To cast the 'unification' component in the street name in relation to Beit Safafa is of little symbolic consequence to the Palestinians. Beit Safafa does not have the emblematic power in the construction of Palestinian national identity that Jerusalem possesses. This is why the 'Unification of the Village Street' is tolerated as a place name in Beit Safafa to avoid confrontation with a superior enemy.

Umm al-Fahm, a Palestinian border town inside the green line, exemplifies a strong awareness of the role of street names in enunciating political ideology. When the town council set about allocating names to its streets in 1993 (Azaryahu and Kook 2002), it chose names with strong Arabo-Islamic resonance to signal the ideology of the dominant Islamic group in the town hall. Some of these names referred to early battles in Islam – including al-Khandaq, in which the early Arab Muslims fought the Jews of Medina for failing to keep the pledges they made to the Prophet. Names commemorating Arab rule in Spain were chosen, no doubt because of their strong nationalist connotations in modern Palestinian consciousness. Another interesting name is that of Baybars, the Mamluk sultan (1228–77) who contributed substantially to the elimination of the Crusader presence in Palestine. Considering the resonance of the Crusades in Arab and, especially, modern Palestinian consciousness, the symbolic meaning of this name will not have been lost on the residents of Umm al-Fahm. More significant in this respect is the use of the name of the Palestinian national hero Izz al-Din al-Qassam, who fell in battle at the hand of the British in 1935.[42] The fact that al-Qassam had as his aim fighting the Zionist project in Palestine indicates a commitment in the

[42] Pinchevski and Torgovnik (2002: 386) report another attempt to use the name of this Palestinian figure in a Palestinian town in Israel, Kufr Qar':

> In July 1996, the municipal council of the Arab-Israeli town Kafar-Kara decided to commemorate the mythological Muslim warrior 'Az-El-Din El-Kassam'. The act, probably initiated to attract public attention to the poor financial situation of the municipality, caused a torrent of commentary and even resulted in a special discussion in the Knesset, held on 14 January 1998, in which the Minister of the Interior claimed he had known about another initiative to commemorate the name of the Hamas suicide-terrorist Ichia [Yahya?] Ayash. Both cases were then passed to legal investigation.

Umm al-Fahm town hall to inscribe a Palestinian narrative of courage, resistance and martyrdom.[43] The project of creating a town-text, through the map of Umm al-Fahm, to inscribe a Palestinian narrative against the hegemonic power of the state is a reflection of the rising interest among the Palestinians in exploiting the power of cartography in pursuing their claims over the landscape. It is in the coalescence of these factors that place names, as linguistic artefacts, can be fully appreciated.

Interest in the importance of names as constructs of national identity and as the means of laying a claim of authentic proprietorship over the indigenous landscape is the subject of Mustafa Murad al-Dabbagh's book *al-Mamlakatān al-nabātiyya wa-l-ḥayawāniyya fī bilādina filasṭīn wa-atharuhā fī tasmiyat amkinatihā* (The plant and animal kingdoms in our homeland Palestine and their reflection in its place names, 1985). In a short preface, the author states that the aim of the book is to list the Arabic names of all the locations in Palestine that carry the names of native plant and animal species. The author also declares that the motive behind the book is to preserve these names for the future generations, particularly as the 'enemy' had destroyed many of these places and 'wilfully' gave them, and some of those that remained, other names. The message behind this work is overtly political. It is meant to press the claim that the Palestinians have expressed their unity with, and love of, the land by giving the names of their native fauna and flora to the places in which they had lived. Arabic place names are pictured as a 'natural growth' from the soil of Palestine in a way that authenticates the Palestinian claim to the land.[44]

Note the use of the Hebrew rendering of the town name, Kafar-Kara, not its Arabic name Kufr Qar', and the description of the Palestinian national hero Izz al-Din al-Qassam as a 'mythological Muslim warrior'. Readers unfamiliar with this name would be excused if, on the basis of this description, they thought that al-Qassam never existed (mythological), that he was not a Palestinian (Muslim), and that he belonged to an ancient sword-and-spear past (warrior). This is another example of the strategy of erasure to which the Palestinians are exposed in the academic literature. Witness also the interpretation of the proposal to name the street after al-Qassam as 'an attempt to attract public attention to the poor financial situation of the municipality' of Kufr Qar'.

[43] See Swedenburg (1995: 117–18) for the meaning of Qassam's memory in the Palestinian popular imagination.

[44] Palestinians and Israeli Jews have vied with each other in recent years in expressing their love for Palestine/Israel. The idea behind this is that those who excel over the Other in the intensity of their love of the land must have a stronger claim to it. It is possible to read al-Dabbagh's book as part of this 'emotional competition'. The following quotation from Benvenisti (2000: 49–50) explains an aspect of this phenomenon:

> 'One who lives with his heart's beloved does not feel the need to express his feelings for her in poetry, since she is tangible to him,' claimed a [an Israeli] Palestinian in response to a Jew who mocked him, saying that he had not found expressions of feeling for the homeland in Arabic literature like those to be found in Hebrew writings, both ancient and modern. 'Only one who lost his beloved or is far from her needs to give poetic

A similar mission lies behind the two magisterial volumes, one in English and the other in Arabic, in which the highly respected Palestinian scholar Walid Khalidi (1982, 1997), aided by a team of researchers, documented the villages occupied and destroyed by Israel in 1948. The entry for each village consists of its location on a skeletal map, its elevation, land ownership and use in 1944/5 divided among Arabs and Jews (where appropriate), population and number of houses. In addition, each entry provides a narrative with information about the village before 1948, its occupation and depopulation by Israeli forces, the name(s) of the Israeli settlement(s) built on village lands, and any parts of the village (mosque, church, school, graveyard, olive press, etc.) that are still standing or are in existence as heaps of stone. The dedication in the English volume reads: 'To all those for whom these villages were home and to their descendants'. The Arabic version differs in three symbolic ways: (1) it contains a larger number of maps, setting out patterns of land ownership to show that the Jews possessed only a small part of Palestine; (2) it gives the names of those Palestinian martyrs (*shuhadā'*) who fell in battle defending their villages against the Israeli forces; and (3) its dedication sets out its dual aim as a celebration of the lives of those Palestinian villagers who were 'diasporized' by Israel, and as an exhortation to their descendants to preserve and cherish the memory of a lost cartographic text of Palestine: (*ilā al-ladhīna shurridū min qurāhum fa-hāmū fī al-arḍ; ilā dhurriyātihim jamī'an* ***kay lā yansū***: To those who were driven away from their villages to roam the earth, and to their descendants lest they forget). To signal the role of the map and memory, and hence of language, in keeping the aspirations of Palestinians alive, the editor sets out the last three words in bold.[45]

In spite of the above references, there is a paucity of Arab studies on place names in Palestine. This phenomenon needs explanation. It is not that the Palestinians are less interested than the Israeli Jews in

expression to his longing for her. We are connected to the stone fence that our father built and the fig tree that our great-grandfather planted. One doesn't write poems about such connections'.

[45] This insistence on remembering through naming practices has become a feature of 'online identities' for Palestinians in the refugee camps in Lebanon. In her study of Palestinian cyberculture in these camps, Khalili (forthcoming) writes:

> In numerous instances, the grandchildren and great-grandchildren of the men and women who left their villages in Palestine in 1948 choose to name their email addresses after [their] lost and in many [cases] destroyed villages; SAFFURIEH 2001@XXX.com commemorates the village of Ṣaffūrieh in the Galilee, whereas WALID FARA@XXX.com combines the real name of the young man and the name of his grandfather's village in the Safad province. Additionally, the number 48 appears again and again in the email addresses and Instant Messenger (IM) names, denoting and commemorating the year of the *Nakba* with each evocation.

allocating names to features of their landscape, but that their conditions differ in two fundamental ways. On the one hand, the Palestinians possessed established names for their cities, towns and villages, so they were not in need of creating new names.[46] In addition, the land of each village has been given names that were common currency among the villagers. This practice continues to this day. If anything, the Palestinians had an abundance of names to describe almost every valley, hill, cave, spring, plain or rock formation in their environment, and they often had traditions, mythic or real, to explain the reasons behind these names.[47] What they did not do is to create a cartographic record of these place names. As McCarthy (1979) points out in his study of Beirut, the Ottomans, the ruling authority before the British, attached little or no importance to the allocation of street names even in their major cities. This of course does not mean that the local inhabitants lacked the means of identifying their streets.[48] Names for the different parts of a city or town emerged naturally. Even when new names were officially introduced by the British and French colonial authorities in the countries of the Levant, the traditional, community-based names continued to compete with them.

On the other hand, whereas names among the incoming Jews in Palestine were part of an ideological movement that was linked to the Hebrew language revival and to the politically motivated project of returning to the land, Arabic place names as lived linguistic realities did not have the same ideological potency. Nor could they have been imbued with such potency as long as the Palestinians continued to live as a majority population on their own land. Moreover, the issue of immediate concern for the Palestinians was not the ideological content of the new names, but the fact that the land on which they lived was gradually snatched from under their feet. Fighting against the 'alien' names could not therefore be accorded the importance that it later assumed in Palestinian politics, life and culture. When the Palestinians were faced with the loss of their country, names as a linguistic means of denoting attachment, aspirations and proprietorship started to gain greater importance in the symbolic construction of their national identity and in the preservation of their

[46] In a not-so-well-known case, a large village in the coastal plain between Ramle and Jaffa changed its name in the 1930s from Yahudiyya to 'Abbasiyya in response to the Zionist expansion in Palestine. All the villagers were Palestinian Muslims.

[47] See Benvenisti (2000: 49–52) for some of these traditions and explanations.

[48] There is a tendency in the literature on street names to treat a street for which there is no official name on the map, if a map existed at all, as nameless. This tendency privileges town planning, map making and the written word over local knowledge, mental maps and oral tradition. Many of the streets in Palestinian cities inside or outside Israel had/have local names of one kind or another, but Israeli (and other) scholars invariably refer to these streets as 'nameless'.

territorial memories. In Jordan, a trend of using family names that are derived from the names of villages and towns in Palestine has been in existence for over thirty years now. A Palestinian village inside Israel may no longer exist, but its memory lives on through those who bear its name and still treat it as their home town. Inside Israel, Palestinians have become more aware of the importance of place names as constructs of ideological and political contestation.

Two further reasons may be added. First, allocating new names to places is often associated with urbanization and modernization. Before 1948, most of the Palestinians lived in small villages and towns in close-knit communities. There were few paved roads linking these villages and towns to each other or to the main cities. The cities were small in size, and their expansion outside the traditional city boundaries was recent. Literacy was very low, and services to these villages and towns were very limited. These conditions could not generate a strong interest in allocating names to places or in recording existing ones. Linguistic practices typically expand to meet the needs of the communities they serve. And since there was not a perceived need for naming places or signposting existing ones, the Palestinians did not embark on a cartographic project of the kind witnessed among the ideologically driven Jewish incomers to Palestine.

The second reason is more culturally embedded. A person's instrumental need for maps and road signs increases in foreign or unfamiliar places. Locals do not normally resort to maps or street signs to navigate their way in places that are familiar to them. However, this utilitarian function of maps and place names has an additional symbolic meaning: it brands the map user as foreigner or stranger, a person who does not belong to the place in which he is. This is particularly true in a small and compact country such as Palestine. Palestinians therefore read the Jewish obsession with maps and place names in Palestine as a reflection of their 'alien' and 'foreign' status. There is in fact an expression of this element in Palestinian culture in one of the best-known poems by the Palestinian poet Mahmud Darwish (1981). In his poem 'Biṭāqat huwiyya' (Identity card), Darwish tells his Israeli interlocutor that he (the poet) lives in an isolated and forgotten village 'whose streets bear no names'. I believe this is intended not only to convey the discrimination against the Palestinians in Israel, but also to contrast their cultural and linguistic practices with those of Israeli Jews. Unlike the Israeli Jew, the Palestinian lives close to the land and he can find his way around his native environment without having to use maps or resort to street signs. It is interesting that, after more than twenty-five years in the UK, I still find it difficult to remember street names and that, whenever I see a person using a map,

I do not read this as showing that the person concerned is lost and is looking for directions, but that he does not belong to the place (be it a city, town or part thereof) in which he is. In this respect at least, I still seem to act like a traditional Palestinian rather than as an acculturated Westerner.

The Shakespearian adage that a 'rose by any other name would smell as sweet' does not translate easily when assessing the symbolic meaning of place names in the land that constitutes the substance of the Arab–Israeli conflict. Names in this conflict are ideologically loaded linguistic constructs. They are used to validate or contest claims of proprietorship over the landscape. In the Arab–Israeli conflict, the map is a cartographic and linguistic record that inscribes a narrative of the nation. A map is a 'spatial-text' (Pinchevski and Torgovnik 2002), whose cartographic configuration should not obscure its linguistic content. It is a loaded weapon, as it is sometimes represented in children's drawings of the map of Israel (*Jewish Chronicle*, 21 June 2002). That is why it becomes a site of contestation in which different versions of history and different memories are ranged against each other. The fact that the Israeli map records its version of history and the memory of its people in Hebrew, and that the Palestinian map does so in Arabic, brings the two languages into a contact situation where hegemony and resistance define the rules of the engagement. We will see how this occurs in the street signs in Jerusalem in the next section.

Street signs in Jerusalem: the battle of hierarchical representation

We have seen above how street names serve as a site of national and ideological contestation in Israel/Palestine. The purge of Arab street names in Haifa in 1951 (Azaryahu 1992) and their introduction into Umm al-Fahm in 1993 (Azaryahu and Kook 2002) exemplify this facet of the Arab–Israeli conflict.[49] The 'tug of war' over street names between the Israeli authorities and the Palestinian residents of Beit Safafa and Beit

[49] In their study of Israeli street names, Pinchevski and Torgovnik (2002: 366–7) locate the political nature of street naming in the following factors:

> Firstly, being the result of a political struggle in which one option defeated several others, naming streets is like any other political contest in having a potential for conflict . . . Secondly, the decision is made by political-bureaucratic institutions having the *legitimate monopoly to name*, and as such, they hold what Pierre Bourdieu calls a 'means of symbolic violence' . . . And finally, decisions over street names are conducted by political actors who endeavour to engrave their ideological views in the social space, and further into the collective memory. [emphasis in original]

Hanina provides further evidence of the use of the map as a field of symbolic exploitation in promoting competing nationalist ideologies. In this section, I will discuss how public signs are used representationally to act out the Arab–Israeli conflict. Most of the data will be drawn from Jerusalem.[50] The term 'routine' will be used in discussing the corpus of signs in this study to signal the regular and widespread use of a limited set of orthographic-cum-cartographic practices that express the changes in political structure in historical Palestine.[51] More extensive research is necessary to test the findings of this study and to establish the extent to which they can be generalized to other signs. Some of the remarks that follow are therefore provisional in nature.

The first public sign (plate 1) is taken from the old city of Acre, and is dated 1919. This date is significant for three reasons: (1) it post-dates the expulsion of the Ottoman authorities from Palestine; (2) it coincides with the imposition of British control in Palestine which started in December 1917; and (3) it pre-dates the formal imposition of the British mandate in Palestine in 1922. These facts help explain the linguistic character of the sign. The absence of Turkish from this sign is explained by the first point above, although the sign alludes to the cooperation of the Turks and the British in defeating Napoleon outside the walls of Acre. Point (3) explains the absence of Hebrew, for it was not until the imposition of the mandate that Hebrew acquired an official status in Palestine. English, which occupies half of this commemorative plaque, is present in its capacity as the language of the ruling power. As the language of the vast majority of the people of Palestine (Palestinian Jews totalled around 66,000 out of 650,000 in 1914),[52] Arabic occupies the other half. The parity between the two languages is exhibited in the fact that English and Arabic appear

Achieving this ideological objective meant in Israel 'erasing traces' of the Palestinian past in such cities as Ramleh and 'constituting a new horizon of signification' (Pinchevski and Torgovnik 2002: 374). Thus, although one-third of the population of Ramleh are Palestinians, there is not a single street in the city that carries an Arabic name. And in the one quarter of the city in which the Palestinians live, the Juraish neighbourhood, not a single street is named. We can only speculate that the municipal authorities have shied away from doing this because, among other things, the imposition of non-Arab names might be met with local resistance, and that the local residents have not pressed for their streets to be named to avoid having Hebrew/Jewish names imposed on them. Avoidance may therefore be the preferred option for both parties in managing the conflict that may emerge as a result of any street-naming initiative.

[50] See Spolsky and Cooper (1991) for a similar study. The present work will, however, go beyond the parameters set by Spolsky and Cooper in terms of both the data it uses and the categories of analysis it invokes.

[51] I have collected images of hundreds of signs from Israel/Palestine over the past eight years. The data in this study represent the major routines I have observed. The study excludes signs that appear on religious buildings.

[52] See Tibawi (1969) for more details.

Plate 1 An English plaque: old city, Acre

Plate 2 Jaffa Road: West Jerusalem

on the left and the right sides of the plaque respectively, reflecting the orthographic direction of the two languages.

However, the plaque contains two clues which signal the dominance of English, the language of the ruling power, over Arabic, the language of the indigenous population.[53] The first pertains to the faulty lexical and grammatical structure of the Arabic. The use of *tārīkh* for 'tablet' and *inḥiṣār* for 'besieged' is lexically unwarranted. The Arabic corresponding to 'who fell in leading a sortie from the garrison when . . .' is ungrammatical. It is therefore most likely that the Arabic is a poor translation of the English, thus signalling the textual precedence of the one language over the other. To use the terminology of translation theory, the Arabic in the

[53] The term 'indigenous population' is synonymous with what is called the 'local population' or the 'public' in the correspondence between Jerusalem (government of Palestine) and London (the mandatory power). Nadia Abu El-Haj (2001) examined the meaning of these two terms in this correspondence and in official reports. She has established that they are almost exclusively used to refer to the Arabs (Palestinians) in Palestine.

Plate 3 Nablus Road: East Jerusalem

plaque is a mutilated target text of the English source text in a relationship in which the former is a derivative of the latter. The second clue pertains to the dates of the First World War at the bottom of the plaque. Whereas the ordering of the dates is correct in English, the Arabic reproduces a mirror image of these dates. A literal reading of these dates would lead to the ludicrous conclusion that the First World War started in 1918 and ended in 1914. Here the English source text totally dominates its Arabic counterpart. Arabic in this plaque is no longer the linguistic master in its own house. Its orthographic visibility must, however, be contrasted with the invisibility of Hebrew in a way that echoes the demographic structure of Palestine.

The establishment of Hebrew as one of the official languages of Palestine by the mandate authority enabled it to appear alongside English and Arabic in public notices, including road signs. However, Hebrew was subordinated to these two languages, which appeared above it, in these signs. Two road signs from this period have survived to this day: the Jaffa Road sign (plate 2) in West Jerusalem and the Nablus Road sign (plate 3) in East Jerusalem. The latter is interesting because the English reproduces the Arab name of the town (Nablus) rather than its Hebrew name (Shechem). There is therefore a sense in which Arabic dominates English lexically, although it occurs below it in the plaque. As mentioned earlier, Zionist leaders objected to this vertical ordering of the languages, treating it as a 'national insult', in spite of the fact that Hebrew was neither the language of the ruling power nor that of the majority indigenous population.[54] The Zionist leaders demanded that the three languages be represented alongside each other on a horizontal plane.

[54] Early Zionist settlers in Palestine looked upon the Palestinian Arabs very much as the native population of the country they had come to 'colonize'. Netiva Ben-Yehuda, a member of the Palmach (underground Jewish military organization in Palestine), talks in her autobiography, published in 1981, about how the ideal of the early Zionist 'colonists' was the native Palestinian Arab. She writes (cited in Katriel and Greifat 1988: 303–4):

> We were concerned with only this: to talk like them [Palestinian Arabs], walk like them, behave like them, in the sun, in the wind, in the field, at night, to dress like them. We imitated them in everything . . . They were for us *the model for the natives of the land*, and we – perhaps did not even come close to something defined, but we were certainly 'non-Diaspora Jews.' So what does a native of the land look like, a 'non-Diaspora Jew'? as an Arab, no question. Anyone who could chatter in Arabic was highly esteemed by us, and whoever had Arab friends – a real king. Even one Bedouin would be enough . . . I think whoever does not understand this cannot even begin to understand that period [the months preceding the 'outbreak of the state' as she puts it]. [emphasis in original]

The terms 'colony' and 'colonist' used to introduce the preceding quotation may strike the reader as less appropriate than other terms that one might have used – for example, 'settlement' and 'settler'. I have used these terms, however, because there is evidence that this is how some leading Zionists, particularly those working in the cultural domain, conceptualized themselves and their activity. The captions of some of the illustrations in a volume entitled *Zionist Work in Palestine*, edited by Israel Cohen and published on behalf of the Zionist Central Office in 1911, refer to this: 'Vine plantation in a colony' (p. 142); 'Young colonists in Rishin Le Zion' (p. 157); and 'Zichron Jacob colony' (p. 165). One Arab TV station, Sharjah TV in the United Arab Emirates, calls the Israeli settlement in the Occupied Territories *mughtaṣabāt*, not *mustawṭanāt*, which is the prevalent term in the Arab media. The former term is derived from the root *ghaṣaba*, the meaning of which incorporates the ideas of taking away by force, extortion, coercion, abduction and rape. This range of meanings is closer to how the Arabs conceptualize the Israeli settlements, and is closer to the status of the settlements in international law than the normal Arabic term.

The following comment from Cleary's study of literature and partition establishes the double-sided nature of Zionist ideology (2002: 6): 'In the early twentieth century especially, Israeli Zionists [this is a strange concept since Israel did not come into existence until 1948] maintained a complex and contradictory identification with both white-settler and anti-colonial nationalisms. Zionists watched Irish nationalism, in particular, with considerable interest and frequently asserted similarities between the plight of the Irish under British rule and that of the Jews under imperial rule in mandate Palestine.' Cleary gives the following as an example of this identification (2002: 6–7):

> An early Israeli film, made in 1955, called *Hill 24 doesn't Answer* (Giva 24 Eina Ona), is set during the 1948 war, and tells the story of four fighters – an American Jew, an Israeli-born Sabra, a Sephardi Jew and an Irishman – assigned to defend a strategic hill outside Jerusalem. The apparently anomalous presence of the Irishman in this narrative is explained by the desire of those who made the film to suggest that . . . Zionism was not a regressive colonial nationalism but a revolutionary anti-colonial national liberation struggle which, like its Irish counterpart, deserved international sympathy and support.

Their efforts seem to have borne fruit, as is clear from the King George V Avenue plaque in West Jerusalem, dated 1924 (plate 4). Here English is situated in the middle, between Arabic and Hebrew; the fact that three languages appear on the same horizontal plane gives an impression of equality between them. However, a close reading of the semiotics of representation in this plaque contradicts this impression. English dominates Arabic and Hebrew in two ways. On the one hand, it occurs in the centre of the plaque, thus enjoying greater visibility than its two partners. On the other hand, whereas English occupies 40 per cent of the space area of the plaque, Arabic and Hebrew equally share the remaining space at 30 per cent each. Nevertheless, this equality between the two languages conceals a discrepancy in status between them. Both Arabic and Hebrew are right-to-left languages in their modes of orthographic representation. By virtue of appearing on the right of the plaque, Arabic must therefore be judged to dominate Hebrew. The plaque lost its demographic meaning after 1948 owing to the dominance of Hebrew over Arabic in West Jerusalem, which came under Israeli control. However, this plaque stands to this day as a reminder of the balance of linguistic power between Arabic and English in Palestine before the establishment of the state of Israel. In this respect, it signals a narrative from the past that challenges the empirical reality of the present.

The division of Jerusalem in 1948 into a western part controlled by Israel, and an eastern part controlled by Jordan, was marked by further changes in the semiotics of the road signs. Plate 5 shows the Via Dolorosa sign. The bottom section of this sign, bordered by an ornamental frieze, gives the Arabic and English names of the road arranged vertically in that order. This order of representation reflects the status of Arabic as the official language of Jordan – and that of the population of the Old City – and of English as the language of the ex-mandatory power and the international lingua franca. The absence of Hebrew reflects the political realities of East Jerusalem between 1948 and 1967. As the language of the enemy, Hebrew was denied any cartographic legitimacy in East Jerusalem, except in the Nablus Road sign (plate 3), which – to the best of my knowledge – was the only sign to survive from the mandate period.[55]

This situation changed after the Israeli occupation of East Jerusalem in 1967. Plate 5 marks this change in a very interesting way. The top section of the sign, appearing in its own frieze, is in Hebrew. Both the Hebrew name of the road and the frieze surrounding it are placed above the Arabic and English names to signify the new political realities of

[55] The bullet holes in this sign provide a perfect representation of the subject matter of this book: language and conflict in the Middle East.

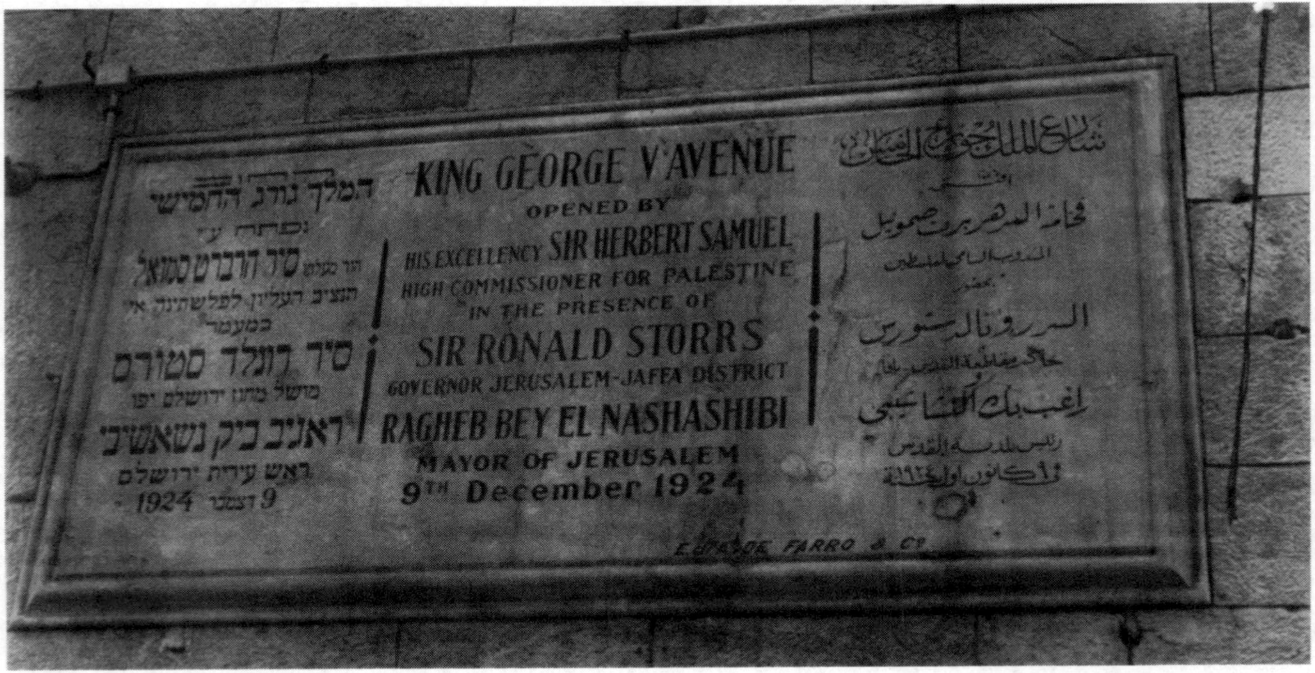

Plate 4 King George V Avenue: West Jerusalem

Plate 5 Via Dolorosa: East Jerusalem

the city. As in the mandate period, Arabic and Hebrew are allowed to coexist, but their status in the semiotics of representation is reversed in favour of Hebrew. This routine of imposing a Hebrew frieze on top of the Arabic and English frieze from the Jordanian period is repeated in many parts of East Jerusalem. What is, however, particularly interesting about road signs of this type is their ability to provide a historical narrative of the structure of political power in the Old City. Both the absence of Hebrew and its reimposition in this plate sum up the violent changes in the fortunes of the Old City between 1948 and 1967.

The Malak Road sign (plates 6a and b) provides a more complex example of how linguistic power and conflict operate in the cartographic domain. Plate 6a exhibits the following routines: the vertical representation of Arabic over English in a frieze dating back to the Jordanian period; the absence of Hebrew from this period; and the imposition of Hebrew above Arabic and English in a separate bordered frieze after 1967. So far, this road sign is consistent with the routines we witnessed in plate 5. An important difference between the two does, however, exist. Although Hebrew dominates Arabic and English in this sign (in its final shape), still Arabic manages to subvert this dominance. The morphology of the English transliteration contains the crucial clue: the definite

Plates 6a and 6b El-Malak Road: East Jerusalem

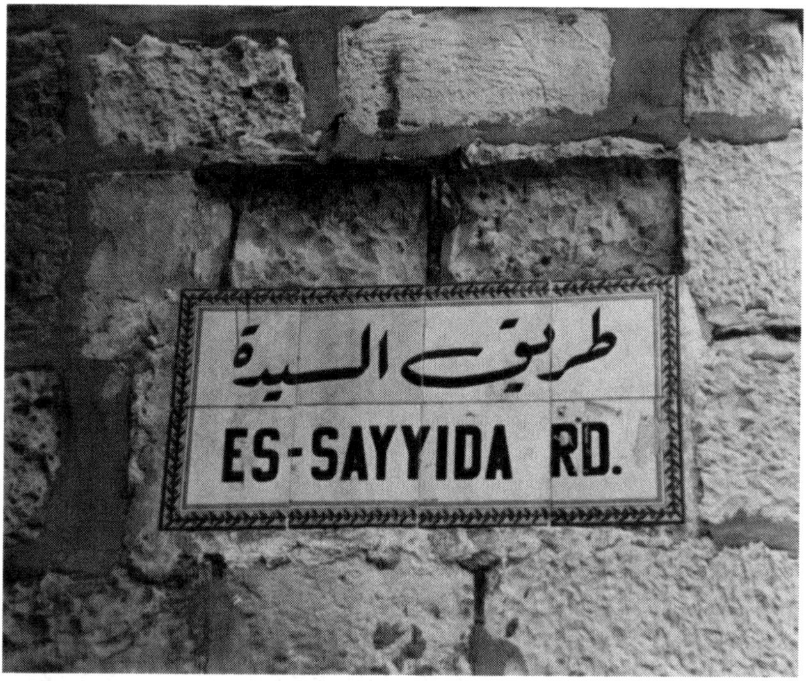

Plate 7 Es-Sayyida Road: East Jerusalem

article is given as 'El-'. This is changed in plate 6b, where the definite article is a transliteration of Hebrew 'Ha-'. The dominance of Hebrew in this sign is further reflected in the transliteration of the final consonant in the name of the road as 'kh', not 'k' as in plate 6a. Plate 6b represents the new style of road sign in the Old City. In signs of this kind, Hebrew occurs above Arabic and English in one single bordered frieze. However, Hebrew does not always dominate English morphologically in these signs, as plate 7 reveals. In this sign, the definite-article morphology in the English transliteration reflects the influence of Arabic, not Hebrew.

The subordination of Arabic to Hebrew is signalled through a variety of routines in plate 8 (al-'Umariyya Public Primary School for Boys). First, Arabic is subordinated to Hebrew along the horizontal plane by virtue of its appearing in the left part of the sign. This is a reversal of the situation in plate 4. Second, the sign in this plate is superimposed on the original (engraved) Arabic inscription bearing the name of the school, parts of which are still visible on the right of the new sign. Third, the name of Jerusalem in the Arabic part of the sign is given as Urshalim al-Quds, in which the priority is given to the Hebrew name of the city over its Arabic

Plate 8 Al-'Umariyya School for Boys: East Jerusalem

counterpart. Fourth, the background of the sign is in blue, the Israeli national colour. Fifth, the Arabic word *rasmiyya* (public, state school) represents an extension of the authority of the occupying power over the city.

The subordination of Arabic to Hebrew in East Jerusalem is signalled through other routines. In plate 9, from the Dome of the Rock area, Arabic is absent, in spite of the fact that this is the one part of East Jerusalem where the language seems to be most relevant. The absence of Arabic from this sign perhaps reflects the feeling that the Palestinians are unlikely to use the services of the Israeli police, whose primary responsibility is to protect the non-Arabic-speaking visitors to the Haram al-Sharif (the noble sanctuary) complex.[56] In plate 10 Arabic is dominated by Hebrew

[56] There is a general feeling among the Palestinians in occupied East Jerusalem that the Israeli police are not there to help or protect them, but to prevent any demonstrations against the Israeli authorities. In the Haram al-Sharif area the police provide some protection for the Muslim holy places against radical Jewish groups that aim to blow up these places and build the Jewish Temple instead.

Plate 9 Police station: al-Haram al-Sharif in East Jerusalem

and English. Its subordinate status is expressed in two additional routines. First, Arabic occupies a fraction of the space allocated to Hebrew in this commemorative plaque. It occupies even a smaller space than English. Second, Arabic is badly written in comparison with both Hebrew and English. In fact, the slapdash manner in which the Arabic on this plaque is produced may be regarded as an insult to the long and celebrated tradition of using Arabic for calligraphic representation. The pointed angularity of the script and its amateurish character are anathema to the established norms of Arab culture. They convey to the reader that the sign writer and the commissioning authority do not hold Arabic and its aesthetic values in high esteem. In fact, this is not the worst example of this routine in my corpus. Plate 11, from Haifa bus station, provides an even worse example. The word for 'Coke' in Arabic is barely legible in this sign.

Many of the routines described above are repeated in West Jerusalem, in which Hebrew is the dominant language. Plate 12 provides an example of two of these routines: the vertical ordering of the three languages, with Hebrew at the top; and the allocation of a smaller space to Arabic in relation to Hebrew and English. The space allocated to Arabic in the sign, combined with the mutilation of the Arabic script (see below),

Plate 10 Damascus Gate Park: East Jerusalem

undermines the instrumental purpose of the sign. However, plate 12 provides three further routines that are largely absent from East Jerusalem, but are characteristic of road signs in West Jerusalem. The first is the rendering of the Arabic script in a way that replicates the image of the Hebrew script. The acute angular nature of the Arabic is unusual in road signs in the Arabic-speaking countries, even when a Kufic script is used. This routine is similar to the well-known practice of rendering the English letters in

Plate 11 Haifa bus station

Plate 12 Hahistadrut Street: West Jerusalem

the names of Chinese restaurants in Britain in a manner suggestive of the shapes of Chinese characters.

The second feature consists of the absence of dots on the Arabic letters corresponding to the first and second 'T' in the English. My corpus contains at least ten examples of this orthographic practice where the absence of dots in Arabic contrasts with the carefully pointed nature of the Hebrew script. When this happens the name in Arabic is almost unrecognizable without the help of either the Hebrew or the English. The same result obtains when the Arabic is morphologically and orthographically misspelled, as in plate 13, from Tiberias.[57]

The third feature consists of imposing Hebrew morphology on the Arabic name of the street. Instead of using the Arabic definite article 'al-' in the second word in the Arabic name, Hebrew 'ha-' is used. In some cases, Hebrew in its Ashkenazi form dominates Arabic phonology, as in plate 14. The name of the mosque in Tiberias is rendered with 'kh' (voiceless velar fricative) instead of Arabic 'ḥ' (Voiceless pharyngeal fricative), through a process which identifies the latter phoneme with its stigmatized Mizrahi counterpart in Hebrew. The combination of all these routines means that Hebrew dominates Arabic in order of presentation, size, orthography, phonology and morphology.

Plate 15, from the northern border point between Israel and Jordan, presents another routine. The orthography and phonology in this plate are free from error. However, the instruction to the travellers is grammatically incorrect in several places. The first line, *musāfir karīm*, is normally rendered in Arabic in the definite, preceded by the vocative *ayyuhā* (*ayyuhā al-musāfir al-karīm*), or with the first word only in the definite, preceded by the word *akhī*, literally 'brother' (*akhī al-musāfir*). The second line contains a number of mistakes. The word *bi-jawāzātika* (literally 'in' + singular 'your' + passports + singular possessive pronoun) is lexically nonsensical (second word in line 2), since it is unlikely that those travellers who would wish to smuggle 'firearms, ammunition or weapons' into Israel would try to do so in their passports. The sign writer must have been aiming at *bi-ḥawzatika* (have on you, carry), but produced *bi-jawāzātika* because of the context (a border point where passports are an essential document) and the orthographic similarity in Arabic between the target word and the word that actually appears on the sign. But even if we were to replace *bi-jawāzātika* by *bi-ḥawzatika* we would still end up with a grammatically incorrect expression, since *idhā* ('if', first word in

[57] This sign has been recently removed and replaced by a new sign, from which the Arabic has been eliminated. However, the English transliteration does not render the correct Arabic name: it is given as al-Amri instead of al-'Umari. In 1999, I saw the old discarded sign inside the half-ruined mosque with the Hebrew name blotted out, presumably as a sign of respect to the sacred nature of the language.

Plate 13 Al-Bahri Mosque: Tiberias

Plate 14 Al-Bahri Mosque: Tiberias

line 2) requires the verb *kāna* to occur after it to make the if-clause grammatically correct. The word *rajā'* ('please', fourth word in line 2) is also incorrect: it should be in the definite, *al-rajā'*. The word *i'lim* ('inform', fifth word in line 2) should be rendered as a verbal noun, *i'lām* (make known). Alternatively, the sign writer could have deleted *rajā'* ('please') and kept *i'lim* in the imperative, although this would be a little impolite at the border point to a country. Finally, *fawran* ('immediately', sixth word in line 2) should be placed at the end of the construction in this context to convey a neutral (non-marked) message, after the last two words *ḍābiṭ al-amn* (security officer) instead of occurring before them. A correct rendering of the first two lines in the sign may take one of the following forms:

(1) *Ayyuhā al-musāfir al-karīm*
Idhā kāna bi-ḥawzatika silāḥ al-rajā' i'lām ḍābiṭ al-amn fawran
(2) *Akhī al-musāfir*
Idhā kāna bi-ḥawzatika silāḥ al-rajā' i'lām ḍābiṭ al-amn fawran
(3) *Ayyuhā al-musāfir al-karīm*
Idhā kāna bi-ḥawzatika silāḥ a'lim ḍābiṭ al-amn fawran
(4) *Akhī al-musāfir*
Idhā kāna bi-ḥawzatika silāḥ a'lim ḍābiṭ al-amn fawran[58]

[58] Although suggestions (3) amd (4) are grammatically correct, they are stylistically less polite than (1) and (2).

Plate 15 Border sign: Israeli–Jordanian border

The dominance of Hebrew over Arabic in cartographic terms, both with respect to the vertical ordering of the two languages and the space allocated to them in signs, is further signalled in the imposition of Hebrew orthography, phonology and grammar on Arabic. The presence of Arabic in these signs in East Jerusalem and Israel reflects a fundamental contradiction between policy and practice. On the level of policy, the use of Arabic in the signs serves three purposes: (1) it expresses its status as an official language in Israel; (2) it represents a gesture of goodwill towards the Palestinians in the state; and (3) it (intentionally or unintentionally) recognizes the status of the Palestinians in East Jerusalem as the majority of the inhabitants of the Old City. On the level of practice, the poor state of the Arabic in the signs indicates that the recognition accorded to it is tokenistic in nature. The authorities seem to think that what matters is the presence of some Arabic in the signs, regardless of whether or not the Arabic is grammatically correct or aesthetically pleasing.

This is more or less the response I received from most Palestinians when I asked them about the state of the Arabic in the signs. They are, however, reluctant to do anything to change this situation. In both East Jerusalem and Israel, Palestinians treat the linguistic infringements against Arabic as no more than an irritation when compared with the serious Israeli violations against them in the form of land confiscation and house demolition

Plate 16 Post Office: West Jerusalem

(in East Jerusalem). Palestinians in this part of Jerusalem are particularly reluctant to make representations to the municipality, in order not to accord it any legitimacy over their occupied city. As a result, Hebrew hegemony over Arabic is achieved by default, although it is driven by the intention to resist on the part of the Palestinians. In some cases, however, resistance does take place by defacing the road signs. In plate 7 (Old City) the Hebrew has been removed, leaving a gap in its place. Israeli Jews in West Jerusalem subject Arabic to similar practices, as plate 16 illustrates. These practices stem from the desire to deny the legitimacy of the Other in the cartography of the city. They are, in effect, reflexes of the Arab–Israeli conflict in the linguistic domain. None of the routines I have outlined above would be adequately comprehensible without placing them within the facts of this conflict.

The conflict between Arabic and Hebrew in Israel and Palestine is part of a wider struggle over the symbols of political control, national authentication and territorial branding (van Ham 2002).[59] The Palestinians have turned the map of historical Palestine into a gold necklace

[59] See Olins (1999) and Kotler et al. (1997) for a discussion of the connection between branding and the construction of national identity.

Plate 17 Israeli millennium wine

which the women wear. The Israeli Jews have turned the same map into an eraser for use in Israeli schools. The Palestinians have used the Dome of the Rock as a symbol of national identity on the stamps of the Palestinian National Authority, continuing a long tradition in this area (Katz 1999; Abuljebain 2001). The Israeli Tourist Board in London used the same symbol to promote tourism to Israel at the turn of the millennium. The Palestinians have created models of the Dome of the Rock using olive wood and mother-of-pearl. Some Israeli Jews have used the same image to promote a special edition of Israeli wine to celebrate the new millennium (plate 17). The Palestinians have promoted their traditional embroidery to underline their rootedness in the land through the stylized images of its

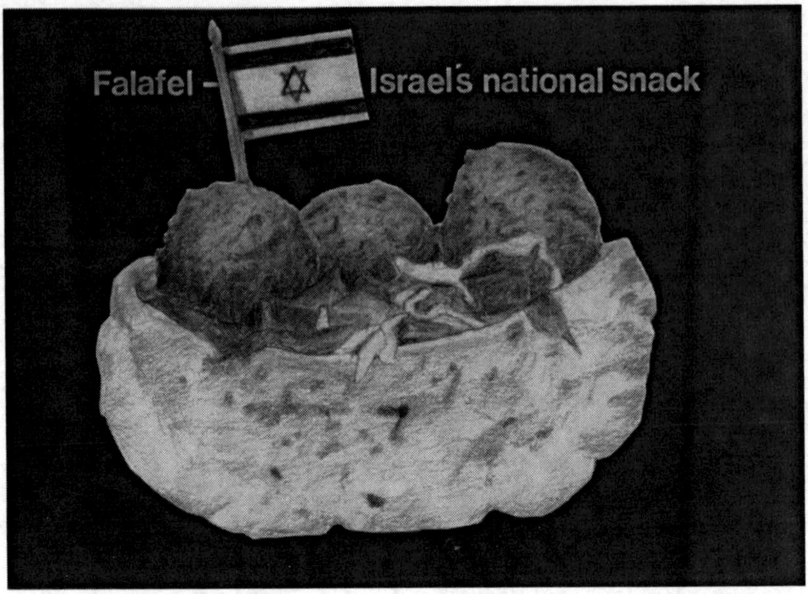

Plate 18 *Falafel* postcard

fauna and flora. The Israeli Jews have appropriated the traditional Arab *falafel* sandwich and dubbed it 'Israel's national snack' (plate 18).

This struggle over symbols is a struggle between two competing national semiologies. The conflict between Arabic and Hebrew is part of this semiological struggle over the symbolic means of national-identity construction. Although this aspect of the struggle is never the cause of political or military conflict per se, it is nevertheless an important element in the Arab–Israeli conflict. It is in fact so important that it extends to the time systems of the Palestinians and Israelis. The following story from *To Rule Jerusalem*, by Roger Friedland and Richard Hecht (1996: 289), illustrates this aspect of the semiological struggle between the two competing nationalities:

> We [Friedland and Hecht] arrived for our appointment at Nusseibeh's [mayor of East Jerusalem before its occupation in 1967] office promptly at 9:30 on Monday 22 May, 1984. The big clock in his office showed 8:30. We checked our watches, thinking the electricity had stopped functioning in East Jerusalem or perhaps his clock was broken. The clocks were working fine. Israel had just introduced daylight saving time. Nusseibeh's office, like all other Palestinian institutions, refused to set its clocks forward. East Jerusalem would run on Arab time. It was a foretaste of the struggle over time that would soon explode on Jerusalem's streets.

A question of linguistic asymmetry: political conflict and linguistic vitality

One of the most important features of the linguistic conflict between Hebrew and Arabic is the asymmetry in the ideological intensities they have within their respective national movements. Hebrew enjoys a higher intensity than Arabic, hence its greater vitality as a symbol of national identity and mass mobilization in the Israeli Jewish context. Zionists promoted Hebrew as the symbol and vehicle for continuity with the past, in its capacity as an authenticating factor in the national revival of the Jewish people. On its way to actually assuming this role, Hebrew had to fight off challenges from a host of languages, including German and French, that enjoyed the support of strong patrons. But the biggest challenge to Hebrew came from Yiddish, the language of the Jewish enlightenment in Europe. The First Zionist Congress held in Basle in 1897 in fact voted to adopt Yiddish, not Hebrew, as the language of the Jewish national movement. Supporters of Hebrew opposed this decision. The struggle between the two languages was eventually won by Hebrew, whose status as an official language in Palestine was inscribed in the instruments of the British mandate in 1922. This struggle did not represent a difference over political objectives, but over the character of the Zionist movement and the future state it set out to achieve. Whereas Yiddish represented the ideals of change and secularism, Hebrew signified those of continuity and emancipation from the Diaspora. Taking these facts into consideration, we may describe Hebrew as the 'daughter of ideological battles', which endowed it with a strong political meaning. As an ideologically loaded weapon, Hebrew was therefore able to engage Arabic in linguistic battles, to its advantage.

The ideological significance of Hebrew for the waves of Jewish immigrants into Israel associated its use on the individual level with being a 'good [and] loyal citizen' of the state (Katz 1982: 102). For the immigrants who represented different ethnicities and different language backgrounds Hebrew came to symbolize their unity as members of an emerging polity. The *ulpanim* (adult language classes in Hebrew) played an important role in transforming the ethnicities of the new immigrants into a Hebrew-based national identity. In these classes, as Katz points out (1982: 102), 'ethnic differences and tensions among immigrants were negotiated in Hebrew. Particularistic ethnic symbols were expressed in Hebrew. Secular Jews argued with religious Jews in Hebrew; Yemenites disagreed with Russian Jews in Hebrew; and radical Jews argued with conservative Jews in Hebrew.'

A similar role is played by the Israeli army through its system of universal conscription and active reserve duty (Spolsky and Shohamy 1999).

Azarya (1989: 119) characterizes the Israeli military as the 'principal carriers of national goals and identity, the inculcators of national consciousness, the integrators of various sectors of the population, and the most genuine representatives of the new culture and generation'. The use of Hebrew as a means of acculturation in the *ulpanim* and, to a lesser extent, in the military endowed the language with social, cultural and political significance in a context which emphasized the emergence of a new Jew in a new nation whose homogeneity was being created against the diversities of the Diaspora. This motif of the 'rebirth' of the individual and the 're-emergence' of the nation was signalled in the adoption of new names by the immigrants as a 'rite of passage' that represented the discontinuity between a 'discredited recent past' and a 'proud future'. In all of this, the *ulpanim* linked the new immigrant, through the language, to a host of national symbols and national practices. Criticism of the national heroes was frowned upon in these classes. Katz (1982: 104) relates how an *ulpan* teacher voiced her displeasure at an immigrant who expressed concern about the welfare of Ben-Yehuda's family (the father of modern Hebrew) because they were forced to speak only Hebrew when the language was not in daily use by the Jews in Palestine. The immigrant was told that the hardship was an insignificant price to pay for the Jews who were trying to revive the language and build a Jewish nation. Katz sums up the ideologization of Hebrew in the *ulpanim* as follows (1982: 107):

> In these language classes, immigrants learn values about Israeli society under the auspices of learning the highly valued language. Immigrants learn to identify as Israelis by interpreting symbols of national unity, such as national heroes, national holidays and ancient and modern history. Through the teacher as a cultural broker they also learn about Israeli ethnic prejudices and conflicts, particularly the higher value placed upon Western culture and immigrants from Western countries [Ashkenazi Jews]. In addition, the Ulpanim reflect the ways in which a revitalization movement in a new national state attempts to denigrate its recent past and the past of its immigrants in order to inculcate new national loyalties.

As an instrument of ideological and political contestation, Arabic in Palestine did not enjoy the same 'nationalist charge' as did Hebrew, at least until recently and mainly among the Palestinians in Israel whose position as a national minority has given an added urgency to the language issue. It is true that Arabic acquired its nationalist credentials in the modern period through conflicts with its colloquial varieties, the Turkish language of the ruling elite and the colonial languages (mainly French in North Africa), but none of these conflicts had the same ideological load and political intensity that characterized the struggle between Hebrew and its rivals. The Arabic language renaissance in the nineteenth century could never be described as a 'revival' of the language in the same way the concept applies to Hebrew.[60] Interest in Arabic in the emerging national movement was therefore not pursued with the same ideological zeal, and the same political determination, as the interest in Hebrew was in Zionism. In Palestine, Arabic had a secure place as an official language in the mandate for purely instrumental reasons: it was the language of the vast majority of the population who were linguistically homogeneous. Hebrew owes its position as an official language in Palestine to British political expediency, the imperatives of Zionist ideology and the need to promote it as an intra-community language among a linguistically heterogeneous population. The fact that the Zionists in Palestine had to fight for equality with Arabic in road signs explains the disparity in the status of the two languages. The weaker position of Hebrew sharpened the awareness of its ideological and political value among the Zionists, and gave a degree of urgency to the nationalist enterprise of increasing its visibility in the public domain. None of these conditions pertained to Arabic.

Furthermore, the Palestinians saw the linguistic challenge posed by Hebrew as a low-priority issue when compared with the danger they faced of losing their control over their own land and their own destiny. The fact that the level of literacy among the Palestinians was significantly lower than among the Jewish immigrants to Palestine made the ideologizing of Arabic more difficult than that of Hebrew. But even among the elite, Arabic could not be established as a specific marker of a Palestinian national identity because this elite was strongly pan-Arabist in its political orientations. Arabic belonged to all the Arabic-speaking peoples, not just to the Palestinians, and this limited its potential for being projected as an exclusive marker of Palestinian national identity in the way Hebrew acted among the Jews in Palestine. This fact made the Palestinians look outside Palestine for the configuration of their national identity as a constituent people within the Arab nation. The combination of these factors may give the impression that Arabic was an undervalued nationalist resource among the Palestinians. This is not true: the above-mentioned conditions created a feeling of linguistic security among them that was so strong they felt no need to ideologize their language the way the Jews in Palestine had done with respect to Hebrew. This situation started to change after the creation of Israel, as the following examples will reveal.

One of the interesting features of Palestinian prose literature in Israel is the strategic use of colloquial Palestinian Arabic to signify the link between the people and the land (Taha 1995). The use of peculiarly

[60] Blau's (1969) use of the term 'revival' to refer to the linguistic renaissance of Arabic in the nineteenth century is in my view unwarranted. See Paulston et al. (1993) for the theoretical background to this view.

Palestinian words, fossilized expressions and proverbs creates a communion between the reader and the text in a way that preserves and celebrates Palestinian culture. The fact that most of this linguistic material is culled from the rural Arabic of Palestine signifies the symbiotic relationship between the land, the people and the language that mediates the connection between the other two constructs. This is done intentionally to assert that the land of Palestine speaks in its own dialect. While still committed to the range of ideological meanings that are associated with Standard Arabic, Palestinian writers use the colloquial to particularize their relationship with their national territory within the overarching Arab nation. For many Palestinians, Sheikh Imam's song 'l-arḍ b-titkallim 'arbī' (The land speaks Arabic) resonates in a way that perhaps has a greater meaning than for other Arabs.[61] I have seen Palestinians listen to this song, and hum its words, with tears in their eyes. This is because the language (Arabic) and the land (Palestine) are brought into a nationalist duality to articulate the feelings of yearning, belonging and dispossession. Expressions of this duality occur in sociolinguistic studies. In his study of variation in Palestinian Arabic, Shorrab (1981: 160) quotes one of his rural Palestinian respondents as saying that 'any Fallahi speaker who substitutes his [stigmatized] *ch* [as in English 'church'] with [the standard phoneme] *k* is a traitor and is . . . less of a Palestinian'.

This duality of language and national territory finds expression in Palestinian poetry in Israel (al-Qadi 1982: 171–5). Samih al-Qasim, one of the best-known Palestinian poets, tells his readers that Palestine was made to learn many languages in its long history. However, whenever the country is asked to give its name it does so in Arabic, declaring that it is Arab. In another poem, al-Qasim describes how the valleys, streams and mountains of Palestine exchange news about the weather in Arabic, and how the orchards, vineyards and vegetable fields think in the language about the harvest and the songs that accompany it. The poet then tells us how he has memorized his homeland, its songs, the map of Palestine and Palestinian folklore in their own language to commemorate the identity of his own people.

Mahmud Darwish makes similar links between national territory and language. However, unlike Samih al-Qasim he does so by lamenting the interruption of the link between the two after the establishment of Israel in 1948. In one of his poems he describes Jaffa (an Arab city on the outskirts of Tel Aviv) as a city that has been translated into another language (*wa-yāfā turjimat ḥattā al-nukhā'*), presumably Hebrew, as a result of the influx of Jewish immigrants to replace the Palestinians who fled their homes

[61] Sheikh Imam is a blind Egyptian singer. Almost all of the song, around ten minutes long, consists of repeating one line: *l-arḍ b-titkallim 'arbī, l-arḍ l-arḍ* (The land speaks Arabic, the land . . . the land . . .).

in 1948. However, by using 'translation' as a metaphor here Darwish suggests that Arab and Arabic Jaffa are the original text from which Jewish and Hebrew Jaffa are derived but can never obliterate. In another poem, Darwish (1981: 258–60) laments the fact that his homeland has forgotten the dialect of its own absent people. Fadwa Tuqan, the leading Palestinian woman poet, expresses how sad she was – on her first visit to Jaffa after the 1967 war – to find that the city was full of people with strange faces, behaviour and languages (*ghrīb al-wajh wa-l-yad wa-l-lisān*).

The utilization of Arabic as an ingredient in the Arab–Israeli conflict is sometimes expressed through the terminology of Arabic grammar. Mu'in Bsisu, a Palestinian poet from Gaza, used this terminology to signify the asymmetrical power relations between Israel as the agent or doer of the action (*fā'il*), and the Arabs as the patient or receiver of the action (*maf'ūl bihi*), during the negotiations between Egypt and Israel for military disengagement in Sinai after the 1973 October war (Bsisu 1974). The use of Arabic grammar to talk about this event in the Arab–Israeli conflict is characterized by sarcasm and irony, the intention being to describe the talks as a deviation (solecism) from the national and grammatical norm. This pessimistic tone of the poem contrasts with Salih Baransi's (1981) use of grammatical terminology to articulate to his students the fate of those who collaborate with the enemy, and the rewards that await those who refuse to deal with him. At the time (1951), the Palestinians in Israel were living under military rule. The resort to Arabic grammatical terminology to communicate a political message therefore represents one of the most ingenious ways of (1) subverting the harsh nature of Israeli military rule; (2) challenging the ban it imposed on all political activity among Palestinians; and (3) avoiding the censorship it imposed on all forms of Palestinian nationalist expression. Before setting out how Baransi did this (1981: 30–1), I will explain the syntactic structures and functions he invoked.[62]

[62] The following transliteration of the full text from Salih Baransi is given for the benefit of readers who know Arabic (1981: 30–1):

Kunt attakhidh min tadrāis al-adab al-'arabī wa-tārīkhih manfadhan li-tadrīs al-siyāsa. Wa 'alā sabīl al-mithāl fa-qad kunt udarris mawḍū' kāna wa-akhawātihā 'alā i'tibār annahā majmū'at al-duwal al-imbiryāliyya allatī taḥtall bilād shu'ūb ukhrā (hiya al-jumal al-ismiyya) li-istighlālihā fa-tarfa' man yataqarrab ilayhā wa-tusmmīh bi-ismihā, wa-tanṣib 'alā al-mashāniq man yujāfīhā wa-yuqāwimuhā wa-yabta'id 'anhā, wa dhālik ta'bīran 'an ann kāna wa-akhawātihā tadkhul 'alā al-jumla al-ismiyya fa-tarfa' al-mubtada' wa-tanṣib al-khabar.

Wa-ammā inna wa-akhwātihā, fa-innī kunt uqaddimuhā li-l-ṭullāb 'alā i'tibār annahā ḥarakāt al-taḥarrur allatī tathūr 'alā al-musta'mirīn wa-taṭruduhum fa-tanṣib 'alā al-mashāniq al-mubtada' alladhī yata'āwan ma' al-isti'mār ta'bīran 'an anna inna wa-akhawātihā tanṣib al-mubtada' wa tarfa' al-khabar. Wa-istaṭa'tu khilāl fatrat 'amalī ka-mudarris an uqīm ma' ṭullābī 'alāqat wudd wa-ṣadāqa makkanatnī min an infatiḥ ma'ahaum wa-uḥaddithahum fī kull al-mawḍū'āt bi-ṣarāḥa wa-wuḍūḥ.

The main structure he utilized is the nominal sentence (*jumla ismiyya*) in which the first constituent is the subject (*mubtada'*) and the second is the predicate (*khabar*). Both constituents occur in the nominative. The Arabic term for this is *raf'*, which is derived from a root meaning 'to elevate, to raise'. When the nominal sentence is governed by the defective verb *kāna* (was), the subject remains in the nominative (*raf'*, elevation, high status) but the predicate takes the accusative. The Arabic term for the accusative is (*naṣb*), which is derived from a root that also signifies 'hanging from the gallows'. The opposite case markings obtain when the nominal sentence is governed by *inna* (an article of assertion): the subject takes the accusative (*naṣb*) and the predicate the nominative (*raf'*). The following examples set out the three cases:

(1)	*al-*	*walad-*	*u*	*shujā'*	*-un*
	the	boy	nom.	brave	nom.
	The boy is brave				
(2) *kāna*	*al-*	*walad-*	*u*	*shujā'*	*-an*
	the	boy	nom.	brave	acc.
			(*raf'*, elevation)		(*naṣb*, hanging)
	The boy was brave				
(3) *inna*	*al-*	*walad-*	*a*	*shujā'*	*-un*
	the	boy	acc.	brave	nom.
			(*naṣb*, hanging)		(*raf'*, elevation)
	The boy *is* brave				

Baransi utilized this information to convey the following set of political messages to his students with respect to *kāna*:

(1a) *kāna* and its sisters (verbs that behave in the same manner) represent the imperialist powers that occupy the land of other people, a clear reference to Israel;

(2a) just as these verbs make the subject (*mubtada'*) take the nominative (*raf'*), the imperialist and occupying powers elevate it in status (*raf'*) because it is adjacent to (collaborates with) them;

(3a) just as *kāna* and its sisters make the predicate take the accusative (*naṣb*), the imperialist powers hang it from the gallows (*naṣb*) because it is not adjacent to (refuses to collaborate with) them.

As far as *inna* is concerned, Baransi launches the following set of statements:

(1b) *inna* and its sisters (particles that behave in the same manner) represent the liberation movements (a clear reference to the struggle of the Palestinians) that seek to free their homelands from the imperialist and occupying powers;

(2b) just as these particles make the subject take the accusative (*naṣb*), the liberation movements will hang it from the gallows (*naṣb*) because it was adjacent to (collaborated with) the imperialist and occupying powers;

(3b) just as *inna* and its sisters make the predicate take the nominative (*raf*ʿ), the liberation movements will elevate its status (*raf*ʿ) because it kept its distance from (refused to collaborate with) the imperialist and occupying powers.

Furthermore, the fact that *kāna* shifts the meaning of the nominal sentence to the past shows that imperialism and occupation belong to a bygone age. Similarly, the fact that *inna* restores and asserts the original meaning of the nominal sentence indicates that the liberation movements will restore to the colonized people the freedoms they had had before the imperialist encounter. This example shows the sophistication with which Arabic can be used to articulate a Palestinian political agenda. This is in large part due to the new status of Arabic as the stigmatized language of a low-status national minority in Israel.

Conclusion

The collision between Arabic and Hebrew is one of the least-studied aspects of the Arab–Israeli conflict. This collision involves the instrumental and symbolic roles of the two languages as the vehicles of ideological contestation, mass mobilization and political action. Influenced by the German Romantics, Zionist leaders understood the significance of language in nation building, and they set about trying to revive Hebrew as a medium of everyday communication among the Jews in Palestine. Achieving this aim required determination and the will to fight off other contenders for linguistic legitimacy among the Jews. It also required political action to ensure that the language was given official status in Palestine. This was secured in 1922 when the British bestowed this status on Hebrew, alongside English and Arabic. Zionist efforts to promote Hebrew in the public sphere continued in the form of letters to the British authorities demanding that the language be given the same rights and privileges as English and Arabic – for example, by abandoning the vertical arrangement of the languages, with Hebrew at the bottom below English and Arabic, in favour of a horizontal mode of representation in which the three languages were linearly represented. The point at stake here was not instrumentality, but symbolic parity as a socio-political index of granting the Jews the same status as the Arabs of Palestine, although the former were mostly recent European immigrants who represented less than 10 per cent of the total population.

The revival of Hebrew as the language of everyday communication allowed it to be used as the medium for the delivery of education at all levels in the ever-growing Jewish community. Under the mandate, the Jews of Palestine enjoyed complete autonomy in the educational field. As a result, they were able to deploy Hebrew as the medium of teaching, as well as for both ideological and political mobilization away from the eyes of the British mandate authorities. When the Hebrew University was established in Jerusalem in 1924, Hebrew was declared the language of instruction in all fields of study, including medicine and the exact sciences. This was a bold educational and political move; it reflected the understanding that ideological commitment to Hebrew must be converted into a practical measure that signalled a new reality in Palestine. And to underline the break with the diversities of the Diaspora, in 1927 the university authorities refused to allow a chair of Yiddish to be established at their new institution (see Wright 1996).

These developments endowed Hebrew with heightened ideological relevance and political vigour. Loyalty to Hebrew came to represent loyalty to the ideals and objectives of the Zionist movement itself. Under this, the 'return' of the Jews to Palestine had to be accompanied by their 'return' to the language of their forefathers. Tilling the land required that Jewish labour restore to it the Hebrew names of its fauna and flora as an act of symbolic bonding in the nationalist enterprise. Hebrew was the 'stuff' and the means from and through which the Zionist dream of establishing a Jewish national home in Palestine had to be fashioned. This is why the Zionist movement referred to the emerging Jewish nation in Palestine as the 'Hebrew Nation' (Even-Zohar, cited in HaCohen 1997: 390).

The Zionist philosophy of reclaiming the land for the Jews went hand in hand with the effort of cartographers to create a model of the landscape in which Hebrew designated all features of the topography. A similar strategy operated in Israeli Jewish archaeology, although this will not detain us here.[63] This strategy brought Hebrew into contact and conflict with Arabic. The Zionists fired the first salvo by acting on their intention 'to restore' to the land the Hebrew names it lost, most of which they claimed had survived in a 'corrupt' form in Arabic. Imposing Hebrew on the landscape was therefore projected as an act of purification, a return to

[63] See Abu El-Haj (1998, 2001) for a fascinating account of how Israeli archaeology was and is still used in the service of Zionist ideology. Renaming the Citadel – built by the Mamluks on Crusader-period foundations – inside Jaffa Gate in the Old City as the 'Tower of David' is an act of cultural appropriation. The museum inside the Citadel tells the story of the city from a Jewish perspective, without any reference to the history of the Citadel itself. This is an act of cultural subversion. Both strategies, appropriation and subversion, are employed for political and ideological reasons in the service of the Zionist project of projecting the present onto the past. See Meskell (1998) for a collection of interesting studies on the interaction between nationalism, politics and archaeology in the Middle East.

the *status quo ante*, rather than as an act of linguistic and cartographic appropriation of the Arabic names. For the Zionists, the Arabic names acted as a semantic palimpsest: they did not designate the landscape directly, but did so through the Hebrew names they absorbed and preserved in a 'mutilated' form. Hebrew cartography is therefore a supreme act of national self-assertion whose aim was to draw up a contract of ownership, a linguistic title deed, to legitimize the claims of the Jews while, at the same time, delegitimizing the rights of the Palestinians in the struggle over Palestine.

This strategy of using linguistic cartography in support of the Zionist political aims and objectives is still in existence to this day. The use of Hebrew names to designate the Occupied Territories is a form of political action. It is intended to create an imagined political geography from which the occupation is absent. The Israelis have been extremely successful in this enterprise. Many people in the West have succumbed to the mistaken view that Gilo is a 'neighbourhood' of Jerusalem rather than an illegal settlement built on occupied Palestinian land; that Har Homa is another such 'neighbourhood' rather than an illegal settlement built on an occupied hill outside Jerusalem, which the Palestinians call Jabal Abu-Ghneim; and that East Jerusalem (including the Old City) is part of the 'unified' capital of Israel rather than a city illegally annexed by Israel in defiance of UN resolutions.

The deployment of language to create and legitimize illegalities on the ground is so pervasive that it has entered 'scientific' discourse. The main culprits have been (some) Israeli geographers. The failure in the literature on place names in Israel to respect the principles of international law has become an established practice in international journals. Similar practices are common in the Western media, which often give currency to the Hebrew name of a place against its Arabic name. In reports about the peace negotiations between Israel and the Palestinians, one often reads references to the 'Temple Mount' rather than to 'al-Haram al-Sharif', or to East Jerusalem as a 'contested city' rather than as an 'occupied city'. Similar practices are found in a major sociolinguistic study of the Old City. In addition, this study paints a picture of the linguistic situation in East Jerusalem that gives greater visibility to Hebrew than Arabic, although the latter is said to be the language of the majority in the Old City. The clash over names and modes of linguistic representation is replicated in the street signs of Jerusalem. As a sphere of contested ideologies, street and other public signs provide a vivid expression of the collision between Arabic and Hebrew. Although the Palestinians have tried to counter Hebrew hegemony in this and other domains of linguistic practice, the balance of linguistic power is far from tilting to their advantage. The occupation of Palestinian lands seems to go hand in hand with the command of the linguistic means to describe this occupation.

The Arab–Israeli conflict is responsible for a set of linguistic attitudes and practices among Arabs and Israeli Jews. The latter treat Arabic as the language of a 'hostile enemy'. Some also treat it as the language of a low-status national minority, the Palestinians in Israel, whom they consider as a fifth column. Arabic is further treated as a backward language of a backward people.[64] HaCohen (1997: 392) refers to a set of oppositional terms that describe the Palestinians in the Occupied Territories in an unflattering manner in comparison with the Israeli Jews: 'The Palestinians are portrayed as "rural", "traditional", "oriental", "primitive", in comparison to the Jews, who are "urban", "modern", "western" and "sophisticated".'[65] In an interesting twist of terminology, the application of the pejorative term 'native' (*mekomiyyim*) to refer to the Palestinians has led some to ask what the Jews would be if the Palestinians are the 'natives' in Israel. The combination of these attitudes explains the lack of motivation among Mizrahi Jews to maintain competence in the language of their fathers. The motivation to learn Arabic in Israel is therefore driven mainly by security considerations; hence the strong involvement of the Israeli military and intelligence services in teaching the language. In fact, some people in Israel believe that the primary responsibility for teaching Arabic belongs to the army and the security services. It is therefore not surprising that the most competent speakers of Arabic in the young age group are members or ex-members of the Israeli military establishment. This is indeed the association that Israelis and Palestinians in the Occupied Territories make in reflecting on Arabic language competence among young Jews in Israel.

The Arabs' views of Hebrew are equally unflattering. Hebrew is treated as the language of a colonial-style enemy who occupies Arab lands, oppresses the Palestinian people and conspires with the West against Arab

[64] See Rabinowitz (2002: 318) for a set of contrasting features between the Palestinians and their culture, on the one hand, and the Israeli Jews and theirs, on the other. These features are part of a dichotomy of negativity (represented by the Palestinians) and positivity (represented by the Israeli Jews).

[65] HaCohen (1997: 392) gives other examples of these terms in Israeli discourse:

> Palestinians . . . are usually 'villagers' (*kafriyyim*), whereas Jews who live in rural communities are *kibuzniks, moshavniks* etc. Palestinians are led by their 'notables' (*nikhbadim*), Jews have political leaders. Jews have intellectuals and professors, Palestinians have 'learned men' (*mashikilim*). Palestinians are *po'alim* 'workers', Jews are *ovidim* 'employees'. Palestinians are *soḥarim* 'merchants', Jews are *anshe asakim* 'businessmen'. A Palestinian university used to be called *mikhlala* 'college', unlike Israeli *universita* (a differentiation dropped in recent years, when American modelled colleges entered the Israeli higher education system).

interests. The presence of Hebrew in the Middle East is therefore delegitimized as an intrusion from the outside, aided and abetted by the colonial aspirations of Britain as a mandatory authority. Consequently, interest in Hebrew is driven by security considerations. Those who bewail the low competence in Hebrew among the Arabs do so because the national interest demands knowing the language of the enemy, who seem to be more aware of the value of learning the Other's language than the Arabs are (Abd-el-Jawad and al-Haq 1997). The Arab attitude towards Hebrew extends to the strong opposition to translating works from this language into Arabic and, in some cases, the other way round.[66] This opposition is strong in Egypt and Jordan, in spite of the fact that these countries have peace treaties with Israel. Arab intellectuals give as the reason for this position the belief that Israeli Hebrew culture does not have anything of positive value to contribute to the development of Arabic culture. The true reason, however, is the desire by these intellectuals to voice their opposition to what they see as the defective nature of the peace treaties with Israel. We may therefore ask whether Jordan and Egypt's peace treaties with Israel are likely to lead to conflict resolution on the linguistic front.

Evidence from Jordan seems to suggest that the peace treaty between Israel and Jordan in 1994 has led to a thaw in the linguistic conflict between them. The treaty stipulated that the two countries undertake to remove all hostile language from their media and school curricula. Abd-el-Jawad and al-Haq (1997) provide many examples of the linguistic cull implemented by the Jordanian government in education and the media. Israel is no longer referred to, among other things, as the 'Zionist enemy/entity' (*al-ʿaduww/al-kiyān al-ṣuhyūnī*), the 'colonizing entity' (*al-kiyān al-isṭīṭānī*), 'the occupation authority' (*al-sulṭāt al-muḥtalla*). The terms 'occupation' (*iḥtilāl*) and 'invasion' (*ghazw*) are now reserved for Israeli incursions into the areas controlled by the Palestinian National Authority. Whereas before the peace treaty operations against Israeli targets, ending in the death of the Palestinians who carried them out, were called 'resistance operations' (*ʿamaliyyāt muqāwama*), 'heroic operations' (*ʿamaliyyāt buṭūliyya*) or 'martyrdom operations' (*ʿamaliyyāt istishhādiyya*), they are now called 'terrorist operations' (*ʿamaliyyāt irhābiyya*), 'criminal operations' (*ʿamaliyyāt ijrāmiyya*), 'disgraceful operations' (*ʿamaliyyāt mushīna*) or, in a less critical mode,

[66] Edward Said (http://www.amin.org/eyejrs/0501/free-240501.htm) criticizes this practice among Arab intellectuals. He says that Hebrew translations of Arabic literature can have a positive effect on the attitude towards the Arabs in Israel. He cites as evidence in support of this the fact that most of this literature is published by Israeli publishers whose aim is to challenge the oppressive policies of their country towards the Palestinians.

'suicide bombings' (*'amaliyyāt intiḥāriyya*). Similar practices are in evidence in Egypt, although the Egyptian media enjoy greater freedom in their choice of terminology to describe the Israeli actions against the Palestinians.

The peace treaties with Jordan and Egypt have led to a reduction of the linguistic tensions with these two countries. Until recently, the same was true between Israel and the Palestinian National Authority (PNA) after the Oslo Accords in 1993 and 1995. During this period, Yasser Arafat was described as chairman of the PLO and the PNA, in contrast to previous references to him as a terrorist. However, this term returned during the second Palestinian intifada, which started in September 2000. The peace negotiations between Israel and the Palestinians in September 2000 – which took place at Camp David with the direct involvement of the American president, Bill Clinton – were responsible for the appearance of a new set of terminology to describe various proposals for resolving the Israeli–Palestinian dispute over East Jerusalem. Suzanne Goldenberg, *The Guardian's* correspondent in Israel, exemplified this by providing a list of the various terms referring to the sovereignty over the holy sites in occupied East Jerusalem (13 September 2000):

> If all had gone according to plan, today, September 13, would have been the birth of the state of Palestine, after a gestation period of more than 50 years.
>
> But instead of a state – whose due date was delayed for the second time at the weekend – there is the birth of a strange new vocabulary, the creation of those trying to solve the Israeli–Palestinian conflict.
>
> Their offerings include: divided sovereignty, joint sovereignty, shared sovereignty, delayed sovereignty, suspended sovereignty, functional sovereignty, custodial sovereignty and extraterritorial sovereignty.

Suzanne Goldenberg might have also added other terms: vertical sovereignty, horizontal sovereignty, above-ground sovereignty, and below-ground sovereignty – which made a fleeting appearance in some English newspapers. Discussions in Israeli circles about the shape of the future solution with the Palestinians employed other terminologies. One such term was 'unilateral separation' which had no precise meaning, although it generally referred to the imposition of a (territorial and demographic) de facto or interim solution on the Palestinians.[67] In spite of this terminological vagueness, political analysts used it to classify politicians and activists into 'right' and 'left wing', or into those who shifted their earlier positions to the right or left.[68]

[67] See Selwyn (2001) for some comments on 'separation' as a policy objective in Israel.

[68] See Lily Galili in Ha'aretz 27 June 2001: http://www.haaretzdaily.com/htmls/kat 10-2.htm.

The much-hoped-for thaw in the linguistic conflict between Israel and the Arabs has had limited success, and only on the official level during the last few years.[69] Progress on this front, at the popular level, will depend on whether a just and durable peace for the Arab–Israeli conflict can be found.[70] It therefore seems very likely that as long as Israel continues to occupy Arab lands in Palestine, Syria and Lebanon, the linguistic conflict between Hebrew and Arabic will continue.[71]

[69] Studies by social psychologists show that the desired reconciliation between the Israeli Jews and the Palestinians is beset by many problems whose roots lie in the 'structural inequality and domination' existing between them (see Helman 2002: 327). As long as these conditions apply, it is unlikely that the situation will change, even if peace is formally achieved. See Gur-Ze'ev (2001) and Maoz (2001) for the obstacles to the reconciliation between the Palestinians/Arabs and the Israeli Jews.

[70] To gauge the level of opposition to the normalization of relations at the popular level, we may cite the example of the Jordanian who was ostracized and hounded by his community for wanting to give his baby boy the name of the late Israeli prime minister Yitzhak Rabin. The boy was born on the day Rabin was assassinated in November 1995 (cited in Abd-el-Jawad and al-Haq 1997: 429–30).

[71] David Grossman (cited in HaCohen 1997: 393) hints at the major nature of this challenge when he points out that 'ten columns in a well known Hebrew Dictionary are dedicated to the entry "war", whereas only two columns [are dedicated] to "peace" '. I have checked a number of Arabic dictionaries, modern and pre-modern, for the entry 'war'. It seems that Arabic is no lexical match to Hebrew in this area.

6 Language and conflict in the Middle East: a conclusion

Between instrumentality and symbolism: the politics of language in the Middle East

Language is an important resource in any society. It is the means by which the members of a group communicate with each other in conducting their daily lives. But it is also an instrument for shaping reality by influencing people's perceptions of that reality, and of what counts as reality. Words are not empty talk; they are a form of action. When used in situations of political conflict, language can emerge as a loaded weapon: it can motivate people to act in pursuit of particular goals to deadly effect, or it can dissuade them from doing so by appealing to their better natures, or by invoking the principle of enlightened self-interest that allows compromise and reconciliation to occur. Either way, language is 'doing'. The Arabic grammatical maxim that speech is an act of the speaker (*al-kalām min fi'l al-mutakallim*), enunciated by the famous linguist Ibn Jinni a millennium ago (see Suleiman 1999c), is one of the guiding principles of this study. It enables us to take the rhetorical use of language very seriously, rather than dismissing it as 'hot air'. This is particularly pertinent when rhetoric is backed by material or physical force, or when the power between the contestants in a conflict is distributed asymmetrically. In such a relationship, the weaker party may in fact try to redress the balance of power in its favour by engaging in rhetorical acts on which it cannot deliver. It is this practice that gives rhetoric its 'bad name' in the court of public opinion. Whenever rhetoric becomes a substitute for action, rhetoric ceases to be a form of 'action'.

The use of language for ideological and political goals is a prime example of this instrumentality of language. We have seen many examples of this phenomenon in the present study. In prosecuting their political aims in Palestine, Zionist leaders showed an acute awareness of this role of language. They treated the map of Palestine as a site of linguistic contestation in which Hebrew had to dominate and would eliminate Arabic through acts of suppression, erasure and self-inscription. The mapping of the nation for these leaders was a linguistic one, which could proceed only by unmapping the Other. In pressing their case, Zionist leaders lobbied the mandatory power, appealed to the authority of the Bible as a source for naming the topography of the present in the image of a distant and (at least) hazy past, sought to set out their own counter-proposals on naming methodology, produced rules of conversion between the existing Arabic names and the putative Hebrew names that correspond to them, and attempted to inscribe these on the landscape of Palestine through acts of nationalist cartography.

Guided by the Orwellian maxims which stipulate that 'Who controls the past controls the future' and 'Who controls the present controls the past', this enterprise intensified after the establishment of the state of Israel in 1948. It included the linguistic cleansing of the maps of the main cities in Palestine by removing their Arabic street names, removing not only the names but all the cultural and nationalist connotations these names carried. Ramleh, a Palestinian town captured by Israeli Jewish forces in July 1948, provides an excellent example of how this was done. The six streets that bore Arab names on the map of the city in 1947 (the rest were not named) acquired Hebrew-Jewish names, including that of one of the most right-wing leaders in the history of the Zionist movement, Vladimir Jabotinsky (see Pinchevski and Torgovnik 2002).

This 'semantic blitzkrieg' reflected the depopulation of the country of its Palestinian inhabitants, and their replacement with new Jewish immigrants for whom Hebrew, not Arabic, was the language of national identity. Thus, what started in the pre-state period as a model for the future turned in the post-state era into a model of the present projected onto the past. The Palestinians mounted acts of cartographic resistance in which they sought to inscribe their memory of a Palestine dominated by Arabic names. They have also engaged in personal-names practices that signal the commitment to resisting the Israeli Jewish control of their country. Names such as *Kifāḥ* (struggle), *Thā'ir* (revolutionary), *Intiṣār* (victory) exemplify this trend. I hope to deal with this issue at length in a future study. In some cases, Palestinians in the Diaspora turned the names of their Palestinian villages inside Israel, including those that were destroyed in 1948, into 'objects of memory' by giving them to their offspring (see Slyomovics 1998: 202).

The instrumentality of language in the above examples is heavily laced with symbolism. When deployed in the prosecution of socio-political conflicts, language derives much of its power from this symbolism. As a marker of personal and collective identity, language encapsulates the values of a group, expresses its connectedness with the past and articulates its aspirations for the future. The intimacy of language and its ability to mark group boundaries endow it with socio-political meanings of inclusion and exclusion. This power of language as a border-guard comes to the fore when its ability to act in this way is infringed by outsiders who are projected as the quintessentially Other, the necessary counterpoint for a vis-à-vis mode of defining the nation and its national identity. Anton Shammas's *Arabesques* provides an example of this complex situation. Its Hebrew idiom challenges the link between people, language, territory and faith among Israeli Jews.

Anton Shammas wrote in Hebrew as a Christian and as a Palestinian in Israel, inscribing a narrative of a pre-state Palestine that challenged the received Zionist discourse on Palestine and punctured the view that Hebrew is the language of the Jews only. Some Israeli critics treated him as an intruder in the body of the Israeli Jewish nation, who they believed must be resisted and evicted by discursive means. Had Shammas written his novel in Arabic or in another language, this would not have mattered to Israeli Jews. And had the novel been written in Hebrew, but by another writer who did not belong to the 'enemy', this would not have mattered as much either. What gives the novel its politically induced linguistic charge in the Israeli milieu is its ability to demolish a set of culturally conceived dichotomies by making the voice of the out-group resonate in the ear of the in-group in its own idiom. By taking the linguistic-cum-ideological battle to the Other, Shammas provided an excellent illustration of the power of language in both its instrumental and symbolic connotations.

Language symbolism is at the heart of the language situation in Jordan. As we have seen in chapter 4, language (more correctly, dialect) in this context acts as a symbol of the state, separating those who are indigenous members of its national territory from those who are not. But language–dialect borders are always brittle and porous, even in cases of entrenched political conflict of the kind that exists in Israel/Palestine. In Jordan, this fact allows acts of code-switching where the male members of the out-group signal their membership in the state by shifting to those features that are constructed as emblematic of the linguistic repertoire of the in-group. As a cultural product, language is a valuable commodity in the symbolic domain. Its exchange in empirical transactions will therefore depend on who speaks to whom, when, where and under what conditions. These variables define the direction of code-switching, which is always subject to an assessment by the interlocutors of the balance of power between them. The greater the asymmetry of power between the interlocutors, the greater the unidirectionality of the code-switching. Jordan presents an excellent illustration of this principle. A similar situation exists in Romema in Israel (chapter 5), except that the Romemites switch to a *stigmatized* language (Moroccan Judeo-Arabic) to distinguish themselves from the Ashkenazi Jews.

The above examples resonate with heightened sociolinguistic meanings because of their embeddedness in situations of datable and overt political conflict. The fact that the political dominates the linguistic in these conflicts does not mean that the linguistic is unimportant or inoperative. Although language is not the cause of conflicts in the Middle East, it is nevertheless a symptom of these conflicts. It indexes them in socio-political terms and allows for their continuation at a level of tolerable intensity in intra- and interstate relations. Language acts as a safety valve in this domain. As a proxy for extra-linguistic concerns, language provides the politically disenfranchised with a channel for articulating a variety of what would otherwise be regarded as openly 'subversive' political messages. Language here acts as an instrument, as a symbol and as a buffer that disables the application of naked power against those whose real aim is to resist the hegemony of the state outside the linguistic domain. This is why when the state acquiesces to the linguistic demands of the disenfranchised under its rule, all it does in fact is to call their bluff and to cause a shift in their resistance to other domains of semiotic contestation. It is therefore unlikely that the Palestinians in East Jerusalem would cease their opposition to the Israeli rule over their city if Israel granted them a free hand in naming their streets and over the way the road signs for these streets are produced. It is also unlikely that the Palestinians in Israel would give the state their unquestioning loyalty even if it granted them a school curriculum that gave full expression to their Arabic-based culture and national identity. Landau (1987) was aware of this, which explains the attitude implicit in his discourse that granting Arabic equal rights with Hebrew in Israel would advance the Palestinization of the Palestinians rather than strengthen their loyalty to the state.

In his book on the symbolic construction of community, Anthony Cohen (2000: 14) makes the valid point that symbols 'do more than stand for or represent something else'. Unlike linguistic signs in the Saussurean sense, symbols are not governed by overtly fixed conventions that restrict their meaning in an invariable manner. Names are linguistic symbols par excellence. They are the quintessential symbols within language as a semiotic system that can in turn serve as a symbol in its own right in the socio-political world. Although the conventions of the English language 'stipulate' that 'John' is a male name for a human being, this does not preclude applying it to non-humans, animate or inanimate. The same does not hold equally for the linguistic sign 'car'. Applying this word outside its tightly circumscribed conventional meaning requires greater explanation and justification. Symbols are an effective means of communication precisely because they are semantically imprecise. This lack of precision allows those who use them to 'make meaning', to decant their own subjectivity into them, without feeling a total rupture with others in their group who endow the same symbols with quite different meanings.

Symbols are an important element of any culture because they enable people to express their commonality and individuality at the same time. They allow belonging and difference within a community to coexist without any feeling of contradiction. As Cohen tells us (2000: 16), 'the sharing of symbol is not necessarily the sharing of meaning'. This is why symbols have the ability to negotiate difference and to gloss it over. Commenting on this versatility of symbols, Cohen says (2000: 16): 'People of radically opposed views can find their own meanings in what nevertheless remain common symbols.' Symbols are also important because, as reified abstractions, they can encompass semantic terrains that work in unison through the power of imagination. They can also help the members of the nation to 'conceptualize their own disappointments and humiliations' (Sleeboom 2002: 301), as well as to celebrate their successes and connections with the past.

I think the above characterization of symbols is eminently applicable to language in any context. However, its validity strikes us most when languages or dialects exist in a state of conflict with each other. In Jordan, Arabic is a common symbol between Palestinians and East Jordanians. It expresses their membership in the Arab nation. Both groups are proud of the heritage and the culture for which this language is the medium. But this does not stop them from viewing their respective dialects differently under the impact of political conflict. And what unites the two groups also includes ingredients that drive them apart. We must also recognize that the same dialect may not hold the same meaning for all those who think of it as their native tongue. It is therefore not true that all Palestinians hold the same view of their local dialects, or that all East Jordanians hold the same view of their local dialects either. It is also not true that the members of each group hold uniform attitudes towards the dialect of the other group. Yet there are enough commonalities in each group to make it act as a reasonably cohesive unit in relation to the other group. Conflict accentuates these attitudes and the meanings they express. Language communicates these meanings and symbolizes them. It is both the means and, at the same time, an end.

Israel provides other examples of the way in which what is sociopolitically stigmatized is invoked to express meanings of difference within the body politic. That Palestinians in Israel use Arabic in this way is not surprising. What is, however, interesting is how Mizrahi Jews use their

Arabic vernaculars to express difference from their Ashkenazi compatriots in situations of socio-economic conflict. Moroccan Jews in Romema provide an interesting application of this practice (see p. 155), as do the Iraqi Jews who fall back on old discredited symbols to express their opposition to the Ashkenazi hegemony in the state. The temporary utilization of these symbols points to their existence as a latent resource in their communities. There is, however, a limit to the way in which these symbols can be utilized to express ethnic difference. This difference is still controlled by the Hebrew-language ideology. United with Ashkenazi Jews under the banner of Hebrew, Mizrahi Jews can dissent; but not to the extent of replacing the ties of faith and culture by those of an 'external' language. Although there is a sense in which Arabic speakers in Israel, Arabs and non-Arabs or Jews and non-Jews, can be made to share a common symbol – the Arabic language – the fact of the matter is that this is not possible because faith and national identity among the Mizrahi Jews override any ties of affinity that Arabic can forge between them and the Palestinians in Israel. Among the Israeli Jews, Arabic is a symbol of difference and division. But it is not a symbol of unity among *all* those who speak it in Israel.

The conflict between Arabic and Hebrew is a conflict between symbols. In this sense it is subject to variability and change. Palestinians in Israel do not relate to Hebrew in the way that Palestinians in the Occupied Territories do, and the latter also differ in their relation to the language from the Palestinians in the Diaspora. This situation of symbolic variability obtains again within Israel towards Arabic. Sociolinguistic studies of Israeli society reveal that the Ashkenazi Jews tend to be more accepting of Arabic than their Mizrahi compatriots, although the latter are native speakers of Arabic or descend from families who spoke the language until recently, or still speak it, as a native tongue (Ben-Rafael 1994). Evidence also exists, some of it tentative in nature, to the effect that the ethno-linguistic vitality of Arabic among Israeli Jews increases when the Palestinians mount acts of successful resistance to the Israeli occupation of the West Bank and Gaza. This seems to have happened in the wake of the first Palestinian intifada that erupted in 1987. And whether this will be sustained in the wake of the second intifada that started in September 2000 is an issue in need of empirical investigation. Whether peace can lead to radical and positive changes in linguistic attitudes on both sides is a moot point at the moment of writing. All will, however, depend on whether the peace between Israel and the Palestinians is a formal one, of the kind that exists between Egypt (or even Jordan at the popular level) and Israel, or is a lasting peace based on justice and the principles of international legality.

Tradition, modernity and coloniality: the socio-politics of language in the Middle East

As a symbol, Arabic in the Middle East is part of a triadic conflict involving tradition, modernity and coloniality. Some modernizers believe that the modernization of Arab society and culture must begin by modernizing the language itself. Script and grammatical reforms constitute the main and most immediate ingredients in the proposals to modernize the language. Proposals for reforming the script vary between wholesale Romanization and the modification of the current writing system by adding new symbols. Grammatical-reform proposals vary between those that aim at producing more or less new grammars of the language and those that seek to rearrange traditional grammar for pedagogic purposes. But some modernizers believe that the linguistic malaise in Arab life runs much deeper and is much more diffuse. They point to diglossia as the main problem facing the Arabs in the linguistic field. For this group, linguistic modernization in the form of grammatical and script reforms cannot on their own achieve real and lasting success without tackling the problem of diglossia in the first place. One solution consists of adopting a standard Arabic form of the language that is closer to the colloquial than it is to the erstwhile *fuṣḥā*. Another solution calls for the wholesale rejection of SA as an ossified language of the past in favour of the colloquials, the living and real mother tongues of the Arabs. Supporters of this solution are a vociferous minority who believe that nothing less than a linguistic divorce with the past can release the Arabs from the shackles of SA. At least this is their rhetoric as exhibited in, for example, the writings of the Egyptian essayist Salama Musa. People of this persuasion tend to be state nationalists who wish to weaken, or even eradicate, the link between Arabic and membership in an all-embracing Arab nation. It is no surprise therefore that Egypt, the longest-established nation-state in the Arab Middle East, produced some of best-known figures in this camp. Lebanon, with its complex ethnic and religious mix, comes a close second.

The call for linguistic reforms and the support for the colloquials against SA is a highly charged issue for many Arabic speakers, both culturally and politically. Touching on some of the most cherished values in Arab culture, the modernizers' agenda was bound to produce a counter-reaction. This was complicated by the belief that, intentionally or unintentionally, the modernizers have allied themselves to the colonialists who sought to undermine the cultural and political integrity of the language by (1) promoting their own languages in education and the administration at its expense; (2) supporting the call for the Romanization of the script;

and (3) encouraging through practical measures the use of the colloquial in writing. William Willcocks, a colonial administrator in Egypt, achieved great notoriety in the Arabic-speaking world in the nineteenth and twentieth centuries for blaming the lack of creativity among the Egyptians (and by implication the Arabs) on SA, and for making available a monthly magazine for publishing articles in the colloquial. The colonial involvement was thought to have been even more pervasive. It included the academy, members of which offered their extra-linguistic views dressed in the garb of objectivity and the idiom of pedagogic concern for the Egyptians. This interpretation, which has some validity, was cast in a 'conspiracy-theory' framework by highly respected Arab scholars. Naffusa Zakariyya Saʿid's book on the subject (1964) is still a classic forty years after its publication (see pp. 62–72).

Regardless of their source, the various calls and proposals for modernization were treated as an attack on the integrity of the Arabic language. The language-defenders read the modernizers' agenda as an attack on the range of historically sanctioned meanings the language carries. The attack on the language was therefore seen as an attack on Islam and on the Qur'an as its founding text. It was also interpreted as an attack on the set of values Arabic symbolizes, including the myth of election – the belief that the Arabs' exceptional qualities are encoded in the very structure of their language. Destroy this structure by grammatical reforms, and you will destroy the evidence for the uniqueness of the Arabs as an identifiable group that has a divine mission to fulfil on this earth (see Suleiman 2002 and 2003 for how this argument is made, although it may not apply to all those who call Arabic a native language). The language-defenders also argued that the linguistic fragmentation that would be ushered in by the colloquials does indeed have the capacity to lead to political and national fragmentation beyond the levels that already exist in the Arabic-speaking world. The fight against the modernizers was therefore projected as a noble battle for Islam, for the uniqueness of the Arabs and for their national aspirations: as misguided and dangerous individuals, the modernizers must be defeated to prevent them from destroying one of the foundations of Arab culture. This is what the language-defenders stood for and what they set out to achieve.

This fight against the modernizers was first and foremost an ideological battle. The modernizers were attacked with all the venom that ideologies can muster when they feel threatened or have come under fire. Rhetoric was the ultimate weapon of the language-defenders (although they had others at their disposal). Through it they could present their case in the court of public opinion. Using the power of language to defend language, the language-defenders adopted a variety of strategies.

To begin with, they had to make the difference between themselves and the modernizers seem as sharp as possible. Intermediate modernizing positions had therefore to be projected as the first step on a slippery slope whose ultimate destination is the full rejection of tradition, authenticity and continuity with the past. According to this, all modernizers are the same in spite of the differences that exist between them. For the language-defenders (for example Umar Farrukh 1961), the difference between Salama Musa, a radical modernizer, and Anis Frayha, a moderate modernizer, was more or less eliminated. In fact, Frayha was judged to be more dangerous than Musa because he preferred a covert mode of action to the overtly strident agenda espoused by Musa. When the battle lines are drawn sharply, the fight can begin in earnest. But when they are not, as in Frayha's case, there may be a quixotic feel to the charge. This is why the language-defenders prefer clarity to ambiguity.

After that, the language-defenders sought to draw attention to language as a symbol which could 'condense an enormous mass of information and experience in a single bit . . . for me or against me, right or wrong' (Boulding 1962: 281). The battle against the modernizers was therefore displayed as a battle about where one belongs in the full sweep of history, and to which morality one subscribes. This is clearly reflected in the dedications in some of the anti-modernizing books I have examined in this work. It is also clearly to be seen in some of the intertextual references the language-defenders made to the foundational texts of Arabic and Islamic culture. The language-defender usually presents himself as an embattled soldier defending his nation against unscrupulous opponents who are hell-bent (in the literal sense of 'hell', for that is their destination) on destroying one of the foundations of Arab and Islamic culture. In spite of this, the best and by far the most effective example of this intertextuality belongs to a modernizer, Gibran Khalil Gibran. To press their claim in the court of public opinion, the language-defenders marshalled the power of poetry, whose cultural meaning and emotional effect they exploited in compositions that extolled the virtues of Arabic and lamented the ingratitude and lack of concern Arabs displayed towards it. The personification and sublime objectification of the language in this poetry makes it both living and abstract, a target for love and respect, empathy and veneration.

Finally, the language-defenders invoked the trope of treason to silence the modernizers. They depicted them as members of a fifth column who worked against their people and culture in the service of the colonialists and neo-imperialists. Imputing these political intentions to the modernizers was the defenders' way of engaging the full meaning of language as a cultural symbol. In particular, this strategy drew attention to the political nature of language in a world where it is often taken for granted. It also created a sense of drama and spectacle where the cut and thrust of the battle can be witnessed and reproduced in other discursive battles in different places and times – as, for example, happened in Saudi Arabia in the debate over vernacular poetry in the 1980s.

In recent years, the language-defenders have turned their rhetorical firepower against the practice of code-switching in Arab societies. Code-switching was projected as a form of colonial penetration, cultural invasion and linguistic bastardization at whose roots lies a feeling of inferiority among the Arabs towards the West. As an aping behaviour, code-switching has been projected as a false form of linguistic modernization. One writer refers to code-switching as linguistic prostitution. Another refers to it as linguistic tarting up. These epithets are intended to signal the morally repugnant nature of code-switching, the fact that it involves giving up linguistic respectability in the cause of a veneer-thin modernity. Code-switching is therefore conceptualized as a form of linguistic impurity that challenges the verbal hygiene of the Arabic language. According to this view, code-switchers are linguistic defecators who pollute their verbal environments with colonial and neo-imperialist lexical excrement. The strong moral tones of these attacks may reflect the popularity of code-switching in some Arabic-speaking regions – North Africa and parts of the Levant, in particular – as a form of display that makes a statement about the self (see Eastman and Stein 1993).

It is, however, interesting to note here that code-switchers are often critical of their own linguistic behaviour, while this does not stop them from persisting in it. Most do not feel that there is any contradiction between their disapproving of code-switching and practising it. As long as they think that their loyalty to Arabic is attitudinally intact, and that code-switching is a harmless mode of speaking, code-switchers carry on in their happy ways irrespective of the accusations of affectation and inferiority that are levelled against them by the purists and the language-defenders. For these code-switchers, Arabic is no less a symbol of identity than it is for the purists. This is yet another illustration of how language as a symbol allows for diversity within commonality. Both the purists and the code-switchers feel they belong to the community of Arabic speakers, although they act differently towards the language.

In spite of their differences, the modernizers and the language-defenders, the code-switchers and the purists, are all the product of the same condition: the encounter between the past and the present, or between tradition and modernity, with all the tensions and social dislocations this encounter generates. Both camps are oriented towards the future, but they differ on the means of achieving it. In reality, both camps are cultural syncretists, but they differ on the mix of continuity and change in the syntheses they advocate. Both camps believe in a bounded identity, but they differ on where the boundary for this identity should be drawn. These differences are responsible for the tensions that exist between them. Nevertheless, there are usually enough commonalities between the two camps to justify their continuing to hang together, and to act together, in relating to outsiders in their environment. Symbols are an important element in the negotiation of difference and in the assertion of commonality. The language of a group communicates and enacts this process, combining its instrumentality with its ability to make meaning as a symbol.

Closing remarks

In this book, I have chosen to study language and socio-political conflict by examining various kinds of data. Some of the data are drawn from actual linguistic behaviour – for example, the code-switching in male speech in Jordan from the Fallahi and Madani varieties to the Bedouin variety. There is considerable scope for similar studies among the Palestinians in Israel, the Occupied Territories and Lebanon, three places where political conflict is a pervasive daily reality. North Africa, particularly Algeria and Morocco (see Bentahila 1983; al-Jabiri 1990; Tilmatine and Suleiman 1996), can provide extensive information on the topic. We must, however, make sure that in any such study conflict is not reduced to a background impulse that plays second fiddle to the usual demographic factors (age, sex, education and so on) that constitute a major part of the staple diet of Arab sociolinguistics. Other data involving code-switching that I have studied in this work relate to the attitudinal evaluation of this phenomenon in the Arabic-speaking countries. These are data about data, what may be called meta-data. It is actually at this level of discourse that the study of language and socio-political conflict can really come into its own, as it would in any major study of the conflict between the traditionalists and the modernizers at the institutional level – for example, in the Arab language academies or the institutions of higher learning. The third type of data I have utilized in this study is the map as a site of linguistic and ideological contestation.

Treating the map as a cartographic text, the sociolinguist can uncover a world of political meanings, in both the technical and general sense of the political. Studies of street names can yield further insights on the realities of power, hegemony, memory and resistance. Work in this field has so far been the preserve of the geographer, the anthropologist and (to a lesser extent) the social historian and the media specialist. Arab (not Arabic) sociolinguistics, relating both to Arabic and to other languages that fall within the domain of the Arab world, would be significantly enriched as an empirical and politically relevant discipline if it treated the map as part of its data. After all, the map is linguistic material which the sociolinguist must bring into his purview. There is a case, I believe, for treating the map as a semiotic system of signification, just as road signs and traffic lights are such systems. If so, the map has a degree of systemic affinity with language in its capacity as the semiotic system par excellence. Approached from this direction, the sociolinguist would not be stepping outside his disciplinary domain if he ventured into the socio-politics of map making. He would still be working in a way that is consistent with the major insights of his discipline.

Three further points need highlighting here. The first point concerns the need to increase the pool of data for the study of language and socio-political conflict. One obvious source of data is discourse itself. How is conflict represented in discourse? What strategies are deployed to articulate conflict? What is the context, historical and situational, for those texts that encode conflict? These and other questions can guide us in data selection and in the choice of approach for the study of conflict in language. By talking about 'language and political conflict in the Middle East' we can open the door for the involvement of languages other than those that are indigenous to the area in the study of conflict. In the case of the Arab–Israeli conflict, English can be engaged as a major player, and the internet can produce a very rich catch. The lexical domain may serve as a convenient starting point in any such study, but there are other more subtle ways in which conflict can be marked in discourse. The media can provide valuable data for this, as would the translation of conflict-related documents.

The second point concerns the importance of engaging a variety of approaches in studying language and socio-political conflict. In addition to sociolinguistics, these include cultural theory, media studies, urban geography, speech-accommodation theory, pedagogy and so on. Some of the references in this work testify to this variety of approaches. Language and socio-political conflict constitute a multidisciplinary enterprise; this enterprise must therefore engage as many disciplines as can shed light on it.

The third point concerns the importance of monitoring our discourse as scholars lest it be absorbed in the very ideological terrain it seeks to make manifest. We may not always succeed in doing this, but we have a responsibility to try. I have provided a few examples in this work of how ideology can permeate our thinking about language, making our 'objective' discourse on ideology itself ideological (see Liebes 1997 for interesting comments on the topic in the media and academia). This can happen at the level of terminology. But it can also happen at a more abstract and sophisticated level, involving erasure, self-censorship and the very way in which a scholarly work is organized. I hope to return to this fascinating issue, which touches on 'science as practice', in a future study.

Appendix 1
Letter to Robin Cook, British Foreign Secretary in 1998

Rt. Hon. Robin Cook PC MP
Foreign Secretary
House of Commons
London SW1A 0AA

22 March 1998

Dear Mr Cook

We, the undersigned, are writing to express our support and appreciation for the courageous step you have taken to visit Jabal Abu Ghneim in the Israeli Occupied Palestinian Territories during your last diplomatic tour of the Middle East. We believe that the visit has highlighted the illegality of the Israeli settlements on occupied Palestinian lands and Israel's blatant violations of International Law and United Nations resolutions concerning Jerusalem.

Enjoying the unquestioning support of the Americans in international fora, Israeli governments over the past few decades have continued to behave as though they were exempt from the provisions of international legality. Successive Israeli governments of all political colours have consistently refused to accept the will of the international community that settlements are illegal and that they are a very serious obstacle to peace. We believe that this has severely undermined the authority and effectiveness of the United Nations in the area and elsewhere in the world. Witness the reactions in the Arab world to the recent crisis in the Gulf where the firmness of the Americans, with robust British support, has been contrasted with the way Israel is allowed to act outside the law.

Great Britain has an historical responsibility towards Palestine and the Palestinians. There is no need for us to remind you that it was a Scottish Foreign Secretary, Lord Balfour, who was responsible through his famous declaration in 1917 for starting the ball of the Middle East conflict rolling. Instead of being grateful to Britain for its role in creating Israel, Mr Netanyaho has shown ingratitude and a crass lack of diplomatic decorum during your visit. We also believe that the description of you in sectors of the Israeli media and officialdom as an 'anti-Semite' shows the extent to which some Israelis are prepared to go to silence any criticism of their country's policies, no matter how right and well-justified this criticism is. This probably gives you a taste of what it is like to be a Palestinian living under Israeli occupation.

The European Union cannot afford to act indecisively while Israel, with American support, continues to wreck the search for a durable and just peace in the Middle East. The suffering and humiliation of the Palestinian people cannot be allowed to continue. There is also too much at stake strategically in the Middle East for Europe to adopt a policy of lukewarm engagement in the area. The argument that Israel does not respond well to public pressure has run its course. The European Union must therefore act firmly in dealing with both Israel and America if it is to contribute positively to achieving peace in the Middle East. As President of the European Union, Britain has a special duty and an historical responsibility to make sure that this happens. We therefore look to you and to the Prime Minister to provide the missing Western leadership in the pursuit of peace with justice between the Israelis and the Palestinians. We would be very grateful if we could be assured that this will indeed be the policy of HM government during its Presidency of Europe and beyond. As the minister in charge of British foreign policy we all look to you to provide the vigour that is your wont in pursuing this objective.

Yours sincerely
Professor Yasir Suleiman

Appendix 2
Letter from the Foreign and Commonwealth Office

2 April 1998
Professor Yasir Suleiman

Foreign & Commonwealth Office
London SW1A 2AH
Telephone: 0171

Dear Professor Suleiman,

Thank you for your letter of 22 March to the Foreign Secretary in support of his recent visit to Har Homa. I have been asked to reply. He is grateful for your supportive comments.

The objective of the visit to Har Homa was to underline the extent to which the expansion of settlements is undermining the Peace Process (there has been no progress in the Peace Process since the announcement that Har Homa was to go ahead). The Secretary of State wanted to make clear the concern of the international community, and especially the EU, at the expansion of settlements. By going to Har Homa, the Foreign Secretary also emphasised our strong support for the American call for time-out on settlement expansion. The visit, therefore, was in no way a distraction from the main issues of the Peace Process. On the contrary, it was a reminder that the main issue is land and the need to respect commitments under the Oslo Process.

UK/Israeli relations are sound and have stood the test of time and politics. We have no doubt that they will remain so. We will continue the important business of working for a successful outcome to the Middle East Peace Process and look forward to a successful visit to Israel by the Prime Minister later this month.

Yours Sincerely
Mohammed Toafiq Wahab
Near East and North Africa Department

References

WORKS IN ARABIC CITED IN THE TEXT

'Abbās, 'Abd al-Jabbār. 1967. al-Lugha 'ind Yūsuf Idrīs. *al-Ādāb*, 1: 29–31.

'Abbūd, Mārūn. 1968. *al-Shi'r al-'āmmī: amthāl al-qarya al-lubnāniyya wa-aghānīhā wa-saharātihā wa-l-lugha al-'āmiyya fīhā*. Beirut: Dār al-Thaqāfa.

'Abd al-Ghanī, Muṣṭafā. 1999. *al-Gāt wa-l-tabi'iyya al-thaqāfiyya*. Cairo: al-Hay'a al-Miṣriyya al-'Āmma li-l-Kitāb.

'Abd al-Laṭīf, Sanā'. n.d. al-Tarjama 'an al-'ibriyya wājib qawmī wa-risāla sāmiya. In *Qaḍāyā al-tarjama wa-ishkāliyyātihā*. Cairo: al-Majlas al-A'lā li-l-Thaqāfa, pp. 161–70.

'Abd al-Mawlā, Maḥmūd. 1980. al-Lahajāt khaṭar 'alā al-fuṣḥā. *Qaḍāyā 'arabiyya*, 8: 125–32.

'Abd al-Raḥmān, 'Ā'isha (Bint al-Shāṭi'). 1969. *Lughatunā wa-l-ḥayā*. Cairo: Dār al-Ma'ārif.

al-Abṭaḥ, Sawsan. 2001. al-Tabarruj al-lughawī: al-ṭarīq al-asra' ilā al-hāwiya. *Asharq al-Awsat*, 13 August 2001.

al-'Ālim, Maḥmūd Amīn (ed.). 1997. *Lughatunā al-'arabiyya fī ma'rakat al-ḥaḍāra* (Special issue of *Qaḍāyā fikriyya*). Cairo: Qaḍāyā Fikriyya li-l-Nashr wa-l-Tawzī'.

'Amāmra, Turkī Rābiḥ. 1995. Dawr al-isti'mār fī ib'ād al-lugha al-'arabiyya 'an majālāt al-ḥayā al-thaqāfiyya wa-l-tarbawiyya wa-l-idāriyya. *Asharq al-Awsat*, 7 March 1995.

al-Anbārī, Muḥammad Ibn al-Qāsim. 1987. *Kitāb al-aḍdād*, ed. Muḥammad Abū al-Faḍl Ibrāhīm. Sidon and Beirut: al-Maktaba al-'Aṣriyya.

Anīs, Ibrāhīm. 1970. *al-Lugha bayn al-qawmiyya wa-l-'ālamiyya*. Cairo: Dār al-Ma'ārif.

al-Atharī, Muḥammad Bahjat. 1984. (A poem in praise of Arabic: untitled). *Majallat majma' al-lugha al-'arabiyya al-urdunī*, 25/6: 112–14.

'Aṭṭār, Aḥmad 'Abd al-Ghafūr. 1964. *Ārā' fī al-lugha*. Jedda: al-Mu'assasa al-'Arabiyya li-l-Ṭibā'a.

1966. *al-Zaḥf 'alā lughat al-Qur'ān*. Beirut: Dār al-'Ilm li-l-Malāyīn.

1979. *Wafā' al-lugha al-'arabiyya bi-ḥājāt hādhā al-'aṣr wa-kull 'aṣr*. Mecca (no publisher).

1982. *Qaḍāyā wa-mushkilāt lughawiyya*. Jedda: Tihāma.

'Awaḍ, Luwīs. 1947. *Plutoland wa qaṣā'id ukhrā*. Cairo: Maṭba'at al-Karnak.

1965. *Mudhakkirāt ṭālib baʿtha*. Cairo: al-Kitāb al-Dhahabī.
1980. *Muqaddima fī fiqh al-lugha al-ʿarabiyya*. Cairo: Sīnā li-l-Nashr.
Badawī, El-Saʿīd Muḥammad. 1973. *Mustawayāt al-ʿarabiyya al-muʿāṣira fī miṣr*. Cairo: Dār al-Maʿārif.
al-Baḥrāwī, Sayyid. 1997. Lughat al-salām shopping centre li-l-muḥajjabāt. In al-ʿĀlim (ed.), *Lughtatunā al-ʿarabiyya*, pp. 135–8.
Barānsī, Ṣāliḥ. 1981. *al-Niḍāl al-ṣāmit: thalāthūn sana taḥt al-iḥtilāl al-ṣuhyūnī*. Beirut: Dār al-Ṭalīʿa.
al-Barāzī, Majd Muḥammad al-Bākīr. 1989. *Mushkilāt al-lugha al-ʿarabiyya al-muʿāṣira*. Amman: Maktabat al-Risāla al-Ḥadītha.
al-Bayyārī, Maʿn. 2001. al-Lugha al-ʿarabiyya tatadahwar fī dawlat al-imārāt. *al-Quds al-ʿArabī*, 14 July 2001.
al-Bazzāz, ʿAbd al-Raḥmān. 1956. *al-Tarbiya al-qawmiyya*. Baghdad: Maṭbaʿat al-ʿĀnī. (Pages 9–47 are reproduced in *Qirāʾāt fī al-fikr al-qawmī*, vol. I: *al-Qawmiyya al-ʿarabiyya, fikratuhā wa-nahḍatuhā*. Beirut: Markiz Dirāsāt al-Waḥda al-ʿArabiyya, 1993, pp. 259–79.)
bin Salāma, al-Bashīr. 1974. *al-Shakhṣiyya al-tūnisiyya: khaṣāʾiṣuhā wa-muqawwimātuhā*. Tunis: Muʾassasāt ʿAbd al-Karīm bin ʿAbdalla.
Bsīsū, Muʿīn. 1974. Muḥāwalat fakk al-irtibāṭ bayn al-fāʿil wa-l-mafʿūl bihi fī al-lugh al-ʿarabiyya. *Dirāsāt ʿarabiyya*, 8: 2–4.
al-Dabbāgh, Muṣṭafā Murād. 1985. *al-Mamlakatān al-nabātiyya wa-l-ḥayāwaniyya fi bilādina filasṭīn wa-atharuhā fī tasmiyat amkinatihā*. Beirut: Dār al-Ṭalīʿa.
Darwīsh, Maḥmūd. 1981. *Dīwān Maḥmūd Darwīsh*. Beirut: Dār al-ʿAwda.
Ḍayf, Shawqī. 1986a. *Tajdīd al-naḥw*. Cairo: Dār al-Maʿārif.
1986b. *Taysīr al-naḥw al-taʿlīmī qadīman wa-ḥadīthan maʿ nahj tajdīdih*. Cairo: Dār al-Maʿārif.
1990. *Taysīrāt lughawiyya*. Cairo: Dār al-Maʿārif.
1994. *Taḥrīfāt al-ʿāmiyya li-l-fuṣḥā fī al-qawāʿid wa-l-binyāt wa-l-ḥurūf wa-l-ḥarakāt*. Cairo: Dār al-Maʿārif.
al-Dhwādī, Maḥmūd. 1981. Judhūr al-franco-arab al-unthawiyya bi-l-mahgrib al-ʿarabī. *Shuʾūn ʿarabiyya*, 22: 124–37.
1983. al-Takhalluf al-ākhar fī al-maghrib al-ʿarabī. *al-Mustaqbal al-ʿarabī*, 47: 20–41.
1986. al-Mazj al-lughawī ka-sulūk lughawī li-l-insān al-maghribī al-maghlūb. *al-Majalla al-ʿarabiyya li-l-ʿulūm al-insāniyya*, 6: 46–66.
1988. Baʿḍ al-jawānib al-ukhrā li-mafhūm al-takhalluf al-ākhar fī al-waṭan al-ʿarabī. *al-Waḥda*, 50: 79–94.
1996. al-Franco-arab al-unthawiyya al-maghāribiyya ka-sulūk iḥtijājī ʿalā al-lāmusāwā maʿ al-rajul wa-ka-ramz li-kasb rihān al-ḥadātha. *Dirāsāt ʿarabiyya*, 3/4: 81–9.
al-Dibl, Muḥammad Ibn Saʿd. 1997. Risāla min umm al-lughāt. *Buḥūth nadwat ẓāhirat al-ḍaʿf al-lughawī fī al-marḥala al-jāmiʿiyya* (Special issue). Riyadh: Jāmiʿat al-Imām Muḥammad Ibn Saʿūd al-Islāmiyya, pp. 51–4.
al-Dūrī, ʿAbd al-ʿAzīz. 1960. *al-Judhūr al-tārīkiyya li-l-qawmiyya al-ʿarabiyya*. Beirut: Dār al-ʿIlm li-l-Malāyīn.
Farrūkh, ʿUmar. 1961. *al-Qawmiyya al-fuṣḥā*. Beirut: Dār al-ʿIlm li-l-Malāyīn.

Fayṣal, Rawḥī. 1989. al-Fuṣḥā wa-l-ʿāmiyyāt al-ʿarabiyya. *Shu'ūn 'arabiyya*, 59: 168–80.

Frayḥa, Anīs. 1955. *Naḥw 'arabiyya muyassara*. Beirut: Dār al-Thaqāfa.

1956. *Yassirū asālīb ta'līm al-'arabiyya: hādhā aysar*. Junyeh: Matābiʿ Karīm.

1959. *Tabsīṭ qawā'id al-lugha al-'arabiyya 'alā usus jadīda: iqtirāḥ wa namūdhaj*. Beirut: American University.

1966. *Fī al-lugha al-'arabiyya wa ba'ḍ mushkilātihā*. Beirut: Dār al-Nahār li-l-Nashr.

Ghanāyim, Muḥammad Ḥamza. 2001. *Wajhan li-wajh: sijālāt ma' muthaqqafīn yahūd*. Ramalla: Palestinian Forum for Israeli Studies (MADAR).

al-Ghazālī, Muḥammad. 1998. *Ḥaqīqat al-qawmiyya al-'arabiyya wa-usṭūrat al-ba'th al-'arabī*. Cairo: Dār Nahḍat Miṣr li-l-Nashr wa-l-Tawzīʿ.

al-Ḥājj, Kamāl Yūsuf. 1978. *Fī falsafat al-lugha*. Beirut: Dār al-Nahār li-l-Nashr (second printing; first published 1956).

Ḥamādī, Muḥammad Ḍārī. 1981. *Ḥarakat al-taṣḥīḥ al-lughawī fī al-'aṣr al-ḥadīth*. Baghdad: Dār al-Rashīd.

Ḥasan, Muḥammad ʿAbd al-Ghanī. 1979. Lugha tajmaʿ al-qulūb ʿalā al-ḥubb. *Majallat majma' al-lugha al-'arabiyya*, 43: 65–8.

Ḥusayn, Muḥammad Muḥammad. 1979. *al-Islām wa-l-ḥaḍāra al-gharbiyya*. Beirut: al-Maktab al-Islāmī.

n.d. *Ḥuṣūnunā muhaddada min dākhilihā*. Beirut: Mu'assasat al-Risāla.

Ibn Durayd, Abū Bakr Muḥammad Ibn al-Ḥasan. 1958. *al-Ishtiqāq*, ed. ʿAbd al-Salām Muḥammad Hārūn. Cairo: Maktabat al-Khānjī.

Ibn Fāris, Abū al-Ḥusayn Aḥmad. 1993. *al-Ṣāḥibī fī fiqh al-lugha wa-masā'ilihā wa-sunan al-'arab fī kalāmihā*, ed. ʿUmar Fārūq al-Ṭabbāʿ. Beirut: Maktabat al-Maʿārif.

Ibn Khaldūn, ʿAbd al-Raḥmān Ibn Muḥammad. 1958. *The Muqaddimah: An Introduction to History*, translated from the Arabic by Franz Rosenthal (3 vols.). New York: Pantheon Books.

Ibn Tinbāk, Marzūq Ibn Ṣnaytān. 1988. *al-Fuṣḥā wa-naẓariyyat al-fikr al-'āmmī*. Riyadh.

Ibrāhīm, Ḥāfiẓ. 1903. Shakwā al-lugha al-ʿarabiyya. *al-Muqtaṭaf*, 28: 552.

ʿĪd, Muḥammad. 1980. *al-Maẓāhir al-ṭāri'a 'alā al-fuṣḥā*. Cairo: ʿĀlam al-Kutub.

ʿIrsān, ʿAlī ʿUqla. 1992. al-Fuṣḥā wa-l-ʿāmiyya wa-lughat al-ḥiwār al-masraḥī. *al-Majalla al-'arabiyya li-l-thaqāfa*, 22: 116–43.

al-Jābirī, Muḥammad ʿĀbid. 1990. *al-Siyāsāt al-ta'līmiyya fī aqṭār al-maghrib al-'arabī*. Amman: Muntadā al-Fikr al-ʿArabī.

1991. *al-Turāth wa-l-ḥadātha: dirāsāt wa-munāqashāt*. Beirut: Markiz Dirāsāt al-Waḥda al-ʿArabiyya.

al-Jamālī, Fāḍil. 1996. *Difā'an 'an al-'arabiyya*. Tunis: Mu'assasat ʿAbd al-Karīm bin ʿAbdalla.

al-Jārim, ʿAlī. 1935. (A poem in praise of Arabic: untitled). *Majallat majma' al-lugha al-'arabiyya al-malakī*, 22–7.

al-Jawārī, Aḥmad ʿAbd al-Sattār. 1984. *Naḥw al-Taysīr: dirāsa wa-naqd manhajī*. Baghdad: al-Majmaʿ al-ʿIlmī al-ʿIrāqī.

al-Jundī, Anwar. 1982. *al-Fuṣḥā lughat al-Qur'ān*. Beirut: Dār al-Kitāb al-Lubnānī.

n.d. *al-Madd al-islāmī fī maṭāliʿ al-qarn al-khāmis ʿashar*. Dār al-Iʿtiṣām.
Khālidī, Muṣṭafā and ʿUmar Farrūkh. 1982. *al-Tabshīr wa-l-istiʿmār fī al-bilād al-ʿarabiyya: ʿarḍ li-juhūd al-mubashshirīn allatī tarmī ilā ikhḍāʿ al-sharq li-l-istiʿmār al-gharbī*. Beirut and Sidon: Manshūrāt al-Maktaba al-ʿAṣriyya (first published 1953).
Khalidī, Walīd (ed.). 1997. *Kay lā nansā: qurā filasṭīn allatī dammarathā isrāʾīl sanat 1948 wa-asmāʾ shuhadāʾihā*. Beirut: Institute for Palestine Studies.
Khalīfa, ʿAbd al-Karīm. 1986. *Taysīr al-ʿarabiyya bayn al-qadīm wa-l-ḥadīth*. Amman: Majmaʿ al-Lugha al-ʿArabiyya al-Urdunī.
Khamīs, ʿAbdalla (Ibn). 1984. (A poem in praise of Arabic: untitled). *Majallat majmaʿ al-lugha al-ʿarabiyya al-urdunī*, 25/6: 115–16.
Khūrī, Yūsuf Qazmā. 1991. *Najāḥ al-umma al-ʿarabiyya fī lughatihā al-aṣliyya*. Beirut: Dār al-Ḥamrāʾ.
Laʿībī, Shākir. 2001. al-Frānkūfūniyya wa-l-ʿarabūfūniyya: malāyīn al-ʿarab al-mansiyyīn fī turkiyyā. *al-Quds al-ʿArabī*, 23 August 2001.
al-Lugha al-ʿarabiyya fī miḥna wa-lā budd min inqādhihā. HTTP://www.middle-east-online.com/Features/May2001/arabic/language-14-5-2001.htm.
Luṭfī al-Sayyid, Aḥmad. 1945. *al-Muntakhabāt* (2 vols.). Cairo: Maktabat al-Anglū al-Miṣriyya.
Maḥfūẓ, Ḥusayn ʿAlī. 1990. Khams wa-thalāthūn ʿām fī majmaʿ al-lugha al-ʿarabiyya fī al-qāhira. *Majallat majmaʿ al-lugha al-ʿarabiyya al-urdunī*, 38: 108–9.
Marḥabā, Muḥammad ʿAbd al-Raḥmān. 1990. al-Lugha al-ʿarabiyya wa mā alḥaqathā bihā al-tarjama min tashwīhāt. *al-Fikr al-ʿarabī*, 61: 69–86.
Maṭar, ʿAbd al-ʿAzīz. 1966. *Laḥn al-ʿāmma fī ḍawʾ al-dirāsāt al-lughawwiya al-ḥadītha*. Cairo: Dār al-Kātib al-ʿArabī li-l-Ṭibāʿa wa-l-Nashr.
Mijlī, Nasīm. 1995. *Luwīs ʿAwaḍ wa-maʿārikuh al-adabiyya*. Cairo: al-Hayʾa al-Miṣriyya al-ʿĀmma li-l-Kitāb.
Munīf, ʿAbd al-Raḥmān. 1994. *al-Kātib wa-l-manfā*. Beirut: al-Muʾassasa al-ʿArabiyya li-l-Dirāsāt wa-l-Nashr.
al-Mūsā, Nihād. 1987. *Qaḍiyyat al-taḥawwul ilā al-fuṣḥā fī al-ʿālam al-ʿarabī al-ḥadīth*. Amman: Dār al-Fikr li-l-Nashr wa-l-Tawzīʿ.
1990. *al-Lugha al-ʿarabiyya wa-abnāʾuhā: abḥāth fī qaḍiyyat al-khaṭaʾ wa-ḍaʿf al-ṭalaba fī al-lugha al-ʿarabiyya*. Amman: Maktabat Wisām.
Mūsā, Salāma. 1964. *al-Balāgha al-ʿaṣriyya wa-l-lugha al-ʿarabiyya*. Cairo: Salāma Mūsā li-l-Nashr wa-l-Tawzīʿ (first edition published 1945).
Muṣṭafā, Ibrāhīm. 1959. *Iḥyāʾ al-naḥw*. Cairo: Lajnat al-Taʾlīf wa-l-Tarjama wa-l-Nashr (first published 1937).
al-Naḥawī, ʿAdnān ʿAlī Riḍā. 1998. *Limādhā al-lugha al-ʿarabiyya?* Riyadh: Dār al-Naḥawī li-l-Nashr wa-l-Tawzīʿ.
Nuʿmān, Aḥmad (Ibn). 1992. al-Lugha wa-l-thaqāfa fī ẓurūf al-ghazw. *al-Fikr al-ʿarabī*, 70: 91–108.
Qaddūra, Zāhiya. 1972. *al-Shuʿūbiyya wa-atharuhā al-ijtimāʿī wa-l-siyāsī fī al-ḥayāt al-islāmiyya fī al-ʿaṣr al-ʿabbāsī al-awwal*. Beirut: Dār al-Kitāb al-Lubnānī.
al-Qāḍī, Maḥmūd. 1982. *al-Arḍ fī shiʿr al-muqāwama al-filasṭīniyya*. Libya and Tunis: al-Dār al-ʿArabiyya li-l-Kitāb.

Qaṣṣāb, Walīd Ibrāhīm. 1994. Jināyat al-ḥadātha ʿalā al-lugha al-ʿarabiyya. *Majallat kulliyat al-dirāsāt al-islāmiyya wa-l-ʿarabiyya*, 9: 201–32.

al-Qurashī, Ḥasan ʿAbdalla. 1990. Fī āfāq al-waḥy. *Majallat majmaʿ al-lugha al-ʿarabiyya al-urdunī*, 38: 104–6.

al-Rāfiʿī, Muṣṭafā Ṣādiq. 1974. *Taḥt rāyat al-Qurʾān*. Beirut: Dār al-Kitāb al-Lubnānī.

Rashīd, Amīna (ed.). 1999. *al-Tabiʿiyya al-thaqāfiyya: mafāhīm wa-abʿād*. Cairo: Dār al-Amīn.

Rukaybī, ʿAbdalla. 1992. *al-Frānkūfūniyya mashriqan wa-maghriban*. Beirut: al-Ruwwād li-l-Nashr wa-l-Tawzīʿ.

al-Ruṣāfī, Maʿrūf. 2000. *al-Aʿmāl al-shiʿriyya al-kāmila*. Beirut: Dār al-ʿAwda.

al-Saftī, Madīḥa. 1982. al-Taʿlīm al-ajnabī fī al-bilād al-ʿarabiyya: al-izdiwājiyya fī al-nasaq al-taʿlīmī wa-qaḍiyyat al-intimāʾ al-qawmī. *Shuʾūn ʿarabiyya*, 22: 13–26.

Saʿīd, Naffūsa Zakariyyā. 1964. *Tārīkh al-daʿwa ilā al-ʿāmmiyya wa-āthāruhā fī miṣr*. Cairo: Maṭbaʿat Dār Nashr al-Thaqāfa.

Samʿān, Khalīl. 1967. Daʿwā al-ṣuʿūba fī taʿallum al-ʿarabiyya (part I). *Majallat majmaʿ al-lugha al-ʿarabiyya bi-Dimashq*, 42: 749–804.

1968. Daʿwā al-ṣuʿūba fī taʿallum al-ʿarabiyya (part II). *Majallat majmaʿ al-lugha al-ʿarabiyya bi-Dimashq*, 43: 166–78.

al-Sāmirrāʾī, Ibrāhīm. 1979. al-Lugha al-ʿarabiyya wa-wasāʾil al-iʿlām: a-tarjama am ʿadwā lughawiyya? *Majallat majmaʿ al-lugha al-ʿarabiyya*, 43: 99–110.

1990. Maʿ al-ʿarabiyya wa-majmaʿ al-lugha fī al-qāhira. *Majallat majmaʿ al-lugha al-ʿarabiyya al-urdunī*, 38: 106–8.

Shaʿbān, ʿAwaḍ. 1994. Muʾāmarat anṣār al-ʿāmiyya ʿalā al-fuṣḥā. *al-Fikr al-ʿarabī*, 75: 155–60.

al-Shakʿa, Muṣṭafā. 1970. *Muṣṭafā Ṣādiq al-Rāfiʿī kātiban ʿarabiyyan wa-mufakkiran islāmiyyan*. Beirut: Arab University of Beirut.

Shākir, Maḥmūd Muḥammad. 1972. *Abāṭīl wa-asmār*. Cairo: Maṭbaʿat al-Madanī.

al-Ṣuwayyān, Saʿd al-ʿAbdalla. 2000. *al-Shiʿr al-nabaṭī*. Beirut: Dār al-Sāqī.

Ṭarābīshī, George. 1982. *al-Dawla al-quṭriyya wa-l-naẓariyya al-qawmiyya*. Beirut: Dār al-Ṭalīʿa.

al-Ṭawīl, al-Sayyid Rizq. 1986. *al-Lisān al-ʿarabī wa-l-islām maʿan fī maʿrakat al-muwājaha*. Daʿwat al-Ḥaqq (vol. 60).

al-Ṭayyib, ʿAbdalla. 1984. (A poem in praise of Arabic: untitled). *Majallat majmaʿ al-lugha al-ʿarabiyya al-urdunī*, 25/6: 139–40.

ʿUmar, Muḥammad Ṣāliḥ. 1987. Muʾāmarat istibdāl al-ḥurūf al-ʿarabiyya bi-l-ḥurūf al-lātīniyya fī ʿahd al-ḥimāya fī tūnis. *al-Mustaqbal al-ʿarabī*, 99: 65–76.

Wahba, Tawfīq ʿAlī. 1983. *al-Shiʿr al-Shaʿbī: shiʿr am zajal?*. Riyadh.

Willcocks, William. 1893. Lima lam tūjad quwwat al-ikhtirāʿ ladā al-miṣriyyīn al-ān? *al-Azhar*, 6: 1–10.

Yaʿqūb, Emile Badīʿ. 1985. *Gibran wa-l-lugha al-ʿarabiyya*. Tripoli, Lebanon: Jarrūs Press.

Zahrān, al-Badrāwī ʿAbd al-Wahhāb. 1985. *Daḥd muftarayāt ḍidd iʿjāz al-qurʾān wa-abāṭīl ukhrā ikhtalaqahā al-ṣalībī al-mustaghrib al-duktūr Luwīs ʿAwaḍ*. Mecca: Rābiṭat al-ʿĀlam al-Islāmī.

al-Zamakhsharī, Abū al-Qāsim Maḥmūd Ibn ʿUmar. 1840. *al-Mufaṣṣal fī al-naḥw*, ed. J. P. Broch. Oslo: Libraria P. T. Mallingii.

Zughoul, Muḥammad Rājī. 1988. al-Lāfitāt fī al-urdun: dirāsa lughawiyya ijtimāʿiyya li-baʿḍ jawānib ghurbatinā al-ḥaḍāriyya. In *Nadwat al-izdiwājiyya fī al-lugha al-ʿarabiyya* (Special issue). Amman: University of Jordan Press, pp. 25–36.

WORKS IN OTHER LANGUAGES CITED IN THE TEXT

Abdel-Jawad, Hassan Rashid E. 1981. Lexical and Phonological Variation in Spoken Arabic in Amman. University of Pennsylvania: Ph.d. thesis.

Abd-el-Jawad, Hassan R. S. and Fawwaz al-Abed al-Haq. 1997. The Impact of the Peace Process in the Middle East on Arabic. In Michael Clyne (ed.), *Undoing and Redoing Corpus Planning*. Berlin and New York: Mouton de Gruyter, pp. 415–43.

Abdel-Malek, Zaki. 1972. The Influence of Diglossia on the Novels of Yusif al-Sibāʿī. *Journal of Arabic Literature*, 3: 132–41.

Abdul-Fattah, H. and M. Zoghoul. 1996. Business Signs in Jordan: A Sociolinguistic Perspective. *al-Abhath*, 44: 59–88.

Abu-Absi, Samir. 1990. A Characterization of the Language of *Iftaḥ Yā Simsim*: Sociolinguistic and Educational Implications for Arabic. *Language Planning and Language Problems*, 14: 33–46.

1991. The 'Simplified Arabic' of *Iftaḥ Yā Simsim*: Pedagogical and Sociolinguistic Implications. *al-ʿArabiyya*, 24: 111–21.

Abu El-Haj, Nadia. 1998. Translating Truths: Nationalism, the Practice of Archaeology, and the Remaking of Past and Present in Contemporary Jerusalem. *American Ethnologist*, 25: 166–88.

2001. *Facts on the Ground: Archaeological Practice and Territorial Self-Fashioning in Israeli Society*. Chicago: Chicago University Press.

Abuljebain, Nader Khairiddine. 2001. *Palestine History in Postage Stamps: Collection of Nader Khairiddine Abuljebain*. Beirut: Institute for Palestine Studies.

Abu-Melhim, Abdel-Rahman. 1991. Code-switching and Linguistic Accommodation in Arabic. In Bernard Comrie and Mushira Eid (eds.), *Perspectives on Arabic Linguistics III: Papers from the Third Annual Symposium on Arabic Linguistics*. Amsterdam and Philadelphia: John Benjamins Publishing Company, pp. 231–50.

Abu-Odeh, Adnan. 1999. *Jordanians, Palestinians and the Hashemite Kingdom in the Middle East Peace Process*. Washington, DC: United States Institute of Peace Press.

Agius, Dionisius A. 1980. The Shuʿūbiyya Movement and its Literary Manifestation. *The Islamic Quarterly*, 24: 76–87.

Ahlqvist, Anders. 1993. Language Conflict and Language Planning. In Ernst Håkon Jahr (ed.), *Language Conflict and Language Planning*. Berlin: Mouton de Gruyter, pp. 7–20.

Aitcheson, Jean. 2001. Misunderstandings about Language: A Historical View. *Journal of Sociolinguistics*, 5: 611–19.

Allen, Irving Lewis. 1983. *The Language of Ethnic Conflict: Social Organization and Lexical Culture*. New York: Columbia University Press.

Alosh, Muhammad al-Mahdi. 1984. Implications of the Use of Modern Standard Arabic in the Arabic Adaptation of 'Sesame Street'. Ohio State University: MA dissertation.

al-Amadidhi, Darwish G. 1985. Lexical and Sociolinguistic Variation in Qatari Arabic. University of Edinburgh: Ph.d. thesis.

Amara, Muhammad Hasan. 1999. *Politics and Sociolinguistic Reflexes: Palestinian Border Villages*. Amsterdam and Philadelphia: John Benjamins Publishing Company.

Amara, Muhammad and Bernard Spolsky. 1996. The Construction of Identity in a Divided Palestinian Village: Sociolinguistic Evidence. In Yasir Suleiman (ed.), *Language and Identity in the Middle East and North Africa*. Richmond: Curzon Press, pp. 81–98.

Arnold, Werner. 2002. Code-switching and Code-mixing in the Arabic Dialects of Antioch. In Ibrahim Youssi, Fouzia Benjelloun, Mohamed Dahbi and Zakia Iraqui-Sinacer (eds.), *Aspects of the Dialects of Arabic Today* (Proceedings of the Fourth Conference of the International Arabic Dialectology Association (AIDA), Marrakesh, 1–4 April 2000), pp. 163–8.

Azarya, Victor. 1989. Civil Education in the Israeli Armed Forces. In Ernest Krausz and David Glanz (eds.), *Education in a Comparative Context*. New Brunswick: Transaction Publishers, pp. 119–47.

Azaryahu, Maoz. 1992. The Purge of Bismarck and Saladin: The Renaming of Streets in East Berlin and Haifa: A Comparative Study in Culture-Planning. *Poetics Today*, 13: 350–67.

Azaryahu, Maoz and Rebecca Kook. 2002. Mapping the Nation: Street Names and Arab Palestinian Identity: Three Case Studies. *Nations and Nationalism*, 8: 195–212.

Badawi, M. M. 1985. *Modern Arabic Literature and the West*. London: Ithaca Press.

Bader, Yousef and Radwan Mahadin. 1996. Arabic Borrowings and Code-switches in the Speech of English Native Speakers Living in Jordan. *Multilingual*, 15: 35–53.

Baker, Colin. 1992. *Attitudes and Language*. Clevedon: Multilingual Matters Ltd.

Bakhtin, M. M. 1981. *The Dialogic Imagination*. Austin: University of Texas Press.

Bamia, Aida Adib. 2001. *The Graying of the Raven: Cultural and Socio-political Significance of Algerian Folk Poetry*. Cairo and New York: American University in Cairo Press.

Bardenstein, Carol B. 1999. Trees, Forests, and the Shaping of Palestinian and Israeli Collective Memory. In M. Bal, J. Crewe and L. Spiter (eds.), *Acts of Memory*. Hanover: University Press of New England, pp. 148–68.

Bar-Gal, Yoram. 1989. Cultural–Geographical Aspects of Street Names in the Towns of Israel. *Names*, 37: 329–44.

Barhoum, Khalil. 1994. English–Arabic Code-switching as a Form of Bilingual Discourse. In Raji M. Rammuny and Dilworth B. Parkinson (eds.), *Investigating Arabic: Linguistic, Pedagogical and Literary Studies in Honour of Ernest N. MacCarus*. Columbus, OH: Greyden Press, pp. 95–109.

Barnes, Barry. 1988. *The Nature of Power*. Cambridge: Polity Press.

Barth, Fredrik. 1969. Introduction. In Fredrik Barth (ed.), *Ethnic Groups and Boundaries*. Boston: Little, Brown, pp. 9–38.
Bauer, Laurie and Peter Trudgill (eds.). 1998. *Language Myths*. London: Penguin Books.
Ben Artzi-Pelossof, Noa. 1996. *In the Name of Sorrow and Hope*. New York: Alfred A. Knopf.
Ben-Rafael, Eliezer. 1994. *Language, Identity and Social Division: The Case of Israel*. Oxford: Clarendon Press.
2001. A Sociological Paradigm of Bilingualism: English, French, Yiddish and Arabic in Israel. In Hanna Herzog and Eliezer Ben-Rafael (eds.), *Language and Communication in Israel*. New Brunswick and London: Transaction Publications, pp. 175–205.
Ben-Rafael, Eliezer and Hezi Brosh. 1991. A Sociolinguistic Study of Second Language Diffusion: The Obstacles to Teaching Arabic in the Israeli Schools. *Language Planning and Language Problems*, 15: 1–24.
2001. Jews and Arabs in Israel: The Cultural Convergence of Divergent Identities. In Hanna Herzog and Eliezer Ben-Rafael (eds.), *Language and Communication in Israel*. New Brunswick and London: Transaction Publications, pp. 289–310.
Benson, Phil. 2001. *Ethnocentricism and the English Dictionary*. London and New York: Routledge.
Bentahila, Abdelali. 1983. *Language Attitudes among Arabic–French Bilinguals in Morocco*. Clevedon: Multilingual Matters Ltd.
Bentolila, Yaakov. 2001. Bilingualism in a Moroccan Settlement in the South of Israel. In Hanna Herzog and Eliezer Ben-Rafael (eds.), *Language and Communication in Israel*. New Brunswick and London: Transaction Publications, pp. 243–58.
Benvenisti, Meron. 2000. *Sacred Landscape: The Buried History of the Holy Land since 1948*, translated from the Hebrew by Maxine Kaufman-Lacusta. Berkeley: University of California Press.
Berg, Nancy E. 1996. *Exile from Exile: Israeli Writers from Iraq*. Albany: State University of New York Press.
Birks, J. S. 1988. The Demographic Challenge in the Arab Gulf. In B. R. Pridham (ed.), *The Gulf and the Arab World*. London: Croom Helm, pp. 131–52.
Blanc, Haim. 1964. *Communal Dialects in Baghdad*. Cambridge, MA: Harvard University Press.
Blau, Joshua. 1969. *The Renaissance of Modern Hebrew and Modern Standard Arabic: Parallels and Differences in the Revival of Two Semitic Languages*. Berkeley: University of California Press.
Blommaert, Jan (ed.). 1999. *Language Ideological Debates*. Berlin and New York: Mouton de Gruyter.
Bolinger, Dwight. 1980. *Language: The Loaded Weapon*. London: Longman.
Boulding, Kenneth E. 1962. *Conflict and Defense: A General Theory*. New York: Harper & Row.
Bourdieu, Pierre. 1992. *Language and Symbolic Power*. Cambridge: Polity Press.
Bourhis, Richard Yvon. 1979. Language in Ethnic Interaction: A Social Psychological Approach. In Howard Giles and Bernard Saint-Jacques (eds.), *Language and Ethnic Relations*. Oxford: Pergamon Press, pp. 117–41.

1997. Language Policies and Language Attitudes: Le Monde de la Francophonie. In Nikolas Coupland and Adam Jaworski (eds.), *Sociolinguistics: A Reader and a Coursebook*. New York: St Martin's Press, Inc. pp. 306–22 (first published in 1982).

Bourhis, Richard Yvon, Howard Giles, Jacques P. Leyens and Henri Tajfel. 1979. Psycholinguistic Distinctiveness: Language Divergence in Belgium. In Howard Giles and Robert N. St Clair (eds.), *Language and Social Psychology*. Oxford: Basil Blackwell, pp. 158–85.

Bowman, Glenn. 1988. Tales of the Lost Land: Palestinian Identity and the Formation of Nationalist Consciousness. *New Formations*, 4: 31–52.

Brenner, Rachel Feldhay. 1993. In Search of Identity: The Israeli Arab Artist in Anton Shammas's *Arabesques*. *Proceedings of the Modern Language Association*, 18: 431–45.

Cachia, Pierre. 1990. *An Overview of Modern Arabic Literature*. Edinburgh: Edinburgh University Press.

Cadora, Frederic J. 1970. Some Linguistic Concomitants of Contractual Factors of Urbanization. *Anthropological Linguistics*, 12: 10–19.

1992. *Bedouin, Village and Urban Arabic: An Ecolinguistic Study*. Leiden: E.J. Brill.

Calvet, Louis-Jean. 1998. *Language Wars and Linguistic Politics*, translated from the French by Michel Petheram. Oxford: Oxford University Press.

Cameron, Deborah. 1995. *Verbal Hygiene*. London and New York: Routledge.

1997. Demythologizing Sociolinguistics. In Nikolas Coupland and Adam Jaworski (eds.), *Sociolinguistics: A Reader and a Coursebook*. New York: St Martin's Press, Inc., pp. 55–67 (first published in 1990).

Cameron, Deborah and Jill Bourne. 1988. No Common Ground: Kingman, Grammar and the Nation. *Language and Education*, 2: 147–60.

Cheshin, Amir S., Bill Hutman and Avi Melamed. 1999. *Separate and Unequal: The Inside Story of Israeli Rule in East Jerusalem*. Cambridge, MA: Harvard University Press.

Cleary, Joe. 2002. *Literature, Partition and the Nation State: Culture and Conflict in Ireland, Israel and Palestine*. Cambridge: Cambridge University Press.

Cleveland, Ray C. 1963. A Classification of the Arabic Dialects of Jordan. *Bulletin of the American Schools of Oriental Research*, 17: 56–63.

Cohen, Anthony P. 2000. *The Symbolic Construction of Community*. London and New York: Routledge (first published in 1985).

Cohen, Israel. 1911. *Zionist Work in Palestine*. London and Leipzig: Zionist Central Office and T. Fisher Unwin.

1918. *The German Attack on the Hebrew Schools in Palestine*. London: Offices of the Jewish Chronicle and the Jewish World.

Cohen, Saul B. and Nurit Kliot. 1981. Israel's Place-names as Reflection of Continuity and Change in Nation-building. *Names*, 29: 227–48.

1992. Place-names in Israel's Ideological Struggle over the Administered Territories. *Annals of the Association of American Geographers*, 82: 653–80.

Cooper, Robert. 1989. *Language Planning and Social Change*. Cambridge: Cambridge University Press.

Coulombe, Pierre A. 1993. Language Rights, Individual and Communal. *Language Planning and Language Problems*, 17: 140–52.
Crowley, Tony. 1989. *The Politics of Discourse: The Standard Language Question in British Cultural Debates*. London: Macmillan.
Daniels, Helge. 2002. Debating Variability in Arabic: *Fuṣḥā* versus *'āmiyyah*. University of Antwerp: Ph.d. thesis.
Das Gupta, Jyotirindra. 1970. *Language Conflict and National Development: Group Politics and National Language Policy in India*. Berkeley: University of California Press.
Davison, Roderic H. 1963. *Reform in the Ottoman Empire, 1856–1876*. Princeton: Princeton University Press.
Douglas, Mary. 1966. *Purity and Danger: An Analysis of Concepts of Pollution and Taboo*. New York: Praeger.
Dua, Hans Raj. 1996. The Politics of Language Conflict: Implications for Language Planning and Political Theory. *Language Planning and Language Problems*, 20: 1–17.
Eastman, Carol M. and Roberta F. Stein. 1993. Language Display: Authenticating Claims to Social Identity. *Journal of Multilingual and Multicultural Development*, 14: 187–202.
Edwards, John. 1988. *Language, Society and Identity*. Oxford: Basil Blackwell.
Eisele, John. 2001. Representations of Arabic in Egypt, 1940–1990. *Arab Studies Journal*, 8/9: 47–60.
Elad-Bouskila, Ami. 1999. *Modern Palestinian Literature and Culture*. London: Frank Cass.
Eminov, Ali. 1997. *Turkish and Other Muslim Minorities in Bulgaria*. London: Hurst & Company.
Fairclough, Norman. 1989. *Language and Power*. London: Longman.
Faraco, J. Carlos González and Michael Dean Murphy. 1997. Street Names and Political Regimes in an Andalusian Town. *Ethnology*, 36: 123–48.
Ferguson, Charles. 1959. Diglossia. *Word*, 15: 325–40.
1972. Myths about Arabic. In Joshua A. Fishman (ed.), *Readings in the Sociology of Language*. The Hague: Mouton, pp. 375–81.
1990. 'Come Forth with a Surah Like It': Arabic as a Measure of Arab Society. In Mushira Eid (ed.), *Perspectives on Arabic Linguistics I: Papers from the First Annual Conference of Arabic Linguistics*. Amsterdam and Philadelphia: John Benjamins Publishing Company, pp. 39–51.
1996. Diglossia Revisited. In Alaa El-Jibali (ed.), *Understanding Arabic: Essays in Contemporary Arabic Linguistics in Honour of El-Said Badawi*. Cairo: American University in Cairo Press, pp. 49–64.
Fernandez, Mauro. 1993. *Diglossia: A Comprehensive Bibliography 1960–1990, and Supplement*. Amsterdam and Philadelphia: John Benjamins Publishing Company.
Fisherman, Haya and Joshua Fishman. 1975. The 'Official Languages' of Israel: Their Status in Law and Police Attitudes and Knowledge Concerning Them. In Jean-Guy Savard and Richard Vigneault (eds.), *Multilingual Political Systems: Problems and Solutions*. Quebec: Les Presses de l'Université Laval, pp. 497–535.

Fishman, Joshua. 1972. *Language and Nationalism: Two Integrative Essays*. Rowley, MA: Newbury House Publishers.

1997. The Sociology of Language. In Nikolas Coupland and Adam Jaworski (eds.), *Sociolinguistics: A Reader and a Coursebook*. New York: St Martin's Press, Inc., pp. 25–30 (first published in 1972).

Friedland, Roger and Richard Hecht. 1996. *To Rule Jerusalem*. Cambridge: Cambridge University Press.

Galtung, John. 1980. *The True Worlds: A Transnational Perspective*. New York: Free Press.

Garrett, Peter. 2001. Language Attitudes and Sociolinguistics. *Journal of Sociolinguistics*, 5: 626–31.

Gershoni, Israel and James Jankowski. 1986. *Egypt, Islam and the Arabs: The Search for Egyptian Nationalism 1900–1930*. New York and Oxford: Oxford University Press.

Gibb, H. A. R. 1962. *Studies on the Civilization of Islam*, eds. Stanford J. Shaw & William R. Polk. London: Routledge and Kegan Paul.

Giles, Howard, Richard Yvon Bourhis and D. M. Taylor. 1977. Towards a Theory of Language in Ethnic Group Relations. In Howard Giles (ed.), *Language, Ethnicity and Intergroup Relations*. London, New York and San Francisco: Academic Press, pp. 307–48.

Giles, Howard and Peter F. Powesland. 1975. *Speech Style and Social Evaluation*. London, New York and San Francisco: Academic Press.

Giles, Howard and Philip Smith. 1979. Accommodation Theory: Optimal Levels of Convergence. In Howard Giles and Robert N. St Clair (eds.), *Language and Social Psychology*. Oxford: Basil Blackwell, pp. 45–65.

Goffman, E. 1959. *The Presentation of Self in Everyday Life*. New York: Doubleday Anchor Books.

Goldziher, Ignaz. 1966. *Muslim Studies*, ed. Samuel M. Stern and translated from German by G. R. Barber and Samuel M. Stern, (2 vols.). London: George Allen & Unwin.

Gramsci, Antonio. 1985. *Selections from Cultural Writings*, translated from the Italian by W. Boelhower. London: Lawrence & Wishart.

Grossman, David. 1993. *Sleeping on a Wire: Conversations with Palestinians in Israel*, translated from the Hebrew by Haim Watzman. London: Jonathan Cape.

Gully, Adrian. 1997. Arabic Linguistic Issues and Controversies of the Late Nineteenth and Early Twentieth Centuries. *Journal of Semitic Studies*, 42: 75–120.

Gur-Ze'ev, Ilan. 2001. The Production of Self and the Destruction of the Other's Memory and Identity in Israeli/Palestinian Education on the Holocaust/Nakbah. *Studies in Philosophy and Education*, 20: 255–66.

HaCohen, Ran. 1997. Influence of the Middle East Process on the Hebrew Language. In Michael Clyne (ed.), *Undoing and Redoing Corpus Planning*. Berlin and New York: Mouton de Gruyter, pp. 385–414.

Haeri, Niloofar. 1996. *The Sociolinguistic Market of Cairo: Gender, Class, and Education*. London and New York: Kegan Paul International.

al-Haj, Majid. 1995. *Education, Empowerment and Control: The Case of the Arabs in Israel*. Albany: State University of New York Press.

al-Hamad, Mohamed Qasim. 2001. Translation and Censorship with Special Reference to Jordan. Edinburgh University: Ph.d. thesis.

al-Haq, Fawwaz al-Abed. 1999. A Sociolinguistic Study of Hebrew in Jordan: Implications for Language Planning. *International Journal of the Sociology of Language*, 140: 45–58.

Hary, Benjamin. 1996. The Importance of the Language Continuum in Arabic Multiglossia. In Alaa El-Jibali (ed.), *Understanding Arabic: Essays in Contemporary Arabic Linguistics in Honour of El-Said Badawi*. Cairo: American University in Cairo Press, pp. 69–90.

El-Hassan, S. 1977. Educated Spoken Arabic in Egypt and the Levant: A Critical Review of Diglossia and Related Concepts. *Archivum Linguisticum*, 8: 112–32.

1978. Variation in the Demonstrative System in Educated Spoken Arabic. *Archivum Linguisticum*, 9: 32–57.

Heller, Monica (ed.). 1988. *Code-switching: Anthropological and Sociolinguistic Perspectives*. Berlin: Walter de Gruyter & Co.

1995. Code-switching and the Politics of Language. In Lesley Milroy and Pieter Muysken (eds.), *One Speaker, Two Languages: Cross-disciplinary Perspectives on Code-switching*. Cambridge: Cambridge University Press, pp. 158–74.

1999. Ebonics, Language Revival, la qualité de la langue and More: What do we Have to Say about the Language Debates of our Time? *Journal of Sociolinguistics*, 3: 260–6.

Helman, Sara. 2002. Monologic Results of Dialogue: Jewish–Palestinian Encounter Groups as Sites of Essentialization. *Identities: Global Studies in Culture and Power*, 9: 327–54.

Hever, Hannan. 1987. Hebrew in an Arab Israeli Hand: Six Miniatures on Anton Shammas's *Arabesques*. *Cultural Critique*, 7: 47–76.

Hindess, Barry. 1996. *Discourses of Power: From Hobbes to Foucault*. Oxford: Basil Blackwell.

Holes, Clive. 1983. Patterns of Communal Language Variation in Bahrain. *Language in Society*, 12: 433–57.

1987. *Language Variation and Change in a Modernizing Arab State*. London: Kegan Paul International.

1993. The Uses of Variation: A Study of the Political Speeches of Gamal Abdul-Nasir. In Mushira Eid and Clive Holes (eds.), *Perspectives on Arabic Linguistics V*. Amsterdam and Philadelphia: John Benjamins Publishing Company, pp. 13–45.

1995. *Modern Arabic: Structures, Functions and Varieties*. London and New York: Longman.

Honey, John. 1997. *Language is Power: The Story of Standard English and its Enemies*. London and Boston: Faber & Faber.

Hourani, Albert. 1983. *Arabic Thought in the Liberal Age, 1789–1939*. Cambridge: Cambridge University Press.

Hudson, Alan. 1992. Diglossia: A Bibliographic Review. *Language in Society*, 21: 611–74.

Hussein, Riad Fayez Issa. 1980. The Case of Triglossia in Arabic with Special Emphasis on Jordan. State University of New York: Ph.d. thesis.

Hussein, Riad F. and Nasr El-Ali. 1988. Subjective Reactions Towards Different Varieties of Arabic. *al-Lisān al-arabī*, 30: 7–17.

Ibrahim, Mohammad H. 1981. Language and Politics in Modern Palestine. *Arab Journal for the Humanities*, 1: 323–41.

1986. Standard and Prestige Language: A Problem in Arabic Sociolinguistics. *Anthropological Linguistics*, 26: 115–26.

Ibrahim, Zeinab. 2000. Myths about Arabic Revisited. *al-'Arabiyya*, 33: 13–27.

Inglehart, R. F. and M. Woodward. 1972. Language Conflict and Political Community. In Pier Paolo Giglioli (ed.), *Language and Social Contexts: Selected Readings*. Harmondsworth: Penguin, pp. 358–77.

Ivanic, Roz. 1997. *Writing and Identity: The Discoursal Construction of Identity in Academic Writing*. Amsterdam and Philadelphia: John Benjamins Publishing Company.

Jabeur, M. 1987. A Sociolinguistic Study in Tunisia: Rades. University of Reading: unpublished Ph.d. thesis.

Jahr, Ernst Håkon (ed.). 1993. *Language Conflict and Language Planning*. Berlin: Mouton de Gruyter.

Janicki, Karol. 1993. From Small to Large-scale Language Conflicts: A Philosophical Perspective. In Jahr (ed.), *Language Conflict and Language Planning*, pp. 99–113.

Jassem, Zaidan Ali. 1993. *Impact of the Arab Israeli Wars on Language and Social Change in the Arab World: The Case of Syrian Arabic*. Kuala Lumpur: Pustaka Antara.

Johnson, Sally. 2001. Who's Misunderstanding Whom? Sociolinguistics, Public Debate and the Media. *Journal of Sociolinguistics*, 5: 591–610.

Joseph, John Earl. 1987. *Eloquence and Power: The Rise of Language Standards and Standard Languages*. New York: Basil Blackwell.

Kamhawi, Dania L. W. 2000. Code-switching: A Social Phenomenon in Jordanian Society. Edinburgh University M.Litt. thesis.

Katriel, Tamar. 1986. *Talking Straight: Dugri Speech in Israeli Sabra Culture*. Cambridge: Cambridge University Press.

Katriel, Tamar and Yusuf Greifat. 1988. Cultural Borrowings: A Sociolinguistic Approach. In John E. Hofman (ed.), *Arab–Jewish Relations in Israel: A Quest in Human Understanding*. Bristol: Wyndham Hall Press, pp. 301–21.

Kattan, Naim. 1976. *Farewell, Babylon*, translated from the French by Sheila Fischman. Toronto: McClelland & Stewart.

Katz, Kimberly. 1999. Jordanian Jerusalem: Postage Stamps and Identity Construction. *Jerusalem Quarterly File*, 5 (http://www.jqf-jerusalem.org./journal/1999/jqf5/katz.html).

Katz, Pearl. 1982. Ethnicity Transformed: Acculturation in Language Classes in Israel. *Anthropological Quarterly*, 55: 99–111.

Kaye, Alan. 1972. Remarks on Diglossia in Arabic: Well-defined vs ill-defined. *Linguistics*, 81: 32–48.

1994. Formal vs. Informal in Arabic: Diglossia, Triglossia, Tetraglossia, etc.: Polyglossia-multiglossia Viewed as a Continuum. *Zeitschrift für arabische Linguistik*, 27: 47–66.

2001. Diglossia: The State of the Art. *International Journal of the Sociology of Language*, 152: 117–29.

Khalidi, Rashid. 1997. *Palestinian Identity: The Construction of Modern National Consciousness*. New York: Columbia University Press.
Khalidi, Walid (ed.). 1982. *All that Remains: The Palestinian Villages Occupied and Depopulated by Israel in 1948*. Washington, DC: Institute for Palestine Studies.
Khalili, Laleh. Forthcoming. Virtual Nation: Palestinian Cyberculture in Lebanese Camps.
al-Khatib, Mahmoud Abed Ahmad. 1988. Sociolinguistic Change in an Expanding Context: A Case Study of Irbid City, Jordan. University of Durham: unpublishd Ph.d. thesis.
Khleif, Bud B. 1979. Insiders, Outsiders, and Renegades: Towards a Classification of Ethnolinguistic Labels. In Howard Giles and Bernard Saint-Jacques (eds.), *Language and Ethnic Relations*. Oxford: Pergamon Press, pp. 159–77.
Kia, Mehrdad. 1998. Persian Nationalism and the Campaign for Language Purification. *Middle Eastern Studies*, 34: 9–36.
Kinberg, Naphtali and Rafael Talmon. 1994. Learning of Arabic by Jews and the Use of Hebrew among Arabs in Israel. *Indian Journal of Applied Linguistics*, 20: 37–54.
Koplewitz, Immanuel. 1992. Arabic in Israel: The Sociolinguistic Situation of Israel's Linguistic Minority. *International Journal of the Sociology of Language*, 98: 29–66.
Kotler, Philip, Somkid Jatusripitak and Suvit Mausincee. 1997. *The Marketing of Nations: A Strategic Approach to Building National Wealth*. New York: Free Press.
Kraemer, Roberta and Elite Olshtain. 1989. Perceived Ethnolinguistic Vitality and Language Attitudes: The Israeli Setting. *Journal of Multilingual and Multicultural Development*, 10: 197–212.
Kramarae, Cheris, Muriel Schulz and William M. O'Bar. 1984. Toward an Understanding of Language and Power. In Cheris Kramarae, Muriel Schulz and William M. O'Bar (eds.), *Language and Power*. Beverly Hills: Sage Publications, pp. 9–22.
Kuzar, Ron. 2001. *Hebrew and Zionism: A Discourse Analytic Cultural Study*. Berlin and New York: Mouton de Gruyter.
Laforest, Marty. 1999. Can a Sociolinguist Venture outside the University? *Journal of Sociolinguistics*, 3: 276–81.
Laitin, David D. 1987. Linguistic Conflict in Catalonia. *Language Planning and Language Problems*, 11: 129–47.
Lakoff, Robin Tolmach. 1990. *Talking Power: The Politics of Language*. New York: Basic Books.
2000. *The Language War*. Berkeley: University of California Press.
Lalor, Paul. 1997. Naming Jordanian–Palestinian Relations. Paper presented at the Third Symposium on Language and Society in the Middle East and North Africa, 1–4 July, Edinburgh.
Lambert, Wallace E. 1979. Language as a Factor in Intergroup Relations. In Howard Giles and Robert N. St Clair (eds.), *Language and Social Psychology*. Oxford: Basil Blackwell, pp. 186–92.
Landau, Jacob M. 1970. Language Study in Israel. In Thomas A. Sebeok (ed.), *Current Trends in Linguistics, VI*. The Hague: Mouton, pp. 721–45.

1987. Hebrew and Arabic in the State of Israel: Political Aspects of the Language Issue. *International Journal of the Sociology of Language*, 67: 117–33.

Layne, Linda L. 1994. *Home and Homeland: The Dialogics of Tribal and National Identities in Jordan*. Princeton: Princeton University Press.

Lefkowitz, Daniel. 1993. On the Social Meaning of Code Choice in an Israeli City. *Proceedings of the First Annual Symposium about Language and Society-Austin (SALSA I)*, 89–100.

Lehn, Walter. 1980. West Bank Sojourn. *Journal of Palestine Studies*, 9: 1–16.

Liebes, Tamar. 1997. *Reporting the Arab–Israeli Conflict: How Hegemony Works*. London and New York: Routledge.

Lodge, Anthony. 1998. French is a Logical Language. In Laurie Bauer and Peter Trudgill (eds.), *Language Myths*. London: Penguin, pp. 23–30.

Makdisi, Ned. 1955. Arabic Type Simplified. *Middle Eastern Affairs*, 16: 51–3.

Maoz, Ifat. 2001. Power Relations in Intergroup Encounters: A Case Study of Jewish–Arab Encounters in Israel. *International Journal of Intercultural Studies*, 24: 259–77.

Mar'i, Sami Khalil. 1978. *Arab Education in Israel*. Syracuse: Syracuse University Press.

1989. Arab Education in Israel. In Ernest Krausz and David Glanz (eds.), *Education in a Comparative Context*. New Brunswick: Transaction Publishers, pp. 91–118.

Massad, Joseph A. 2001. *Colonial Effects: The Making of National Identity in Jordan*. New York: Columbia University Press.

Massey, Doreen. 1995. Places and their Pasts. *History Workshop Journal*, 39: 182–92.

May, Stephen. 2001. *Language and Minority Rights: Ethnicity, Nationalism and the Politics of Language*. Harlow: Longman.

Mazrui, Ali and Alamin M. Mazrui. 1998. *The Power of Babel: Language and Governance in the African Experience*. Oxford: James Currey Ltd.

McCarthy, Kevin M. 1979. Street Names in Beirut, Lebanon. *Names*, 23: 74–88.

Meskell, Lynn (ed.). 1998. *Archaeology under Fire: Nationalism, Politics, and Heritage in the Eastern Mediterranean and Middle East*. London and New York: Routledge.

Milroy, James. 2001a. Language Ideologies and the Consequences of Standardization. *Journal of Sociolinguistics*, 5: 530–55.

2001b. Response to Sally Johnson: Misunderstanding Language? *Journal of Sociolinguistics*, 5: 620–5.

Milroy, James and Lesley Milroy. 1999. *Authority in Language: Investigating Standard English*. London: Routledge (third edition).

Mitchell, T. F. 1978. Educated Spoken Arabic in Egypt and the Levant, with Special Reference to Participle and Tense. *Journal of Linguistics*, 14: 227–58.

1986. What is Educated Spoken Arabic? *International Journal of the Sociology of Language*, 61: 7–32.

Musa, Salama. 1955. Arabic Language Problems. *Middle Eastern Affairs*, 16: 41–4.

Myers-Scotton, Carol. 1993. *Social Motivations for Code-switching: Evidence from Africa*. Oxford: Clarendon Press.
Newman, Francis W. 1895. *Handbook of Modern Arabic: Consisting of Practical Grammar with Numerous Examples, Dialogues, and Newspaper Extracts in a European Type*. Nottingham: Stevenson, Bailey & Smith.
Niedzielski, Nancy A. and Dennis R. Preston. 2000. *Folk Linguistics*. Berlin and New York: Mouton de Gruyter.
Norris, H. T. 1990. *Shu'ūbiyya* in Arabic Literature. In Julia Ashtiany, T. M. Johnstone, J. D. Letham, R. B. Serjeant and G. Rex Smith (eds.), *The Cambridge History of Arabic Literature: 'Abbasid Belles-Lettres*. Cambridge: Cambridge University Press, pp. 31–47.
O'Leary, de Lacy Evans. 1872. *Colloquial Arabic*. London: Kegan Paul, Trench, Trubner & Co.
Olins, Wally. 1999. *Trading Identities: Why Countries and Companies are Taking on Each Others' Roles*. London: Foreign Policy Centre.
Omran, Elsayed M. H. 1991. Arabic Grammar: Problems and Reform Efforts. In Kinga Dévényi and Tamás Iványi (eds.), *Proceedings of the Colloquium on Arabic Grammar* (Special issue of *The Arabist: Budapest Studies in Arabic*, 34) Budapest: Eötvös Lorànd University, Department of Arabic Studies, and Csoma De Körös Society, Islamic Studies Section, pp. 297–311.
Palmer, Edward L. 1979. Linguistic Innovation in the Arabic Adaptation of 'Sesame Street'. In James E. Altais and G. Richard Tucker (eds.), *Language in Public Life: Georgetown University Round Table on Languages and Linguistics 1979*. Washington, DC: Georgetown University Press, pp. 287–94.
Patai, Raphael. 1977. *The Jewish Mind*. New York: Charles Scribner's Sons.
Paulston, Christina Bratt, Pow Chee Chen and Mary C. Connerty. 1993. Language Regenesis: A Conceptual Overview of Language Revival, Revitalization and Reversal. *Journal of Multilingual and Multicultural Development*, 14: 275–86.
Paxman, Jeremy. 1999. *The English: The Portrait of a People*. London: Penguin Books.
Peake, Roderick. 1958. *History and Tribes of Jordan*. Coral Gables, FL: University of Miami Press.
Peres, Yochanan, Avishai Erlich and Nira Yuval-Davis. 1970. National Education for Arab Youth in Israel: A Comparative Analysis of Curricula. *Jewish Journal of Sociology*, 12: 147–63.
Piamenta, Moshe. 1979. Jerusalem Sub-standard Arabic: Linguistic Analysis of an Idiolect. *Jerusalem Studies in Arabic and Islam*, 1: 263–85.
1992. Notes on the Decay of Jerusalem Judaeo-Arabic under the Impact of Socio-political Transformation. *Asian and African Studies*, 26: 81–88.
Pinchevski, Amit and Efraim Torgovnik. 2002. Signifying Passages: The Signs of Change in Israeli Street Names. *Media, Culture and Society*, 24: 365–88.
Rabinowitz, Dan. 2002. Oriental Othering and National Identity: A Review of Early Israeli Anthropological Studies of Palestinians. *Identities: Global Studies in Culture and Power*, 9: 305–25.
Reiter, Yitzhak. 2002. Higher Education and Socio-political Transformation in Jordan. *British Journal of Middle Eastern Studies*, 29: 137–64.

Rickford, John. 1999. The Ebonics Controversy in my Backyard: A Sociolinguist's Experiences and Reflections. *Journal of Sociolinguistics*, 3: 267–75.

Rouhana, Nadim. 1997. *Palestinian Citizens in an Ethnic Jewish State*. New Haven and London: Yale University Press.

Rudin, Catherine and Ali Eminov. 1990. Bulgarian Turkish: The Linguistic Effects of Recent Nationality Policy. *Anthropological Linguistics*, 32: 149–62.

Saatci, Mustafa. 2002. Nation-states and Ethnic Boundaries: Modern Turkish Identity and Turkish–Kurdish Conflict. *Nations and Nationalism*, 8: 549–64.

Safi, Sabah. 1992. Functions of Code-switching: Saudi Arabic in the United States. In Aleya Rouchdy (ed.), *The Arabic Language in America*. Detroit: Wayne State University Press, pp. 72–80.

Said, Edward. 1978. *Orientalism*. London and Henley: Routledge & Kegan Paul.

Salih, Mahmud and Mohammed El-Yasin. 1994. The Spread of Foreign Business Names in Jordan: A Sociolinguistic Perspective. *Abhath al-Yarmouk*, 12: 37–50.

Sallam, A. 1979. Concordial Relations within the Noun Phrase in ESA. *Archivum Linguisticum*, 10: 20–56.

1980. Phonological Variation in Educated Spoken Arabic: A Study of the Uvular and Related Plosive Types. *Bulletin of the School of Oriental and African Studies*, 42: 77–100.

Sarsour, Saad. 1983. Arab Education in a Jewish State: Major Dilemmas. In Alouph Hareven (ed.), *Every Sixth Israeli: Relations between Jewish Majority and the Arab Minority in Israel*. Jerusalem: Van Leer Jerusalem Foundation, pp. 113–32.

Saulson, Scott B. 1979. *Institutionalized Language Planning: Documents and Analysis of the Revival of Hebrew*. The Hague, Paris and New York: Mouton Publishers.

Sawaie, Mohammed. 1986. A Sociolinguistic Study of Classical and Colloquial Arabic Varieties: A Preliminary Investigation into Some Arabic Speakers' Attitudes. *al-Lisān al-arabī*, 26: 1–19.

1994. *Linguistic Variation and Speakers' Attitudes: A Sociolinguistic Study of Some Arabic Dialects*. Damascus: al-Jaffan and al-Jabi Publishers.

Schmid, Carol L. 2001. *The Politics of Language: Conflict, Identity and Cultural Pluralism in Comparative Perspective*. Oxford: Oxford University Press.

Seccombe, I. I. 1988. International Migration, Arabization and Localization in the Gulf Labour Market. In B. R. Pridham (ed.), *The Gulf and the Arab World*. London: Croom Helm, pp. 153–88.

Selwyn, Tom. 2001. Landscapes of Separation: Reflections on the Symbolism of By-pass Roads in Palestine. In Barbara Bender and Margot Winer (eds.), *Contested Landscapes: Movement, Exile and Place*. Oxford and New York: Berg, pp. 225–40.

Shammas, Anton. 1991. Cultural Identity and the Crisis of Representation. In Miriana Philomena (ed.), *Critical Fictions: The Politics of Imaginative Writing*. Seattle: Bay Press, pp. 75–9.

Shohamy, Elena. 1994. Issues of Language Planning in Israel: Language and Ideology. In Richard D. Lambert (ed.), *Language Planning around the World:*

Contexts and Systemic Change. Washington, DC: Johns Hopkins University, National Foreign Language Center, pp. 131–42.

Shohat, Ella. 1989. *Israeli Cinema: East/West and the Politics of Representation*. Austin: University of Texas Press.

Shorrab, Ghazi Abd-El-Jabbar. 1981. Models of Socially Significant Linguistic Variation: The Case of Palestinian Arabic. State University of New York at Buffalo: Ph.d. thesis.

Shryock, Andrew. 1997. *Nationalism and the Genealogical Imagination: Oral History and Textual Authority in Tribal Jordan*. Berkeley: University of California Press.

Simmel, Georg. 1955a. *Conflict*. Glencoe, IL: Free Press.

1955b. *The Web of Group Affiliations*. Glencoe, IL: Free Press.

Skutnabb-Kangas, Tove and Sertaç Bucak. 1994. Killing a Mother Tongue: How the Kurds are Deprived of Linguistic Human Rights. In Tove Skutnabb-Kangas and Robert Phillipson (eds.), *Linguistic Human Rights: Overcoming Linguistic Discrimination*. Berlin: Mouton de Gruyter, pp. 347–71.

Sleeboom, Margaret. 2002. The Power of National Symbols: The Credibility of a Dragon's Efficacy. *Nations and Nationalism*, 8: 299–313.

Sluglett, Peter and Marion Farouk-Sluglett (eds.). 1996. *Guide to the Middle East: The Arab World and its Neighbours*. London: Times Books.

Slyomovics, Susan. 1998. *The Object of Memory: Arab and Jew Narrate the Palestinian Village*. Philadelphia: University of Pennsylvania Press.

Smart, J. R. 1990. Pidginization in Gulf Arabic: A First Report. *Anthropological Linguistics*, 32: 83–119.

Smith, Anthony D. 2001. *Nationalism*. Cambridge: Polity.

Smith-Kocamahhul, Joan. 2001. In the Shadow of Kurdish: The Silence of Other Ethnolinguistic Minorities in Turkey. *Middle East Report*, 219: 45–7.

Sowayan, Saad Abdullah. 1985. *Nabaṭi Poetry: The Oral Poetry of Arabia*. Berkeley: University of California Press.

Spolsky, Bernard. 1993. Language Conflict in Jerusalem, 1880–1980. In Jahr (ed.), *Language Conflict and Language Planning*, pp. 179–92.

1996. Hebrew and Israeli Identity. In Yasir Suleiman (ed.), *Language and Identity in the Middle East and North Africa*. Richmond: Curzon Press, pp. 181–92.

Spolsky, Bernard and Muhammad Amara. 1995. *Sociolinguistic Reflexes of Political Division: A Study of a Divided Village*. Ramat Gan: Bar Ilan University, Language Policy Research Centre.

Spolsky, Bernard, Muhammad Amara, Hanna Tushyeh and Kees de Bot. n.d. Language, Education and Identity in a Palestinian Town: The Case of Bethlehem. Unpublished manuscript.

Spolsky, Bernard and Robert Cooper. 1991. *The Languages of Jerusalem*. Oxford: Clarendon Press.

Spolsky, Bernard and Elana Shohamy. 1999. *The Languages of Israel: Policy, Ideology and Practice*. Clevedon: Multilingual Matters.

Suleiman, Saleh M. 1985. *Jordanian Arabic between Diglossia and Bilingualism: Linguistic Analysis*. Amsterdam and Philadelphia: John Benjamins Publishing Company.

Suleiman, Yasir. 1993. The Language Situation in Jordan and Code-switching: A New Interpretation. *New Arabian Studies*, 1: 1–20.
1994. Nationalism and the Arabic Language: An Historical Overview. In Yasir Suleiman (ed.), *Arabic Sociolinguistics: Issues and Perspectives*. Richmond: Curzon Press, pp. 3–24.
1996a. The Simplification of Arabic Grammar and the Problematic Nature of the Sources. *Journal of Semitic Studies*, 41: 99–119.
1996b. Language and Identity in Egyptian Nationalism. In Yasir Suleiman (ed.), *Language and Identity in the Middle East and North Africa*. Richmond: Curzon Press, pp. 25–37.
1997. The Arabic Language in the Fray: A Sphere of Contested Identities. In Alan Jones (ed.), *University Lectures in Islamic Studies I*. London: Altajir World of Islam Trust, pp. 127–48.
1999a. Language and Political Conflict in the Middle East: A Study in Symbolic Sociolinguistics. In Yasir Suleiman (ed.), *Language and Society in the Middle East and North Africa: Studies in Variation and Identity*. Richmond: Curzon Press, pp. 10–37.
1999b. Language Education Policies: Arabic-speaking Countries. In Bernard Spolsky (ed.), *Concise Encyclopedia of Educational Linguistics*. Oxford: Elsevier/Pergamon, pp. 106–16.
1999c. *The Arabic Grammatical Tradition: A Study in Taʿlīl*. Edinburgh: Edinburgh University Press.
2000. Under the Spell of Language: Arabic between Linguistic Determinism and Linguistic Relativity. In Ian Richard Netton (ed.), *Studies in Honour of Clifford Edmund Bosworth*, vol. I: *Hunter of the East*. Leiden: E. J. Brill, pp. 113–37.
2002. Bayān as a Principle of Taxonomy: Linguistic Elements in Jāḥiẓ's Thinking. In J. F. Healey and V. Porter (eds.), *Studies on Arabic in Honour of G. Rex Smith*. Oxford: Oxford University Press, pp. 273–95. (*Journal of Semitic Studies*, Supplement 14.)
2003. *The Arabic Language and National Identity: A Study in Ideology*. Washington, DC: Georgetown University Press.
Swedenburg, Ted. 1995. *Memories of Revolt: The 1936–1939 Rebellion and the Palestinian National Past*. Minneapolis and London: University of Minnesota Press.
Tabory, Mala. 1981. Language Rights in Israel. *Israel Yearbook on Human Rights*, 11: 272–306.
Taha, Ibrahim. 1995. Elements of Dialects in Palestinian Literature in Israel. In Nadia Anghelescu and Andrei A. Avram (eds.), *Proceedings of the Colloquium on Arabic Linguistics* (Bucharest) 29 August to 2 September 1994, part 1. Bucharest: University of Bucharest, Centre for Arab Studies, pp. 267–73.
Talmon, Rafael. 2000. Arabic as a Minority Language in Israel. In Jonathan Owen (ed.), *Arabic as a Minority Language*. Berlin and New York: Mouton de Gruyter, pp. 199–220.
Thomas, George. 1991. *Linguistic Purism*. London and New York: Longman.
Tibawi, A. L. 1956. *Arab Education in Mandatory Palestine*. London: Luzac.

1969. *A Modern History of Syria including Lebanon and Palestine*. London: Macmillan.
Tilmatine, Mohamed and Yasir Suleiman. 1996. Language and Identity: The Case of the Berber. In Yasir Suleiman (ed.), *Language and Identity in the Middle East and North Africa*. Richmond: Curzon Press, pp. 165–79.
al-Toma, Salih J. 1961. The Arabic Writing System and Proposals for its Reform. *The Middle East Journal*, 15: 403–15.
Trudgill, Peter. 1986. *Dialects in Contact*. Oxford: Blackwell.
Turki, Fawaz. 1999. Roundtable Discussion on Israeli and Palestinian Literature. In Kamal Abdel-Malek and David C. Jacobson (eds.), *Israeli and Palestinian Identities in History and Literature*. London: Macmillan, pp. 198–211.
van Ham, Peter. 2002. Branding Territory: Inside the Wonderful Worlds of PR and IR Theory. *Millennium: Journal of International Studies*, 31: 249–69.
Vikør, Lars S. 1993. Principles of Corpus-planning as Applied to the Spelling Reforms of Indonesia and Malaysia. In Jahr (ed.), *Language Conflict and Language Planning*, pp. 278–98.
Vollers, K. 1895. *The Modern Egyptian Dialect of Arabic: A Grammar with Exercises, Reading Lessons and Glossaries*, translated from the German by F. C. Burkitt. Cambridge: Cambridge University Press.
Wardhaugh, Ronald. 1987. *Languages in Competition: Dominance, Diversity and Decline*. Oxford: Basil Blackwell.
Weber, Jonathan. 1979. The Status of English as a Lingua Franca in Contemporary Jerusalem. University of Oxford: D.Phil. thesis.
Weinreich, Uriel. 1966. *Languages in Contact: Findings and Problems*. The Hague: Mouton.
Wendell, Charles. 1972. *The Evolution of the Egyptian National Image: From its Origins to Aḥmad Luṭfī al-Sayyid*. Berkeley: University of California Press.
al-Wer, Enam Essa. 1991. Phonological Variation in the Speech of Women from Three Urban Areas in Jordan. University of Essex: Ph.d. thesis.
1999. Why do Different Variables Behave Differently? Data from Arabic. In Yasir Suleiman (ed.), *Language and Society in the Middle East and North Africa: Studies in Variation and Identity*. Richmond: Curzon Press, pp. 38–57.
Wernberg-Møller, Alison. 1994. A Sociolinguistic Study of the Moroccan Community of Edinburgh. University of Edinburgh: Ph.d. thesis.
1999. Sociolinguistic Meaning in Code-switching: The Case of Moroccans in Edinburgh. In Yasir Suleiman (ed.), *Language and Society in the Middle East and North Africa: Studies in Variation and Identity*. Richmond: Curzon Press, pp. 234–58.
Wexler, Paul. 1990. *The Schizoid Nature of Modern Hebrew: A Slavic Language in Search of a Semitic Past*. Wiesbaden: Otto Harrassowitz.
Willmore, Seldon. 1901. *The Spoken Arabic of Egypt*. London.
Wilson, Zara Jacqueline. 2002. Invisible Racism: The Language and Ontology of 'White Trash'. *Critique of Anthropology*, 22: 387–401.
Winter, Michael. 1979. Arab Education in Israel. *Jerusalem Quarterly*, 12: 112–22.
Wright, Sue. 1996. *Language and the State: Revitalization and Revival in Israel and Ireland*. Clevedon: Multilingual Matters.

El-Yasin, Mohammed K. and Radwan S. Mahadin. 1996. On the Pragmatics of Shop Signs in Jordan. *Journal of Pragmatics*, 26: 407–16.

Zerubavel, Yael. 1991. New Beginning, Old Past: The Collective Memory of Pioneering in Israeli Culture. In Laurence J. Silberstein (ed.), *New Perspectives on Israeli History: The Early Years of the State*. New York and London: New York University Press, pp. 193–215.

Index

al-Abbadi, Ahmad Uwaydi 123
Abbas, A. 82
'Abbasiyya (was Yahudiyya) 181
Abbud, Marun 73
Abd al-Ghani, M. 28
Abd al-Latif, S. 143
Abd al-Rahman, A. 68
Abd-el-Jawad, H. and al-Haq, F. 141, 143, 153, 215
Abdel-Jawad, H. R. E. 99, 104, 105, 108, 111, 114, 121
Abdel-Malek, Z. 82
Abdul-Fattah, H. and Zoghoul, M. 27
Abdul-Nasir, Gamal, Egyptian President 59
Abdullah II, King, of Jordan 97, 124
Abdullah, Emir (King), of Transjordan (Jordan) 100
Abu Sa'd, Khalil 42
Abu-Absi, S. 90
Abu-Melhim, A.-R. 109
Abu-Odeh, Adnan 118, 124, 129, 133, 136
  Jordanians, Palestinians and the Hashemite Kingdom . . . 97, 102
Abu-Shawar, Rashad 132
Abuljebain, N. K. 203
Acre 145
  street sign 184–187
Administered Territories, use of term 166
affect 54, 59
  and cognition 107
age, factor in code-switching 110, 112, 113, 126
agriculture, negative view of 106
Ahlam, Bahraini singer 132
Ahlqvist, A. 16
Air France 174
Aitcheson, Jean 61
'ajam (non-Arab) 75, 78
Ajloun, Jordan 103, 105, 111
Alexandretta, Sanjak of 23
Algeria 30, 32
al-Alim, Mahmud Amin 47, 50–51
Allen, I. L. 116
Alosh, M. 90, 91
al-Amadidhi, D. G. 99
Amamra, T. R. 47
Amara, M. 139
Amara, M. and Spolsky, B. 143
Amin, Qasim 66
Amman
  amphitheatre 129
  female code-switching in 108, 111
  linguistic variation in 104
  Palestinians in 101, 105
  population 100, 101
Amman Baccalaureate School, code-switching 29, 30
al-Anbari, Muhammad Ibn al-Qasim 78
Anis, I. 78
anṣār ('supporters') 48, 50
anthropology 143
Aql, Sa'id 39, 62, 74, 78
al-Aqqad, Abbas Mahmud 79
Arab identity 19–20, 48, 52
  and cultural continuity 74–75
  in Israel 149
  and Standard Arabic 77
  see also Palestinian identity
Arab League 131
Arab nationalism 54, 131
  as cultural 38–39
  role of Arabic language 48, 149
  view of religious belief 40
Arab renaissance (*nahḍa*) 41, 206, 207
Arab-Israeli conflict
  linguistic dimension of 138, 141, 153, 214–215, 221
  obstacles to reconciliation 217
  semiological struggle 204, 229
  terminology of 138, 166, 173, 214, 215–216
  see also place names

(Q) variable
[?] variant *see* Madani dialect
context of prestige 100
[g] variant *see* Bedouin dialect
[k] variant *see* Fallahi dialect
and power asymmetry 133
[q] variant (SA) 98
salience as factor in dialect maintenance 111
as sociolinguistic marker 98–100
see also Jordan
Qaḍāyā fikriyya, Egyptian journal 46
al-Qadi, M. 208
al-Qasim, Samih 208
al-Qassam, Izz al-Din 178
al-Quds al-Arabi 2, 132
Qur'an 40, 45, 46, 59
inimitability 74
linguistic integrity of 84
and solecism 75
and support for dialects 74–75
al-Qurashi, H. A. 54

Rabat, Arab Summit (1974) 129
Rabin, Yitzhak 217
racism, and folk belief about language 61
Rae, John 93
al-Rafi'i, Mustafa Sadiq 51, 75
Ramleh 145
street names 184, 219
Rania, Queen, of Jordan 102
Rashid, A. 27
Raxiel-Naor, Esther, MK 146
Reiter, Y. 102
religion
and language 40, 84, 158
see also doctrine
'response', use of term 138
Ribāṭ al-Kurd building complex 175
Rickford, J. 58, 79
Rida, Muhammad Rashid 19
al-Rishani, Ilyas 43
Roman alphabet 44, 225
for colloquial Arabic 39
for Egyptian Arabic 68
for maps 65
Newman's call to use 64, 65
threat to inimitability of Qur'an 74
in Turkey 74
Romema, Negev, Moroccan Jews in 155, 156, 158, 220, 223
Rouhana, N. 158
Royal Geographical Society 160
Rudin, C. and Eminov, A. 23, 24
Rukaybi, A. 32
al-Rusafi, Ma'ruf 132

Sa'ada, Antun 39
Saatci, M. 23
Sadat, Anwar, President of Egypt 2, 28, 29, 37
Safi, S. 43
al-Safti, M. 27
Said, Edward 63, 215
Sa'id, Naffusa Zakariyya 27, 29, 63–64, 65, 68, 71, 72, 76, 225
al-Salām Shopping Centre li-l-Muḥajjabāt 28, 37
Salih, M. and El-Yasin, M. 26
Sallam, A. 100, 109
Sam'an, K. 53
al-Samirra'i, Ibrahim 52, 54, 93
Samuel, Herbert, British High Commissioner 145
satire 2–3
Saudi Arabia 82–87
Islamic and Arab identity 84, 85, 86
use of Gulf Pidgin 34
vernacular poetry 82, 84, 85–86, 227
Saulson, S. B. 140
Saussure, Ferdinand de 61
Sawaie, M. 98, 100, 103, 105, 111, 115, 122, 123
Sayce, A. H. 68
Schmid, C. L. 11, 16
schools
Hebrew compulsory in 150, 151
mixed (in Israel) 141
subordinate position of Arabic in (Israel) 150, 153, 157
in UAE 36
science
use of Arabic for teaching of 42
use of colloquial for 68
use of German for teaching 17
Seccombe, I. I. 35
sedentary people, effeminate qualities ascribed to 103
Sephardim, in Jerusalem 170
Sesame Street, Arabic version 90
settlements
illegal (Gilo) 173, 213
illegal (on Jabal Abu-Ghneim) 172–173, 213
naming of 163
use of term 167
al-Shak'a, M. 75
Shakir, Mahmud Muhammad 79

Cambridge Middle East Studies 19

1 Parvin Paidar, *Women and the Political Process in Twentieth-Century Iran*
0 521 47340 3 hardback 0 521 59572 X paperback
2 Israel Gershoni and James Jankowski, *Redefining the Egyptian Nation, 1930–1945* 0 521 47535 X hardback 0 521 52330 3 paperback
3 Annelies Moors, *Women, Property and Islam: Palestinian Experiences, 1920–1990* 0 521 47497 3 hardback 0 521 48355 7 paperback
4 Paul Kingston, *Britain and the Politics of Modernization in the Middle East, 1945–1958* 0 521 56346 1 hardback 0 521 89439 5 paperback
5 Daniel Brown, *Rethinking Tradition in Modern Islamic Thought*
0 521 57077 8 hardback 0 521 65394 0 paperback
6 Nathan J. Brown, *The Rule of Law in the Arab World: Courts in Egypt and the Gulf* 0 521 59026 4
7 Richard Tapper, *Frontier Nomads of Iran: The Political and Social History of the Shahsevan* 0 521 58336 5
8 Khaled Fahmy, *All the Pasha's Men: Mehmed Ali, his Army and the Making of Modern Egypt* 0 521 56007 1
9 Sheila Carapico, *Civil Society in Yemen: The Political Economy of Activism in Arabia* 0 521 59098 1
10 Meir Litvak, *Shi'i Scholars in Nineteenth-Century Iraq: The* Ulama *of Najaf and Karbala* 0 521 62356 1 hardback 0 521 89296 1 paperback
11 Jacob Metzer, *The Divided Economy of Mandatory Palestine* 0 521 46550 8
12 Eugene L. Rogan, *Frontiers of the State in the Late Ottoman Empire: Transjordan, 1850–1921* 0 521 66312 1 hardback 0 521 89223 6 paperback
13 Eliz Sanasarin, *Religious Minorities in Iran* 0 521 77073 4
14 Nadje Al-Ali, *Secularism, Gender and the State in the Middle East: The Egyptian Women's Movement* 0 521 78022 5 hardback 0 521 78504 9 paperback
15 Eugene L. Rogan and Avi Shlaim (eds.), *The War for Palestine: Rewriting the History of 1948* 0 521 79139 1 hardback 0 521 79476 5 paperback
16 Gershon Shafir and Yoav Paled, *Being Israeli: The Dynamics of Multiple Citizenship* 0 521 79224 X hardback 0 521 79672 5 paperback
17 A. J. Racy, *Making Music in the Arab World: The Culture and Artistry of* Tarab
0 521 30414 8 hardback 0 521 31685 5 paperback
18 Benny Morris, *The Birth of the Palestinian Refugee Problem Revisited*
0 521 81120 1 hardback 0 521 00967 7 paperback

Lightning Source UK Ltd.
Milton Keynes UK
UKOW05f0743230114

225096UK00008B/66/P

9 780521 5465